SCHOLARS' GUIDE TO WASHINGTON, D.C. FOR AFRICAN STUDIES

THE WILSON CENTER

SCHOLARS' GUIDE

TO WASHINGTON, D.C.

FOR

AFRICAN STUDIES

PURNIMA MEHTA BHATT

Consultants
DANIEL G. MATTHEWS
MICHAEL R. WINSTON
JULIAN W. WITHERELL

Series Editor
ZDENĚK V. DAVID

WOODROW WILSON INTERNATIONAL CENTER FOR SCHOLARS

SMITHSONIAN INSTITUTION PRESS
WASHINGTON, D.C.
1980

Scholars' Guide to Washington, D.C.   No. 4

This work was developed under a grant from the U.S. Office of Education, Department of Health, Education, and Welfare. However, the content does not necessarily reflect the position or policy of that agency, and no official endorsement of these materials should be inferred.

Library of Congress Cataloging in Publication Data

Bhatt, Purnima Mehta.

    Scholars' guide to Washington, D.C. for African studies.
    At head of title: Woodrow Wilson International Center for Scholars,
       Washington, D.C.
    Bibliography: p.
    Includes indexes.
    1. Africa—Library resources—Washington, D.C.
    2. Africa—Archival resources—Washington, D.C.

I. Woodrow Wilson International Center for Scholars.
II. Title.
Z3501.B48 [DT3]   026'.96   79–607774
ISBN 0-87474-238-2
ISBN 0-87474-239-0 pbk.

CONTENTS

FOREWORD

This is the fourth in a series of *Guides* to the scholarly riches of the Washington area, published by the Woodrow Wilson International Center for Scholars. The series exemplifies the center's "switchboard function" of facilitating connections between the vast resources of the nation's capital and individuals with scholarly or practical needs—or simple curiosity. Like the center's annual fellowship program, these *Guides* are designed largely to serve the national and international scholarly communities. Approximately 20,000 visiting scholars come each year to Washington from elsewhere in America and abroad. It is hoped that the *Guides* will inform these scholars, many of them outside the major university research centers in the United States, about the possibilities for engaging in research on particular topics in Washington.

The series of *Guides* is under the general editorship of Dr. Zdeněk V. David, the Wilson Center librarian. Elizabeth Dixon is largely responsible for the design and publication arrangements. Dr. Prosser Gifford of the Wilson Center, and Dr. Brian Weinstein of Howard University helped with the initial stages of this project. The author of this particular volume, Dr. Purnima M. Bhatt, is assistant professor of anthropology and interdisciplinary studies at Hood College.

The center wishes to thank the U.S. Office of Education for its indispensable financial support of the *Guide's* preparation (under the authority of Title VI, Section 602, NDEA), as well as the Morris and Gwendolyn Cafritz Foundation for additional support.

So far the center has prepared *Guides* for scholars in the fields of Russian/ Soviet (1977), Latin American and Caribbean (1979), and East Asian (1979) studies. All were published by the Smithsonian Institution Press. Forthcoming volumes will include surveys of resources in the Washington area for scholars interested in the study of Central and Eastern Europe, the Middle East, South Asia, and film and video materials.

James H. Billington, *Director*
Woodrow Wilson International Center for Scholars

INTRODUCTION

Purpose. This *Guide* is intended to serve as a basic reference aid for scholars who wish to utilize the unique resources of the nation's capital for research on Africa. Although aimed primarily at serious researchers, it is hoped that this volume will also prove valuable and informative to a broad reading audience with an interest in Africa.

It is a well-known fact that the Washington, D.C., area abounds in fine collections and offers remarkably rich opportunities for scholarly research in many fields. However, until a few decades ago there was a general lack of interest in Africa and a paucity of materials concerning it. African studies had not received due recognition and Africa was regarded by many as an appendage to Europe. Fortunately, the continent has acquired a new significance in recent years. In the last few decades there has been a phenomenal increase in the interest in Africa and a corresponding growth in source materials available for its study. There is an urgent need to identify these resources and make them available to scholars for purposes of study and research.

Scope and Content. This *Guide* was designed to be more than a rudimentary directory of names and addresses. While it cannot claim to be an exhaustive inventory of all source materials, efforts have been made to make it as comprehensive as possible. Its primary purpose is to survey the resource materials in the field of African studies and indicate the scope and extent of research facilities in the area.

The *Guide* focuses on African studies; therefore, coverage does not generally include research materials for the study of Afro-Americans and people of African descent in the New World. However, recognizing that a clear demarcation between the two is impossible, if not unwise, the author has included some Afro-American sources where it was regarded as necessary.

At the very outset, it was decided to analyze certain sources from the viewpoint of geographic regions rather than individual countries. (For the regional breakdown see the "Libraries" entry format at the beginning of the "A" section of this *Guide.*) Though the issue of regional groupings, particularly for the evaluation of the strength of collections, was by no means an easy one, the decision to retain them was justified on two grounds—first, most African countries are inadequately represented in library and archival collections; second, an overwhelming number of books deal with geographical regions rather than individual countries in Africa.

In preparing this volume, virtually all subjects of potential interest to Africanists have been considered, though the emphasis is on the social sciences, arts, and humanities. Because science and technology are more universal and transcend geographic and demographic boundaries, they have been treated somewhat differently and included only in the case of significant collections. The subject index at the back of the book shows the scope of the materials sought. Similarly, the table of contents reveals the range of agencies, institutions, organizations, facilities, and collections investigated.

Methodology. Preparation of the volume began with a compilation of a list of all Washington-area collections and organizations considered potentially relevant for research on Africa. All these were contacted in person and/or by telephone. Pertinent information for each was obtained from on-site examinations, discussions with staff members, and from printed materials. Information contained in the *Guide* should be considered up-to-date as of mid-to-late 1978.

Though attempts have been made to make this *Guide* as accurate and inclusive as possible, certain resources may have been overlooked, while descriptions of some collections may not be as complete as might be desirable. Data on reference materials has been made as complete as possible; in some instances, however, complete citations were unavailable. For possible future revision of this work, any suggestions by readers for additions, changes, and improvements will be greatly appreciated. Please notify the Librarian, Wilson Center, Smithsonian Institution Building, 1000 Jefferson Drive, SW, Washington, D.C. 20560.

ACKNOWLEDGMENTS

The author gratefully acknowledges her indebtedness to the U.S. Office of Education (Department of Health, Education, and Welfare) for the grant which made this project possible. The author would also like to thank Zdeněk V. David, editor of the Wilson Center's *Scholars' Guide* series, for his aid; Daniel G. Matthews, Michael R. Winston, and Julian W. Witherell for advice and counsel; and most of all, the authors of the other *Guides* in the series: Steven A. Grant, Michael Grow, Hong N. Kim, Kenneth J. Dillon, Steven R. Dorr, and Bonnie Rowan. The author would also like to extend her appreciation to the staff members of the various institutions discussed in the following pages for their assistance and cooperation. Finally, this *Guide* could not have been compiled without the support and understanding of my husband, Kiran.

HOW TO USE THE *GUIDE*

Format. The main body of this work is divided into 2 parts. The first deals with the resource *collections* in the Washington area which include libraries; archives; museums; music, film, and map collections; and data banks. The second part focuses on Washington-based *organizations,* both public and private, which have Africa-related interests and are potential sources of information for researchers. Included are sections on research centers and information offices; academic programs; U.S. government agencies; African embassies and international organizations; associations; cultural-exchange and technical-assistance organizations; religious organizations; and publications and media. Within each section, entries are arranged alphabetically by the name of the collection or organization.

Libraries. African book holdings in most of the large collections and in the smaller but more specialized ones are evaluated on a scale of A to D. These rankings are based on the quantity and quality of holdings for 15 subject categories. The Library of Congress was taken as a standard for A collections. Comprehensive collections of primary and secondary sources roughly one-tenth the size of the Library of Congress holdings and sufficient for original research, were defined as B collections. Collections which contain substantial secondary sources and some primary materials (about one-half the size of a B collection) sufficient for graduate instruction, were categorized as C collections, while those which contain sufficient materials to support undergraduate teaching were defined as D collections. Collections rated below D are indicated by a "D–."

The numerical strength of each major collection was derived from measurements of the shelflists in the libraries. The number of book titles was calculated on the basis of 100 index cards per inch and 85 titles per 100 cards.

Users of this *Guide* will find that in the case of the larger and more general collections, shelflist measurements have been given for the major geographical regions in Africa and also for individual African countries when sufficient numbers of books justified such treatment. However, this numerical breakdown by regions and countries has been provided primarily for the subject category of history. This decision was based on 3 considerations: (a) a preliminary survey of African holdings in various collections revealed that virtually all libraries, with the exception of a few specialized ones, had the richest and most extensive holdings in the subject category of history. It was assumed, therefore, that the holdings in this category would, by and large, reflect the overall numerical strength of Africa-related holdings in any given collection; (b) most libraries surveyed had very limited holdings in many subject categories. Furthermore, a large number of books dealing with travel and exploration, geography, and politics are classed under the subject category of history. (This may also explain the relatively small number of holdings in the subject categories of geography, foreign relations, sociology, etc., in most area collections.); and (c) the Library of Congress classification schedule was found to vary with the subject, making it virtually impossible to obtain regional and country breakdowns for the various subject categories (for example, under the subject category of geography, Zaire is classified under Central Africa, while elsewhere it is included in Southern Africa).

It was also difficult to measure law holdings in many general collections because of the unavailability of a well-developed Library of Congress classification schedule for African law. In such instances, the word "unmeasured" or "insignificant" appears in the subject category listings. As a consequence of the inherent shortcomings in the methods used for shelflist measurement, the size of all collections tends to be understated rather than overstated. Furthermore, researchers should bear in mind that collections tend to increase and expand at a very rapid rate.

Standard Entry Forms. At the beginning of each section of the *Guide* (and in Appendix IV), a standard entry form is provided which indicates the numerical sequence of information contained within each entry. Users of the *Guide* should consult these entry forms prior to perusing each section. The sequence of data presented in each entry corresponds to the standard entry form. Where a number is omitted in the entry, it means that the information was not relevant to the particular collection or organization.

Names, Addresses, and Telephone Numbers. All of these are subject to frequent change. The most ephemeral are data for government agencies and associations. All telephone numbers without an area code are assumed to be in the District of Columbia (area code 202). For numbers in Maryland and Virginia, the area codes 301 and 703, respectively, are included at the start of the entry.

Indexes. The Name Index contains the names of organizations and institutions, but not of individuals. The Personal-Papers Index includes the names of individuals whose papers and manuscripts are located in libraries or depositories surveyed. The Library Subject-Strength Index is based on the method of evaluation described above under the heading of "Libraries." Categorization is based on standard Library of Congress subject headings, or, in the case of geographic headings, on regional and country holdings in selected subcategories such as history, economics, political science, and literature. The Subject Index covers rather broad categories and, where necessary, is broken down by geographic region or country. However, the majority of collections focus on all the countries of Africa, rather than concentrating on any single nation or regional grouping.

Transliteration. The system used in this book is essentially that of the Library of Congress. Certain inconsistencies may be inevitable due to the author's policy to spell names and titles as they appear in the catalogs or other materials surveyed. Likewise, some organizations appear under their own transliteration.

COLLECTIONS

A Libraries

Libraries Entry Format (A)

1. General information
   a. *address; telephone number(s)*
   b. hours of service
   c. conditions of access (including availability of interlibrary loan [ILL] and reproduction facilities)
   d. name/title of director and heads of relevant divisions

2. Size of collection

3. Description of holdings/Evaluation of subject strength

Subject Category	*Number of Titles*	*Evaluation (A-D)* *
History		
Philosophy and Religion		
Geography		
Anthropology		
Economics		
Sociology		
Politics and Government		
Foreign Relations		
Law		
Education		
Fine Arts		
Language		
Literature		
Military		
Bibliography and Reference		

North Africa
    Algeria, Canary Islands, Egypt, Libya, Morocco, Sahara, Tunisia
West Africa
    Benin, Cameroon, Cape Verde Islands, Dahomey, Gambia, Ghana, Guinea, Guinea-Bissau, Ivory Coast, Liberia, Mali, Mauritania, Niger, Nigeria, Senegal, Sierra Leone, Sudan, Togo, Upper Volta

Central Africa
>Angola, Burundi, Central African Empire, Chad, Congo, Equatorial Guinea, Gabon, Rwanda, São Tomé and Principé, Zaire

East Africa
>Comoro Islands, Ethiopia, Kenya, Madagascar, Mauritius, Mozambique, Reunion, Seychelles, Somalia, Tanzania, Uganda

Southern Africa
>Botswana, Lesotho, Malawi, Namibia (Southwest Africa), Republic of South Africa, Swaziland, Zambia, Zimbabwe (Rhodesia)

>*A—comprehensive collection of primary and secondary sources (Library of Congress collection to serve as standard of evaluation)

>B—substantial collection of primary and secondary sources; sufficient for some original research (holdings roughly one-tenth those of the Library of Congress)

>C—substantial collection of secondary sources, some primary; sufficient to support graduate instruction (holdings roughly one-half those of B collection)

>D—collection of secondary sources, mostly in English; sufficient to support undergraduate instruction (holdings roughly one-half those of C collection); collections rated below D indicated by a "D–"

4. Special collections (periodicals, newspapers, government documents, maps, films, tapes)

5. Noteworthy holdings

6. Bibliographic aids facilitating use of collection (guides, catalogs, computerized retrieval systems)

Academy for Educational Development, Inc. Library See entry M1.

A1 Action Library (formerly Peace Corps Library)

1. a. *806 Connecticut Avenue, Room M-407*
        Washington, D.C. 20525
        254-3307

    b. 9:30 A.M.-4:00 P.M.   Monday-Friday

    c. Open to the public for on-site use. ILL available.

    d. Rita Warpeha, Chief Librarian
        Victoria Fries, Reference Librarian

2. The library, the bulk of which consists of the holdings of the former Peace Corps Library, contains some 38,000 books and documents and several hundred periodicals. Since the library's main function is to serve the needs of the Action staff, its acquisitions policy is not directed at building a comprehensive collection but at providing selective background materials on various countries. As a consequence, most of the materials in the library deal with subjects such as developing countries,

agriculture, rural development, health and education, poverty, technology, women, and related topics.

The library's African holdings comprise over 4,050 volumes and 18 periodical titles.

3. The book/document collection has been cataloged using the Library of Congress classification scheme. For African materials, a prefix has been added to the call number so that all materials on Africa in general are shelved together, followed by materials on each African country of interest to the Peace Corps. Examples of call numbers: AFRICA/ DS405/S25 or GHANA/DS432/W4.

The number of book titles in the various subject categories given below pertains to Africa in general and does not include titles listed under the individual countries. Section (b) lists the total number of titles in all subject categories for the major regions and selected countries in Africa.

(a) Subject categories and numbers of titles for Africa (General):

History	340
Philosophy and Religion	insignificant
Geography	—
Anthropology and Sociology	100
Politics and Government	50
Education	85
Fine Arts	30
Language and Literature	85
Military	—
Bibliography and Reference	72
Economics	390

(b) Number of titles in all subject categories for major regions and selected countries:

North	*East*	*West*	*Central*	*Southern*
187	*637*	*1,161*	*187*	*100*
Morocco	Ethiopia	Nigeria	Malawi	Botswana
85	195	340	80	63
Tunisia	Kenya	Ghana	Zaire	Lesotho
68	178	144	42	63
Libya	Tanzania	Liberia		Swaziland
34	102	144		20
	Uganda	Sierra Leone		
	85	85		
	Somalia	Cameroon		
	51	76		
		Senegal		
		59		
		Ivory Coast		
		59		

4-5.   The major resource in this library consists of the extensive collection of Peace Corps program documents dating from the organization's inception to the present. These include country training manuals, country program evaluations, project reports, articles by Peace Corps volunteers, and technical manuals. Much of the material here is unique and not available elsewhere. The Africanist may also discover substantial materials in the extensive folder (vertical file) collection, which contains newspaper and magazine clippings, Peace Corps news releases, planning documents, State Department reports, and other pamphlets. Folders for Africa are arranged alphabetically by country.

6.   There are two card catalogs:

    a. The one for the book/document collection is an alphabetically arranged index by author, title, and subject. For instance, by looking under "GHANA" one can find general materials on that country; by looking under "U.S. PEACE CORPS—GHANA" one can identify materials relating to the Peace Corps in Ghana.

    b. The smaller catalog for the folder collection is arranged alphabetically by the topic heading for each folder. There are entries under "AFRICA" and under the various Peace Corps African countries. No title or author entries for specific materials in the folders are included.

African Bibliographic Center, Inc. Library See entry H2.

A2 Agency for International Development (AID)—Development Information Center (DIC)

1. a. *Development Information Center*
1601 North Kent Street
Rosslyn Plaza Tower C
Arlington, Virginia
(703) 235-8936

State Department Branch
Room 1656, State Department Building
320 21st Street, NW
Washington, D.C. 20523
632-8571

    b. Central and Branch Hours:
8:45 A.M.-5:30 P.M.   Monday-Friday

    c. The primary purpose of DIC is to service AID personnel. Private researchers may gain access to the facility by obtaining prior permission either from the Development Information Center chief or from the AID Office of Public Affairs. Borrowing privileges are limited to AID personnel and there is no ILL service. Photoreproduction services are available.

d. Edna A. Falbo, Chief

2. The collection totals approximately 125,000 titles (reports and documents) and an indeterminate amount of uncataloged material. Cataloged African holdings number more than 3,900 titles.

3. The Development Information Center is the agency's unit for gathering information on development sciences and services. It is the primary collection point for program and technical documentation generated by AID. In addition, DIC also accessions relevant documents produced by non-AID sources such as other U.S. government agencies, research institutions, professional and development assistance organizations, and commercial publishers. As such, DIC is a major resource for African development studies, particularly in the fields of agriculture/rural development, population/family planning, health/nutrition, education, economics, development administration, and technical assistance methodology. The Development Information Center's collection contains both classified and unclassified reports. Included are: AID Program and Project Documentation (project reports, evaluations, etc.); AID-generated technical information (contract and consultant reports, feasibility studies, country analyses, sector assessments); and non-AID materials.

   A survey of the center's holdings revealed the following numbers of Africa-related titles, virtually all of which focus on development-related topics: Africa—General, 950; Algeria, 10; Angola, 6; Botswana, 30; Burundi, 10; Central African Republic, 15; Chad, 8; Egypt, 175; Ethiopia, 300; Ghana, 300; Kenya, 250; Liberia, 400; Nigeria, 975; Tunisia, 240; and Uganda, 130.

6. Access to the DIC's collection varies. In the central DIC, access is provided through a book catalog, AID's *Catalogue of Research Literature for Development*.

   In the DIC State Department Branch there is a dictionary card catalog arranged by author, title, subject, geographic designation, and contract. Plans are underway for centralized on-line retrieval.

Note: The DIC (235-1000) maintains a separate collection of over 6,000 monographs, periodical articles, and research reports dealing with population, family planning, and related topics.

Agriculture Department Library See National Agricultural Library, entry A30.

A3 American University Library

1. a. *Massachusetts and Nebraska Avenues, NW*
      Washington, D.C. 20016
      686-2325

   b. Fall and spring semesters:
      8:00 A.M.-Midnight   Monday-Friday
      9:00 A.M.-6:00 P.M.   Saturday
      1:00 P.M.-Midnight   Sunday

Summer sessions:
9:00 A.M.-11:00 P.M.   Monday-Thursday
9:00 A.M.-5:00 P.M.   Friday-Saturday
Closed Sunday

c. Open to the public for reference use. ILL and photoreproduction facilities available.

d. Donald D. Dennis, Director

2. There are approximately 400,000 volumes in the collections. The holdings on Africa, however, are insignificant.

3. Subject categories, numbers of titles, and evaluations:

Subject Category	Total	North	West	Central	East	Southern	Evaluation
History	2,610	405	340	170	320	445	B/C

Egypt	Nigeria	Congo	Ethiopia	R.S.A.
270	125	60	45	125

Algeria	Ghana	Angola	Kenya	Rhodesia
30	45	25	25	45

Subject Category	Total	Evaluation
Philosophy and Religion	50	D–
Geography	30	B/C
Anthropology	125	B
Economics	275	C
Sociology	35	C
Politics and Government	190	B/C
Foreign Relations	75	B
Law	*	
Education	65	C/D
Fine Arts	40	C
Language	60	C
Literature	405	C
Military	3	D–
Bibliography and Reference	4	D–

* Insignificant

4. The library currently receives about 35 periodicals pertaining to Africa.

A4 Army Library (Department of the Army)

1. a. *The Pentagon, Room 1A518*
   Washington, D.C. 20310
   697-4301 (Reference)

   b. 9:30 A.M.-4.00 P.M.   Monday-Friday

   c. Entrance to the Pentagon is restricted. The library serves the needs of military and civil personnel assigned to the Pentagon. Private researchers may use the library at the discretion of its staff. ILL and photocopying facilities are available.

   d. Mary L. Shaffer, Director

2-3.   The Army Library's holdings total some 275,000 titles and over 2,000 periodicals. The subject matter of the collection focuses on the military arts and sciences, international relations, political science, history, economics, and law. A few hundred volumes pertain specifically to Africa.

6.   Card catalogs and a list of currently received periodicals and recent acquisitions are available.

Brookings Institution Library See entry H8.

A5 The Catholic University of America—Mullen Library

1. a. *620 Michigan Avenue, NE*
   Washington, D.C. 20064
   635-5077 (General reference)

   b. 9:00 A.M.-10:00 P.M.   Monday-Thursday
   9:00 A.M.-6:00 P.M.   Friday
   9:00 A.M.-5:00 P.M.   Saturday
   1:00 P.M.-10:00 P.M.   Sunday
   Call for holiday and intersession hours.

   c. Open to any serious reader. ILL is available. Materials may be reproduced on photocopy machines, or they may be left with the reproduction service.

   d. Shannon Macioroski, Head, General Reference and College Library
   Thomas Schmidt, Assistant Head
   Barbara Pruett, Head, Social Sciences
   Betty Gutekunst, Head, Humanities

2.   The number of volumes totals about 1,000,000 now. The goal is to provide a good general collection for the use of undergraduates and to provide specialized titles in theology, church history, philosophy, and the missions for graduate students.
      As a result, the holdings on Africa are slim. Students in the occasional course on Africa (one is listed in anthropology at the graduate level)

are encouraged to go to Founders Library, Howard University. Many of the books on anthropology are kept in the Anthropology Library on the third floor, which has periodicals and volumes put on reserve for courses currently offered.

3. Subject categories, numbers of titles, and evaluations:

History	1,035 (Egypt 148, Nigeria 42, Zaire 44, Ethiopia 31, Republic of South Africa 104)	C/D
Philosophy and Religion	94 (Egypt 25)	D
Geography	19 (12 atlases)	C
Anthropology	487 (Egypt 11, Nigeria 36, Zaire 107, Republic of South Africa 27)	A/B
Economics	82	D–
Sociology	84	B
Politics and Government	66	D
Foreign Relations	10	D
Law	negligible	D–
Education	25	D–
Fine Arts	43 (Egypt 20)	C
Language and Literature	253 (Egypt 52, Arabic 100)	C
Military	insignificant	D–
Bibliography and Reference	50	D–

Note: The Mullen Library has many publications of the *Annales du Musée Royal du Congo Belge* (Tervuren), which accounts for the strength of Zaire in Anthropology and History.

4. THE OLIVEIRA LIMA LIBRARY

Room 7, Ground Floor
Mullen Library
635-5059

1:00 P.M.-8:00 P.M.   Tuesday
Noon-7:00 P.M.   Wednesday-Friday
9:00 A.M.-1:00 P.M., 2:00 P.M.-5:00 P.M.   Saturday

Manoel Cardozo, Curator and Professor of Luso-Brazilian History, Catholic University
Ralph Annicharico, Library Assistant

This library was opened in 1924 after Manoel de Oliveira Lima, Brazilian historian and diplomat, donated his large collection of books, pictures, correspondence, and memorabilia to Catholic University. The library continues to grow by donations and purchases of materials dealing with Portuguese-speaking peoples throughout the world.

All serious researchers are enthusiastically welcomed in the elegant reading and study room. No original work may circulate through inter-library loan, but if the condition of the book is satisfactory, a copy may be made for loan.

The total printed material is about 52,000 volumes. It is difficult to make a satisfactory estimate of the size of the African holdings because many books primarily about Brazil or Portugal contain chapters on Africa or the slave trade. The curator is strengthening titles on Africa, decolonization, and the slave trade, and there are 110 titles currently cataloged which deal with African history.

Nine periodicals were received from Mozambique, Angola, and Guinea-Bissau until recent disruptions in service. These are mainly government publications. No Portuguese-language newspapers are currently received. Brazilian transcripts of legislative debates have been continuously received, and the collection is complete from 1823 to the present. The Portuguese law-book holdings are impressive.

Miscellaneous vertical files contain numerous uncataloged pamphlets from the early 19th-century "Liberal Period" in Portugal, and a number of document boxes in the stacks contain a wide range of pamphlet materials on Portugal. According to the staff estimate, the library possesses 200,000 pages of original manuscript material dealing with Luso-Brazilian subjects. The wide-ranging correspondence of the donor is also here, but one must have the name of a correspondent in order to make use of it as no subject categories have been used in classifying the letters. Hundreds of photos of life in Brazil, Portugal, and of important people are available in storage boxes, but they are not completely organized.

Noteworthy for the African specialist are the following items:

Boletim Geral Ultramar das Colónias (news from African colonies);

Collecão das Leis do Brasil (some legislation dealing with slavery);

Nova Legislacão Ultramarina (Lisbon: Agencia Geral do Ultramar, 1950–65) (colonial laws);

Manoel Ribeiro Rocha, *Ethiope Resgatado* . . . (Lisbon, 1758), dealing with the institution of slavery;

about 150 uncataloged books on Africa;

many books on Portuguese explorations, "discoveries" which are not in the shelflist. Also, much on religious syncretism in Brazil;

numerous travel books—18th- and 19th-century Brazil, with considerable information on the slave trade and slavery;

publications of the Junta de Investigacao do Ultramar: about 80 titles dealing with colonial geography, zoology, but rarely with social issues.

Most of the library's holdings are not indicated in the general Mullen Library catalogs. It is better to consult the following:

Manoel S. Cardozo, "A Guide to the Manuscripts in the Lima Library . . ." in *Handbook of Latin American Studies,* no. 6 (1940), pp. 471–504;

Catalog of the Oliveira Lima Library, The Catholic University of America (Boston: G.K. Hall & Co., 1970);

Ruth E.V. Holmes, *Bibliographical and Historical Description of the Rarest Books in the Oliveira Lima Collection at The Catholic University of America* (Washington, D.C., 1926);

card dictionary catalog divided into acquisitions up to 1970 and acquisitions since 1970;

correspondence card catalog, arranged by name of person writing to Oliveira Lima;

introductory brochures;

lists of photos, paintings, engravings, and medallions;

serial card catalog;

shelflist, modified Library of Congress classification scheme.

INSTITUTE OF CHRISTIAN ORIENTAL RESEARCH—
DEPARTMENT OF SEMITIC AND EGYPTIAN LANGUAGES
AND LITERATURES

Mullen Library
Room 18, Ground Floor
635-5083

9:00 A.M.-5:00 P.M.   Monday-Friday

Aloysius Fitzgerald, Head of Institute and Department Chairman
Patrick Skehan, Coptic Specialist
Carolyn T. Lee, Librarian

The Institute of Christian Oriental Research is essentially the library of
the Department of Semitic and Egyptian Languages and Literatures. It
has a separate existence because of an endowment and because it was
founded by a most extraordinary scholar, Henri Hyvernat.

Father Hyvernat began teaching at Catholic University in 1889, and
he founded the department shortly thereafter. He founded the institute
several decades later on the basis of his own private library, memorabilia
collected on trips to the Middle East and North Africa, and his research
materials. His main interest was the Coptic language and Christian
Egypt; this led him to a close association with J.P. Morgan, Sr., who
purchased a large find of Coptic materials. He also worked with other
scholars in order to publish works of the Eastern Churches in a series
called the *Corpus Scriptorum Christianorum Orientalium*. The languages
of works in this project were Coptic, Arabic, Ge'ez from Ethiopia, and
other languages from the Levant.

Because of its history, a vast amount of material in the collection is
uncataloged, and a very advanced scholar interested in Christianity in
North Africa and the Middle East should find valuable books, manuscripts, and artifacts here. It is not possible to assess properly the importance of individual items, but a sampling of them should give the
more qualified person an idea of the holdings.

The institute is open to serious researchers who would be well advised
to write or telephone in advance of arrival. Decisions concerning interlibrary loan are made on a case-by-case basis. Microfilming and photocopy services are available.

The whole collection contains about 30,000 titles of printed books
and periodicals. The emphasis of the holdings is on Christian Egypt, old
literature produced by Christian Arabs, some Muslim literature, Ethiopian materials, and pharaonic Egypt. The 120 periodicals include English, German, and French items not easily accessible elsewhere (the
following are not necessarily complete collections): *Annales d'Ethiopie,
Acta Orientalia, Aegyptus, Aethiopica, Ancient Egypt, Annales du Service des Antiquités de l'Egypte, Archaeological Reports of the Egypt
Exploration Fund, Archiv für Payprusforschung, Bulletin de l'Association des Amis des Eglises et de l'Art Copte, Bulletin de la Société
d'Archéologie Copte, Bulletin de l'Institut d'Egypt, Memoires de l'Institut d'Egypte, Revue des Manuscrits Arabes, Die Welt des Islam,* and
Zeitschrift für Agyptische Sprache und Altertumskunde.

All periodicals are easily accessible, as are the books. Desks are arranged around the rooms mainly for the use of the 15 Ph.D. students in the department. A section of reference books contains encyclopedias, dictionaries, church directories, commentaries on the Bible, and related volumes. The main collection of other books is arranged according to the Dewey Decimal System, which has been somewhat altered, but there is no subject or title card catalog. To find a book one must know the author or the general number, as there is an author card catalog and a shelflist.

A walk through the library brought the following items to my attention:

Many Arabic texts, histories of Arabic literature;

Louis Brunot, *Introduction à l'Arabe Marocain* (Paris: G.P. Maisoneuve, 1950);

Catalogue de la Bibliothèque Khédiviale du Caire;

Catalogue des Manuscrits Arabes de Rabat;

Catalogue of the Arabic Manuscripts in the John Rylah Library at Manchester;

Hartwig Derenbourg, *Les Manuscrits Arabes de l'Escurial* . . . (Paris, 1884);

Ibn Khaldun, *The Muqaddimah: An Introduction to History* (sets in Arabic and in English);

Elisée Reclus, *Nouvelle Géographie Universelle* . . . (Paris, 1876–94);

Carl Reinhardt, *Ein Arabischer Dialekt Gesprochen In Oman Und Zanzibar* (Amsterdam: Philo Press, 1972);

Arab literature—books of proverbs;

atlases, polyglot Bibles;

Berber life and times;

books on hieroglyphics, histories of Egypt, art of Egypt;

Ethiopic, No. 278: 191 titles including catalogs of other libraries and manuscript collections in France and Germany, texts in Amharic, Ge'ez (called Ethiopic), and a few in Tigrinya, *Evangelia Sancta* (1824, in Amharic), *The Contendings of the Apostles* (in Ge'ez and English), and *The Ethiopic Liturgy* (Ge'ez). One of the most beautiful books I have ever seen is E.A. Wallis Budge, ed., *The Life of Takla Hâymânôt* . . . *The Miracles of Taklah and The Book of the Riches of Kings* (London, 1906), in Ge'ez and English. Taken from a manuscript in the British Museum, the book reproduces illuminated pages;

histories of the caliphates.

Along the far wall are Hyvernat's travel books; grammars, and the following histories of church missions to Ethiopia:

Karl Baedeker, *Egypt and the Sudan* (New York, 1908);

Frédéric Cailliaud, *Voyage à Meroé, au Fleuve Blanc au delà de Fazoql* . . . (Paris, 1826–27);

Abbé de Marigny, *Histoire des Arabes* (Paris, 1750);

Louis Piesse, *Algérie et Tunisie* (Paris, 1906);

P. Vansleb, *Nouvelle Relation en Forme de Journal d'Un Voyage Fait en Egypte en 1672 et 1673* (Paris, 1677);

books on Coptic liturgy and ritual.

In another room nearby, 19 drawers of vertical files, numbered the same way the library books are numbered, contain offprints of articles, short studies, and other useful materials. Another 14 drawers contain the notes of Theodore C. Petersen, Coptic scholar, who was particularly interested in Coptic bookbindings, of which there are many photos and sketches. Petersen's manuscripts, pictures, and correspondence are also here. The Morgan collection of Coptic material is here in photographic form.

Along the walls are placed wooden cabinets and flat files containing a vast assortment of uncataloged materials: a set of the scientific studies done during Napoleon's expedition to Egypt (in several cases); 35 Arabic manuscripts (case 22); 7 boxes of lantern slides of Greek and Roman antiquities; 11 volumes of Lepsius, *Denkmaeler aus Aegypten un Aethiopien;* a Ge'ez prayer book (17th or 18th century, case 22); Arabic scrolls (22); ancient coins (some are in the university vault); artifacts such as potsherds, coins, amulets, pieces of an Egyptian wooden sarcophagus (16, 17); Mohammad ibn'Abd al-Mo'tial-Ishak, *Beauties of the Ancient History or Notices of the Sovereigns that Ruled over Egypt* (in Arabic, 1734); 56 document boxes of Hyvernat correspondence, research notes ("L'Absolution chez les Coptes," "Notes on Coptic Church History . . .," maps, atlases, photos); and so forth.

The institute has not had the resources to prepare many finding aids to this fascinating collection, but they include: an author card catalog, a loose-leaf guide to the numbering system for books, and a list of periodicals and serials holdings. In the periodical room one finds a shelflist, an index for some periodicals, and cards for folios and small books. In another room a book catalog includes holdings of the New York Public Library and the Jewish Institute of Religion of the Hebrew Union College. A card catalog contains an "Analytical Index of the Coptic Manuscripts in Libraries other than the Bibliothèque Nationale, Paris." T.C. Petersen began a "Catalogue of Manuscripts Belonging to Professor H. Hyvernat" (in case 23), but unfortunately he did not complete it.

SPECIAL COLLECTIONS

See Carolyn T. Lee, Theology-Philosophic Library

Mullen Library
Third Floor
635-5088

The Special Collections consist of about 20,000 partially cataloged volumes currently divided in 3 parts in different locations. Researchers should confer with C. T. Lee regarding African holdings.

The first collection is called "Dewey" because books are classified by the Dewey Decimal System. It includes books on Roman Catholic missions around the world and Church history. Of particular note is the *Annales de la Propagation de la Foi,* of the Society for the Propagation of the Faith. Sets exist for the offices in Quebec, Dublin, Lyons, and New York. They contain much information on activities in Africa. There are a few annual reports of the American Colonization Society; the Foster-Sterns collection of books on the history of the Knights of Malta, going back to the 16th century; books on Africa by Richard Burton; many old travel books (Thomas Herbert, *Some Yeares Travels Into Divers Parts of Asia and Afrique,* revised and enlarged [London,

1638]); and atlases such as a version of *Mercators Atlas* (1635). Other books worth noting are Ramussio, ed., *Viagi* (1554) and P. Apianus, ed., *Cosmographia sive Descriptia* (1584). In general history one finds a very large collection of pamphlets which do not seem to have been bound together in any logical way; also about 45 monographs *(The Ruined Cities of Mashonaland)*.

The second collection is in the vault and contains very rare items such as the magnificent *Nuremburg Chronicle* (*Liber Cronicarum*, 1493) with material on Egypt; an atlas dating from 1601; a *Book of Islands* (1534); and *Mercator Atlases*.

The third collection is the Clementine Library purchased from the family of Pope Clement XI. Volumes in this collection are in the process of being cataloged. They include a Ge'ez lexicon (1638); other materials for the propagation of Christianity in Ethiopia; a book on the Jesuits in Egypt (1725); as well as Solinus, *Memorabilium Mundi, Africa* (1603), with descriptions of pyramids, funeral arrangements, Ethiopic priests, and holy persons.

In sum, researchers analyzing church histories, missionary activity, and religious leaders will find considerable material in this collection, which may be seen by appointment.

The Theology-Philosophy Library receives 6 journals currently of interest to African researchers, such as *Revue du Clergé Africain.*

5. Noteworthy holdings are indicated above.

6. Bibliographic aids not mentioned above include handouts with library hours and rules for use; dictionary card catalog; shelflists which are not complete for the collections; printed catalogs for the Bibliothèque Nationale (Paris) and for the British Library or British Museum—each by author only; a card catalog of masters theses and doctoral dissertations at Catholic University; and a *Comprehensive Dissertation Index, 1861–Present.*

A6 Census Bureau Library (Department of Commerce)

1. a. *Federal Office Building 3, Wing 4, Room 2451*
   Suitland, Maryland 20233
   (301) 763-5042

   Mail: *Department of Commerce*
   Washington, D.C. 20233

   (Note: A daily Commerce Department shuttle-service operates between the Main Commerce Building in downtown Washington and the Census Bureau Library.)

   b. 8:00 A.M.-5:00 P.M. Monday-Friday

   c. Open to the public. ILL and photoreproduction services are available.

   d. Betty Baxtresser, Chief of the Library Branch

2. The library's total holdings consist of over 375,000 volumes and approximately 3,400 current periodicals. Subjects include demography, population studies, economics, political science, education, and certain social sciences. The bulk of the collection comprises U.S. and foreign statistical materials (censuses, yearbooks, and bulletins).

3. Many current items in the collection are on permanent loan to the Census Bureau's International Demographic Statistics staff.

6. There are 2 separate dictionary card catalogs, both of which should be consulted by the researcher: a catalog for holdings cataloged prior to 1976, and an active catalog for acquisitions since 1976. The pre-1976 materials are listed in *Catalogs of the Bureau of the Census Library*, 20 volumes (Boston: G.K. Hall & Co., 1976). A monthly list of acquisitions and current periodicals is available to researchers.

Note: Also see entry A7.

Central Intelligence Agency Library See entry K5.

A7 Commerce Department Library

1. a. *14th Street and Constitution Avenue, NW, Room 7046*
   Washington, D.C. 20230
   377-5511

   b. 8:30 A.M.-5:00 P.M.   Monday-Friday

   c. Open to the public for on-site use. ILL and photoduplication facilities.

   d. Stanley J. Bougas, Librarian

2. The holdings consist of some 350,000 volumes and over 1,400 periodical titles. The library's collection is strong in the subject category of economics, law, legislation, and allied fields. Holdings pertaining to Africa number approximately 530 volumes.

3. The shelflist shows approximately 350 volumes in the economics category consisting mainly of census statistics, economic reports, government documents, and commercial directories. In addition there are over 150 books in the fields of history and foreign relations. (Note: much of the pre-1940 material has been discarded and thus the shelflist does not provide an accurate count of the Africa holdings.)

4. For the past few years, the library has been receiving some select foreign serials and official government documents, mainly from Angola, Cameroon, Ethiopia, Ghana, and Kenya. These holdings consist of annual reports on banking, economics, trade, and varied statistics.

6. *Commerce Library Bulletin*, issued periodically, gives a list of recent acquisitions.

A8 Congressional Quarterly, Inc.—Editorial Reports Library

1. a. *1414 22nd Street, NW*
      Washington, D.C. 20037
      296-6800

   b. 9:30 A.M.-5:30 P.M.   Monday-Friday

   c. Closed to the public. Serious scholars may obtain special permission from the librarian to use the collection. Limited ILL and photoreproduction services.

   d. Edna M. Frazier, Librarian

2. The library's holdings consist of approximately 18,000 bound volumes (including *Congressional Records*) and 5,000 microfilms. The library also receives over 200 periodicals and serials. Most of the items in the collection deal with current events, domestic politics, and international relations.

3-4. Though it is not possible to assess the size and strength of holdings on Africa, there is considerable material here which would interest the Africanist, especially in the realm of U.S. policy toward Africa. The 2 valuable sources of information are the *Congressional Quarterly* and the *Editorial Research Reports*. The former provides specific coverage of Congress, government, politics, etc., while the latter covers topics beyond the specialized scope of the *Congressional Quarterly* and contains in-depth analysis of current events. The Africanist can find useful material on subjects such as Angolan independence, Mozambique elections, OAU summit meetings, Rhodesian negotiations, war in Sahel, Cuban expansionism in Africa, the Republic of South Africa, refugees, drought, and Arab unity.

5. The library has an extensive vertical file collection which consists of newspaper clippings, periodical articles, government documents, and White House releases. There are numerous folders on Africa both in the subject file as well as the biographical files.

6. See *Editorial Research Reports: Index* (January 1974-March 1978).

A9 District of Columbia Public Library

1. a. *901 G Street, NW*
      Washington, D.C. 20001
      727-1111

   b. 9:00 A.M.-9:00 P.M.   Monday-Thursday
      9:00 A.M.-5:30 P.M.   Friday-Saturday
      Closed Sunday

   c. Open to the public. ILL and reproduction services.

   d. Jewel Ogonji, Central Librarian
      Alice Robinson, Chief of Black Studies Division

2. The total holdings of the library consist of books, some 300 current periodical titles, films, slides, tapes, records, and art reproductions. African material in the collections is estimated at some 2,000 volumes and approximately 37 periodical titles.

3. Subject categories, numbers of titles, and evaluations:

Subject Category	Total	North	East	West	Southern	Central	Evaluation
History	1,010	150	175	200	150	155	D
		Egypt 50	Ethiopia 25	Nigeria 40	Zaire 55		
				Ghana 25			
Philosophy and Religion	50						D–
Geography	20						—
Anthropology	*						—
Economics	100						D–
Sociology	25						C
Politics and Government	50						D–
Foreign Relations	*						D–
Law	*						D–
Education	*						D–
Fine Arts	105						B
Language and Literature	211						C/D
Military	*						D–
Bibliography and Reference	35						D–

* Insignificant   ** Unmeasured

4. Each division of the library maintains its own vertical file collection. The researcher can find scattered material on Africa in the pamphlets, brochures, newspaper clippings, and government documents in these files. The Africanist will find considerable secondary material in the Black Studies Division, which focuses on African and Afro-American history, literature, music, art, and biographies.

    The Audio-Visual Division, Room 226, has over 45 films and filmstrips pertaining to Africa. The Music and Recreation Division's collection includes some 50 records of African music. The Art Division has a picture file containing over 350 reproductions of African sculpture and Egyptian art.

6. No bibliography of the library's holdings exists. Researchers may find the following publications useful in locating materials in the library: *Films: A Descriptive Catalog of 16mm Sound Films for Free Loan* (Film Division, D.C. Public Library, 1971) and *Potpourri 1: A List of Recent Acquisitions of the Black Studies Division.*

A10 Dumbarton Oaks Research Library (Trustees for Harvard University)

1. a. *1703 32nd Street, NW*
        Washington, D.C. 20007
        342-3240

    b. 9:00 A.M.-5:00 P.M.   Monday-Friday

    c. Open to qualified researchers for on-site use. Prior permission required from the librarian. Photoreproduction services available.

    d. Irene Vaslef, Librarian

2-3. The library's total holdings consist of over 95,000 volumes and 800 current periodical titles. The primary focus of the collection is on Byzantine civilization and related topics. African holdings in the collection consist of several thousand volumes on North Africa, specifically during the Byzantine period.
      Because this is a specialized library, the usual subject categories are not germane here. It may, however, be pointed out that researchers with an interest in North Africa will find useful material here in the areas of history, language, art, archeology, and religion.

6. The following catalogs and guides should facilitate access to the collections: *Dictionary Catalogue of the Byzantine Collection of the Dumbarton Oaks Research Library,* 12 volumes (Boston: G.K. Hall & Co., 1975); and *Dumbarton Oaks Bibliographies* (London: Mansell, 1973), a continuing series (3 volumes already published).

Embassy of Nigeria Library See entry L27.

Embassy of South Africa Library See entry L32.

Energy Department Library See entry K10.

Environmental Protection Agency Library See entry K11.

A11 Export-Import Bank Library

1. a. *811 Vermont Avenue, NW*
        Washington, D.C. 20571
        566-8320

b. 7:45 A.M.-5:00 P.M.   Monday-Friday

c. Open to the public. ILL, but no reproduction facilities available.

d. Theodora McGill, Librarian

2-3.   The Export-Import Bank Library Collection totals over 15,000 books and some 950 periodical titles. African holdings consist of approximately 400 items, most of which deal with the subject categories of economics and finance and include agriculture, trade, and economic bulletins; reports; economic surveys; statistical abstracts; and bank newsletters. The greatest number of titles are from Nigeria (50), South Africa (25), Tanzania (20), Morocco (20), Ghana (16), Malawi (15), Sudan (15), and Kenya (15).

4.   The library receives a large number of African-related economic periodicals, which include the *Marches Tropicaux et Méditerranéens,* a weekly economic review with special issues on African nations; *Middle East and African Economist; Middle East Economic Digest;* and the *Quarterly Economic Reviews,* providing economic coverage of some 53 African countries.

6.   The library mantains a card catalog arranged alphabetically by country.

A12 Folger Shakespeare Library

1. a. *201 East Capitol Street, SE*
Washington, D.C. 20003
546-4800 (Information)

b. 8:45 A.M.-4:30 P.M.   Monday-Saturday

c. The reading room and library are open to advanced scholars and qualified researchers. Persons wishing to engage in research at the Folger should bring proper identification from an academic institution or other acceptable source.

d. O.B. Hardison, Jr., Director

2-5.   The library has one of the finest collections of rare books and manuscripts dealing with the Renaissance. Its holdings comprise 200,000 books and 40,000 manuscripts.

The Folger's collection focuses on Shakespeare and the world in which he lived. he majority of its holdings center on the Renaissance and fall in the subject categories of drama, philosophy, music, exploration, and the history of science. The majority of Africa-related holdings in the library deal with early travels in Africa and exploration of the continent and thus come under the subject category of geography.

The Folger's African holdings consist of some rare and unique materials, many being descriptions and journals of travel and exploration dating from the 16th to the 19th centuries. Some of the more important ones are: Luis del Marmol Carvajal, *L'Afrique de Marmol* (1667); Gomes Eannes de Azurara, *The Chronicle of the Discovery and Conquest of Guinea* (London: Hakluyt Society, 1896); João de Barros,

L'Asia . . . de' Fatti de' Portoghesi nello Scoprimento, and Conquista de' Mari and Terre di Oriente . . . (Venice, 1562); Allessandro Geraldini, *Itinerarium ad Regiones sub Acquinoctiali Plaga Constitutas . . . Opus Antiquitates, Ritus, Mores, and Religiones Populoru, Aethiopie, Africae, Atlantici Oceani, Indicarumque Regionum Complectens . . .* (Rome, 1631); James Houstoun, *The Works of James Houstoun . . . Containing Memoirs of His Life and Travels in Asia, Africa, America . . .* (London, 1753); *Libretto Nuouo del Sito, delle Città, delli Monti, Fiumi, Isole, and Porti di Tutta la Barbaria* (1535); Martin Lipen, *Navigatio Salomonis Ophiritica Illustrata a M. Martino Lipenio . . .* (1660); Livio Sanuto (ca. 1530–86), *Geografia dell' Africa, Venice 1588* (Amsterdam: Theatrum Orbis Terrarum, 1965).

Other noteworthy items include extensive publications of the Hakluyt Society (which contains over 100 volumes from 1847 to 1908 and some 147 volumes from 1909 onwards); a 1513 edition of the *Geographia* of Claudius Ptolemaeus; Antony's oration from *Julius Caesar* (act 3, scene 2) translated into pidgin English by a mission-trained boy of New Guinea; and translations of several Shakespearean works into Arabic and one into Xhosa.

Scholars should note that the Folger Library is a valuable resource for research on Africa and Africans in Renaissance literature, art, and drama.

The Folger Library collection also holds several hundred maps of Africa dating from the 12th to the 18th centuries.

Other items of interest to Africanists consist of: collection of leaflets relating to the Royal African Company and Britain's trade with Africa, 1709–50, and an uncataloged collection of over 2,000 pamphlets dealing with 17th-century Dutch history. The latter may contain scattered but useful material on Africa.

6. Researchers should find the following bibliographies useful in locating materials in the Folger Library: *Catalog of Manuscripts of the Folger Shakespeare Library*, 3 volumes (Boston: G.K. Hall & Co., 1971); *Catalog of Printed Books of the Folger Shakespeare Library;* and Betty Ann Kane, *The Widening Circle: The Story of the Folger Shakespeare Library and Its Collections* (Washington, D.C.: Folger Shakespeare Library, 1976).

Foreign Service Institute Library See entry K24.

A13 Freer Gallery of Art Library (Smithsonian Institution)

1. a. *12th Street and Jefferson Drive, SW*
    Washington, D.C. 20560
    381-5332

    b. 10:00 A.M.-4:30 P.M.   Monday-Friday

    c. Open to the public. No ILL. Xeroxing facilities available.

    d. Priscilla P. Smith, Librarian

2-3.   The library has a number of fragments of Coptic texts (dating from the 5th to the 10th centuries). These include both biblical and secular material.

6.   A description of the Coptic holdings of the Freer can be found in William H. Worrel, *The Coptic Manuscripts in the Freer Collection* (New York: The Macmillan Company, 1923).

A14 Geological Survey Library (Interior Department)

1. a. *12201 Sunrise Valley Drive*
    Fourth Floor, Room 4A-100
    Reston, Virginia 22092
    (703) 860-6671 (Reference)

    b. 7:45 A.M.-4:15 P.M.   Monday-Friday

    c. Open to the public. ILL and photoreproduction facilities available.

    d. George H. Goodwin, Jr., Chief Librarian

2.   The Geological Survey Library is one of the largest earth science libraries in the world. The main library in Reston, Virginia, contains approximately 700,000 bound and unbound monographs, serials, and government publications, at least 1,500 of which focus on Africa. In addition, the library has an extensive collection of pamphlets, maps, and doctoral dissertations.

3.   The collection is comprehensive in all aspects of the geosciences. The bulk of the African holdings are in the fields of geology, paleontology, petrology, mineralogy, ground and surface water, geochemistry, cartography, and mineral resources.
     The library has its own classification scheme, which is simple and effective to use. Basically a decimal system, this scheme has a geographic breakdown for many of the subjects. For holdings in science, at least certain aspects of it, the library deserves an A rating; however, the collection seems to fall below the D level in all other subject categories used in this guide.

4.   Currently the library maintains more than 9,500 serial and periodical titles, of which some 300 deal with Africa. This extensive collection consists of 3 different types of materials: nonofficial geological publications, nongeological offical publications, and serials on sciences other than geology. (African material in these categories can be located in the shelflist under G 700, P 700, and S 700.)
     Scientific journals and official publications of African government geological services, mining bureaus, and academic institutes are very well represented in the collection, with coverage extending back into the late 19th century in some instances.
     The library's map collection is discussed in entry E2.

6.   The library maintains a subject and an author-title catalog. Within the subject catalog, African materials may appear under country headings

or under geographic subdivisions of scientific subject headings. Researchers who wish to conduct a thorough search of the African materials in the collection should consult the shelflist with the aid of the *Geological Survey Library Classification Scheme and Index.*

The library's card catalog is also available in book form: *Catalog of the United States Geological Survey Library,* 25 volumes (Boston: G.K. Hall & Co., 1964), with continuing supplements.

A brochure, *U.S. Geological Survey Library,* is available free of charge.

A15 George Washington University Library

1. a. *2130 H Street, NW*
    Washington, D.C. 20052
    676-6558

    b. Academic year:
    8:30 A.M.-Midnight   Monday-Friday
    10:00 A.M.-10:00 P.M.   Saturday
    10:00 A.M.-2:00 A.M.   Sunday
    Hours vary during examinations, summer, and intersession periods. Call 676-6845 for information on library hours and schedule changes.

    c. The library is open to the public for reference use. ILL and reproduction facilities available.

    d. Rupert C. Woodward, Librarian

2. The total library collection (excluding the Medical and Law School Libraries) numbers 512,091 volumes. African holdings are generally small and number approximately 2,500-3,000 volumes.

3. Subject categories, numbers of titles, and evaluations:

Subject Category	Total	North	West	Central	East	Southern	Evaluation
History	1,250	395	215	125	170	215	C
		Egypt 225	Nigeria 60		Ethiopia 43	R.S.A. 21	
		Algeria 43	Ghana 17		Kenya 60	Rhodesia 55	
Philosophy and Religion	30 (Egypt 14)						D–
Geography	25						C/D
Anthropology	105						B
Economics	165 (Egypt 20, Nigeria 17)						C/D
Sociology	50						B/C
Politics and Government	110						C

Subject Category	Total	North	West	Central	East	Southern	Evaluation
Foreign Relations	—						D–
Law	—						D–
Education	25						D–
Fine Arts	30						C/D
Language	50						D–
Literature	15						D–
Military	*						D–
Bibliography and Reference	42						D–

* Insignificant

The library has recently been designated as the depository for the Defense Mapping Agency Topographic Center maps in the Washington Consortium of Universities. Among its map holdings are more than 684 maps of Africa, of which 36 are of Africa (General), 225 of North Africa, 149 of West Africa, 194 of East Africa, 60 of Southern Africa, and 20 of Central Africa.

5. A survey of the uncataloged holdings of the Special Collections Division (676–7497) revealed the following items of interest: Andrew Leith Adams, *Notes of a Naturalist in the Nile Valley and Malta* . . . (Edinburgh, 1870); William H. Bartlett, *The Nile Boat: Or, Glimpses of the Land of Egypt* (New York, 1851); Philip Beaver, *African Memoranda: Relative to an Attempt to Establish a British Settlement on the Island of Bulama* . . . *(1792)* (London, 1805); Jacob Bryant, *Observations Upon the Plagues Inflicted upon the Egyptians* (London, 1810); Joseph Corry, *Observations upon the Windward Coast of Africa* (London, 1807); and *Narratives of an Expedition to Explore the River Zaire* . . . (1818).

The Special Collections Division also contains the personal papers of Frederick R. Kuh, an American journalist, which may provide scattered but useful material on Africa.

6. There are no published catalogs for the library. Researchers may obtain some helpful information from the Consortium of Universities' *Guide to Library Resources*.

Note: The Jacob Burns Law Library located at 716 20th Street, NW, has a small collection of books, approximately 120 volumes on African law, foreign relations, and related subjects. For additional information contact James Heller, Reader Services (676-6646).

A16 Georgetown University Library

1. a. *37th and O Streets, NW*
   Washington, D.C. 20057
   625-4173

b. 8:30 A.M.-Midnight   Monday-Thursday
   8:30 A.M.-10:00 P.M.   Friday
   10:00 A.M.-10:00 P.M.   Saturday
   11:00 A.M.-Midnight   Sunday
   For information on summer schedules, call 625-4173.

c. The library and the stacks are open to the public for reference purposes.
   ILL and photoreproduction services available.

d. Joseph E. Jeffs, Librarian

2.   The library collection numbers over 800,000 volumes, with an estimated 4,150 titles for Africa. The library currently receives some 3,450 serials and 25 newspapers.

3.   Subject categories, numbers of titles, and evaluations:

Subject Category	Total	North	West	Central	East	Southern	Evaluation
History	2,715	960	445	130	320	405	B/C
		Egypt 435	Nigeria 105	Congo 40	Ethiopia 85	R.S.A. 70	
		Algeria 155	Ghana 65	Angola 21	Kenya 85	Zambia 30	
						Rhodesia 43	
Philosophy and Religion	45						D–
Geography	25						C
Anthropology	120						B
Economics	270 (Egypt 22, Nigeria 23)						C
Sociology	265						B/C
Politics and Government	150						C
Foreign Relations	10						D
Law	**						—
Education	20						D–
Fine Arts	25						D
Language	305 (Coptic 75, Hausa 17, Yoruba 12)						B/C
Literature	50						B/C
Military	*						D–
Bibliography and Reference	135						C

* Insignificant   ** Unmeasured

4. The library currently receives about 30 periodicals pertaining to Africa. Since 1969 the Georgetown Library has served as a depository for select U.S. government documents. Some of these, especially the *Reports of the Department of State and Congressional Hearings,* contain valuable information for the research scholar. These government publications are on microprint and are located in the Audiovisual Department on the first floor of the library. (Note: The U.S. depository documents are not listed in the library's card catalog.)

5. The library has an extensive collection of books in Arabic, totaling over 5,000 volumes. The interest in Arabic material developed with the founding of the School of Language and Linguistics in 1949 and the establishment of the Center for Contemporary Arab Studies at Georgetown University. The Arabic collection is a valuable resource for the history; social and intellectual life; art; literature; economics; and politics of Egypt, Nubia, Sudan, Libya, Algeria, and Morocco. Pamphlets and documents of the OAU in Arabic and the al-Maktabah-al-Arabiyah series are also included in the holdings. For more information on the Arabic materials, contact Brenda Bickett (625-4175), who is a specialist in this area.

    The Archives, Manuscripts, and Rare Books Division of the library may have a few scattered items on Africa. These include pamphlets of the American Colonization Society and the John Kelly Papers. Kelly, a Catholic missionary at Cape Palmas in Liberia, describes the Catholic Church and missions in Liberia, and his journal is a good source of information on the Grebo people.

6. There are no published catalogs for the library's collections. There is, however, a printed *Guide for Users of the Government Documents Depository,* which is available free of charge from the reference section.

A17 Health, Education, and Welfare Department (HEW) Library

1. a. *330 Independence Avenue, SW*
    Washington, D.C. 20201
    245-6791 (Reference)

    b. 8:30 A.M.-5:30 P.M.   Monday-Friday

    c. Open to the public for on-site use. ILL and limited photoduplication services available.

    d. Charles F. Gately, Director

2. The library contains 400,000 volumes and receives some 9,000 periodicals and serials. Its holdings are strong in the field of the social sciences and include a comprehensive collection of departmental and operating agencies' publications. The library's holdings on Africa are, however, insignificant, totaling some 100 volumes.

3. Some years back all the Africa-related materials in the field of education were transferred to the National Institute of Education Library (see entry A33). The remaining books are general reference works in the fields of history, health, and economics.

6. For a published guide to the library's holdings, see U.S. Department of Health, Education, and Welfare, *Author/Subject Catalog of the Department Library,* 29 volumes (Boston: G.K. Hall & Co., 1965), with a first supplement in 7 volumes (1973).

    The library has recently added the OCLC automated cataloging system and JURIS, for retrieving legal information from the Department of Justice.

___

A18 Housing and Urban Development (HUD) Library

1. a. *451 7th Street, SW, Room 8141*
        Washington, D.C. 20410
        755-6370

    b. 8:30 A.M.-5:15 P.M.   Monday-Friday

    c. Open to the public. ILL and photoreproduction services available.

    d. Elsa Freeman, Director

2. The library's holdings comprise nearly half a million items, including some 2,000 current periodicals. Of these, approximately 150-200 titles pertain to Africa.

3. Most of the books on Africa deal with subjects such as planning and urban development (housing, architecture, new towns, city growth), economic development (agriculture, cooperatives, technical assistance programs, demography), and social conditions. There is substantial data on individual countries of Africa, Nigeria being particularly well represented.

6. The library's holdings are listed in *The Dictionary Catalog of the United States Department of Housing and Urban Development,* 19 volumes (Boston: G.K. Hall & Co., 1972), with 2 supplements. For recent acquisitions the researcher should consult the U.S. Department of Housing and Urban Development, *HUD Library Recent Acquisitions,* a semimonthly listing of books, documents, and reports, and *Housing and Planning Reference,* a bimonthly index to current literature on housing and planning.

Note: Also see entry K14.

___

A19 Howard University—Afro-American Studies Resource Center

1. a. *Afro-American Studies Resource Center*
        Founders Library, Room 300
        500 Howard Place, NW
        Washington, D.C. 20059
        636-7242

    b. 9:00 A.M.-5:00 P.M.   Monday-Friday

    c. Open to the public. ILL and photoreproduction services available.

    d. E. Ethelbert Miller, Director

2. This is the resource center of the Department of Afro-American Studies at Howard University. Its primary purpose is to facilitate research and communication on the black experience via the media of print, sound, and visual materials. The total collection consists of some 20,000 books and a large collection of films, slides, videotapes, records, and periodicals, of which some 1,500 to 2,000 book titles pertain directly to Africa.

3. Africa-related titles in the center's collection cover a wide range of subject matter. These include books on history, politics, economics, education, folklore, religion, literature, and music.

4. The center receives several periodicals, including: *A.F. Press Clips, Africa Report, Africa Today, African Affairs, African Arts, African Forum, African Environment, African Progress, Ba Shiru,* and *Journal of Eastern African Research Development.*

    In addition, the Resource Center has over 50 Africa-related films. The majority of these are commercial films and deal with the history, culture, music, and political development of African nations. The videotape collection of the center includes some unusual materials, such as Chinua Achebe's readings, "Congress and Rhodesian Chrome," coverage of the Second National Black Leadership Symposium on Africa, Leon Dash's "The War in Angola," Angela Gilliam's "Africanisms in the New World," George Shepperson's "Malawi, Independent Africa," and "Washington Task Force on African Affairs."

    The Resource Center periodically sponsors lectures and poetry readings during the school year.

6. The center's card catalog is arranged by subject and author. African holdings are further classified by individual countries.

    For the videotape collection, consult *Afro-American Studies Resource Center Videotape Library,* available on request.

A20 Howard University—Founders Library

1. a. *500 Howard Place, NW*
    Washington, D.C. 20059
    636-7253 (Reference)
    636-7250 (General library information)

    b. 8:00 A.M.-Midnight   Monday-Friday
    8:00 A.M.-5:00 P.M.   Saturday
    Noon-Midnight   Sunday

    c. Open to serious researchers for on-site use. ILL and photoreproduction facilities available.

    d. Binford H. Conley, Director of University Libraries

2. The Founders Library, which houses the University Libraries general collection, contains over 1,000,000 bound volumes; approximately 7,000 current periodical titles; 57,000 items on microfilm; and several thousand other items. African holdings total at least 3,500-4,000 volumes.

3. The African holdings of the Founders Library and the 10 branches which comprise the university libraries system, provide adequate resources to support the university's program of instruction and research. (Most of the primary sources are housed in the Moorland-Spingarn Research Center, see entry A21.) Founders holdings on Africa consist of general reference works and more current materials.

    Subject categories, numbers of titles, and evaluation:*

Subject Category	Total	North	East	West	Central	South-ern	Evalu-ation
History	1,350	255	212	357	212	276	C

	Egypt 234	Ethiopia 55	Nigeria 85	Zaire 51
		Kenya 25	Ghana 64	

Subject Category	Total	Evaluation
Philosophy and Religion	85	D
Geography	42	B/C
Anthropology	64	B/C
Economics	191	C/D
Sociology	149	B
Politics and Government	234	B
Foreign Relations	85	B
Law	†	
Education	42	D
Fine Arts	81	B
Language and Literature	110	D–
Military	10	C
Bibliography and Reference	64	D

---

* The shelflist measurement was complicated by the fact that the Founders Library collection is classified partly under the Library of Congress system and partly under the Dewey Decimal System.

† Insignificant.

4. Most of the African periodicals are available in the Moorland-Spingarn Research Center. Founders Library subscribes to a few African newspapers which include: *African World, Arab News, Ethiopian Herald,* and the *Sunday Times* (Nigeria).

6. The library maintains a subject/author card catalog. A subject listing for periodicals is available. A record of periodical titles currently re-

ceived by all components of the library system is maintained at the reference desk. Additionally, computerized bibliographic searches are also available through the Reference Department of the library.

A21 Howard University—Moorland-Spingarn Research Center

1. a. *Founders Library, Room 109*
   500 Howard Place, NW
   Washington, D.C. 20059
   636-7239/40 (For all services)

   b. For most of the academic year:
   9:00 A.M.-5:00 P.M.   Monday and Friday
   9:00 A.M.-8:00 P.M.   Tuesday, Wednesday, and Thursday
   9:00 A.M.-4:30 P.M.   Saturday
   Summer hours:
   9:00 A.M.-5:00 P.M.   Monday-Friday

   c. Open to the public, but all outside researchers must obtain a visitor research card, which is easily procured on arrival. The card is valid for one academic year. There is no ILL, and no materials may leave the reading room. However, individual items may be microfilmed or photocopied by the library at the researcher's request and expense.

   d. Dr. Michael R. Winston, Director of the Center
   James P. Johnson, Chief Librarian
   Betty M. Culpepper, Head Reference Librarian
   Cornelia R. Stokes, Coordinator of Reader Services
   Ethel M. Ellis, Cataloger

2. The Moorland-Spingarn Research Center Library comprises some 90,000 volumes or approximately 56,000 titles (March 1977 figures) and an additional 8,000 titles in process of classification. Of the Moorland Collection's 40,531 titles, 15,000 deal with Africa, while 25,531 deal with America and foreign areas such as the Caribbean. Of the Spingarn Collection's 12,700 titles, 3,000 deal with Africa, 6,900 with America, and 2,800 with foreign areas such as the Caribbean and other areas connected with the African diaspora.

3. The total collection of the Moorland-Spingarn Research Center Library is the richest and most accessible assemblage of African and African diaspora materials outside the Library of Congress. For researchers interested in Pan-Africanism and intra-diaspora relations, this library may be the most important in the world. A knowledgeable and helpful staff plus a reading room decorated with portraits of former Howard University professors and with artifacts from the manuscript collection or museum make this library a desirable place to work.
   Two separately maintained collections form the core of the library, namely, the gift donated to the university in 1914 by the Reverend Jesse E. Moorland and the purchase by the university in 1946 of the books amassed by attorney Arthur B. Spingarn. Each of these collectors had concentrated on books about Africa and the African diaspora and on

books written by black authors. The Spingarn group, composed exclusively of books by black authors, has remained intact since 1968, while the Moorland group has been growing over the years. Other collections acquired from time to time, such as that of Glen Carrington, are integrated with the Moorland group. The most recent accession is the Jon Bonk Collection, which consists of historical and contemporary Ethiopian materials.

Most growth was due to the efforts of Mrs. Dorothy Burnett Porter, curator from 1930 to 1973, who resides in Washington. Her successor, Dr. Michael R. Winston, director of the Moorland-Spingarn Research Center, has continued her work. A significantly greater financial commitment by the university followed the center's transformation in 1973 from a collection within the main university library into a comprehensive research facility. In addition to the library, the research center is composed of a museum (see entry C6), a manuscript division (see entry B1), a photoduplication center, and a photography section.

The center is constantly expanding with the addition of new collections and by the steady purchase of new books about black Africa, particularly about Chad, Congo, Gabon, Liberia, Sierra Leone, Cameroon, Central African Empire, Ethiopia, Ghana, Nigeria, Senegal, Guinea, Kenya, Tanzania, and Uganda. Plans are being formulated for regular contacts and exchanges with similar centers in Africa and the Caribbean.

Subject categories, number of titles, and evaluations:

Subject Category	Total	North	East	West	Central	Southern	Evaluation
History	7,182	462	1,012	2,422	661	1,108	A/B
		Egypt 125	Ethiopia 250	Nigeria 900	Zaire 581	R.S.A. 380	
Philosophy and Religion	320	45	31	62	10	35	B
		Egypt 4	Ethiopia 11	Nigeria 17	Zaire 3	R.S.A. 19	
Geography	1,051						A/B
Anth. and Soc.	440						A/B
Economics	736	63	162	436	60	139	B
		Egypt 14	Ethiopia 36	Nigeria 250	Zaire 22	R.S.A. 69	
Politics and Government	1,354	62	145	339	99	420	A/B
		Algeria 19	Kenya 46	Nigeria 136	Zaire 61	R.S.A. 346	
Foreign Relations	56						B
Law	125						D–

Subject Category	Total	North	East	West	Central	Southern	Evaluation
Education	335						B/C
Fine Arts	381						B
Language	1,306						A/B
Literature	2,000						A/B
Military	13						B
Bibliography and Reference	587						A/B

Subject Strength—Spingarn Collection

Quantitative measurement of the Spingarn Collection is not very meaningful because the author's name is the primary means of classification, and cross-referencing is limited, as many books fall in the subject categories of fiction and poetry. Among these are many first editions and signed copies. An added feature of the Spingarn Collection is the notation of the citizenship of authors on the cards. Some books are found in both the Spingarn and Moorland collections, but not many. For example, under the subject "Yoruba" Moorland has 72 titles, of which only 8 are duplicated in Spingarn. Under the same subject Spingarn has 64 titles of which only 8 are duplicated in Moorland. Under "Senegal" Moorland has 94 titles of which only 7 are found in Spingarn, and Spingarn has 16 titles not found in Moorland. Thus the 2 collections complement each other.

The Spingarn and Moorland collection of African authors is particularly valuable. For example, of the 12 Yoruba authors listed by Herdeck (*African Authors,* see Bibliography), Moorland-Spingarn has 7 and in addition has at least 11 other Yoruba authors—writing in Yoruba language for the most part—who are not listed by Herdeck. Benedict Vilakazi, an important Zulu writer, has 4 books in the Zulu language in the collection, plus a Zulu-English dictionary. Alexis Kagame, an historian of Rwanda and Burundi, has 3 books in Kinyarwanda and 14 in French in the collection. Zakea Dolphin Mangoaela, writing in Sesotho, has 4 books in the combined collection. Seventy-one different African languages are represented in the form of bilingual dictionaries and grammars, and at least 25 African languages are presented in the form of novels and collections of poetry. Zulu, Luganda, Swahili, Yoruba, and Hausa are particularly well represented.

Numbers of titles of African-language books, by region:

North Africa	12
(Sudan)	(7)
West Africa	927
(Nigeria)	(440)
Central Africa	143
(Zaire)	(55)
East Africa	268
(Uganda)	(103)
South Africa	331
(Republic of South Africa)	(226)

4.   The library possesses 803 different periodicals from Africa and areas connected with the African diaspora. Of these, 345 are currently received on a regular basis, and a total of about 140 come from Africa. Out of 256 regularly received newspapers, 54 are African; 168 out of 440 newspapers on microfilm are African; and 14 out of 217 hard copies (stored newspapers) are African, making a total of 236 titles from Africa. There are plans to increase the number of current subscriptions from 50 to 70, and the library is microfilming many titles.

     With respect to government documents Nigeria and Liberia are particularly well represented. There is a fairly large collection of vertical files. Archives, manuscripts, maps, films, and tapes are primarily in the manuscript division (see entry B1).

5.   Moorland-Spingarn owns several rare books:
     'Abd al-Rahmān ibn 'Abd Allāh al-Sa'di, *Tarikh es Soudan,* in Arabic (Paris, 1898);
     William Bosman, *A New and Accurate Description of the Coast of Guinea* . . . (London, 1705);
     T. Edward Bowditch, *Mission from Cape Coast Castle to Ashantee* (London, 1819);
     Olaudah Equiano, *The Interesting Narrative of the Life of Olaudah Equiano or Gustavus Vassa, the African* (Norwich, 1794);
     Johann M. Hartmann, *Edrisii Africa* (1796); and
     Anders Sparrman, *A Voyage to the Cape of Good Hope* . . . (London, 1785).

     In addition, the library has purchased 276 reels of microfilm containing the records of the Church Missionary Society of London (CMS) covering the period 1803–1914, and it has obtained on microfilm the British Colonial Office *Annual Reports of the Colonies,* 1889–1938/39 for all African and Caribbean colonies. Howard University dissertations and papers given at the International Congress of Africanists (1973) are on microfilm.

     The library has the Albert Porte papers on microfilm, and they contain Liberian newspapers, reports of Liberian political party affairs, Liberia's official gazette, and correspondence about Liberian politics. A microfilm of the C. Abayomi Cassell collection on Liberian affairs is also in the library.

6.   Two separate card catalogs cover the 2 collections of books. In addition, there are separate drawers for periodicals, dissertations done at Howard, and publications by Howard faculty members. Several guides and aids have been prepared over the years and are being prepared now. Among them are:
     Dorothy B. Porter, "The African Collection at Howard University," *African Studies Bulletin* 2 (January 1959): 17–21;
     ———, *Dictionary Catalog of the Arthur B. Spingarn Collection of Negro Authors,* 2 volumes (Boston: G.K. Hall & Co., 1970);
     ———, *Dictionary Catalog of the Jesse E. Moorland Collection of Negro Life and History,* 9 volumes (Boston: G.K. Hall & Co., 1970), with a 3-volume supplement (1977);
     ———, *Howard University Masters' Theses Submitted in Partial Fulfillment of the Requirements for the Master's Degree at Howard University, 1918–1945* (Howard University Graduate School, 1946);

————, "A Library on the Negro," *The American Scholar* 7 (Winter 1938): 115–117.

In addition, the abovementioned microfilm collections are accompanied by lists of contents. Since 1968, books in African languages are listed in a separate file according to language.

Michael R. Winston, "Moorland-Spingarn Research Center: A Past Revisited, A Present Reclaimed," *New Directions* (Summer 1974), is available in reprints in the library. Several other small brochures are printed to explain how to use the library, and ad hoc bibliographic lists on subjects of current interest are prepared by the staff. With the addition of every new major collection a catalog and program are printed. Members of the staff have prepared bibliographies and bibliographic essays, but they are primarily about Afro-American subjects.

Institute of International Law and Economic Development Library
See entry H17.

A22 Interior Department—Natural Resources Library

1. a. *Department of the Interior*
    C Street entrance, between 18th and 19th Streets, NW
    Washington, D.C. 20240
    343-5821
    343-5815 (Reference)

    b. 7:45 A.M.-5:00 P.M.   Monday-Friday

    c. Open to the public for on-site use. ILL and photoreproduction services available.

    d. Mary A. Huffer, Director

2. The library holds over 750,000 volumes and currently receives 4,000 periodicals and 8,000 serials. The majority of the library's holdings relate to natural resources interpreted in terms of the environment as a whole.

3. The library's total holdings on Africa number approximately 300 titles. Though there are a limited number of items in other subject categories, most of the works deal with natural history, geology, mines and mineral resources, ornithology, and wildlife. South Africa, Rhodesia, and Zambia are particularly well represented in the collection.

6. The library's holdings are listed in the *Dictionary Catalog of the Departmental Library*, 37 volumes (Boston: G.K. Hall & Co., 1967), with 4 supplementary volumes. Researchers should also consult the U.S. Department of the Interior, *Natural Resources in Foreign Countries: A Contribution Toward a Bibliography of Bibliographies,* compiled by Mary Anglemyer (January 1968), which is arranged alphabetically by continent and country.

    For a complete list of the serials holdings, see the National Resources Library—Technical Services Division, *Key Title Serial List* (December 1975).

Note: The Interior Department has several branch libraries located throughout the country. Many of their holdings are not duplicated in the main library but can be accessed by means of the interlibrary-transmitted system. (See also Geological Survey Library, entry A14.)

A23 International Communication Agency (ICA) (formerly United States Information Agency) Library

1. a. *1750 Pennsylvania Avenue, NW, Room 1011*
      Washington, D.C. 20547
      724-9214 (Librarian)
      724-9126 (Reference)

   b. 8:45 A.M.-5:30 P.M.   Monday-Friday

   c. Closed to the public. ILL service and photocopying facilities are available.

   d. Jeanne R. Zeydel, Librarian

2. The ICA Library holds approximately 65,000 volumes, some 1,300 of which deal with Africa. The library currently receives an estimated 400 periodicals and a large number of newspapers.

3. Primarily a reference collection for ICA staff members, the library holdings focus on United States foreign relations, international affairs, government and politics, area studies, and communications.
   The book collection of the ICA Library is not a significant resource for Africanists.

   Subject categories, numbers of titles, and evaluations:

Subject Category	Total	Evaluation
History	680 (of which there are 85 for Egypt, 85 for Republic of South Africa, 44 for Nigeria, 42 for Kenya, and 38 for Congo)	D–
Philosophy and Religion	*	
Geography	42	C
Anthropology	13	D–
Economics	71	D–
Sociology	40	B
Politics and Government	111	C
Foreign Relations	25	B
Law	*	
Education	22	D–
Fine Arts	8	D–
Language and Literature	25	D–
Military	*	
Bibliography and Reference	29	D–

* Insignificant.

4-5.   The library receives newspapers and periodicals from Africa. These are not retained in the library but are sent to various African divisions within ICA.

   The Documents Branch of the library (724-9364) contains over 3.5 million items, including U.S. government reports and press releases, issuances from several international organizations, and clippings from U.S. newspapers. This collection is organized by geographic areas and by subject.

   The Propaganda Collection, Room 1014 (724-9292) contains some 25,000 items of communist propaganda in Western languages. Holdings are organized by country.

6.   The library publishes a number of accessions lists on a regular basis, covering books (biweekly), documents (weekly), and classified documents (weekly), all arranged by geographic area.

   In addition, the library also issues bibliographies, such as Joseph L. Dees, comp., *United States Information Agency Library Resources on Africa: An Annotated Selection of 400 Books from the Agency Library's Holdings on Africa*, indexed by region and country.

   An information pamphlet and an index of periodical holdings are available.

A24   International Labour Office (ILO)—Washington Branch Library

1. a. *1750 New York Avenue, NW, Room 330*
    Washington, D.C. 20006
    634-6335

    b. 8:30 A.M.-5:00 P.M.   Monday-Friday

    c. Open to the public. Photoreproduction facilities available.

    d. Patricia S. Hord, Librarian

2.   The library holdings comprise some 13,000 volumes and more than 3,500 ILO documents.

3.   The library's comprehensive collection of ILO publications and documents is an important resource for the researcher. The majority of the holdings fall within the subject categories of economics, law, and sociology. The library's acquisitions are particularly strong in the fields of industrial relations, management, manpower planning, economic and social development, and educational planning and vocational training.

4-5.   The Africanist can find a wealth of material pertaining to Africa in the various ILO studies, monographs, and handbooks, as well as the special reports prepared for International Labour Conferences and other regional meetings. A quick survey of ILO publications revealed over 30 items that focused specifically on Africa. Noteworthy among these were: the African Advisory Committee, *Evaluation of ILO Activities in the African Region* (1975); *Employment Incomes and Equality: A Strategy for Increasing Productive Employment in Kenya* (1972); *ILO, Employment in Africa: Some Critical Issues* (Geneva, 1973); and *Report of the*

Director-General: A Basic-Needs Strategy for Africa (Abidjan, 1977).
There are 2 major resources available to the Africanist. The first is the
Technical Assistance Programme (TAP) Reports, which are arranged
alphabetically by country in vertical files. There are over 400 classified and unclassified reports in this collection. They focus on varied
aspects of labor-related themes, such as development of vocational
training, trade union activities, cooperative education and training, and
rural youth and rehabilitation programs. The second source of information is the ILO periodicals, which include: *Bulletin of Labour Statistics;
International Labour Documentation; International Labour Review;* the
Legislative Series (which lists the important national laws and regulations on labor and social security); the *Official Bulletin,* which provides
information on the activities of the ILO and the texts adopted by the
various conferences; *Social and Labour Bulletin;* and *Yearbook of
Labour Statistics.*

6. Guides for using the ILO library and materials include: *Cumulative
Edition, 1970–1971* (2 volumes), and *International Labour Documentation: Cumulative Edition, 1965–1969* (8 volumes). This extremely useful
bibliographic tool lists all the documents, conference papers, monographs, reports, and other studies, and is arranged by subject, author,
and country. Researchers should also consult the *ILO Catalogue of
Publications in Print, 1977* and the *Subject Guide to Publications of the
International Labour Office, 1919–1964.*

Note: Also see entry F20.

A25 International Trade Commission Library

1. a. *701 E Street, NW*
Washington, D.C. 20436
523-0013

   b. 8:45 A.M.-5:15 P.M.   Monday-Friday

   c. Open to the public. ILL and photoreproduction facilities available in the
building.

   d. Dorothy J. Berkowitz, Chief, Library Division

2-3. The International Trade Commission (formerly Tariff Commission)
Library contains about 75,000 volumes, 1,300 periodical titles, and some
microfilms. The bulk of the collection falls in the broad subject category
of economics (agriculture, econometrics, tariffs, fisheries, forests, commerce, etc.).
The library receives official foreign trade serials and statistical yearbooks from various African countries. Other items of interest include:
official tariff schedules (these are supplemented by the *International
Customs Journal,* by country); *Treaties and Other International Agreement* series; *Overseas Business Reports,* which give the economic outlook
and commercial policies of various countries; and *United Nations International Trade Statistics* series.

4. The library's Foreign Service Reports Collection should be of special interest to researchers. It consists of official airgrams from U.S. diplomatic posts in various countries of the world which contain current information on general economic conditions, trade developments, agricultural and industrial production, investment climate, etc., of the specific country. Many of these reports are classified. Private researchers can, however, gain access to the unclassified reports.

A26 Joint Bank-Fund Library (Library of the International Monetary Fund and the International Bank for Reconstruction and Development)

1. a. *700 19th Street, NW*
    Washington, D.C. 20431
    477-3125 (Librarian)
    477-3167 (Reference)

    b. 9:00 A.M.-5:30 P.M.   Monday-Friday

    c. Open to researchers for on-site use. ILL and photoreproduction services available.

    d. Charles Olsen, Librarian

2. The materials in the Joint Bank-Fund Library consist of over 150,000 cataloged volumes in some 30 languages, and 3,000 current periodical titles and newspapers. The library also maintains a file of 5,000 pamphlets and a rapidly growing microfilm collection. The holdings on Africa number over 11,000 titles, in addition to over 400 serials and periodicals.

3. Most of the items in the library's collection fall in the subject category of economics. Within this broad category there is a heavy concentration in the fields of public finance, planning and development, international commerce, capital investment, banking, statistics, and labor economics. For this category, the collection rates an A. Since this is a specialized library, items in other subject categories are insignificant, and the breakdown of the number of titles is provided on the basis of region and country:

    Subject Category—Economics

Africa—General	1,067
Reference Works	114
North Africa	1,171
Morocco	238
Egypt	357
Algeria	181
Tunisia	223
West Africa	2,631
Nigeria	619
Ghana	303
Liberia	125

Subject Category—Economics

Central Africa	750
Central African Republic	53
Congo	321
Angola	71
East Africa	1,553
Kenya	321
Uganda	232
Ethiopia	153
Southern Africa	1,303
Republic of South Africa	425
Rhodesia	339
Zambia	286

4.   The library receives over 400 serials and periodicals pertaining to Africa and approximately 50 daily newspapers from the major African nations. This extensive list of newspapers includes *Al-Ahram* (Egypt), *Al-Mouharrir Noticias* (Mozambique), *Cameroon Tribune, Ehuzu* (Dahomey), *Ethiopian Herald, Etumba* (Congo), *Fraternité Matin* (Ivory Coast), *El Moudjahid* (Algeria), *Le Sahel* (Niger), *Le Soleil* (Senegal), *Standard* (Kenya), and many others.

A sizable portion of the library collection is made up of reports, publications, and other materials from member countries. These items are also an important resource for the researcher.

6.   The main card catalog in the library is arranged alphabetically by author, title, and subject. However, for the Africanist a far more useful and unique facility is the Geographic Catalog, in which the library's holdings are arranged by regions, subregions, and country.

Bibliographic guides to the library's collection include: *Economics and Finance: Index to Periodical Articles, 1947–71* (Boston: G.K. Hall & Co., 1972) with a *First Supplement, 1972–1974,* and a *Second Supplement, 1975–1977*—a valuable reference tool, especially for locating and identifying material by geographic area and country; Joint Library of the International Monetary Fund and of the International Bank for Reconstruction and Development, *The Developing Areas: A Classed Bibliography of the Joint Bank-Fund Library,* 3 volumes (G.K. Hall & Co., 1976).

The Joint Library also publishes a monthly *List of Recent Periodical Articles.* Two other items of interest are: International Bank for Reconstruction and Development, *Catalog of Publications* (Washington, D.C., 1977), and the *Catalog of Studies* published annually, listing *Economic Staff Reports, Miscellaneous Reports, Working Papers,* and the numerous *World Bank Staff Occasional Papers,* many of which contain material of interest for the Africanist.

A brochure entitled *Guide to the Joint Bank-Fund Library* is available free of charge.

A27 Library of Congress

1. a. *Main Building*
   East Capitol and First Street, SE
   Washington, D.C. 20540

   Thomas Jefferson Building (Annex)
   Second and Independence Avenues, SE
   Washington, D.C. 20540
   287-5000 (For all services)

   b. General Reading Rooms, Main Building and Annex
   8:30 A.M.-9:30 P.M. (Book requests accepted to 7:45 P.M.)   Monday-Friday
   8:30 A.M.-5:00 P.M. (Book requests accepted to 4:00 P.M.)   Saturday
   1:00 P.M.-5:00 P.M. (Book requests accepted to 4:30 P.M.)   Sunday
   Closed Christmas, New Year's Day, Memorial Day, Fourth of July, Labor Day, and Thanksgiving.
   Division hours are noted below.

   c. Reading rooms are open to all adult readers and scholars. No letters of introduction are required, and no permits are issued. Open access sometimes means that it is difficult to find a seat, so that researchers with limited time are advised to arrive early. ILL service operates, and a complete photoduplication service is available.

   d. Daniel J. Boorstin, The Librarian of Congress
   Division chiefs listed below.

2-3.   The total holdings of the Library of Congress have been estimated at about 75 million items. Its collection of Africana—material issued in or relating to Africa—comprises over 33,000 book titles; 6,000 periodicals; 35,000 government publications; and approximately 7,000 titles in African languages (including Arabic). This makes it the largest and most comprehensive collection in the country, and among the finest in the world. Size, however, has its drawbacks. It is often difficult to identify and locate all the available research materials on a given topic, because the holdings are not merely extensive but dispersed among various divisions of the library. A wealth of Africana may be found in the special collections of legal material, manuscripts, maps, microfilm, music, newspapers, prints, photographs, and films in various custodial divisions of the library. In addition, large quantities of materials remain uncataloged. Scholars who wish to utilize these unusually rich research materials should visit the various divisions described in the following pages, undertake a thorough search of the catalogs and other research tools available in each division, and confer with the reference staff members who can answer inquiries and assist in locating materials.

   Readers intending to use the library research facilities for an extended period may want to apply for private desks (there is currently a 6-month waiting list), reserved book shelves, advance book reserve service, and limited stack passes. The Study Facilities Office in the General Reading Rooms Division (287-5530) handles all applications and requests. Complaints regarding stack service should be addressed to the Collections Management Division (287-5455).

Subject categories, numbers of titles, and evaluations:

Subject Category	Total	General	North (Egypt)	West (Nigr.)	Central (Zaire)	East (Ethiop.)	Southern (R.S.A.)	Evaluation
History	28,889	3,734	9,304 (4,006)	4,603 (830)	1,752 (990)	4,355 (1,080)	5,141 (3,301)	A
Phil. and Religion	3,348	2,417	753 (728)	37	16	69 (46)	56 (12)	A
Geography *	250							A
Anthropology	789	400	26 (21)	141	79	71	72	A
Economics	4,745	884	853 (379)	905 (280)	291 (140)	979 (200)	833 (168)	A
Sociology (Slavery)	339							A
Politics and Government	2,510	314	449 (187)	563 (250)	114 (60)	415 (124)	655 (409)	A
For. Relations	250							
† Law	7,302	275	3,395 (2,660)	756 (315)	401 (185)	856 (180)	1,619 (1,415)	A
Education	1,404	348	241 (125)	250 (20)	54 (27)	198 (37)	313 (250)	A
Fine Arts	724	370	354 (199)					A
Language and Literature	6,305							A
Military	133							A
Bibliography and Reference	2,903	1,689	459 (102)	120 (22)	54 (28)	95 (29)	486 (324)	A

* Number includes 100 books on geography and cartography in the reference collection of the division located in Alexandria, Virginia, which will probably be moved to the new Madison Annex. The main collection has an additional 150 titles on cartography.

† In the Law Library. Data do not include European colonial law.

THE AFRICAN AND MIDDLE EASTERN DIVISION

Thomas Jefferson Building (Annex)
First Floor, Room 1040C
287-7937

Julian W. Witherell, Chief

African Section
Room 1940C
287-5528

8:30 A.M.-4:30 P.M.   Monday-Friday

Beverly A. Gray, Head
John B. Howell, Area Specialist
Joanne M. Zellers, Area Specialist
Mattye Laverne Brandon, Senior Reference Librarian/Bibliographer
Fassil Aradoum, Senior Reference Librarian/Bibliographer
H. Dwight Beers, Library Technician

The African Section, established in 1960, is one of the 3 units of the Library of Congress' African and Middle Eastern Division. It serves as a focal point of the library's reference and bibliographic activities on Sub-Saharan Africa. (North Africa—Algeria, Egypt, Libya, Morocco, and Tunisia—is outside its purview.) The section also plays a vital role in the library's acquisitions program and may recommend the purchase or accessioning of other materials. In addition, it handles inquiries from Congress, government agencies, organizations, and the scholarly community.

The Library of Congress' collections of Africana—material from or relating to Africa—are outstanding and include virtually every significant area of study except technical agriculture and clinical medicine. These extensive holdings are dispersed in the library's general book and periodical collections and other numerous special collections, such as manuscripts, maps, newspapers, films, photographs, etc. The African Section's staff of reference specialists is available for consultation and can assist researchers in locating African materials in the library.

The section maintains a small reading room with a basic reference collection of published bibliographies, general studies, dictionaries, yearbooks, unpublished research papers, and biographical materials. Current issues of some 40 major periodicals are displayed for easy access. The section also maintains a vertical file collection comprising mainly pamphlets arranged by region, country, and subject. Some items of interest in this collection include agriculture and trade materials, speeches by political leaders, trade union materials, programs and publications of liberation movements, unpublished papers, and miscellaneous items on the Organization of African Unity.

The section provides a number of unique reference tools and finding aids to facilitate the task of researchers. These include: (1) a monograph and series card catalog which is arranged by area and subject categories and duplicates cards from the main catalog, as well as preliminary cards for uncataloged materials; (2) a card index for African languages (excluding Arabic); (3) a periodical card index of over 100,000 citations from several hundred serials, arranged by area and subject. Much of the material in this index has been published in 4 volumes entitled *Africa South of the Sahara: Index to Periodical Literature, 1900–1970* (Boston: G.K. Hall & Co., 1971). A *First Supplement* for 1971 was issued in 1973 and a second supplement is now in preparation.

The African Section has over the years compiled a number of bibliographic guides with a view to bringing the African material to the attention of scholars and librarians. These range in scope from general and topical guides on Sub-Saharan Africa to bibliographies of official publications of a specific country or region. The publications listed below were prepared between 1965 and 1978:

African Names and Naming Practices: A Selected List of References in English (1977);

African Newspapers in Selected American Libraries: A Union List, 3d ed. (1965), compiled in the library's Serial Division;

The African Section in the Library of Congress (1979);

Africana Acquisitions: Report of a Publication Survey Trip to Nigeria, Southern Africa, and Europe, 1972 (1973);

Africana in the Library of Congress (1977);

Arab-African Relations, 1973–75: A Guide, Maktaba Africana Series (1976);

Botswana, Lesotho, and Swaziland: A Guide to Official Publications, 1868–1968 (1971);

East African Community: Subject Guide to Official Publications (1976);

Folklore from Africa to the United States: An Annotated Bibliography (1976), compiled in the library's Children's Book Section;

French-Speaking Central Africa: A Guide to Official Publications in American Libraries (1973);

French-Speaking West Africa: A Guide to Official Publications (1967);

Ghana: A Guide to Official Publications, 1872–1968 (1969);

Islam in Sub-Saharan Africa: A Partially Annotated Guide (1978);

Kenya: Subject Guide to Official Publications (1978);

Madagascar and Adjacent Islands: A Guide to Official Publications (1965);

Nigeria: A Guide to Official Publications (1966);

The Nigerian Petroleum Industry: A Guide, Maktaba Africana Series (1978);

Portuguese Africa: A Guide to Official Publications (1967);

The Rhodesias and Nyasaland: A Guide to Official Publications (1965);

La Section Africaine de la Bibliothèque du Congress, folder (1975);

Spanish-Speaking Africa: A Guide to Official Publications (1973);

Sub-Saharan Africa: A Guide to Serials (1970);

Tanganyika African National Union: A Guide to Publications by and about TANU, Maktaba Africana Series (1976);

Uganda: Subject Guide to Official Publications (1977);

United States and Africa: Guide to U.S. Official Documents and Government-Sponsored Publications on Africa, 1785–1975 (1978);

Zanzibar's Afro-Shirazi Party, 1957–1977: A Bibliography, Maktaba Africana Series (1978).

Since 1962, the African Section has contributed on a regular basis to the *Joint Acquisitions List of Africana,* a bimonthly publication of Northwestern University Library. Recent acquisitions from East Africa are listed in the *Accessions List: Eastern Africa,* also issued bimonthly.

Microfilm and photoreproduction services are available through the Photoduplication Service of the library.

HEBRAIC SECTION

Thomas Jefferson Building (Annex)
First Floor, Room 1006
287-5422

8:30 A.M.-5:00 P.M.   Monday-Friday

Lawrence Marwick, Head
Myron M. Weinstein, Senior Reference Librarian

The Hebraic Section has custody over the Library of Congress' collection of Hebrew, Yiddish, Aramaic, Syriac, Ethiopic, and cognate languages. Books and periodicals in Coptic and in Ethiopian languages such as Amharic and Ge'ez are available in this section.

The section's total holdings of over 115,000 volumes include an estimated 1,000 items in Amharic. Many of these materials do not appear in the library's main card catalog; therefore, researchers should seek the assistance of the reference staff in locating African materials. Researchers should find substantial material here on subjects such as the history, cultures, and languages of the ancient Near East; Jews and Judaism in Africa; Zionism; anti-semitism; and Ethiopia. There are also several titles on pre-Islamic Egypt in the card catalogs.

Research tools in the section include the *Union Catalog of Hebraica in America* and an unpublished title catalog in card form arranged by Hebrew alphabet.

In addition, Africanists should find useful material in the following reference and bibliographic works. These do not, however, reflect the holdings of the Library of Congress Hebraic collection:

Robert Attal, *Les Juifs D'Afrique du Nord: Bibliographie* (Jerusalem: Institut Ben-Zvi Yad Izhak Ben-Zvi et Université Hébraïque, 1973);

Joseph Ben Naim, *Malkhe rabanan* (Jerusalem, 1930–31);

Solomon Gabre Christos, comp., *A Decade of Ethiopian Language Publications, 1959–1969* (Addis Ababa: Haile Sellassie I University Library, 1971);

Pierre Comba, *List of Books in Amharic in the Ethiopian Collection of the University College of Addis Ababa, April 1959* (Addis Ababa, 1961);

David Corcos, *Studies in the History of the Jews of Morocco* (Jerusalem: Rubin Mass, 1976);

Maurice Eisenbeth, *Les Juifs de L'Afrique du Nord: Démographie et Onomastique* (Alger: Imprimerie du Lycée, 1936);

Leon Feldberg, ed., *South African Jewry* (Johannesburg: Fieldhill Publishing Co., 1965);

Ben-Ami Issachar, *Le Judaisme Marocain: Etudes Ethno-Culturelles* (Jerusalem: Rubin Mass, 1975);

Jacob Moses Toledano, *La Lumière du Maghreb: Histoire des Israélites du Maroc* (Jerusalem, 1911);

Stephen G. Wright, comp., *Ethiopian Incunabula from the Collections in the National Library of Ethiopia and the Haile Sellassie I University* (N.P.: Commercial Printing Press, 1967).

The section also receives a large number of periodicals and daily newspapers.

In Room A1016, shelves are provided for storage of readers' books. A microfilm reader and printer are also available. Materials may be reproduced, subject to copyright laws, through the library's Photoduplication Service.

NEAR EAST SECTION

Thomas Jefferson Building (Annex)
Room 1005, First Floor
287-5421

8:30 A.M.-5:00 P.M.   Monday-Friday
8:30 A.M.-12:30 P.M.   Saturday

George N. Atiyeh, Head
George Dimitri Selim, Arab Area Specialist, General Reference
Fawzi Tadros, Senior Reference Librarian, Periodicals
Karam M. Habashy, Processing and Reference Assistant (Newspapers)

The holdings of the Near East Section consist of materials in Arabic, Turkish, Persian, Armenian, and Central Asian languages. North Africa—Morocco, Algeria, Tunisia, Libya, and Egypt—is within its purview, and all books and periodicals in Arabic come to this section, irrespective of their place of publication.

Researchers who wish to consult books and other materials can use the Asian Reading Room, Room A1016, where reserved shelves are available for storage of books. Microfilm and microfiche readers are also easily accessible. Complete reproduction facilities are available in the building, and the section participates in interlibrary loans.

The estimated total holdings of the Near East Section exceed 108,000 titles, most of which are in the general collection. Of these about 30,000 pertain to Egypt and approximately 15,000 deal with the rest of North Africa. The collection provides a broad coverage of materials relating to the Middle East and North Africa, with special emphasis on area languages, history, the vernacular press, and government publications. Almost all of these publications are kept in the stacks of the Thomas Jefferson Building. The section maintains a reference collection of 2,000 titles in the office.

The section has the records of 250 periodicals received by the Library of Congress and 31 newspapers (19 from Egypt, 4 from Morocco, 4 from Algeria, 2 from Tunisia, and 2 from Libya). Government documents in Arabic are also in the custody of this section. A few vertical files contain pamphlets from North Africa, and although the section has custody of a number of manuscripts, they rarely concern North Africa west of Egypt. It is likely, however, that a researcher interested in linguistic and religious questions in Egypt would find valuable material. For example, the Mansuri Collection contains 1,400 manuscripts covering religious and cultural questions in the world of Islam.

A few maps are available for reference work, and the section has begun an important series of tape recordings by Near Eastern poets and writers. This is part of the Archive of World Literature. Recordings are undertaken in the Cairo office of the library or in Washington if writers and poets visit the library.

Plans are being formulated to expand the North African collection by placing blanket orders with publishing houses and by filling in newspaper and periodical gaps through field trips to the area by section personnel.

Finding aids in the section consist of a visible file of periodicals; an Arabic title catalog; an Arabic subject catalog; and an Arabic author catalog; as well as the Near East National Union List. The following publications may also assist researchers:

Accessions List, Middle East (monthly), available from the Overseas Operations Office, Library of Congress, Washington, D.C. 20540;

Salāh al-Din al-Munajjid, *Arabic Manuscripts at the Library of Congress, Washington, D.C.* (Beirut, 1969);

George Dimitri Selim, *American Doctoral Dissertations on the Arab World, 1883–1974,* 2d ed. (Washington, D.C.: Library of Congress, 1976);

United States Government Publications on the Arab World (in preperation).

HISPANIC DIVISION

Main Building
Room 239, Second Floor
287-5397 (Reference)

8:30 A.M.-5:00 P.M. Monday-Friday

William E. Carter, Chief
John Hebert, Assistant Chief
Georgette M. Dorn, Head of Reference Section
Everette Larson, Reference Librarian

The Hispanic Division (until recently called the Latin American, Portuguese, and Spanish Division) should be of interest to researchers working on Angola, Equatorial Guinea, Guinea-Bissau, Mozambique, Sahara, and other former Spanish and Portuguese possessions.

The division's primary role is to develop the various Hispanic collections which are housed separately in various divisions of the Library of Congress and to interpret them through published guides and bibliographies. Although the division does not have custody of materials, the staff will orient researchers regarding the library's diverse collections and provide bibliographic and reference assistance.

The division maintains a 4,000-volume reference collection which includes some items on Africa, and vertical files containing bibliographies, reference aids, newspaper clippings, and pamphlets. A dossier called "Blacks in the Americas" contains Vicenta Cortes, *La Trata de Esclavos Durante los Primeros Descubrimientos (1489–1516)* (1963); a Cuban study entitled *Los Aportes Culturales Africanos en America Latina;* and mimeographed lists of relevant books. In addition there is a 200-box pamphlet collection arranged geographically and topically. Africanists should find interesting materials here under titles such as "Portuguese Overseas Territories" and "Cuba." The latter contains speeches by Fidel Castro, including some with references to Africa.

The division's Archive of Hispanic Literature on Tape, which was begun in 1943, contains original voice recordings of some 400 contemporary Latin American and Iberian poets and prose writers reading selections from their works. Afro-Latin writers are also represented in this archive collection. Listening equipment is available, along with notebooks containing texts of the recorded selections. A valuable finding aid is Francisco Aguilera and Georgette M. Dorn, eds., *The Archive of Hispanic Literature on Tape: A Descriptive Guide* (Washington, D.C.: Library of Congress, 1974).

Other publications and bibliographies include: the division's *Handbook of Latin American Studies,* an annotated annual bibliography which serves as a basic reference tool; *Latin America, Spain, and Portugal: An Annotated Bibliography of Paperback Books* (1976); and Ira P. Lowenthal and Drexel G. Woodson, eds., *Catalogue de la Collection Mangones-Petionville, Haiti* (New Haven: Yale University Antilles Research Program, 1974). Four editions of this bibliography have been published to date. The latest edition, expanded to include Spain and Portugal, contains annotated references to over 1,500 paperback books on these areas.

A brochure on the Hispanic Division of the Library of Congress is available free, on request.

RARE BOOK AND SPECIAL COLLECTIONS DIVISION

Main Building
Room 256, Second Floor, Rear
287-5434

8:30 A.M.-5:00 P.M.   Monday-Friday (Holidays excepted)

William Matheson, Chief
Thomas D. Burney, Assistant to Chief
Leonard N. Beck, Subject Collections Specialist

The Rare Book and Special Collections Division has custody of over 300,000 volumes and 200,000 other items such as posters, manuscripts, photographs, and prints. Nearly four-fifths of this material is contained in over 50 special collections, none of which pertains directly to Africa. None of the division's holdings is available on interlibrary loan. The division does not have facilities for photocopying, but photoreproduction is available through the library's Photoduplication Service, subject to the physical condition of the item.

According to the shelflist, the division has about 350 titles specifically on Africa. These include the following number of titles by country: Egypt, 35; Republic of South Africa, 25; Sierra Leone, 9; and Zaire, 6. Of particular interest to Africanists are the Early Africana materials, which include:

(1) Ancient papyri fragments, the earliest of which is Egyptian and believed to have been written in the XIIth dynasty or ca. 2000 B.C.; a demotic Egyptian papyrus dating back to ca. 5th century B.C.; 4 Greek papyri from the late 1st century to 4th century A.D., including Isaiah fragments, documents of the "Associated Tax Gatherers" in Egypt, and a letter from Diogenes to Asclepiades and others.

(2) One volume of the Qu'ran dating from the late 14th century, with beautiful decoration and design.

(3) Several editions of Claudius Ptolemaeus's (Ptolemy) *Cosmographia,* the earliest of which dates back to 1478.

(4) Pliny the Elder's *Historia Naturalis.* The library has 10 editions in Latin and 2 in Italian.

(5) Half-a-dozen 15th century Egyptian bindings.

(6) *Sneyd Codex* (ca. 1503). This may contain the earliest extant accounts of early Portuguese voyages to Africa.

The Rare Book and Special Collections Division's holdings are particularly rich for the 16th- and 17th-century period of exploration and discovery. The majority of these are Portuguese, Dutch, and German accounts of travel and exploration in Africa. Notable among them are: Joannes Leo Africanus, *Description of Africa;* Fracanzano da Montalboddo, *Paesi Nuovamente Retrovati* (the division has 7 early 16th-century editions); João de Barros, *L'Asia;* Jan Huygen van Linschoten, *Beschryvinghe van de Gantsche Custe van Guinea, Manicongo, Angola, Monomotapa* (Amsterdam, 1596); and accounts of Lodovico Varthema, Giovanni Battista Ramusio, and Livio Sanuto.

Eighteenth- and 19th-century accounts of Africa include: Jehudi Ashmun, *History of the American Colony in Liberia* (1826); Paul Cuffe, *A Brief Account of the Settlement and Present Situation of the Colony of Sierra Leone* (1812); Jeronymo Lobo, *A Voyage to Abyssinia* (1735); and H.M. Stanley, *How I Found Livingstone* (1874).

In addition to the above holdings, the division has Bibles in 18 African languages (Mpongwe, Zulu, Hausa, etc.) and one Ethiopic text.

The division has its own central card catalog which provides access to most of its collections by author or other form of main entry. In addition, there are vertical files which contain articles about exhibits and special collections, but there is little on Africa. American slave narratives collected by the Federal Writers' Project are here in typescript form, along with photographs (E 444, F27 is the call number). Manuscripts of American plays are stored here, but I could see nothing relating to Africa.

The broadside collection has some Africa-related items. In the geographical shelflist the following are found under "Africa": Ethiopia (1932) 2d anniversary of the crowning of Haile Selassie; Liberia (1917) Deportation of German subjects; and under "Royal African Company" 32 broadsides, such as a 2-page brochure on "Reasons for Establishing the African Trade under a Regulated Company." The chronological volume revealed the following items: "An account of the ships employed in the African trade"; "The African Company's property to the forts and settlements in Guinea"; "American Transvaal League, Chicago Branch"; and several other items on the African slave trade.

The YA pamphlet collection, arranged serially, chronologically, and alphabetically by author or title, contains material on 19th-century American trade and commerce. Inevitably the slave trade dominates: YA 23201 "African Slave Trade in Jamaica and Comparative Treatment of Slaves, Read Before the Maryland Historical Society," October 1854; and YA 20905 "Anti-Imperialism" (1898).

Some material relating to Africa may be found in the Theodore Roosevelt Collection; among the French Revolution pamphlets; and in the Carpenter Kipling Collection of articles, letters, and manuscripts by and about Rudyard Kipling, with such items as his *The Science of Rebellion* . . . of 1901, specifically written for the Imperial South African Association (10 pages).

Two general-information brochures, *Rare Books and Special Collections in the Library of Congress* (September 1978) and *Some Guides to Special Collection in the Rare Book Division* (1974) are available free of charge. Other useful finding aids include: *Catalog of Broadsides in the Rare Book Division,* 4 volumes (Boston: G.K. Hall & Co., 1972); and Frederick R. Goff, "Early Africana in the Rare Book Division," in the *Quarterly Journal of the Library of Congress,* vol. 27, no. 3 (July 1970), pp. 267–76.

SERIAL AND GOVERNMENT PUBLICATIONS DIVISION

Newspaper and Current Periodical Room
Thomas Jefferson Building (Annex), Room 1026
287-5690

8:30 A.M.-9:30 P.M.   Monday-Friday
8:30 A.M.-5:00 P.M.   Saturday
1:00 P.M.-5:00 P.M.   Sunday

Donald F. Wisdom, Chief
Katherine F. Gould, Coordinator of Reference Service
Agnes Ferruso, Head, Government Publications Section
Frank J. Carroll, Head, Newspaper Section
Anthony J. Kostreba, Head, Periodical Section

This division currently receives approximately 75,000 titles of serial publications and 1,500 newspapers. African periodicals number about 6,000 and current newspapers 170. Once periodicals are bound (after about 1 year), they are shifted into the main collection and must be requested in the Main Reading Room. Newspapers—bound, unbound, and on microfilm—remain in the custody of the room. Forty microfilm readers and 3 reader-printers are available.

It is important to note that the room receives government periodicals such as statistical bulletins, and these are classed in the card catalog by country and not by title as is the case for other periodicals and newspapers. Most Arabic titles are in the Near East Section. The card catalog in the room indicates the following number of titles by country: General Africa—300; North Africa—213 (including 70 from Egypt); West Africa—470 (including 140 from Nigeria); Central Africa—181; East Africa—310 (including 105 from Kenya); and Southern Africa—269 (including 65 from the Republic of South Africa). This catalog is not complete as it concentrates on more recent publications, while the periodical catalog in the Main Reading Room concentrates on older publications.

The total African newspaper collection numbers 609 titles (of which 170 are currently received) from 51 countries. This figure may be somewhat misleading because there are many gaps; however, many African and other languages are represented:

Egypt—65 titles (of which 31 in Arabic, 7 in French, 2 in Greek, 1 in Italian);

Nigeria—49 titles (of which 40 in English, 5 in Hausa, 1 in Igbo);

Tanzania—27 titles (of which 9 in English, 11 in Swahili, 4 in Gujarati);

Ethiopia—15 titles (of which 4 in Amharic);

Zaire—30 titles (of which 25 in French, 2 in Swahili, 1 in Luba, 1 in Lingala, 1 in Flemish);

Republic of South Africa—71 titles (of which 47 in English, 11 in Afrikaans, 5 each in English and in Afrikaans, 2 in English and in Zulu, 1 in Tswana, 2 in Xhosa);

Madagascar—27 titles (of which 17 in Malgasy).

There are numerous finding aids in this room. There is a card catalog, as mentioned above, particularly good for current material; about 600 reference books line the walls. For foreign newspapers prior to 1962, a reader is advised to check "Parson's List of Foreign Newspapers" (1929) and the "Supplement" (1929–61) which is kept behind the reference desk in the reading room. Every 2 years the library publishes *Newspapers Received Currently in the Library of Congress;* one was published in 1976 and another in 1978. In addition, a list of African newspapers is printed for library use and may be consulted, although it is not designed for general distribution: "African Newspapers in the Library of Congress" (November 1977). The room possesses the *Index to South African Periodicals* (Johannesburg: Public Library, 1975), and it issues a small brochure on the operation of the Newspaper and Current Periodical Room.

Researchers should note that requests for bound newspapers must be placed at least 24 hours before one wishes to read them and that although the room has custody of African newspapers on microfilm (except those in Arabic), periodicals on microfilm go to the Microfilm Reading Room.

LAW LIBRARY—NEAR EASTERN AND AFRICAN LAW DIVISION

Main Building
Room 212, Second Floor
287-5075

8:30 A.M.-4:15 P.M.   Monday-Friday

Zuhair E. Jwaideh, Chief (Specialist—Middle Eastern and Islamic Law)
Edward Sourian, Assistant to the Chief (Specialist—Turkish Law)
Anton Wekerle, Senior Legal Specialist (Francophone Africa)
Yorguy Hakim, Legal Specialist (Arabic-speaking Countries)

The Near Eastern and African Law Division dates from 1959. It has jurisdiction over a total of 67 countries—almost all of Africa and Western Asia from Afghanistan to the Red Sea. The only exceptions to this great sweep are the Spanish- and Portuguese-speaking countries which, like the Philippines and even Puerto Rico, fall under the Hispanic Law Division.

There is a reading area for visitors who make requests for volumes in the division. Material may circulate under interlibrary loan procedures, and it may be reproduced in any form through the general Photoduplication Service.

The whole collection consists of 30,000 bound volumes, of which about 7,300 deal specifically with Africa. The division also receives 39 periodicals on African law.

Most African states and regions send their official gazettes to the library, and there are currently 103 of them arriving, generally 2 to 3 weeks after publication. Loose-leaf compilations of laws for the Republic of South Africa, Malawi, Zambia, Kenya, and Nigeria (annual volume) permit researchers to be very up to date on legislative changes. Most are in European languages, but Arabic, Swahili, Somali, and Afrikaans documents arrive steadily.

Noteworthy is the collection of legal documents from Zaire and Egypt. The division purchased the important *Mixed Court Gazette of Egypt*, for example, and the holdings on Islamic law are rich. The Library of Congress offices in Cairo and in Nairobi maintain a steady flow of documents, and personnel of the division travel to Africa to fill in gaps.

Several finding aids assist the researcher. The shelflist is very useful because it contains books which are not yet integrated into the main collection, and because an ingeniously organized numbering system indicates at a glance whether a title is a constitution, a compilation of laws, a civil code or other code, individual addition of separate laws, or a treatise. A subject file contains country-by-country entries around a theme such as "hijacking." One file furnishes information on periodicals received; another, on official gazettes received.

The personnel, most of whom are lawyers by training, undertake research into questions of African and Islamic law. The research completed includes: Anton Wekerle, *Guide to the Text of the Criminal Law and Criminal Procedure Codes of Burundi, Rwanda and Zaire* (1975) and the same author's *Guide to the Text of the Criminal Law and Criminal Procedure Codes of Cameroon and Togo* (September 1976). Other research in progress includes investment systems in Francophone countries. All publications are free.

Note: Also see Zuhair E. Jwaideh, "African Law Collections in the Library of Congress," in *Quarterly Journal of the Library of Congress,* vol. 27, no. 3 (July 1970), pp. 213–221, and the same author's *Nature and Scope of Marriage and Divorce Laws in Egypt and Iraq* (1976).

MICROFORM READING ROOM

Main Building
Room 140B, First Floor
287-5471

8:30 A.M.-9:30 P.M.   Monday-Friday
8:30 A.M.-5:30 P.M.   Saturday
1:00 P.M.-5:00 P.M.   Sunday

Robert V. Gross, Head
Robert Costenbader, Assistant Head
Anthony Mullan, Reference Librarian
Pablo Calvan, Reference Librarian

The Microform Reading Room has custody of about 1.5 million items in the form of microfilm, microfiche, ultrafiche, and microcards. With the exception of dissertations and certain restricted collections, material circulates through interlibrary loan.

There is no particular policy concerning African materials—some types or collections are here and some are not. The reading room maintains all dissertations put out by Xerox University Microfilm of Ann Arbor and by the University of Chicago. It has selected inventories from the French National Archives for the pre-1789 period, and one finds references to the old colonies of the Caribbean and Senegal. The reading room possesses all League of Nations documents on microfilm, social and economic plans of African countries (done by Inter-Documentation, Switzerland), documents from the International Women's Year World Conference of 1975, and the translations from Russian newspapers published by the Joint Publication Research Service (the index indicates much material on Africa).

Further, the room receives daily government information bulletins, official gazettes, and scholarly journals from Africa, all on microfilm. Examples are *Etudes Malgaches* and the gazette of the Belgian Congo. Of special interest is material collected by the Cooperative Africana Microform Project (CAMP) from largely private collections of elusive political material.

The most important periodicals received are FBIS reports and transcripts of foreign country broadcasts. The room subscribes to *Microform Review* and *Guide to Microforms in Print*.

Of particular note are the microfiche collections of CBS news broadcasts, microfilms of Afro-American journals such as *Crisis* from 1910 to 1940, the *American Anti-Slavery Reporter*, holdings of the Mother Bethel AME Church Historical Museum, publications of the African Studies Association, the Columbia University Oral History Collection, the Mangones Collection in Haiti, early state records from colonial times, and some British manuscripts (for example, a letter from Mungo Park to Earl Camden "giving an account of a journey to Africa"). In addition, the room owns microforms of the manuscripts in St. Catherine's Monastery on Mount Sinai. The Abbasid Caliphate used this Christian monastery as a document repository, and the collection includes Ethiopian-language manuscripts of prayers, Arabic Old Testament and Gospels, an Arabic-Coptic horologion or devotional book for use at various hours, and "Firmans" or decrees of the Abassid rulers who had control over North Africa during the 12th century.

Several finding aids produced by the Library of Congress should help researchers. Among them are:

"Black Journals: Periodical Resources for Afro-American and African Studies";

CBS News Index;

ERIC, *Resources in Education* (lists everything financed by the Office of Education);

FBIS Index;

"Microformats in the Library of Congress" (brochure);

"Publications of the African Studies Association" (papers given at meetings).

Other publications of interest are:

Lester K. Born, *British Manuscripts Project: A Checklist* . . . (Washington, D.C.: Library of Congress, 1955);

Kenneth W. Clark, *Checklist of Manuscripts in St. Catherine's Monastery, Mount Sinai* (Washington, D.C.: Library of Congress, 1952);

Doctoral Dissertations on Africa (London: University Microfilms International);

Ira P. Lowenthal and Drexel C. Woodson, eds., *Catalogue de la Collection Mangones—Petionville, Haiti* (New Haven: Yale University Antilles Research Program, 1974);

"Reproductions of Manuscript and Rare Printed Books" (PMLA, April 1950);

George Dimitri Selim, *American Doctoral Dissertation on the Arab World* (Washington, D.C.: Library of Congress, 1976);

F. Leonard Williams et al., "The Holdings of the Mother Bethel African Methodist Episcopal Church Historical Museum in Manuscript and Print."

There are also card catalogs arranged by "series" or periodical and by general collection. Thirty-two readers for all formats are available.

LOAN DIVISION

Main Building
Room G153, Ground Floor
287-5448
287-5444 (Emergency out-of-town interlibrary loan)

8:30 A.M.-4:00 P.M.   Monday-Friday

Libraries—not individuals—must make requests for the loan of materials, but not all holdings circulate. Libraries may keep Library of Congress items for two weeks.

American Library Association forms must be used, and they must be sent to the Library of Congress, Loan Division, Washington, D.C. 20540. Urgent requests may be made by telephone (287-5444).

Information brochures explaining this service are available free of charge.

PHOTODUPLICATION SERVICE

Thomas Jefferson Building
Room G1009, Ground Floor
287-5640

8:00 A.M.-4:15 P.M.   Monday-Friday (Except holidays)

The Photoduplication Service is the centralized office for purchase of copies in most visual reproduction formats of items in the library's collections, not subject to copyright or other restrictions.

Certain newspapers, periodicals, and government gazettes (primarily foreign titles) are microfilmed on a continuing basis. Retrospective files of similar publications (including domestic titles) and manuscript collections, such as the papers of 23 U.S. presidents, are filmed as special or cooperative projects and made available for sale. Information on the

Photoduplication Service's microform offerings of monographic or serial titles and foreign and domestic newspapers appears respectively in the *National Register of Microform Masters* and *Newspapers in Microform,* both Library of Congress publications.

Further information on orders and services can be found in the Photoduplication Service's brochures, order forms, and price sheets, and through its Public Services Section staff or the staff of the appropriate reading room.

MAIN READING ROOM—LIBRARY OF CONGRESS BUILDING 100

8:30 A.M.-9:30 P.M.   Monday-Friday
8:30 A.M.-5:00 P.M.   Saturday
1:00 P.M.-5:00 P.M.   Sunday

Most readers and researchers work here or in the Thomas Jefferson Reading Room North, which is room 5010 of the Thomas Jefferson Building. The Main Reading Room contains a collection of about 50,000 reference volumes, including a few periodicals covering all subjects. No newspapers are received, but the following government documents are accessible: Congressional hearings from 1943 to the present; a complete set of *The Congressional Record* and its predecessors; the *Federal Register* from 1936 to the present; foreign statistical abstracts; and business and other directories which happen to be published by governments.

A very small number of miscellaneous vertical files provide clippings on some topics of current interest and assorted publications of the Congressional Research Service. These files are in alcove 3, but one should consult with the reference librarian in order to use them. An adequate collection of atlases covers Africa.

Most bibliographic and finding aids for the entire Library of Congress are located in the Research Guidance Office at the west entrance of the Main Reading Room (the Thomas Jefferson Reading Room North is much smaller and is unable to provide all of these materials). These aids are described under section 6, but one should note that the card catalog for the Main Reading Room reference collection is located outside alcove 4 and consists of an author-title catalog and a shelflist. Katherin Ann Gardner reproduced the data on these cards in her book *The Library of Congress Main Reading Room Reference Collection Subject Catalog* (Washington, D.C.: Library of Congress, 1975). The card catalog for the Thomas Jefferson Reading Room is near the reference librarians' desk.

Researchers who wish to gain access to the stacks should apply for a stack pass by conferring with the reference librarian of the Main Reading Room central desk.

5.   Noteworthy holdings have been covered in the discussion of special collections.

6.   The primary reference tools for the Library of Congress collections are in the Main Reading Room, but, as mentioned earlier, they do not reflect adequately the African holdings of the institution since they do not include the specialized materials in the custody of the Rare Book, Serial, Prints and Photographs, Geography and Map, and Music divi-

sions. There is a dictionary card catalog in which cards are arranged by author, title, and subject, and a periodical catalog which duplicates cards in the main catalog. The latter tends to be better on older journals than the catalog in the Newspaper and Current Periodical Room; it is also larger. Another card catalog is located in the Genealogy Room (5012A of the Thomas Jefferson Building) but as far as can be determined, it is not too valuable for the African researcher.

Presently, the library's two computerized, machine-readable data bases can supplement the existing finding aids. The MARC (Machine-Readable Cataloging) System provides access to the library's Computerized Catalog (LCCC), which contains bibliographic information on books cataloged since 1968. The SCORPIO (Subject-Content-Oriented Retriever for Processing Information On-Line) System can be used for general bibliographic searches by subject (based on LC subject headings) and by LC classification category (call number) as well as by author and title. In addition to books, the computer contains bibliographies of periodical articles; data on some 10,000 organizations which can serve as information resources on topics in the fields of science, technology, and the social sciences (National Referral Center Master File); and Legislative Information Files for the 94th, 95th, and 96th Congresses.

Public computer terminals to MARC and SCORPIO data bases are accessible and may be used free of charge by researchers. Staff members in the Computer Catalog Center (287-6213) are on hand to assist and instruct researchers in the use of the terminals and in the conduct of bibliographic searches by author and title.

The Library of Congress steadily publishes finding aids, most of which have already been noted. In addition, one may care to consult: *Library of Congress Catalog—Book: Subjects, A Cumulative List of Works Represented by the Library of Congress Printed Cards* (1950 to present) and *The National Union Catalog.* It is best to obtain a copy of *Library of Congress Publications in Print* (appears annually), available from the library free of charge. One should also write for the descriptive pamphlets covering the various sections and divisions: Library of Congress, Washington, D.C. 20540.

Note: Also see entries B2, D2, D3, E3, F21, and F22.

A28 Maryland University Libraries

1. a. *College Park, Maryland 20742*

   McKeldin Library (Main Library)
   454-5704 (Reference)

   Architecture Library
   454-4316

   Undergraduate Library

   b. 8:00 A.M.-11:00 P.M.   Monday-Thursday
   8:00 A.M.-6:00 P.M.   Friday
   10:00 A.M.-6:00 P.M.   Saturday
   Noon-11:00 P.M.   Sunday

These hours apply to McKeldin Library. For other schedules, call the above telephone numbers.

c. Libraries and stacks open to all. ILL and photoreproduction facilities available.

d. Dr. Joanne Harrar, Director of Libraries

2. Campus libraries contain some 1,250,000 volumes, with African holdings estimated to be in excess of 9,000 volumes. The libraries currently receive over 15,850 serials and also maintain an extensive collection of microform materials and U.S. government documents.

3. Subject categories, numbers of titles, and evaluations:

Subject Category	Total	North	West	Central	East	Southern	Evaluation
History	4,375	1,054	807	450	570	740	B
		Egypt 612	Nigeria 230	Congo 127	Ethiopia 127	R.S.A. 153	
		Algeria 102	Ghana 110	Angola 34	Kenya 153	Rhodesia 94	
		Moroc. 102	Liberia 42		Uganda 42		
Philosophy and Religion	122						C/D
Geography	142						B
Anthropology	331						B
Economics	529						B
Sociology	238						B
Politics and Government	484						B
Foreign Relations	42						B
Law	*						D–
Education	138						B
Fine Arts	228						B
Language	637						B
Literature	134						B
Military	10						D–
Bibliography and Reference	170						C

* Insignificant.

4. The library's Special Collection Division consists of the Marylandia Department; Archives, Manuscripts, and Rare Books; and Special Collections. The Africanist can find a few items of interest here. In the special collections, there is substantial material on slavery, primarily papers of the Maryland Historical Society and Maryland State Colonization Society. A survey of the card catalog for the rare books revealed the following titles: Leo Africanus, *Ioannia Leonis Africani Africae Descripto IX Libris Absoluta* (1632); Albert Ernest Augustin Baratier, *A Travers l'Afrique* (Paris, ca. 1910 [?]); Rufus Wheelwright Clark, *The African Slave Trade* (Boston, 1860); Edouard Foà, *Résultats Scientifiques des Voyages en Afrique d'Edouard Foà* (Paris, 1908); and Egon Klemp, ed., *Africa on Maps Dating from the Twelfth to the Eighteenth Century* (Leipzig, 1968).

McKeldin Library is a regional depository for U.S. government documents. The majority of these items do not appear in the main card catalog (there is a separate card catalog in the Documents Room on the third floor). Besides an extensive collection of U.S. government documents, United Nations and other international documents are also available here.

The library currently subscribes to over 100 periodicals and serials which are pertinent to Africa. A new serials list is printed monthly and updated by weekly cumulative supplements.

The Fine Arts Collection, presently located in Room 4125 of McKeldin, consists of an Art Library and a Music Room. The holdings of the Art Library, which is located in Room 2213 of the Arts Sociology Building, include some 70 general reference works on African art and sculpture, in addition to various exhibition catalogs and a vertical file collection.

In the Music Room, besides general works on African music, there are over 200 records of African music, notable among them Hugh Tracey's *Sound of Africa* series, prepared under the auspices of the International Library of African Music. For assistance in locating items, researchers should contact Frederick Heutte, 454-3036.

6. There are no published catalogs or descriptions of the Maryland libraries. Visitors may, however, obtain free of charge a printed guide to McKeldin Library and 1-page flyers describing its numerous collections.

Middle East Institute (MEI) Library See entry H21.

A29 Museum of African Art Library (Smithsonian Institution)

1. a. *318 A Street, NE*
Washington, D.C. 20002
547-6222

   b. 11:00 A.M.-5:00 P.M.   Monday-Friday
Noon-5:00 P.M.   Saturday-Sunday

   c. Access is by appointment. ILL service is not available, nor is there a reproduction service. Telephone inquiries will, however, be answered.

    d. Robert Myers, Librarian
       Jacqueline Lee, Assistant Librarian

2.   This small but compact collection contains books on Africa and on Afro-American subjects. It is ancillary to the museum, but because art is an integral aspect of African society and culture, many books would be considered anthropological in orientation. It should be pointed out that for a highly specialized collection of this kind, the subject categories are not germane. On the basis of shelflist measurements, an attempt has been made, however, to provide some idea of subject strength.

Subject categories, numbers of titles, and evaluations (unless otherwise indicated, all evaluations are **D–**):

History	212	
Geography	170	
Anthropology	213	B/C
Economics	10	
Sociology	59	
Politics and Government	85	
Foreign Relations	—	
Law	20	
Education	15	
Fine Arts	289	B
Language and Literature	153	
Military	—	
Bibliography and Reference	34	

4-5.   Many of the titles deal with West and Central Africa, where most of the art of the collection originates.

    Ten periodicals are currently received by the library including *Africa Report, African Arts, Arts d'Afrique Noire,* and *Journal of Negro History.* Miscellaneous vertical files contain uncataloged clippings about African art and artists, loose bibliographies, reading lists, book advertisements for African and Afro-American art, auction catalogs (a valuable resource), and the journal *Negro Artists,* published 40 years ago by the Harmon Foundation. Flat files contain 100 maps, including an imprint from 1600.

    The library also has custody of the museum register, exhibit catalogs of the museum and other collections, and all the museum's own publications.

6.   The library maintains 2 dictionary card catalogs: Africa and Afro-America. It also has 3 shelflists divided into Art Room, Africa, and Afro-America. Personnel have prepared bibliographies and reading lists for distribution and recently have produced *Publications of Exhibit Catalogs by the Museum of African Art.*

    The library of the Museum of African Art is likely to expand considerably in the near future.

Note: Also see entries C8, D4, and F24.

National Aeronautics and Space Administration (NASA) Library
See entry K19.

A30 National Agricultural Library (NAL) (U.S.D.A. Technical Information Systems)

1. a. *Main Library:*
    U.S. Route 1 and Interstate Route 495 (Beltway Exit 27 North)
    Beltsville, Maryland 20705
    (301) 344-3756 (Reference)
    (301) 344-3755 (Information)

    D.C. Branch and Law Library:
    U.S. Department of Agriculture
    South Building
    Independence Avenue and 14th Street, SW
    Room 1052
    Washington, D.C. 20250
    447-3434

    b. Main Library: 8:00 A.M.-4:30 P.M.   Monday-Friday
    D.C. Branch: 8:00 A.M.-5:00 P.M.   Monday-Friday

    c. Open to the public. ILL and photoduplication service available.

    d. Richard A. Farley, Director

2. NAL holds some 1.5 million volumes and approximately 16,000 periodical titles. Its microfilm collection contains some 129,000 items. Library holdings fall mainly in the subject category of agriculture and related fields such as botany, forestry, economics, statistics, entomology, food and nutrition, natural and water resources, and rural health care.

3. NAL is a major resource for Africanists studying economics. The library's holdings in all other subject categories are insignificant.
    An accurate count of NAL's Africa-related holdings is not possible, since there are 2 different cataloging systems. A computer search carried out by the staff revealed that there are 6,689 items under "Africa" alone. In addition, there were 90 items under "South Africa," 1,513 under "Nigeria," 892 under "Kenya," and 1,762 under "Egypt."

4. NAL's collection of active African serials numbers some 400 titles.

6. An extremely useful bibliographic tool at the National Agricultural Library is a computerized information retrieval system, AGRICOLA. There are over 700,000 book and periodical article entries on this data base. AGRICOLA contains all items cataloged and indexed by the library since 1970.
    A search can be carried out by using keywords (geographic codes, language, subject headings, author, etc.).
    The library also has 2 other data bases which researchers will find useful: MEDLINE of the National Library of Medicine (see entry A34) and JURIS, the on-line retrieval system of the Department of Justice (entry K17).
    The Dictionary Catalog of the National Agricultural Library, 1862–1965 in 73 volumes contains all cards cataloged by the library until 1965. The *National Agricultural Library Catalog* is arranged by name and

subject. See also the *Bibliography of Agriculture,* which has annual cumulations.

Users of the library will find the following helpful: *The Card Catalogs of the National Agricultural Library: How to Use Them, The National Agricultural Library: A Guide to Services,* rev. ed. (July 1974), and a volume on AGRICOLA.

A31 National Air and Space Museum Library (Smithsonian Institution)

1. a. *6th Street and Independence Avenue, SW*
      Washington, D.C. 20560
      381-6591

   b. 10:00 A.M.-5:15 P.M.   Monday-Friday

   c. Open to scholars, by appointment only.

   d. Catherine Scott, Librarian

2-3.   The NASM Library is part of the network of Smithsonian libraries that supports research and exhibit programs of the institution. Its collection consists of some 22,000 books; 4,600 bound periodicals; and 500,000 technical reports primarily in the fields of aeronautics, astronautics, and related disciplines. The library is a minor resource for the Africanist, yet a careful search could yield some interesting material.

4-5.   The historical archives of the museum contain scattered but unusual material on Africa, particularly North Africa. The aeronautical, astronautical, and biographical files contain material on topics such as rocket development in the Middle East; the missiles and space program in Egypt; and the National Air and Space Museum's Center for Earth and Planetary Studies' scientific reports on the deserts of North Africa and the Middle East.

   Among the numerous periodicals available in the library, 3 are particularly noteworthy for their frequent coverage of Africa. Two are weekly publications, *Aviation Week and Space Technology* and *Flight International;* and the third, *Interavia,* is a monthly review of aviation, astronautics, and avionics.

6.   A descriptive article on the library and its collections is available free of charge. The library also publishes a quarterly in-house *Bulletin,* which lists the new acquisitions and indexes aerospace journal literature.

A32 National Geographic Society Library

1. a. *1146 16th Street, NW*
      Washington, D.C. 20036
      857-7787

   b. 8:30 A.M.-5:00 P.M.   Monday-Friday

c. Open to the public for on-site use. Loans within metropolitan Washington only. Photoreproduction service for staff members only.

d. Virginia Carter Hills, Head Librarian
   Carolyn Locke, Reference Librarian

2. Primarily a reference facility maintained for the staff of the National Geographic Society, the library contains over 68,200 volumes covering geography and allied sciences, ethnography, travel and exploration, and wildlife.

3. The library holdings show more than 2,350 volumes on Africa. On the basis of the shelflist, it is difficult to estimate the number of volumes in various subject categories. However, the majority of them reflect the specialized nature of the library and pertain to geography, travel, and ethnography. For the subject categories of geography and anthropology, the library merits a B rating.

   The holdings on Africa contain 615 volumes on North Africa (of which 260 are on Egypt, 65 on Morocco, and 26 on Algeria); 340 on West Africa (of which 62 are on Nigeria and 35 on Ghana); 125 on Central Africa (of which 50 are on the Congo); 375 on East Africa (of which 80 are on Ethiopia, 75 on Kenya, and 42 on Uganda); and 412 on Southern Africa (of which 122 are on the Republic of South Africa and 75 on Rhodesia).

4. The library currently receives over 1,800 periodicals, of which approximately 20 pertain to Africa.

   The National Geographic Society owns an extensive map collection (see entry E5), but its use is restricted to members of the society only. It is located in the Membership Center Building, Gaithersburg, Maryland 20760. For further information, contact Margery Barkbull, Librarian.

5. An extremely valuable resource for the researcher is the Library Clipping Service, an extensive collection of vertical file material arranged alphabetically by geographic area and by subject. There are more than 3 drawers on Africa (General) and approximately 25 folders for Egypt, 20 for Nigeria, and 18 for Kenya. These folders contain clippings from newspapers as well as other pertinent information on antiquities, ethnic populations, agriculture and economy, wildlife, flora and fauna, and related topics.

   The library also has a complete set of publications of the Hakluyt Society, which contains much useful information for the Africanist.

6. An important reference tool is the *National Geographic Index,* which lists all the articles and other relevant data published in the *National Geographic.* These include an index for 1888–1946, 1947–76, and a supplement for 1977–78.

   Scholars interested in using these materials should obtain prior authorization from the society by writing to Leonard J. Grant, Associate Secretary, National Geographic Society, 17th and M Streets, NW, Washington, D.C. 20036.

A33 National Institute of Education (Health, Education, and Welfare [HEW] Department)—Educational Research Library

1. a. *1832 M Street, NW, 6th Floor*
   Washington, D.C. 20208
   254-5060

   b. 10:00 A.M.-4:00 P.M.   Monday-Friday

   c. Open to the public. ILL and photoduplication service available.

   d. Charles D. Missar, Director

2. The NIE Educational Research Library provides a unique educational resource to the staff of the HEW Education Division, as well as to educators all over the country. It contains approximately 140,000 items in the fields of education, social science, history of education, and educational psychology, and an extensive reference and microform collection. It currently receives some 1,200 periodicals and newspapers.

3. The total holdings on Africa number some 287 volumes, of which more than 206 pertain to the subject category of education. The extent and quality of holdings make this an important resource in the field of education. The library has very little material in other subject areas; nevertheless, the education category rates a B.

4. Virtually all ERIC (Educational Resources Information Center—see entry G6) publications and materials are available here. The researcher can thus obtain documents, pamphlets, and articles on a wide range of subjects, such as adult education, demographic trends, African culture, history, literature, and languages, as well as textbooks and teacher manuals.

6. A book catalog of the entire collection is expected to be available in the near future. For periodical holdings, consult the National Institute of Education, Educational Research Library, *Periodical Holdings List,* 3d ed. (January 1978).

A34 National Library of Medicine (NLM)

1. a. *8600 Rockville Pike*
   Bethesda, Maryland 20014
   (301) 496-6095 (Reference)
   (301) 496-5405 (History of Medicine Division)

   b. Regular hours:
   8:30 A.M.-9:00 P.M.   Monday-Friday
   8:30 A.M.-5:00 P.M.   Saturday
   Closed Sunday

   Summer hours:
   8:30 A.M.-5:00 P.M.   Monday-Saturday

   History of Medicine Collection:
   8:30 A.M.-4:45 P.M.   Monday-Saturday

c. The library is open to the public. ILL and photoduplication services available.

d. Martin M. Cummings, M.D., Director

2. NLM's primary objective is to collect, preserve, disseminate, and exchange knowledge and information in the field of the health sciences. The largest collection of its kind in the world, the library holds about 2.5 million items. Besides bound volumes, there are monographs and serials; reports and vital statistics; medical theses, prints, and photographs; and micro- and audio-visual materials. The library collects materials in over 40 biomedical areas and other related fields. Currently it receives over 20,000 serial titles.

3. The library's collection is divided largely between the General Collection (comprising monographs and serials published after 1870) and the History of Medicine Collection (pre–1871 material), as well as oral history and manuscripts.

   The major part of the holdings of this library are arranged not primarily by geographic areas but by subject, which is then broken down by geographic areas. As a result, it is difficult, if not impossible, to measure accurately the holdings on Africa. Nevertheless, this library is probably the most important resource for medical literature on Africa.

   A computerized search of the library's holdings shows that since 1965, some 745 items (books and serials) pertaining to Africa have been entered in CATLINE (Catalog On-Line), NLM's data base. The library also has more than 312 serial titles on African medicine and related fields.

   Most of the holdings on Africa fall in the areas of public health, rural health, nutrition and child development, tropical diseases, and medical data and statistics.

4-5. The Documents Collection of the library contains over 7,000 selected serials and monographs, mainly health-related reports and statistics of U.S., foreign, and international agencies. These documents are arranged geographically and so it is relatively simple to locate African materials here. (African materials are shelved under Table H.)

   Measurements of the shelflist in the Documents Collection indicated a total of 350 documents for Africa (of which some 80 pertain to the Union of South Africa, 50 to Egypt, and 30 to Nigeria). These documents consist of *Annual Reports, Reports of the Department of Public Health and the Ministry of Agriculture,* health bulletins, statistics, yearbooks, etc., dating back to 1870.

   NLM has a unique collection of serials on Africa, many of which are not available elsewhere. Publications from South Africa, Egypt, Kenya, Nigeria, and Ghana are especially well represented in the collection.

   The History of Medicine Division also has valuable but scattered material on Africa. The researcher will, however, need to engage in some painstaking digging in order to unearth these materials. Some of the holdings may be located in the *Index-Catalog* (see point 6) and the *Bibliography of the History of Medicine.*

6. The NLM library has 2 catalogs for locating books. The card catalog is arranged by name (author and title) and by subject. The *Current Cata-*

log is NLM's catalog in book form and can be used instead of the card catalog for items entered since 1965.

More significantly, NLM offers several computerized search services for a small fee. CATLINE (Catalog-On-Line) is a computerized data base which contains information on items cataloged since 1965. MED-LINE (MEDLARS-On-Line) is a data base containing citations from biomedical journals. SERLINE (Serials-On-Line) gives bibliographic information on serials.

The *Periodical Locator* in the reading room should also be useful to researchers.

Of the published bibliographic tools available to researchers, the *Index-Catalogue of the Library of the Surgeon General's Office* is the most important for materials in the History of Medicine Division. This multivolume series is arranged by author and subject. A quick survey of some volumes revealed several hundred items pertaining to Africa.

A35 National Museum of Natural History (Smithsonian Institution)— Anthropology Branch Library

1. a. *Constitution Avenue at 10th Street, NW*
      Washington, D.C. 20560
      381-5048

   b. 9:00 A.M.-5:00 P.M.   Monday-Friday

   c. Open to serious researchers, by appointment only. ILL and reproduction services available by contacting the central library in the Natural History Building.

   d. Janette Saquet, Anthropology Librarian

2. The library holds some 50,000 books and currently subscribes to approximately 1,200 periodicals. African holdings total some 1,000 volumes. Since this is a specialized collection, primary emphasis is on anthropology and other allied subjects—ethnology, linguistics, archeology, and history. The library is a valuable resource for Africanists, at least in the fields of anthropology and linguistics.

3. Subject categories, numbers of titles, and evaluations:

Subject Category	Total	North	East	West	Central	South-ern	Evalu-ation
History	750	190	105	140	105	105	D
			Egypt 150	Ethiopia 30	Nigeria 46	Zaire 59	R.S.A. 25	
				Kenya 18		Angola 25	
Philosophy and Religion	36						D–
Geography	30						C

Subject Category	Total	North	East	West	Central	South-ern	Evalu-ation
Anthropology	210						A/B
Economics	26						D–
Sociology	40						B
Politics and Government	*						D–
Foreign Relations	*						D–
Law	*						D–
Education	*						D–
Fine Arts	180						B
Language and Literature	110						D–
Military	*						D–
Bibliography and Reference	50						D–

* Insignificant.

4. The library currently receives about 86 periodicals which pertain to Africa. The majority of these are in the fields of archeology, linguistics, ethnosociology, and anthropology.

5. The library maintains a vertical file collection which consists of 16 boxes for Africa arranged by region and country. This largely uncataloged material dates back to the early 19th century and contains miscellaneous reports, articles, pamphlets, and accounts of archeological excavations in Africa. A careful search of these items should yield interesting information.

6. There is no published catalog or description of the library holdings. Researchers are advised to consult the staff members for further information on Africa-related materials.

Note: Also see entries C11 and F27.

Oliveira Lima Library See Catholic University Library, entry A5.

A36 Pan-American Health Organization (PAHO) Library

1. a. *525 23rd Street, NW*
    Washington, D.C.20037
    331-5388

    b. 8:30 A.M.-5:30 P.M. Monday-Friday

    c. Open to the public for reference use. ILL available; no photocopying machines.

2. PAHO Library holdings consist of some 55,000 bound volumes and several thousand documents. The library currently receives approximately 350 periodicals.

   Though an effective measurement of the African holdings in the shelf-list is not possible, the library is undoubtedly a major resource for African area specialists.

3. The bulk of the collection consists of technical literature in the fields of medicine and public health, which includes materials on family and environmental health, disease control and epidemiology, food and nutrition, and health services. In addition there is valuable demographic and statistical data for African countries, which is not available elsewhere in Washington. Included are annual reports of African public-health agencies; technical papers and reports from PAHO's Regional Office for Africa, *Afro Technical Papers* series (approximately 100 items); public health and nutrition surveys; government documents on population and family planning; legislation pertaining to public health and welfare; statistical yearbooks and bulletins; and reports from conferences.

   The library also maintains a complete collection of Pan American Health Organization official documents and PAHO publications.

   The collection, which is a valuable resource for Africanists, ranks a B rating in the subject category of public health.

4. The library maintains vertical files of miscellaneous pamphlets and family planning documents, by country.

6. Principal finding aids consist of an author/title and a subject card catalog. A periodicals list is also available.

Peace Corps Library See ACTION Library, entry A1.

Population Crisis Committee Library See entry M40.

Population Reference Bureau, Inc. Library See entry H26.

A37 **School of Advanced International Studies (Johns Hopkins University)—Sydney R. and Elsa W. Mason Library**

1. a. *1740 Massachusetts Avenue, NW*
      Eighth floor
      Washington, D.C. 20036
      785-6805 or 785-6296

   b. 8:30 A.M.-10:00 P.M.   Monday-Thursday
      8:30 A.M.-6:00 P.M.   Friday
      10:00 A.M.-5:00 P.M.   Saturday
      Noon-9:00 P.M.   Sunday
      Call for summer intersession and holiday hours.

   c. Open to scholars with permission. ILL is available. There is no photo-duplication service, but coin-operated machines for photocopy are in use.

   d. Peter J. Promen, Director
Linda Carlson, Reader Services Librarian

2.   The whole collection of books is estimated at 55,000 titles, and the library grows by about 2,000 titles each year.

      The African books number 4,500. In addition, there are 1,200 books in the Arabic language which deal with social, political, and cultural questions in North Africa as well as in the Middle East.

3.   SAIS Library specializes in books on history, political science, and economics. The library is designed for students in the graduate programs offered by the school. In the recent past the emphasis in courses has been on American and European politics, foreign policy, and trade. Consequently, there is African material in books primarily about Europe and America. The library has, however, a solid collection of titles dealing specifically with Africa.

Subject categories, numbers of titles, and evaluations:

Subject Category	Total	North	West	Central	East	Southern	Evaluation
History	3,316	593	549	234	462	764	B
		Egypt 161	Nigeria 166	Zaire 127	Ethiopia 77	R.S.A. 475	
Philosophy and Religion	71						D
Geography	10						C/D
Anthropology	53						B/C
Economics	435	(of which Egypt 27, Nigeria 37, Zaire 15, Republic of South Africa 24)					B
Sociology	28						C
Politics and Government	214	(of which Nigeria 31)					B/C
Foreign Relations	25						B
Law	15						D–
Education	69						C
Fine Arts	17						D–
Language and Literature	98						D–
Military	6						C
Bibliography and Reference	140						C

4. About 800 periodicals are received, of which 50 concern Africa. The following African newspapers are regularly received: *Al Ahram* (Cairo), *Daily Times* (Lagos), *East African Standard* (Nairobi), and *Johannesburg Star* (by air).

6. Divided catalog. Shelflist.

Note: Also see entries H30, J12, and J13.

A38 State Department Library

1. a. *State Department Building*
   2201 C Street, NW, Room 3239
   Washington, D.C. 20520
   632-0535/1099

   b. 8:45 A.M.-5:30 P.M.   Monday-Friday

   c. Only State Department, AID, and Arms Control and Disarmament Agency employees have access to the library. However, researchers may obtain special permission to use the library when required material is not otherwise available in the Washington area. Scholars are advised to call ahead for clearance.

   d. Conrad Eaton, Librarian

2. At present, the library contains some 700,000 volumes and over 1,100 periodical titles. Annual accessions approximate 16,000 volumes, 30-40 percent of which are from foreign countries.

3. The African holdings of the library are small compared to those for other parts of the world. There is already a noticeable shift in this trend, and the library is expected to expand its African collections in the future.

   Subject categories, numbers of titles, and evaluations:

Subject Category	Total	North	West	Central	East	South-ern	Evalu-ation
History	5,079	1,445	956	893	850	935	B
		Egypt 595	Nigeria 191	Congo 255	Ethiopia 213	Rhodesia 149	
		Algeria 234	Ghana 128	C.A.E. 85	Kenya 179	S. Africa 106	
			Liberia 85	Angola 75	Uganda 43	Zambia 64	
			S. Leone 43				
Philosophy and Religion	43						D–
Geography	123						B

Subject Category	Total	North	West	Central	East	Southern	Evaluation
Anthropology	123						B/C
Economics	1,934						B
Sociology	213						B
Politics and Government	1,381						B
Foreign Relations	42						B
Law	—						D–
Education	276						B
Fine Arts	*						D–
Language and Literature	170						D
Military	30						B
Bibliography and Reference	213						B/C

* Insignificant.

4. The library currently receives some 36 periodicals pertaining to Africa. It does not subscribe to any newspapers from Africa.

   The library is also a depository for U.S. government documents.

6. There are 2 card catalogs. The first is a regular dictionary catalog arranged alphabetically by author, title, and subject; the second is the geographic catalog, arranged by continent, country, region, etc.

Note: Also see entry K24.

A39 Textile Museum Library

1. a. *2320 S Street, NW*
   Washington, D.C. 20008
   667-0441

   b. 10:00 A.M.-5:00 P.M.   Wednesday-Friday

   c. Open to the public for reference purposes. No ILL; limited reproduction services available.

   d. Katherine Freshley, Librarian

2. There are about 7,000 volumes in the library, of which over 120 would be of interest to the Africanist.

3. Since this is a specialized collection, only the fine arts category applies. Most of the titles are on subjects such as textiles, rugs, tapestries, fabrics, weaving, and sculpture. The library's holdings on Egypt are substantial

and consist of over 70 volumes. Other areas include Algeria, Morocco, Tunisia, and West Africa, which account for about 100 volumes.

4. The library currently receives more than 84 periodicals, few of which may be pertinent to the Africanist.

6. There are no published materials on the library's holdings.

Traditional Music Documentation Project (TMDP) Research Library See entry D6.

A40 Transportation Department Library

1. a. *Main Library*
    U.S. Department of Transportation
    400 7th Street, SW. Room 2200
    Washington, D.C. 20590

    426-2565 (Director)
    426-1792 (Reference)

    Branch (Air Transportation and Aeronautics)
    800 Independence Avenue, SW, Room 930
    Washington, D.C. 20590
    426-3611 (Reference)

    b. Both libraries: 8:30 A.M.-5:00 P.M.   Monday-Friday

    c. Open to the public for on-site use. ILL and photoreproduction services available.

    d. Lucile E. Beaver, Library Director

2. Combined holdings of the libraries number 550,000 documents; 125,000 microform items, and 2,170 journal titles.

3. An accurate count of the African holdings is not possible; however, most of the materials on Africa are in the subject category of economics and deal with topics such as roads, railroads, railways, motor highways, and road research, with a small number of titles on climate, rainfall, and geography. In all, there are approximately 400-450 items pertaining to Africa. The collections thus rank a B for the field of transportation.

5. The library has an extensive and unique file for periodical literature in all fields of transportation. There are over 800,000 cards in this file which are arranged by subject (roads, railroads, air transportation, etc.) and then further subdivided by geographic areas. An estimated 400 cards pertain to Africa.

6. The above-mentioned periodical reference index file has been microfilmed as Transportation Masterfile, 1921–71, in 140 reels, with a supplement covering 1971–74 in 7 reels.

The library publishes *Selected Library Acquisitions* (monthly) and *Transportation: Current Literature* (biweekly). *TRISNET: Directory to Transportation Research Information Services* (May 1976) is a useful guide to materials in the field of transportation.

Note: Also see entry K25.

Treasury Department Library See entry K26.

A41 United Nations Information Centre Library

1. a. *2101 L Street, NW, Suite 209*
      Washington, D.C. 20037
      296-5370

   b. 9:00 A.M.-1:00 P.M.   Monday-Friday

   c. Open to the public. ILL and photoreproduction facilities available.

   d. Marcial Tamayo, Director
      Vera Gathright, Reference Librarian

2-5. The library maintains a collection of official U.N. records and documents going back to 1946, comprising the numerous speeches and resolutions of the Security Council, General Assembly, and the International Court of Justice.

Though it is difficult to assess the extent and size of holdings pertaining to Africa, the researcher can find valuable materials here. These include select documents of the Economic Commission on Africa and the Center against Apartheid; statements and speeches of African delegates at various U.N. sessions; statistical information for various African nations (primarily demographic and industrial data); and pamphlets and documents on decolonization and human rights.

A large number of U.N. serials and publications are also available at the Centre. These include *Agricultural Economics Bulletin for Africa, Decolonization, Economic Bulletin for Africa, Foreign Trade Statistics of Africa, Namibia Bulletin, Objective Justice, Notes and Documents,* and *A Trust Betrayed: Namibia.* Researchers focusing on South Africa should make note of the following: *Apartheid in Practice, Foreign Capital and Forced Labour in South Africa,.Industrialization, Infringement of Trade Union Rights in Southern Africa, Maltreatment and Torture of Prisoners in South Africa,* and *Repressive Legislation of the Republic of South Africa.* For a complete list of publications, see *U.N. Publications in Print,* a catalog published annually.

The Centre's motion picture and still photo collection is another resource for the Africanist. The films, which deal with themes such as apartheid, urbanization, changing status of women, disarmament, refugees, and race relations, are made available on loan to individuals and organizations free of charge. No inventory of the black-and-white photographs exists; however, they cover a spectrum of subjects with which the U.N. is actively involved.

6.　　An extremely useful index to the various documents is *U.N. Documents: Index*, published monthly and annually. The Centre periodically publishes a list of films available for distribution, which can be obtained free of charge.

Woodrow Wilson International Center for Scholars Library
See entry H36.

B Archives

Archives Entry Format (B)

1. General information
   a. *address; telephone number(s)*
   b. hours of service
   c. conditions of access
   d. reproduction services
   e. name/title of director and heads of relevant divisions

2. Size of holdings pertaining to Africa

3. Description of holdings pertaining to Africa

4. Bibliographic aids facilitating use of collection (inventories, finding aids, catalogs, guides)

Eliot Elisofon Archives (Museum of African Art) See entries D4 and F24.

B1 Howard University—Moorland-Spingarn Research Center—Manuscript Division

1. a. *Founders Library Building, Room G-2*
   500 Howard Place, NW
   Washington, D.C. 20059
   636-7239/40 (For all services)

   b. For the whole year:
   9:30 A.M.-1:00 P.M. and 2:00 P.M.-5:00 P.M.   Monday-Friday

   c. Open to all qualified researchers by appointment. Some collections are not yet open or completely classified. Some collections are open but donors have placed specific restrictions on their use.

   d. Complete reproduction services are available. Photocopy, microfilm, and photographic services permit considerable flexibility. Researchers may also bring their own photo equipment, with permission, if there are no restrictions attached to a particular collection. Personnel will answer queries over the telephone.

e. Dr. Michael R. Winston, Director of the Center
Thomas C. Battle, Curator of Manuscripts
Denise Harbin, Senior Manuscript Librarian
Maricia Battle, Prints and Photographs Librarian
Esme Bhan, Manuscript Research Associate

2. Like the Library Division (see entry A21), the Manuscript Division of the Moorland-Spingarn Research Center has existed as a separate entity since 1973. It includes the Manuscript Department, Prints and Photographs Department, the Oral History Department (primarily the Ralph J. Bunche Oral History of the Civil Rights Movement in America), and the Music Department. The university archives will one day be part of this division.

   Most of the collections in the Manuscript Division are the papers of Afro-Americans who had a direct or an indirect interest in Africa. The papers of university administrators, and professors in particular, may contain considerable information about the activities and visits of Africans to Howard University, even if the administrator or professor had no special interest in Africa. On the other hand, some collections, such as that of Dr. Alain Leroy Locke, who was directly interested in African art and culture, contain a wealth of letters, manuscripts, and clippings about Africa.

   According to the director, the division possesses 400 "collections of personal papers and organizational archives." Of this number, 38 are directly or indirectly of interest to researchers in African affairs.

3. Now available to researchers are the following collections:
   (1) *Thomas Clarkson Papers.* Clarkson was an English abolitionist, and his letters from 1814–46 deal with slavery. Letters from Thomas Fowell Buxton to Clarkson deal with the need to organize against the effort to recruit so-called "free labor" in Africa.
   (2) *Frederick Douglass Collection.* Eleven boxes, 400 items. The collection contains speeches, photos, and correspondence, including a letter from Douglass to Lewis Douglass dated February 11, 1887, about a trip to Egypt and Greece.
   (3) *Thomas Montgomery Collection.* Contains an incomplete manuscript of René Maran's *Batouala* and a manuscript of Edward J. McCoo's *Ethiopia at the Bar of Justice.*
   (4) *Archibald Grimké Papers.* Grimké was consul to Santo Domingo from 1894 to 1898, vice president of the NAACP, and president of the American Negro Academy from 1903 to 1916. The 45 boxes with about 4,000 items contain Grimké's articles and addresses about blacks. Included is a 24-page typescript, "The Opening Up of Africa."
   (5) *Charlotte Moton Hubbard Papers.* Box 4—Uganda Bark Cloth Project.
   (6) *William H. Hunt Papers.* Cover period from 1898 to 1941. In 1901, Hunt was American Consul to Madagascar, and in 1931 he was secre-

tary of legation in Liberia. Some correspondence, clippings on Madagascar, and a manuscript, "Our Duty to Liberia."

(7) *Ruffin Family Papers.* Three boxes with 382 items covering the period from 1823 to 1936. George L. Ruffin was a Boston attorney who had correspondence with Edward Wilmot Blyden (1860s). A businessman in Liberia corresponded with Ruffin.

(8) *Joel E. Spingarn Collection.* Twenty boxes with 3,900 items. Spingarn was president of the NAACP and very interested in Africa and African diaspora literature. 800 letters.

(9) *Stewart-Flippin Papers.* From 1883 to 1886, Thomas McCants Stewart lived in Africa, where he was associate justice of the Supreme Court of Liberia. Box 1 contains papers on the "Liberia Controversy." There is also a scrapbook about his career, 1874–1921.

(10) *Mary Church Terrell Papers.* Terrell was the first president of the National Association of Colored Women. Box 2 contains letters concerning the International Council of the Women of the Darker Races.

(11) *Henry McNeal Turner Papers.* Turner, who lived from 1831 to 1915, was a bishop in the AME Church and the first Afro-American chaplain in the U.S. Army. In 1897 he received an honorary degree from Liberia College, and the collection contains manuscripts of speeches given in his honor in Liberia and in South Africa. Also, a diary kept from 1859 to 1862.

(12) *Thomas Narven Lewis Collection.* Covers the period from 1898 to 1934. Lewis, a Liberian, studied in the U.S. and returned to Liberia, where he built a school and hospital and engaged in business. One box contains 78 items, including letters, his work on the Bassa language, and a biographical sketch of Lewis written in 1934.

(13) *Townsend McKinley Lucas Papers.* A Washingtonian who traveled and did business in Liberia, Lucas became director of the Liberian radio station ELBC. Some 57 items include Liberian documents about a matter of treason, a manuscript by Lucas on Liberia's government, a report by the American Colonization Society, and newspaper articles from Liberian publications.

(14) *Kelly Miller Papers.* The 382 items in 4 boxes include correspondence and Miller's project for a National Negro Museum in Washington, D.C. Miller was an important figure at Howard University.

(15) *Daniel Alexander Payne Murray.* Collection covers the period from 1872 to 1937. Murray worked at the Library of Congress from 1871 to 1922. He planned and collected materials for a *Historical and Biographical Encyclopedia of the Colored Race Throughout the World.* Collection includes materials on this effort and the effort to compile a list of books and pamphlets by black authors.

(16) *Freeman Henry Morris Murray Papers.* Consists of 314 items. Murray passed and then taught the first civil-service examination. He owned a printing business in Washington and wrote on art and literature. Box 3 has a manuscript, "The Ethiopian as Pioneer of Civilization and Religion."

(17) *Alain L. Locke Papers.* Semiprocessed. Restricted only insofar as no photoduplication is allowed, and no publication is permitted without the agreement of the Moorland-Spingarn Research Center. Locke was a leading Afro-American intellectual and teacher whose deep interest in

African culture influenced many Afro-Americans at Howard, where he taught, and elsewhere in America. The 220 document boxes have a "location inventory" to assist the researcher. They contain correspondence, clippings, photographs, and manuscripts. Although the box numbers may eventually change, presently they contain the following: 34—Council of African Affairs; 50—René Maran material (correspondence, manuscripts); 51—African correspondence and manuscripts; 102—literature on African art; 106—African collection at Howard, letters from Africans; 126—Races and Peoples Project; 168—clippings on Africa; 181—Locke's photographs of African art; 187—clippings on Ethiopia. There are numerous unpublished short manuscripts, such as "Legacy of the Ancestral Arts." Also, much material for his book *The New Negro.*

(18) *Benjamin E. Mays Papers.* Mays was president of Morehouse College in Atlanta, and his wide-ranging correspondence is included here. Over 40 storage boxes. Material is largely unprocessed.

(19) *E. Franklin Frazier Papers.* Over 100 boxes include 4 document boxes about race and culture, subjects which interested this important Afro-American professor of sociology at Howard. Included are research materials, notes, manuscripts, correspondence. One document box has material on the African Studies Association, American Institute on African Studies, and American Society of African Culture.

(20) *Cape Verdean Collection.* Photocopies of the collection of papers in New Bedford, Massachusetts library. Denise Harbin prepared a finding aid, "Cape Verdean Collection." Contains correspondence and manuscripts about Cape Verdean immigrants to the U.S.A., support given by them to liberation movements in Africa, periodicals, bibliographies, organization affairs.

(21) *Rayford W. Logan Papers.* Important American Negro historian who served as secretary to first Pan-African Congress in Paris and who wrote and taught over several decades at Howard. Professor Logan, who resides in Washington, is in the process of turning over his papers to the Manuscript Division. Items concerning Africa now in the collection are about the African Studies Association, the American Committee on African Affairs, the Njala University in Sierra Leone, and Friends of Africa in America.

(22) *George B. Murphy, Jr. Papers.* Restricted. Murphy is a member of the family that owns the *Washington Afro-American* newspaper, and he has a long-standing interest in Africa. One box of materials is specifically about Africa (mainly published items).

(23) *Sterling A. Brown Papers.* Important Afro-American writer, folklore collector, critic, jazz connoisseur, and professor at Howard University. Brown is in the process of turning his papers over to Howard.

(24) *William Leo Hansberry Papers.* One box. Restricted. Contains a typescript on Africa. Historian at Howard who pioneered in the study of African history. Thus far, Manuscript Division possesses only a small part of his papers.

(25) *Dorothy Burnett Porter Papers.* Restricted. Mrs. Porter was the director of the Moorland-Spingarn Collections for more than 40 years; she travelled to Africa and had an extensive correspondence with Africans and those connected with the African diaspora. Collection contains her office files, which include correspondence with Africans.

(26) *Merze Tate Papers.* Restricted. Tate, a distinguished historian and teacher at Howard University, is in the process of turning over papers to the division. She conducted studies of mineral resources and communication facilities in Africa, and some of these notes, documents, and publications will be in the collection.

(27) *Max Yergan Papers.* Restricted. May be open in 1980. Twenty-three large storage boxes and 2 file drawers. With Paul Robeson, Yergan worked in the Council on African Affairs. He belonged and worked in countless other Africa-related organizations, and his papers are consequently a very important source of information about Afro-American interest in Africa from the 1920s to the 1960s.

(28) *Mordecai W. Johnson Papers.* Restricted. Forty storage boxes of personal papers and large office materials boxes. Johnson was president of Howard for 34 years (1926–60). The collection contains photos of visiting Africans, awards to Africans, and it probably contains correspondence with and about Africans. It is largely unprocessed.

(29) *William Stuart Nelson Papers.* Restricted. Vice-president of Howard University and dean of the School of Religion, Nelson was deeply involved in the nonviolent movement around the world. Collection is unprocessed and very large. It probably contains materials about Africa.

(30) *Monroe Work Papers.* Two document boxes. Bibliographer of the African and the Afro-American. Material is about the bibliographies he prepared, with correspondence and notes.

(31) *John W. Davis.* Restricted. One storage box. Davis was U.S. director of the Technical Cooperation Administration in Liberia from 1953 to 1954. Materials cover African American Institute.

(32) *Paul Cuffe Collection.* Microfilm of papers held in library of New Bedford, Massachusetts. *Cuffe Collection Master Index* was compiled by the Free Public Library of New Bedford, Massachusetts, in 1969. Materials include correspondence relating to Sierre Leone and Cuffe's efforts to transport American blacks there as settlers. Scrapbook concerning Cuffe's sea ventures. Passenger lists of families going to Sierra Leone in 1815. Writing of Cuffe concerning settlement in Africa.

(33) *William Steen Papers.* Restricted. Steen has been an African area specialist in the Department of Labor. As such he helped plan visits to America of African leaders and arrange for labor training programs for Africans. Details are in this collection.

(34) *Charles Diggs Collection.* Restricted. Member of Congress from Michigan, Diggs has been chairman of House International Relations Subcommittee on Africa and has begun to turn over his papers to the center.

The Prints and Photographs Department has a general file of more than 500 African photos, clippings, drawings, and prints. In addition, there is a collection of 573 official Senegalese photos, a collection of photos dating from the 1920s and 1930s used in the preparation of a *National Geographic*-type article, and a series of very old photos from circa 1909 and 1914. Some photos are identified, some are not. There are some maps, but not in one place and not yet inventoried completely. The department has one map of interest, dating from 1831, of Liberia and the Sierra Leone coast. The broadside or poster collection contains a few items about Africa, and there are also a few World War II newspapers from Brazzaville.

In this department of the Manuscript Division one also finds a very interesting collection of phonotapes, largely of lectures and speeches given over the years at Howard University. They include: "African Influence on Chilean Music"; Bassa church music and sermons; Gabriel D'Arboussier on African economic development (1967); Shirley Graham Du Bois, "Africa, the Middle East, and the Western World" (1970); Liberian music; Miriam Makeba singing songs in English and in African languages; Joshua Nkomo, "The Crisis in Central Africa" (1959); J. Osibodu, "Western African Highlife" in English and in African languages; Sidney V. Peterson, "South Africa: The Birth of the New Language" (1939); Mary H. Umolu, "My Experiences in Nigeria" (1967); and other tapes from Liberia.

4.　To assist the researcher there are Collection Registers arranged in alphabetical order with a brief description of each collection; analyses for some collections in card form; a card catalog integrating all manuscript collections; and lists for a few individual collections.

Other finding aids are planned, and a general expansion of the division, as for the whole center, is on the drawing boards. Personnel have advised other institutions on their book and document collections, and internship programs have been organized for Americans. In the future, ties with African institutions and exchanges of microfilm of collections should develop.

Note:　Also see entry A21.

B2 Library of Congress—Manuscript Division

1.　a.　*Thomas Jefferson Building (Annex)*
Third Floor, Room 3005
10 1st Street, SE
Washington, D.C. 20540
287-5387 Reading Room
287-5383 Main Office (Manuscript Historians)

　b.　8:30 A.M.-5:00 P.M.　Monday-Saturday

　c.　Open to all serious researchers. Some holdings are restricted.

　d.　Researchers should consult the staff regarding photocopying procedures.

　e.　Manuscript historians available for consultation.

2.　Current holdings of the Manuscript Division total over 30 million items which encompass approximately 10,000 separate collections. An accurate estimate of the size of African holdings cannot be made, since African materials are not in exclusive units but interspersed among other materials.

3.　More than 110 collections in the Manuscript Division contain African archival material. Researchers should find valuable material in the

Family Papers, Papers of Government Officials, **Presidential Papers,** Organizational Records, Special Collections, and Foreign **Copies.** Some noteworthy items include:

(1) *American Anti-Slavery Society Records.*

(2) *American Colonization Society Records, 1792–1964.* These voluminous records, containing approximately 190,000 items, are an extremely valuable source for the study of the slave trade and the resettlement of free blacks in Liberia. The bulk of the society's records dating back to the early 19th century contain correspondence, reports, financial records, lists of emigrants, and letters from Liberia.

(3) *American Peace Commission to Versailles Papers, 1917–1919.* About 16 studies and reports about Africa.

(4) *Archives Nationales (France) Colonies, Series C C8 A (N.D.).* One reel. Ministère des Affaires Etrangères Records, 1779–1787. 20 reels.

(5) *Black History Miscellany, 1718–1944.* Some 190 items, including documents on Sierra Leone slave trade; the yacht *Wanderer* (slave ship); and letters from emancipated slaves living in Liberia.

(6) *Breckinridge Family, Papers.* Papers of Robert J. Breckinridge, Presbyterian clergyman, deal with the subject of Negro colonization.

(7) *(British) Anti-Slavery and Aborigines Protection Society Records, 1836–1862.* 2 reels.

(8) *Brotherhood of Sleeping Car Porters Records, 1939–68.* An estimated 1,000 items on Africa (counted by Aloha P. South); includes materials on Tom Mboya, American Committee on Africa, and the personal papers of A. P. Randolph.

(9) *Chaille-Long, Charles, Papers, 1963–1918.* Explorer, diplomat, soldier in the Civil War. His personal papers contain correspondence, articles, maps, and photographs relating to his expedition to Lake Victoria Nyanza, his service under Gen. Charles Gordon in Africa, and African geography.

(10) *Coker, Daniel, Journal, 21 April–21 September 1821 in Peter Force Collection.* Coker, an agent of the American Colonization Society, kept a diary at Fourah Bay.

(11) *Croffut, William A., Papers.* Journalist and secretary of Anti-Imperialist League.

(12) *Cuffe, Paul, Papers. 1765–1963.* Seaman and colonist. Two items —a biographical statement and a sermon on the death of the leader of the back-to-Africa movement.

(13) *Crosby, Oscar T., Papers.* Assistant secretary of Treasury and explorer, his papers deal with his travels in Abyssinia, Near East, Tanganyika, Kenya, and Belgian Congo, from 1900 to 1938. Also includes Abyssinian manuscripts.

(14) *Douglass, Frederick, Papers, 1841–1964.* Afro-American abolitionist. Thirty-four reels on microfilm include his diary of a visit to Africa, speeches, and correspondence.

(15) *Durant, William West, Papers, 1850–1934.* Railroad executive and developer, Durant's collection contains some Arabic materials.

(16) *Eaker, Ira Clarence, Papers.* Commander-in-chief of Mediterranean Allied Air Forces in World War II. Some material is classified and restricted.

(17) *Ethiopia Miscellany.* Contains a parchment volume in Amharic on witchcraft and circular letter about Italo-Ethiopian war.

(18) *Foote, Andrew Hull, Papers.* Includes 2 journals, 1849 to 1851, kept by American Rear Admiral Foote during an expedition to the African coast in pursuit of slave ships. Contains accounts of Liberia and St. Helena.

(19) *Force, Peter, Collection.* Contains material relating to the Royal African Company in the 18th century; diary of Christian Wiltberger relating to a voyage to Liberia, colonization, and missionary work; and the George Chalmers Collection, 1742–1825, containing papers of Chalmers, an historian and antiquarian.

(20) *Foreign Copying—France: Archives de la Marine* known as Marine B², "Correspondence General," on slave trade between Senegal and the French West Indies, 1692–93.

(21) *Foreign Office Records (Great Britain).* F.O. 47—Liberian Office 1848–1905 (19 reels); F.O. 84—Slave Trade 1833–1878 (16 reels); and F.O. 115—America, United States 1791–1902 (500 reels).

(22) *Gilchrist, Huntington, Papers, 1891–1975.* Public official and business executive, Huntington's papers contain material relating to international affairs, especially his activities on behalf of the League of Nations and the United Nations.

(23) *Green, Theodore Francis, Papers.* Lawyer, governor, and U.S. senator from Rhode Island.

(24) *Harmon Foundation Records, 1913–1967.* Some 37,800 items, including biographical notes on African artists; also correspondence, lists of works, and materials relating to exhibitions at African art centers.

(25) *Harper, Robert Goodloe, Papers.* Founder and member of the American Colonization Society.

(26) *Harrison, Jesse Burton, Papers.* Contain material relating to his activities on behalf of the American Colonization Society.

(27) *Hughes, Charles Evans, Papers.* Secretary of state, 1921–25. Papers contain correspondence about African mandates.

(28) *Langston, John M., Papers.* (Library of Congress has microfilm copy; original papers are in custody of Fisk University.) Materials pertain to African origins of black Americans.

(29) *Livingston, David, and Family, Papers, 1732–1823.* One reel.

(30) *Moral Re-Armament Records.* These records document the spread of the MRA movement (which sought to prevent war and foster international understanding) from 1938 to 1965. Contains extensive files on Africa, including letters from the founder, Frank Buchman, to Haile Selassie.

(31) *Morgan, John Tyler, Papers.* U.S. senator from Alabama. Contains 4 letters and reports about the Berlin Conference of 1885.

(32) *Nassau, R. H., Notebook.* Missionary in Gabon. Contains Fang language vocabulary.

(33) *National Association for the Advancement of Colored People Records, 1909–1970.* Approximately 2 million items in 8 series. An Administrative File contains general correspondence and materials on Africa. Documents relate to the Pan-African Congresses of 1919 and 1921; meetings on Africa, Italo-Ethiopian War, Garvey Movement, Liberia, Senegalese in the French army; and letters of W. E. B. Du Bois.

Also included are press clippings about Africa and reports on Liberia.
(34) *National Urban League Records, 1910–1960.* Material on Italo-Ethiopian War.
(35) *Phillipps, Thomas, Collection 1792–1872.* 1 reel. Famous nineteenth-century British collector. Materials include colonial records and items on the slave trade.
(36) *Presidential Papers.* The Manuscript Division's holdings include papers of 24 presidents of the United States, and several contain African material, especially the Woodrow Wilson and Theodore Roosevelt Papers.
(37) *Sheldon, Mary (French), Papers, 1885–1936.* Writer and explorer. Her papers consisting of correspondence, literary manuscripts, and other materials contain information on the Belgian Congo, Belgium, and Africa.
(38) *Shufeldt, Robert W., Papers.* Nineteenth-century American naval figure (part of the Naval Historical Foundation Collection). Reports, correspondence, and other items relate to his visits to various African ports and his activities as an arbitrator in a boundary dispute between Liberia and Sierra Leone.
(39) *Smythe, Hugh H., Papers, 1956–1977.* Diplomat and sociologist interested in Africa (not yet available for examination).
(40) *Spence, Robert Traill, Papers, ca. 1785–1827.* Naval officer (part of the Naval Historical Foundation Collection). Papers relating to West Africa, Liberia, and the slave trade.
(41) *Spingarn, Arthur B., Papers.* Lawyer and long-time president of NAACP. Approximately 40,000 items relating primarily to Spingarn's activities in the NAACP from 1911 to 1940.
(42) *Sweetser, Arthur, Papers, 1888-1968.* Public official and journalist. Contain material relating to United States' activities in the United Nations and League of Nations, as well as the Ethiopian crisis.
(43) *Tappan, Benjamin, Papers, 1795–1900.* Ohio lawyer, judge, and U.S. senator. Papers relating to the antislavery movement.
(44) *Tolson, Melvin B., Papers, 1900–1960.* Poet of Liberia. Some 2,800 items including drafts and reviews of *Libretto for the Republic of Liberia;* correspondence with officials and citizens of Liberia; and printed matter pertaining to Liberia.
(45) *Vernon-Wager, Papers, 1654–1773 (in Peter Force Collection).* Material pertaining to British naval operations against the Spanish in the West Indies; items on slave trade.
(46) *Washington, Booker T., Papers.* Educator and black American leader. Contains 3,000 items on Africa between 1900 and 1915 (counted by Aloha P. South) and substantial material pertaining to Liberia.
(47) *Wilberforce, William, Collection.* Abolitionist. A dozen items about Africa.
(48) *Wilkes, Charles, Papers, 1607–1959.* Naval officer. Papers deal with travels and naval expeditions to Africa.
(49) *Wiltberger, Christian, Diary, 1821–22.* Escorted immigrants to Sierra Leone.
(50) *Woodson, Carter G., Collection.* Two dozen letters from Africa and some articles.

In addition to the above, researchers should also consult the papers of journalists and writers such as Joseph W. Alsop, Eric Sevareid, and Joseph Pulitzer, for information pertaining to major political, diplomatic, and international events, many of which relate to Africa.

4. There are several guides that describe the accessions to the Manuscript Division of the Library of Congress. These include: Richard B. Bickel, *Manuscripts on Microfilm; A Checklist of the Holdings in the Manuscript Division* (Washington, D.C.: Library of Congress, 1975); Curtis Wiswell Garrison, *List of Manuscript Collections in the Library of Congress to July, 1931* (Washington, D.C.: United States Government Printing Office, 1932); *Handbook of Manuscripts in the Library of Congress* (Washington, D.C.: Government Printing Office, 1918); *National Union Catalog of Manuscript Collections; Naval Historical Foundation Manuscript Collection Catalog* (Washington, D.C.: Library of Congress, 1974); and C. Percy Powell, comp., *List of Manuscript Collections Received in the Library of Congress, July 1931 to July 1938* (Washington, D.C.: United States Government Printing Office, 1939).

In addition to the above, the *Annual Report of the Librarian of Congress* contains descriptions of manuscript accessions. Since 1943, the *Library of Congress Quarterly Journal of Current Acquisitions* (now the *Quarterly Journal of the Library of Congress*) has reported on the more important accessions. Africanists should consult John McDonough's article "Manuscript Resources for the Study of Negro Life and History" in the *Quarterly Journal of the Library of Congress,* vol. 26, no. 3 (July 1969), pp. 126–48, which contains valuable information relating to African material in the division.

Other finding aids include: published and unpublished registers for most collections; Master Record of Manuscript Collections (available in the Manuscript Reading Room); card catalog of collections, arranged by title; Presidential Paper Indexes and Foreign Copying Program Catalog and Indexes (France, Great Britain, Portugal, and others).

National Anthropological Archives See entry F27.

B3 National Archives and Record Service (NARS) (General Services Administration)

1. a. *8th Street and Pennsylvania Avenue, NW*
   Washington, D.C. 20408
   523-3218 (General information)
   423-3232 (Central Research Room)

   b. Central Research and Microfilm Reading Room
   8:45 A.M.-10:00 P.M.   Monday-Friday
   8:45 A.M.-5:00 P.M.   Saturday
   Branch Research Rooms
   8:45 A.M.-5:00 P.M.   Monday-Friday

c. Open to all serious researchers with a National Archives research pass, which may be obtained from the Central Reference Division, Room 200-B. Suitable identification may be necessary.

d. Extensive photocopying and microfilming services available.

e. James B. Rhoads, Archivist of the United States

2-3.   The National Archives and Records Service is the official depository for the records of the United States government. Records in the Archives span 2 centuries and total billions of pages of textual material, 6 million photographs, 5 million maps and charts, 100,000 films, and over 80,000 sound recordings.

The vast holdings of the archives are arranged not by subject matter but are organized into some 400 "record groups," each of which consists of the records of a particular federal agency, bureau, or other department. The combined records of a particular government entity, such as the Department of State, are referred to as a "record group."

The starting point for scholars undertaking research on Africa should be the 556-page publication compiled by Aloha South, *Guide to Federal Archives Relating to Africa* (1977), which is a unique and invaluable research tool that describes Africa-related material in the National Archives. Additional materials and record groups have been opened since that volume appeared. They are described in the following pages. Significant Africa-related material in the recently accessioned materials includes Record Group 84: Records of the Foreign Service Posts of the Department of State; RG 59: General Records of the Department of State; RG 306: Records of the United States Information Agency; RG 38: Records of the Chief of Naval Operations; RG 200: Records of the American National Red Cross; and RG 330: Records of the Office of the Secretary of Defense. Researchers should consult staff members for advice and guidance concerning holdings, reference tools, finding aids, and recent accessions.

There follows a brief summary of the major African holdings within each record group (RG), grouped according to the archival division or branch which maintains administrative control over that record group. For more detailed information on each record group, scholars should refer to the *Guide to Federal Archives Relating to Africa.*

CIVIL ARCHIVES DIVISION

Jane Smith, Director
523-3239

Diplomatic Branch
Milton Gustafson, Chief
523-3174

RG 11: Records of the United States Government. Laws, treaties, and other international agreements between U.S. and African nations, 1778–1974.
RG 43: Records of International Conferences, Commissions, and Expositions. Materials dealing with the Berlin Conference on West African

Affairs, 1884–85, the Council of Foreign Ministers, and the Paris Peace Conference, 1945–46.

RG 59: General Records of the Department of State. Since the Department of State administers the U.S. Foreign Service and conducts diplomatic and consular correspondence, this record group is perhaps the most important source material for research in U.S.-African diplomatic history and foreign relations from 1789 until 1949. The voluminous material in this group includes diplomatic and consular instructions of the State Department to its officers in various African countries, 1791–1906; despatches from diplomatic and consular officers; notes to and from foreign missions in the United States; communications from heads of foreign states; records of U.S. neutrality in the Boer War; and reports of the secretary of state to the president and Congress, 1790–1906. The Numerical File of the State Department (1906–10) and the Decimal File (1910–49) comprising general correspondence, information sheets, reports, political pamphlets, and clippings, contain a wealth of material on political and socioeconomic conditions in various countries of Africa. Correspondence in the decimal file is generally arranged according to country.

Researchers should note that the newly accessioned material in this record group consists of the Records of the Office of African Affairs, 1944–49 (which contains consolidated files from the Economic Branch, Independent and International Areas Branch, and African Affairs Office dealing primarily with Ethiopia, Eritrea, Somaliland, Libya, Tangier, and trusteeship territories); Records of the Military Adviser to the Office of Near Eastern, South Asian, and African Affairs, 1945–50; Research Reports of the Foreign Policy Studies Branch, 1944–50; Records of the Office of Near Eastern Affairs, 1946–49; Records of the Research and Analysis Branch Office of Strategic Services, and the Bureau of Intelligence and Research, 1941–61; and records of 3 State Department officials, namely Charles E. Bohlen, 1942–52; Arthur Zimmerman Gardiner, 1947–49; and G. Mennen Williams, 1961–66, who was assistant secretary of state for African affairs, 1961–66.

RG 76: Records of Boundary and Claims Commissions and Arbitrations. Chiefly records of international and domestic claims commissions established between 1794 and 1935.

RG 84: Records of the Foreign Service Posts of the Department of State. Field records of all U.S. diplomatic and consular posts in Africa. Contains general correspondence—despatches, memoranda, reports, papers, and telegrams—which provide information about the government, finances, economy, commerce, arts, and conditions in African countries. Much useful material can be found here on local conditions.

RG 256: Records of the American Commission to Negotiate Peace. Reports and related materials on the Paris Peace Conference and the administration of former German colonial possessions in Africa.

RG 353: Records of the Interdepartmental and Intradepartmental Committees.

RG 360: Records of the Continental and Confederation Congresses and the Constitutional Convention. Africa-related items generally pertain to U.S. diplomatic relations with Morocco and the Barbary States, 1774–89.

Judicial and Fiscal Branch
Clarence Lyons, Chief
523-3059

RG 36: Records of the Bureau of Customs. Information on vessels engaged in the African trade, cargoes, passengers, crew lists, and related topics. Researchers will find in this record group useful source material for the slave trade. Records of southern ports like Mobile, Alabama; Savannah; and New Orleans contain slave manifests (1790–1861) and materials relating to the enforcement of laws against the slave trade (1815–1934).

RG 39: Records of the Bureau of Accounts (Treasury). Materials include Treasury Department correspondence concerning African fiscal conditions and diplomatic and consular reports relating to financial conditions, local currency, commerce, industries, and other subjects in Africa.

RG 53: Records of the Bureau of Public Debt. Accounts of expenses incurred in dealing with the Barbary States, 1795–1812 and statements concerning living expenses and expenditures of U.S. ministers and consuls in Africa.

RG 56: General Records of the Department of the Treasury. Contains correspondence of U.S. consuls, commercial agents, and custom officers relating to foreign trade, 1789–1878, as well as lists and information pertaining to the capture of slavers by U.S. Navy vessels, especially in 1860–61.

RG 60: General Records of the Department of Justice. Correspondence of the attorney general contains material relating to the slave trade, enforcement of laws, and the indictment and trial of Marcus Garvey, 1923–29.

RG 154: Records of the War Finance Corporation. Material on post-World War I government loans to U.S. exporters, with information on the commerce and industry of various African countries.

RG 206: Records of the Solicitor of the Treasury. Contains correspondence received by the solicitor of the Treasury from the State and Navy Departments and U.S. district attorneys concerning the capture of vessels engaged in the slave trade.

RG 217: Records of the United States General Accounting Office. Fiscal documents, correspondence, and reports of expenses of U.S. consuls and diplomatic officials assigned to Africa in the 19th century. Also included is substantial material relating to the slave trade, e.g., expenses for the maintenance of captured Africans, bounty paid for the capture of illegal slave ships, and names of captured and capturing ships, 1790–1860.

RG 220: Records of Presidential Committees, Commissions, and Boards. Materials relate to judicial practices in various African countries, 1959–66, and the records of the War Refugee Board, which deal mainly with refugee camps in North Africa, Egypt, Ethiopia, Tanganyika, the Belgian Congo, and South Africa, 1944–45.

RG 267: Records of the Supreme Court of the United States. Materials deal with matters such as foreign commerce, enforcement of slave laws, and ship seizures.

Industrial and Social Branch
Jerome Finster, Chief
523-3119

RG 28: Records of the Post Office Department. Contains copies of conventions for the exchange of money orders between U.S. and some African countries, 1870–1962.

RG 32: Records of the United States Shipping Board. Material relating to steamship lines operating between U.S. and Africa, commercial shipping records, and African trade routes.

RG 40: General Records of the Department of Commerce. The correspondence files of the secretary of commerce contain a limited amount of material on commercial activities and trade with several African nations.

RG 41: Records of the Bureau of Marine Inspection and Navigation. Documents pertaining to African navigation and information about American vessels engaged in African trade, 1815–1958.

RG 90: Records of the Public Health Service. Extensive material on general public health and hygiene, sanitation and water supply, disease incidence and control, and health services in many African countries, 1879–1944.

RG 151: Records of the Bureau of Foreign and Domestic Commerce. Reports of commercial attachés, 1932–40, deal with economic and financial situation and trade opportunities in various African countries, while the general records contain substantial statistical and other material on African trade, 1914–58.

RG 174: General Records of the Department of Labor. Materials deal with technical assistance to African nations, exchange programs, and activities of international trade unions.

RG 178: Records of the United States Maritime Commission. Contains materials concerning merchant shipping and trade with Africa, including information on trade routes, merchant marine casualties during World War II, freight tariffs and rates, exports-imports, and movement of vessels and cargo.

RG 188: Records of the Office of Price Administration. Reports on price and economic controls and rationing measures in African countries during World War II.

RG 200: Records of the American National Red Cross, 1881–1946. Material relating to the relief operations and activities of the Red Cross in various parts of Africa.

RG 207: Records of the Department of Housing and Urban Development. Material on housing, urban development, town planning, and the building industry in different countries of Africa.

RG 234: Records of the Reconstruction Finance Corporation. World War II and postwar records of the Rubber Development Corporation and U.S. Commercial Company. Includes statistical data on exports from African countries and the development of strategic minerals and transport facilities.

RG 235: General Records of the Department of Health, Education, and Welfare. Documents on health, rural development, and education in Egypt, Ethiopia, South Africa, and Liberia.

RG 248: Records of the War Shipping Administration. Reports and statistical data on shipping vessels, cargoes, freight rates, ship warrants, port facilities, and ship operation policies during World War II.

RG 275: Records of the Export-Import Bank of the United States. Case files of Eximbank loan transactions involving Africa, 1934–51.

RG 357: Records of the Maritime Administration. Information on U.S. shipping companies engaged in trade in Africa, 1950–60.

RG 358: Records of the Federal Maritime Commission. Contains information relating to U.S. companies engaged in African trade, 1950–57.

Legislative and Natural Resources Branch
Harold Pinkett, Chief.
523-3238

RG 7: Records of the Bureau of Entomology and Plant Quarantine. Correspondence files contain documents and reports relating to insect control and prevention of plant diseases in African countries.

RG 16: Records of the Office of the Secretary of Agriculture. Material relating to agriculture in Africa, 1893–1966.

RG 22: Records of the Fish and Wildlife Service. Material on fish and game reserves in Africa, 1902–42.

RG 46: Records of the United States Senate. Includes Senate documents, committee reports, and papers relating to specific bills and resolutions pertaining to Africa, 1789–1972.

RG 48: Records of the Office of the Secretary of the Interior. Miscellaneous 19th- and 20th-century materials on Africa, relating to education, medicine, transportation, politics, etc.

Of far greater importance are the records dealing with the suppression of the African slave trade and the colonization movement, 1854–72. Included are papers relating to the slave trade in the South Atlantic states, copies of contracts with the American Colonization Society, and reports on the conditions of liberated Africans.

RG 54: Records of the Bureau of Plant Industry, Soils, and Agricultural Engineering. Material on introduction and development of new plants, crop diseases, cereal control, plant production and science, 1898–1953.

RG 57: Records of the Geological Survey. Contains topographic surveys and reports on mineral and water resources of Africa, 1901–50.

RG 70: Records of the Bureau of Mines. Correspondence, reports, and statistical data on mines, mineral resources, and technical assistance requirements in various African countries, 1913–52.

RG 79: Records of the National Park Service. Materials relating to national parks in Egypt, Kenya, Liberia, the Belgian Congo, Morocco, and the Union of South Africa, 1907–49.

RG 83: Records of the Bureau of Agricultural Economics. Statistical reports dealing with African agricultural production, labor, marketing, etc., 1913–46. Includes substantial material on agriculture and forestry in South Africa.

RG 95: Records of the Forest Service. Material on African forest resources, 1897–1944.

RG 114: Records of the Soil Conservation Service. Contains information relating to soil erosion, control, and conservation in various African countries, 1935–44.

RG 115: Records of the Bureau of Reclamation. Material on reclamation and irrigation projects in Africa, 1919–45; and colonization of new lands.

RG 166: Records of the Foreign Agricultural Service. This record group contains extensive materials on African agriculture and is, therefore, among the more important source materials for Africanists.

Reports of U.S. consular officers, agricultural attachés, and commercial agents relate to production, import-export, economic conditions, market trends, and trade regulations in various African countries, 1904–54.

RG 233: Records of the United States House of Representatives. House files and committee records on African issues. Material on Liberia in the 19th century, slave trade, and political and military conditions in Africa, especially the Congo.

RG 253: Records of the Petroleum Administration for War. World War II materials on petroleum supply, distribution, and requirements in the Belgian Congo, West Africa, and South Africa.

RG 350: Records of the Bureau of Insular Affairs. Miscellaneous records relating to Africa are interspersed throughout the numerous files.

GENERAL ARCHIVES DIVISION

Washington National Records Center
4205 Suitland Road
Suitland, Maryland
Mail: Washington, D.C. 20409
763-7410
Daniel T. Goggin, Director

(Daily shuttle bus service available from main Archives building.)

RG 17: Records of the Bureau of Animal Husbandry. Correspondence on African livestock matters, dealing primarily with North and Southern Africa, 1895–1939.

RG 21: Records of the District Courts of the United States. Case files pertaining to the slave trade and, specifically, proceedings relating to the seizure, condemnation, and sale of vessels involved in the trade.

RG 84: Records of the Foreign Service Posts of the Department of State. These recently accessioned records of diplomatic and consular posts in Africa contain extensive and valuable material for the Africanist. These records date from the period 1930–55; however, researchers presently have access only to materials through 1949. Correspondence, reports, papers, and other items from over 38 diplomatic and consular posts in Africa can be found in this collection, predominantly from Egypt, Kenya, Algeria, Morocco, and the Union of South Africa.

A useful finding aid for these records is James Edward Miller, comp., "List of Foreign Service Post Records in the General Archives Division" (August 1976).

RG 169: Records of the Foreign Economic Administration. Extensive descriptive and statistical material relating to African economic conditions during World War II. These include records concerning food requirements and supply, refugee centers, procurement and availability of various commodities, relief operations, and the lend-lease program in North and West Africa.

RG 181: Records of the Naval Districts and Shore Establishments. Files of the advanced amphibious bases in Algeria, 1942–44, and Port Lyautey, Morocco, 1943–44.

RG 208: Records of the Office of War Information. Materials dealing with the activities of the Office of War Information, as well as intelligence reports and propaganda material from World War II.

RG 313: Records of Naval Operating Forces. Limited material on U.S. naval operations in African waters during the Moroccan crisis, 1904, and the outbreak of Anglo-Egyptian hostilities in 1882.

RG 331: Records of Allied Operational and Occupation Headquarters, World War II. The records of Allied Force Headquarters contain documents relating to the North African campaign, reports on political and military activities, intelligence reports, and papers dealing with repatriation from East Africa, 1944–47, and Eritrea, 1944–46.

MACHINE-READABLE ARCHIVES DIVISION

711 14th Street, NW
Washington, D.C. 20408
724-1080

This division, which stores machine-readable magnetic tapes, reflects the government's increasing utilization of computer technology for data-processing. Materials of interest to Africanists can presently be found in:

RG 77: Records of the Office of the Chief of Engineers.

RG 90: Records of the Public Health Service. Contains reports and correspondence relating to general public-health situation in Africa, sanitation and water supply, and disease incidence and control, 1897–1946.

RG 166: Records of the Foreign Agricultural Service. Reports of U.S. consular officers, agricultural attachés, and commissioners dealing with all aspects of agriculture and agricultural policy in Africa, 1901–54.

A Catalog of Machine-Readable Records in the National Archives of the United States (1977) is available without charge.

4. In addition to the *Guide to Federal Archives Relating to Africa* (1977) and the published "finding aids" referred to above, researchers may find the following National Archives publications useful:

Catalog of National Archives Microfilm Publications (1974) and supplement (1977);

Guide to the National Archives of the United States (1974) and an annually updated loose-leaf version that researchers may consult;

Milton O. Gustafson, ed., *The National Archives and Foreign Relations Research* (1974);

List of Record Groups of the National Archives and Records Service (March 1975). Distributed to staff only; useful in locating divisions wherein individual record groups are maintained.

Other reference information sheets describing specific materials in the archives collection include: *Commerce Data Among State Department Records* (Reference Information Paper No. 53, 1973).

Useful general-information leaflets include: *General Restrictions on Access to Records in the United States* (1976); *Location of Records and Fees for Reproduction Services in the National Archives and Records Service* (1975); and *Regulations for the Public Use of Records in the National Archives and Records Service* (1972).

Information on recent National Archives accessions can be obtained from the staff of the Central Reference Division, Room 200-B, or the respective divisions. It also appears in *Prologue: The Journal of the National Archives* (quarterly), the American Historical Association's *AHA Newsletter,* and Phi Alpha Theta's *The Historian* (quarterly).

Note: Also see entries D5, E4, and F26.

MILITARY ARCHIVES DIVISION
Meyer Fishbein, Director
523-3089

Navy and Old Army Branch
Gary Ryan, Chief
523-3229

RG 24: Records of the Bureau of Naval Personnel. Logs of U.S. naval vessels active in African waters, 1801–1946; and documents relating to U.S. naval activities in Africa, 1889–1945.

RG 38: Records of the Office of the Chief of Naval Operations. Naval intelligence reports contain military, political, and economic information on various African countries, 1886–1940. Recently accessioned material includes Reports of Naval Attachés, 1940–46, which contain valuable material on Africa. See "Folder List of Navy Attaché Reports, Relating to Africa/Arabia Accessioned by the National Archives," prepared by Gibson B. Smith.

RG 45: Naval Records Collection of the Office of Naval Records and Library. Extensive documentation in the correspondence between the secretary of the Navy and officers of the various squadrons, including the African Squadron, 1843–61, and Mediterranean fleet, 1800–04. Also included in this record group are letters relating to the slave trade and colonization of men of African descent; naval intelligence reports; and naval logbooks and private journals. This voluminous record group is a valuable source material for research in late-18th-century and 19th-century Africa.

RG 80: General Records of the Department of the Navy. Documents and reports on military and intelligence activities, 1885–1946.

RG 92: Records of the Office of the Quartermaster General. Limited materials on U.S. Army activities in North and East Africa.

RG 313: Records of the Naval Operating Forces. Correspondence and files contain documentation of the operational activities of the U.S. Fleet in Northwest African waters.

Modern Military Branch
Robert Wolfe, Chief
523-3340

RG 160: Records of Headquarters Army Service Forces. Materials deal with operations in the North African, Mediterranean, Middle Eastern, and Central African theaters during World War II.

RG 165: Records of the War Department General and Special Staffs.

RG 179: Records of the War Production Board. Materials deal with war procurement and production programs of the United States.

RG 218: Records of the United States Joint Chiefs of Staff. Classified and unclassified records concerning military, political, social, and economic matters relating to Africa during World War II.

RG 226: Records of the Office of Strategic Services. Numerous intelligence reports and analyses of African political, economic, social, and military conditions during the war and early postwar years.

RG 242: National Archives Collection of Foreign Records Seized, 1941–Present. Contains records of the German Foreign Office, Reich Ministry of Economics, Office of the Reich Commissioner for the Strengthening of Germandom, Field Commands, Navy, and Army High Command dealing with military and economic conditions and war operations in Africa.

RG 304: Records of the Office of Civil and Defense Mobilization. Limited number of security-classified reports concerning strategic ports in West Africa.

RG 319: Records of the Army Staff. Post-1942 military intelligence reports on Africa including the Historical Manuscript file for Africa-Middle East Theater of Operations.

RG 334: Records of Interservice Agencies. Materials relating to political and military intelligence.

The Modern Military Branch also maintains files which contain recently declassified Central Intelligence Agency and National Security Council documents.

Note: Certain 20th-century U.S. military record groups are administered jointly by the 2 branches of the Military Archives Division, with pre-1940 records assigned to the Navy and Old Army Branch and post-1940 records held by the Modern Military Branch. These include:

RG 18: Records of the Army Air Force. Contains material on Africa relating to aviation, topography, geography, climate, etc.

RG 107: Records of the Office of the Secretary of War.

RG 165: Records of the War Department General and Special Staffs. Documents include general correspondence of the Office of the Chiefs of Staff, 1942–47, relating mainly to North and West Africa; general correspondence of the War Plans Division, 1940–42, dealing with North, Northwest, and West Africa; general correspondence of the Office of the Director of Plans and Operations, 1942–45; general correspondence of the Civil Affairs Division, 1943–49, and Intelligence Reports received from U.S. military attachés, foreign governments, and other sources.

RG 407: Records of the Adjutant General's Office. Materials deal with the war effort in Africa, including extensive reports on World War II combat operations. Also included are a series of records of foreign-occupied areas which provide information on population, social conditions, indigenous African political systems, and economic conditions in North and West Africa.

SCIENCE AND TECHNOLOGICAL ARCHIVES DIVISION

Albert H. Leisinger, Jr., Chief
523-3223

Center for Polar and Scientific Archives
Franklin Burch, Chief

This is a new division which was established quite recently. At the present time, it is a minor resource for the Africanist, since its Africa-related holdings are insignificant. However, the researcher may find some useful material in the following record groups.

RG 23: Records of the Coast and Geodetic Survey. Geographic and cartographic data on Africa, 1866–1905.

RG 27: Records of the Weather Bureau. Meteorological and oceanographic records pertaining to Africa and pre-Civil War ships' logs containing information on voyages along the African coast.

RG 37: Records of the Hydrographic Office. Hydrographic and topographic surveys and related data pertaining to Africa, 1837–1924.

RG 78: Records of the Naval Observatory. Materials relate to astronomical, navigational, and meteorological observations taken in Africa, 1840–85.

RG 307: Records of the National Science Foundation. Some scattered material relating to South Africa.

C Museums, Galleries, and Art Collections

Museums, Galleries, and Art Collections Entry Format (C)

1. General information
   a. *address; telephone number(s)*
   b. hours of service
   c. conditions of access
   d. reproduction services
   e. name/title of director and heads of relevant divisions

2. Size of holdings pertaining to Africa

3. Description of holdings pertaining to Africa

4. Bibliographic aids facilitating use of collection (catalogs, inventories, guides)

C1 African Hands

1. a. *1851 Redwood Terrace, NW*
      Washington, D.C. 20012
      726-2400

   b-c. Not open to the public. Researchers who wish to examine the items must call ahead for an appointment.

   e. Diane Cohen, Owner

2-3. This private art gallery offers African artwork for sale. The number of items varies.

C2 Anacostia Neighborhood Museum (Smithsonian Institution)

1. a. *2405 Martin Luther King, Jr., Avenue, SE*
      Washington, D.C. 20020
      381-5656

   b. 10:00 A.M.-6:00 P.M.   Monday-Friday
      Noon-5:00 P.M.   Saturday, Sunday, and Holidays. Closed Christmas Day.

    c. Open to the public.

    e. John R. Kinard, Director
    Louise Daniel Hutchinson, Historian

2-3.   The Anacostia Neighborhood Museum was established in 1967 to document, collect, and preserve the history of the Anacostia community and emphasize the black heritage. Since its inception, it has played a vital role in the field of ethnic and social history. The museum's primary focus is on the Anacostia community, urban problems, and the Afro-American heritage.

    Periodically, the museum's exhibits focus on Africa. Past exhibits of special interest to Africanists include "This is Africa" (May 1968), "Negro History" (February 1968), "MaKonde Sculpture" (October 1968), "Africa: Three Out of Many—Ethiopia, Ghana, Nigeria" (September 1973), and the recent "Out of Africa: From West African Kingdoms to Colonization," focusing on slavery, the slave trade, and colonization.

    In addition to its traveling exhibits, the museum has a fine educational and research program. The museum sponsors lectures, workshops, seminars, films, and concerts, and the staff has developed educational and curriculum materials, such as the "Kwanza Kit." The Research Center's activities include an oral-history project that contains more than 80 taped interviews with senior residents of the community. The Research Center also maintains its own library consisting of books and documents relating to Afro-American history.

4.   The following publications and catalogs are available:
    Anacostia Neighborhood Museum, Smithsonian Institution 1967/ 1977;
    Louise Daniel Hutchinson, *The Anacostia Story: 1608–1930* (Washington, D.C.: Smithsonian Institution Press, 1977);
    ————, *Out of Africa: From West African Kingdoms to Colonization* (Washington, D.C.: Smithsonian Institution Press, 1979).

District of Columbia Public Library See entry A9.

C3 Freer Gallery of Art (Smithsonian Institution)

1. **a.** *12th Street and Jefferson Drive, SW*
    Washington, D.C. 20560
    381-5344

    b. 10:00 A.M.-5:30 P.M.   Monday-Sunday. Closed Christmas Day.

    c. Open to the public free of charge.

    d. Photography permitted.

    e. Thomas Lawton, Director
    Esin Atil, Curator of Islamic Art

2-3.   The gallery has an extensive and unique collection of Oriental art. Its Near Eastern collection contains more than 1,088 objects from Egypt comprising pottery, bone and ivory carvings, sculpture, and metalwork. The museum's holdings of Egyptian glass are outstanding and consist of over 767 items, mainly beads and fragments, vases, bowls, lamps, and mosaic plaques (the earliest glass vessels are from the 18th dynasty of Ancient Egypt [ca. 1430–1340 B.C.]). Besides the Egyptian objects, the museum has 2 Meroitic sculptures.

4.   A complete inventory of the African holdings of the museum is not available. However, a fairly comprehensive card file is maintained by the staff. A description of the Near Eastern collection can be found in the various publications issued by the Freer, specifically the Freer Gallery of Art Oriental Series and the Occasional Papers, started in 1947. Notable among these are: 2 monographs by Esin Atil, *Art of the Arab World* (Washington, D.C.: Freer Gallery of Art, 1975) and *Ceramics from the World of Islam* (Washington, D.C.: Freer Gallery of Art, 1973); *Medieval Near Eastern Ceramics in the Freer Gallery of Art* (Smithsonian Publication 4420, 1960); and George Steindorff, *A Royal Head from Ancient Egypt* (Freer Gallery of Art, Occasional Papers, vol. 1, no. 5, 1951).

C4 Hirshhorn Museum and Sculpture Garden (Smithsonian Institution)

1. a. *Independence Avenue at 8th Street, SW*
        Washington, D.C. 20560
        381-6753

    b. Fall/Winter:
        10:00 A.M.-5:30 P.M.
        Spring/Summer:
        10:00 A.M.-9:00 P.M.
        Open 7 days a week. Closed Christmas Day.

    c. Open to the public, free of charge. Most of the pertinent holdings are not on display but in storage. Scholars interested in studying these objects should call for an appointment.

    d. Limited reproduction facilities.

    e. Abram Lerner, Director

2-3.   The museum has one of the most comprehensive collections of 20th-century art. Its permanent holdings comprise 4,000 paintings and 2,000 sculptures. Since the emphasis is on contemporary and modern art, African art does not figure prominently in the collections, nor is it on permanent display. The African collection consists of 48 objects from West and Central Africa, including 25 Benin, 6 Ashanti, and 5 Senufo works. The Benin group comprises mainly bronzes, notably plaques, masks, heads, and figures, as well as miscellaneous pieces in bronze, wood, and terra-cotta.
       The museum also owns 20 examples of ancient Egyptian art of which 16 are mummy masks. Especially noteworthy among these is an Egyptian head from the XXII-XXVI dynasty, a standing figure of Osiris

from the Saite period, and a bronze Ptolemaic Osiris dating to ca. 4th century B.C.

4.   At present, no comprehensive guide to the holdings exists.

C5   Howard University Gallery of Art

1. a. *Fine Arts Building*
    Howard University
    Washington, D.C. 20059
    636-7047

    b. 9:00 A.M.-4:00 P.M.   Monday-Friday
    Closed on weekends.

    c. Open to the public. Researchers wanting to study items that are not on permanent display should call ahead to make an appointment.

    d. No reproduction facilities available.

    e. Starmanda Bullock, Director

2.   The James V. Herring Heritage Gallery is the home of a permanent collection of traditional African art consisting of some 1,000 items. This collection comprises works from over 19 African countries and 47 peoples. In addition, Howard's art holdings also include a small but unique collection of contemporary African art which is, however, not on permanent display.

3.   The collection of traditional African art, though relatively small in size, is unique due to the exceptionally high quality and beauty of the items. These include over 373 Ashanti and Baoule goldweights (the finest collection in the Washington area), jewelry, weapons, rare Congolese sculptures; Ibo, Yoruba, Bambara, Senufo, Baoule, and Dogon masks; ceremonial drums; ancestor figures; bowls, textiles, handicrafts, and sculptures, many of which predate the present century.

Examples of traditional art from all of Africa can be found in this collection, with the exception of North Afrcia, Ethiopia, Nubia, and Southern Africa, which are not represented in the collection. Wood sculptures and the numerous goldweights which figure prominently in the collection are of high quality and exceptional beauty and workmanship.

The permanent collection of contemporary African art includes works of well-known artists from Senegal, Sudan, Zaire, Sierra Leone, Togo, and Cameroon. It consists of paintings, sculptures, and solar etchings.

4.   At the present time, there is no complete inventory of the holdings, published or unpublished. However, the staff is currently engaged in cataloging the collection. Researchers may find the following 2 sources useful in locating the various holdings: Scott Baker, "A Descriptive Catalogue of the African and African-American Collection: Howard University, Gallery of Art," M.A. thesis (Howard University, 1974), and Kojo

Fosu, *The Final Implementation Report: Exhibition of African Contemporary Art* (Howard University, 1977).

Note: Also see Howard University Museum entry C6.

C6 Howard University Museum

1. a. *Howard University Museum*
   Founders Library
   Howard University
   Washington, D.C. 20059
   636-7266

   b. 9:30 A.M.-4:30 P.M.   Monday-Friday

   c. Open to the public, free of charge.

   d. Limited reproduction facilities.

   e. Thomas Battle, Acting Curator
   Scott Baker, Docent

2-3.   The museum, which had its official opening in February 1979, is a unit of the Moorland-Spingarn Research Center. The primary purpose of the collection is to exhibit artifacts and documents that illustrate the history of black people and to facilitate serious research and interpretation of their historical and cultural development.
   The collection contains a broad variety of African materials, including sculpture, masks, textiles, trading beads, and jewelry from West and East Africa and Ethiopia.

4.   At present, there is no published bibliography of the museum's holdings. Plans to prepare catalogs and published guides are, however, under way. A printed catalog of the inaugural exhibition is available.

Note: Guided tours of the museum are available on request.

C7 Miya Gallery

1. a. *720 11th Street, NW*
   Washington, D.C. 20005
   347-6076

   b. 11:00 A.M.-7:00 P.M.   Monday-Saturday

   c. Open to the public. Many of the pertinent holdings are not on permanent display. Scholars wishing to examine these items should call ahead for appointment.

   d. Visitors may take their own photographs of gallery items.

   e. Vernard R. Gray, Director

2-3. Miya Gallery's small but growing permanent collection of art objects includes some examples of traditional African art such as textiles, musical instruments, and sculptures.

Once or twice each year, the gallery shows African art, both traditional and contemporary. A recent exhibit focused on MaKonde sculptures from East Africa.

C8 Museum of African Art (Smithsonian Institution)

1. a. *318 A Street, NE*
Washington, D.C. 20002
547-6222

b. 11:00 A.M.-5:00 P.M.   Monday-Friday
12:00 P.M.-5:00 P.M.   Saturday-Sunday

c. Open to the public without charge, although visitors are encouraged to contribute a donation: $1.00 for adults and $.50 for children.

d. Rather than reproducing its objects, the museum concentrates on circulating a select number of pieces to other museums and to schools. This program is an essential component of the museum's activities, in that the director and his colleagues have made education their highest priority. For example, "The Language of African Art," a group of 100 pieces, 4 large photos, and a catalog, circulates mainly to Afro-American colleges and universities.

In recent years the museum has sent out as many as 50 exhibitions. About 500 elementary school children each week visit the 12 public galleries. School groups that cannot afford transportation can be picked up by the museum's bus. The Department of Elementary and Secondary Education runs workshops for children, and it sends staff members to schools to lecture.

The Department of Higher Education concentrates on university programs and adult education. For example, it supplies personnel to teach courses in universities, and visiting professors and specialists come to the museum to lecture.

Each February, Black History Month brings in a full range of activities, but it is only part of a general effort, the purpose of which is to show the richness of African culture and history to Afro-Americans and others.

e. Warren M. Robbins, Director and Founder
Jean Salan, Deputy Director
Lydia Puccinelli, Curator of Collections
Edward Lifschitz, Photo-Archivist and Coordinator, Department of Higher Education
Amina Dickerson, Department of Education Director

2. The museum's permanent collection consists of about 7,500 African art objects and about 300 19th-century paintings by Afro-American artists. At any one time about 500 objects are on display. Exhibits change,

and different countries or themes are emphasized: Nigerian art, Southern African beadwork, and West African sculpture, for example. One gallery is devoted to the life and work of Frederick Douglass, the great Afro-American abolitionist and statesman, whose first Washington residence is the museum's central building. Another gallery is devoted to the African sources in modern European and American art.

3. The Museum of African Art is the only museum in America devoted solely to African art. All holdings have been donated to the museum, and they are particularly rich in sculptures, textiles, musical instruments, and utilitarian objects from West and Central Africa. Of particular importance are a "Chi-wara," or antelope headdress, from Mali; a spoon from Nigeria; and an ivory amulet in the form of a kneeling woman. The 19th-century Afro-American paintings and sculptures—by Roberts Duncanson, Henry O. Tanner, Edmonia Lewis, and others—constitute the largest collection of this kind in existence.

Objects are attractively exhibited and are augmented by films and color photographs; African music plays in the background. The popularity of the museum has grown significantly in the last 10 years, and today, largely through the efforts of its director, its work is widely known. Embassies, schools, clubs, and government agencies interested in Africa often have evening functions at the museum; the Fourth Triennial Symposium on African Art was held there.

4. Twenty-two catalogs of museum exhibits have been published between 1964 and 1978. They are available in the library, and certain publications are available for sale in the museum's bookstore. The following published and unpublished bibliographic and finding aids should also be of use to researchers:

"Classification Code—Art in Collections";
"Film Holdings" (some available for rent);
"Publications of Exhibit Catalogs by the Museum of African Art," on sale;
"Recorded Tapes" and records;
Tribute to Africa: The Photography and the Collection of Eliot Elisofon (Washington, D.C.: Museum of African Art, 1974), available for rent or purchase as a slide show or a 16mm film with soundtrack.

In addition to the bibliographic and finding aids described above, the museum encourages contributions to an information bank on African art. Visiting experts and graduate students write their remarks, and these are kept in vertical files. In this way, descriptive material increases.

An intern program operates in all sections of the museum. Participants come from Africa and the United States.

Even if one is not doing research on African art, a trip to Washington for Africa-related matters is not complete without a visit to this museum.

Note: Also see entries A29, D4, and F24.

C9 National Air and Space Museum (Smithsonian Institution)

1. a. *6th Street and Independence Avenue, SW*
   Washington, D.C. 20560
   381-6264

   b. Fall/Winter:
   10:00 A.M.-5:30 P.M.
   Spring/Summer:
   10:00 A.M.-9:00 P.M.
   Open 7 days a week. Closed Christmas Day.

   c. Open to the public free of charge.

   d. Photoreproduction services available.

   e. Noel Hinners, Director

2-3. The Africanist should contact the Center for Earth and Planetary Studies. One of the many concerns of the center is the contribution of the space program to desert studies. The center's activities include a research project in Egypt and one soon to be initiated in the Sahel. The primary objective of the Sahel program is to identify border areas threatened by the encroaching desert. For more information on these programs, contact Dr. Farouk El-Baz, research director (381-4081).

C10 National Museum of History and Technology (Smithsonian Institution)

1. a. *Constitution Avenue between 12 and 14th Streets, NW*
   Washington, D.C. 20560
   381-5017 (Information)

   b. Fall/Winter:
   10:00 A.M.-5:30 P.M.
   Spring/Summer:
   10:00 A.M.-9:00 P.M.
   Open 7 days a week. Closed Christmas Day.

   c. Open to the public free of charge. Many pertinent items are not on permanent display. Researchers should make appointments in advance to view these items.

   d. Museum holdings may be photographed. Photos intended for publication must be cleared with the Public Affairs Office.

   e. Roger G. Kennedy, Director

2. This is primarily a museum of American history with a focus on national and cultural history and the history of science and technology. As a result, it is not a major resource for the Africanist. The limited holdings on Africa are, moreover, scattered among many different divisions,

which makes it difficult to obtain an accurate count of documents and artifacts. The following description, though by no means comprehensive, attempts to identify and list the various African holdings.

3. *Department of National History*
    Dr. Vladimir Clain-Stefanelli, Chairman
    381-6230

    Division of Numismatics
    381-5026

    Coins from North Africa, particularly Egypt, are well represented in this collection. There are about 400 coins struck with Greek legends dating to the time when Egypt was a Roman province, about 100 Ptolemaic coins, and more than 500 Islamic coins from Morocco, Tunisia, and Algeria. The collection also contains some 30 rare and valuable gold coins from Axum. Besides these ancient coins, the division's holdings also include coins issued by various African nations.

    Division of Naval History
    381-5505

    The only item of note is an engraved elephant tusk brought to the United States in the mid-19th century.

    Division of Political History
    381-5532

    The one single item of interest for the Africanist is a rare Coptic Bible from Ethiopia presented to General Ulysses S. Grant.

    Division of Postal History
    381-5024

    This division holds several thousand stamps of great value and interest to the Africanist. The special collections include: the Puttkammer Collection, a comprehensive collection of stamps from the German states and colonies; the Hoover Collection, which is virtually complete and has stamps from every part of the world, but is particularly valuable for Eritrean stamps; the Transvaal Collection, 2 volumes; the Liberian Collection; the Michel Collection, 144 volumes, which contains many stamps from Africa; and the Egyptian Royal Imperforates, dating from 1926 to 1954. In addition, the division's holdings consist of 4 volumes for independent Africa and 2 others for British and French Africa. Researchers requiring further information and assistance should contact Lowell Newman of the division staff.

Department of Cultural History
Richard E. Ahlborn, Chairman
381-6112

Division of Community Life
381-4101

This division is an important resource for Afro-American history. Its holdings include some 100–150 items which focus on the Afro-American tradition in the decorative arts. Most of these materials are from the late 17th century and comprise slave drums, tags, locks, bells, mortars, and pestles. In addition to these items, the division also holds more than 5 shelfs of material on Afro-Americans. These consist of over 1,500 photographs (on all aspects of Afro-American life, particularly slavery) and numerous articles, bibliographies, biographical data, and publications.

Division of Ceramics and Glass
381-5014

The only items of interest here are 14 Islamic glassweights dating from ca. A.D. 700 to 1500.

4.   There is no comprehensive guide to the museum as a whole. Perhaps the most complete listing of holdings is the Bicentennial exhibition catalog *A Nation of Nations,* edited by Peter Marzio (1976). For the numismatic collections, researchers may refer to Vladimir Clain-Stefanelli, "History of the National Numismatic Collections," in *Contributions from the Museum of History and Technology,* Paper 31 (Washington, D.C.: Smithsonian Institution Press, 1968).

C11 National Museum of Natural History (Smithsonian Institution)

1. a. *Constitution Avenue at 10th Street, NW*
       Washington, D.C. 20560
       628-4422

    b. Fall/Winter:
       10:00 A.M.-5:30 P.M.
       Spring/Summer:
       10:00 A.M.-9:00 P.M.
       Open 7 days a week. Closed Christmas Day.

    c. Open to the public for museum exhibits. Scholars who wish to examine items not on permanent display must make appointments in advance.

    d. Visitors are permitted to take photographs of exhibits.

    e. Dr. James F. Mello, Acting Director
       Gordon Gibson, Curator, African Ethnology

2.   A large number of the holdings are not arranged geographically and, therefore, the researcher must search for pertinent material in the numerous divisions of the museum. There is a wealth of material here for the Africanist.

3.   The Department of Anthropology and Ethnology has more than 500,000 cataloged entries representing several million specimens. Though an accurate count of the African items is virtually impossible, there are substantial resources here on the material cultures of Africa. The Hall of the Cultures of Africa and Asia is well worth a visit, for many important specimens are on display here. These include tools, weapons, pottery, jewelry, garments, and musical instruments.

The museum's outstanding collections include:

(1) The Herbert Ward Collection, which is an extensive collection of specimens from the Congo. It contains over 200,000 items such as weapons, masks, figures, baskets, clothing, and utensils donated by Mr. Ward, an associate of Stanley's, and other materials acquired as gifts from missionaries and travelers who lived in Central Africa in the mid-19th century.

(2) Collection of Gordon D. Gibson from Namibia (Southwest Africa), Angola, and Botswana. Dr. Gibson has undertaken extensive research on the Herero-speaking peoples, and his interest is reflected in the collection that includes materials from other areas of Central and Southern Africa.

(3) West African Collection of Captain C. C. Roberts. Most of the items in this collection date back to the 1920s.

(4) Items collected during Theodore Roosevelt's expedition to East Africa in 1909–10.

(5) Hoffman Phillip Collection from Ethiopia.

(6) Talcott Williams Collection from Morocco.

Archeological specimens from Africa in the museum are neither numerous nor unique, except for those from North Africa (mainly Egypt) and some from Southern Africa.

In the field of physical anthropology there are scattered specimens from Africa. This is because the museum's primary focus is not on fossil man but on bone biology, population variations, and paleopathology.

The Department of Mineral Sciences also has several interesting items from Africa. Its mineral collection contains virtually every mineral found in the African continent. Outstanding items in the collection include: a comprehensive collection of minerals from the Tsumeb mine in Namibia, an extraordinary collection of beautiful specimens; a good collection of rocks from the diamond pipe in Southern Africa; and a collection of desert glass from North Africa.

In addition, the museum collects flora and fauna specimens from all over the world, including the continent of Africa. The Departments of Botany, Vertebrate Zoology, and Paleo-Biology have many items which should interest the Africanist. These include specimens of plants and animals from Africa. The Department of Zoology has an outstanding collection of small African mammals. Other unique specimens include the Cape Buffalo, white rhinoceros from Sudan, and dik dik. Researchers may also find it worthwhile to visit the Naturalist Center located in Room C-219 of the museum. The center, which contains materials on every aspect of natural history—minerals, rocks, plants, animals, etc.—also maintains a reference library which has books on various fields to accommodate different levels of interest. For further information, call Irene Magyar (381-4164).

4.   No published catalogs are available at present. However, the museum maintains several different card catalogs and the Ethnology Division's Tribal File on Africa should prove particularly useful to the researcher in identifying holdings. This file is arranged by different ethnic groups. The Anthropology Department is currently in the process of computer-

izing its holdings, which once completed should provide an efficient automatic indexing system.

In addition to the display items and the research collections, the expertise of the staff members will be of importance to Africanists who wish to undertake research in the field.

C12 Sun Gallery

1. a. *2324 18th Street, NW*
Washington, D.C. 20009
265-9224

   b. Noon-7:00 P.M.   Tuesday-Saturday
Closed Sunday and Monday

   c. Open to the public. Most of the African holdings are not on permanent display. Researchers who want to examine these items should write or call ahead for appointment.

   d. Selected items can be purchased. Arrangements can be made to photograph items on display.

   e. Charles Mitchell and Jamal Mims, Directors

2-3. This private art gallery shows the work of Third World artists. The number of African items on hand and on display varies from time to time. The gallery also maintains a small permanent collection of traditional African art which consists of sculptures, masks, gourds, baskets, and a few Benin bronzes.

C13 Textile Museum

1. a. *2320 S Street, NW*
Washington, D.C. 20008
667-0441

   b. 10:00 A.M.-5:00 P.M.   Tuesday-Saturday

   c. Open to the public, free of charge

   d. Limited reproduction service available.

   e. Andrew Oliver, Jr., Director
Louise Mackie, Curator, Old World

2. There are about 1,180 items pertaining to Africa, the majority of them from Egypt.

3. The museum's collection, which consists mainly of textiles, rugs, and tapestries, is particularly rich in items from countries influenced by Islamic culture. Its Coptic collection is outstanding and ranked among the best in the world. It comprises about 350 textiles and select large tapestries. Islamic Egypt is represented by over 750 items, mainly textiles

called "Tiraz" (with Arabic inscriptions). The museum also has about 30 carpets (from the 15th and 16th centuries), one of the most extensive collections of Mamluk carpets in the world. Besides this, there are over 30 items from Algeria and Morocco and about 20 textiles from West Africa. Many of these items are not on permanent display and interested persons should make arrangements with the curator to view them.

4.   Published descriptions of the museum's collection valuable to the Africanist include: R. Ettinghausen et al., *Prayer Rugs* (1974); and Ernst Kühnel, *Catalogue of Dated Tiraz Fabrics* (Washington, D.C.: Textile Museum, 1952) and *Cairene Rugs* (Washington, D.C.: Textile Museum, 1957).

Note: For the past several years, the museum has sponsored an annual "Rug Convention" and the "Irene Emery Roundtable," the latter featuring lectures and discussions on a selected topic which varies from year to year. Only professional scholars may attend these meetings.

D Collections of Music and Other Sound Recordings

Collections of Music and Other Sound Recordings Entry Format (D)

1. General information
   a. *address; telephone number(s)*
   b. hours of service
   c. conditions of access
   d. name/title of director and key staff members

2. Size of collection pertaining to Africa

3. Description of holdings pertaining to Africa

4. Facilities for study and use
   a. availability of audio-visual equipment
   b. reservation requirements
   c. fees charged
   d. reproduction services

5. Bibliographic aids facilitating use of collection

District of Columbia Public Library See entry A9.

D1 Howard University—Center for Ethnic Music

1. a. *Fine Arts Building, Room 3036*
      Howard University
      Washington, D.C. 20059
      636-7080

   b. 9:00 A.M.-5:00 P.M.   Monday-Friday

   c. Open to the public.

   d. Wanda L. Brown, Director

2. An accurate count of the center's African holdings is not possible as the African collection is found interspersed with the Afro-American and other collections. There is no question, however, that the unique ma-

terials housed in the center are an extremely valuable resource for the Africanist.

3. The Research Laboratory in the Center for Ethnic Music consists of an extensive collection of commercial recordings; numerous field recordings; and some 70 authentic African instruments. Its comprehensive collection of recordings (including the entire catalog of the African Library Association) includes music from virtually all parts of the African continent. The Africanist will find among the holdings Ethiopian urban and tribal music; Mbira music of Rhodesia; music and chants from Niger, Dahomey, Upper Volta, Malagasy, Kongo, Cameroon, Chad, Gabon, Nigeria-Hausa, Rwanda, Kanem, Central African Republic, Togo, and Kenya; and representations of the music of Ba-Benzele Pygmies, Senufo, Dan, Dogon, and many other ethnic groups.

    In addition to the recordings, the African tapes collection includes interesting items such as original compositions by Nigerian artists; tribal, folk, and café music of West Africa; and demonstrations of Nupe and Ewe music and of African rhythms and drumming.

4. a. Listening equipment is available free of charge, for virtually every form of recorded sound.

    b. Prior reservation is advisable to ensure the availability of equipment.

    c. No fee for listening to items in the collection.

    d. The center has facilities for reproducing and recording sound. The staff will also tape materials free of charge provided they are supplied with the tapes.

5. A detailed description of the center's African holdings can be found in their *Final Report,* volume 4: *Activities and Acquisitions* (August 1977).

Note: Also see entry B1.

D2 Library of Congress—American Folk Life Center—Archive of Folk Song

1. a. *Library of Congress, Main Building*
        Room G 152, Ground Floor
        287-5510

    b. 8:30 A.M.-5:00 P.M.   Monday-Friday

    c. Open to the public.

    d. Joseph C. Hickerson, Head of Archive
       Gerald Parsons, Reference Libarian

2-3. The archive receives and holds noncommercial recordings made in the field on tape, record, wire, cylinder, and cassette. They include all forms of verbal art such as songs, narratives, storytelling, games, and proverbs.

The total general collection is 200,000 titles or recordings and 2,500 reference titles (including 200 periodicals), which are in the reading room.

African materials include 54 collections among which are:

13 cylinders of music of Kenya (1913);

120 cylinders of music from the Erich von Hornbostel collection of the University of Berlin (1902–13);

1 cassette interview with Charlie Smith, "130-year-old African-born ex-slave and former cowboy" (1975);

9 aluminum discs, Laura Bolton Collection, Nyasaland and the Congo;

116 records of Afro-Bahian songs made by Melville and Frances Herskovits (1941–42);

21 tapes of sacred and secular music of Ethiopia, recorded by Halim El-Dabh in 1964;

several tapes of Upper Volta music recorded by Rosellini and Johnson, 1973–75;

8 tapes of Coptic mass in Egypt, recorded by John Gillespie in 1970;

12 tapes of Sephardic Jewish liturgical music from Morocco, with some Berber music from Morocco, recorded by Abraham Pinto in 1970;

"Primitive groups from various parts of the world . . . ," Helen Roberts, 1936–37, 1955;

Voice of America recordings of African music.

Vertical files contain information about holdings such as names of songs that are sung, African bibliographies, clippings, and record catalogs. The archive has the entire collection of slave narratives from the WPA collection, which is going to be indexed soon. It has in its collection 2 dissertations: Thomas F. Johnston, *The Music of the Shangana-Tsonga* (Mozambique-N. Transvaal) and Richard Alan Waterman, *African Patterns in Trinidad Negro Music* (1943). The field notes accompanying the Rosellini- Johnson recordings in Upper Volta are also available here.

The reference collection holds a complete list of items published in the bibliographies of *Ethnomusicology* by Joseph C. Hickerson. They are arranged alphabetically by author.

The archive holds a huge collection of Afro-American songs, and it also has videotapes of blues musicians.

4. a. Listening equipment available, free of charge.

   b. Reservations advisable.

   c. No fee for listening to items in the collections.

   d. Reproduction facilities available.

5. Numerous finding aids and printed descriptions of the collections are available. Researchers should first consult *An Inventory of the Bibliographies and Other Reference and Finding Aids Prepared by the Archive of Folk Song, Library of Congress.* The archive maintains a file of bibliographies and related lists covering over 100 areas and subjects

in the fields of folklore, folk music, and ethnomusicology. Most of these listings have been compiled over the past several years by the archive's former librarian and current head, Joseph C. Hickerson. A limited number of copies of these lists are available on request. Items of interest to Africanists in this inventory include: "African Material in the Archive of Folk Song" (1970); "The Archive of Folk Song: A Bibliography" (1978); "Bibliographies and Discographies of African Music" (1975); "Commercially Issued Recordings of Material from the Archive of Folk Song" (1978); "A Guide to the Collections of Recorded Folk Music and Folk Lore in the Library of Congress" (1976); "Music of Morocco" (1972); "Recording of Slave Narratives and Related Material in the Archive of Folk Song" (1971); and "Talking Drums" (1964).

Researchers should also consult Alan Jabbour and Joseph C. Hickerson, "African Recordings in the Archive of Folk Song," in the *Quarterly Journal of the Library of Congress,* vol. 27, no. 3 (July 1970), pp. 282-88.

In addition to the above, researchers should note that card files are arranged generically (e.g., drum) by location, ethnic group, and name of collector. Field notes of collectors correspond to recordings. Correspondence files contain biographical information about artists. A partial shelflist maintained from 1934 to 1950 is arranged item by item, alphabetically by title of song, then alphabetically by state or region, and then by performer.

Note: An intern program allows students and others to work without pay in the preparation of bibliographies, filing, cataloging, and so forth. The program carries academic credit for some institutions.

D3 Library of Congress—Motion Picture, Broadcasting, and Recorded Sound Division—Reference Section

1. a. *Library of Congress, Main Building*
      Room G 152
      287-5509

   b. 8:30 A.M.-5:00 P.M.   Monday-Friday
      Music Reading Room, G 144
      8:30 A.M.-5:00 P.M.   Monday-Saturday

   c. Open to the public.

   d. Patrick Sheehan, Head, Reference Section
      James R. Smart, Assistant Head

2-3.   The MBRS Division differs from the Archive of Folk Song in that it mainly collects commercially produced recorded material, although there are other items such as interviews and speeches.

No meaningful assessment of African holdings in the Recorded Sound Section is possible, as the majority of the estimated 900,000 items in the collection is uncataloged and the available card catalog for processed items is not arranged geographically. As a result, researchers must rely on staff members for assistance in locating and retrieving African materials. Card catalogs in the Music Reading Room (G 144) and in the Reference Section indicate there are some 900 African items. Commercial recordings include Afrikaaner as well as Black African music. Sources of the recordings are: the Center for the Study of Democratic Institutions (discussions), Washington Tapes, the French OCORA, UNESCO, Kaleidaphone, Folkways, and the International Library of African Music, as well as numerous Hugh Tracey recordings.

The Music Reading Room contains some 50 titles on African music. Researchers can listen to recordings here. Perhaps the best way to identify and locate materials is to survey the available manufacturers' catalogs and locate relevant label numbers. With these label numbers, a search can then be undertaken in Landover, Maryland, where the recordings are stored.

In addition to commercially produced music, the division also has custody of the following interviews and speeches: H. K. Banda at the National Press Club (1960); conversations with African writers (Voice of America, 1975–77): Grace Ogot, Flora Nwapa, Steve Chimambo, Ezekiel Mphahlele, and Ndabaningi Sithole, among others; Alex Haley lecture, September 1972; Langston Hughes poetry readings; Tom Mboya on "Meet the Press" (1959); B. Nabwera, "Kenya, an Emerging Nation"; Sylvanus Olympio on "Meet the Press" (1962); F. D. Roosevelt, "Report on the Casablanca Conference" (1943); Albert Schweitzer's 90th birthday celebration; Haile Selassie on "Meet the Press" (1963); and war broadcasts from Algiers.

The Music Reading Room catalog indicates the division holds sheet music mainly from the Republic of South Africa.

There are few vertical files of interest except for a folder called "African Music Society" in a subject file. This folder has material relating to the work of Hugh Tracey.

4. a. Listening equipment is available, free of charge.

   b. Reservations advisable.

   c. No fee for listening to items in the collection.

   d. Tape duplicates can be made for a fee. Recordings can be purchased. Items of special interest include a 2-record LP set of *Music of Morocco* recorded by Paul Bowles (1959) and *Afro-Bahian Religious Songs from Brazil* recorded by Melville J. and Frances S. Herskovits (1941–42).

5. There are various ways to find recordings and to use the facilities. The following are helpful:

   Brochures: "The Library of Congress Music Division," and "The Music Division: A Guide to Its Collections and Services," and Darious Louis Thieme, *African Music: A Briefly Annotated Bibliography* (Washington, D.C.: Library of Congress, 1964).

   Card catalogs: scores and sheet music, books, and catalogs (more complete than the main catalog), catalog for books about music and education methods, recorded sound catalog, class catalog to locate combinations of musical instruments, libretto catalog, periodicals (articles are cataloged for period before 1949), post-1949 *Music Index* (a reference book).

A list of recorded LP albums for sale is also available on request.

D4 Museum of African Art—Eliot Elisofon Archives—Music Collection

1. a. *330 A Street, NE*
   Washington, D.C. 20002
   547-6222

   b. 9:00 A.M.-5:30 P.M.   Monday-Friday

   c. Researchers should call in advance for appointment.

   d. Edward Liftschitz, Archivist

2-3.   The Eliot Elisofon Archives Collection contains a small number of music and sound recordings. In addition to recorded tapes made by Elisofon during his many visits to Africa, the following items should be of value to researchers: "Fourth Triennial Symposium of Traditional African Art" (April 1-4, 1977); "Francis Bebey Recital" (June 23, 1974); and "Frere Cornet and William Fagg Lecture" (March 1976).

4.   Listening equipment is available.

5.   Researchers should seek the assistance of the staff in identifying materials in the collection.

Note: Also see entries A29, C8, and F24.

D5 National Archives and Records Service (NARS) (General Services Administration [GSA])—Audio-visual Archives

1. a. *8th Street and Pennsylvania Avenue, NW*
   Washington, D.C. 20408
   523-3208 (Sound recordings)

   b. 8:45 A.M.-5:00 P.M.   Monday-Friday

   c. Open to researchers. Users must first obtain an identification pass from the Central Research Staff in Room 200B. Some materials may be restricted.

   d. William T. Murphy, Director
   Les Waffen, Head of Sound Recording

2.   The NARS collection consists of over 100,000 sound recordings, with an undetermined number of items for Africa.

3.   Africa-related items can be found in several record groups:
   RG 43: Records of International Conferences, Commissions, and Expositions. Contains recordings of the Agency for International Development comprising speeches, interviews, press conferences, programs, and related events.

RG 48: Records of the Office of the Secretary of the Interior. Contains Drew Pearson's reports on Vichy France's support of General Rommel in North Africa; a discussion of Washington's response to the British takeover in Madagascar; and a broadcast on soil erosion control programs in South Africa, Kenya, Uganda, and Tanganyika, and their relationship to the war effort.

RG 59: General Records of the Department of State. Contains sound recordings of John Foster Dulles discussing his Middle East trip in 1953 and his interviews with leaders; and a speech by Christian A. Herter defending U.S. and U.N. roles in the Congo crisis and a reexamination of the U.S. stand on the Algerian question.

RG 200: National Archives Gift Collection. Contains sound recordings (1929–67) of speeches, interviews, and addresses by prominent figures in the fields of politics and broadcasting. Included among these numerous items are President Franklin D. Roosevelt's fireside chat on the Tehran and Cairo conferences (December 24, 1943); speeches of Presidents Harry S. Truman and Herbert Hoover on famine; President Eisenhower's address to the nation on the Suez Canal (October 31, 1956); Emperor Haile Selassie's speech on Italo-Ethiopian negotiations (1935); and sound recordings featuring newscasters commenting on World War II events.

RG 262: Records of the Foreign Broadcast Intelligence Service. Contains broadcasts from Brazzaville and Leopoldville, and from Berlin to Africa.

RG 330: Records of the Office of the Secretary of Defense. Sound recording in the long-running series "The Cavalcade of America" recreates General Mark Clark's secret mission to the pro-Allied French in North Africa in 1942 to set up the Operation TORCH invasion.

RG 407: Records of the Adjutant General's Office. "Action in North Africa" describes a battle along the beaches leading to Casablanca; "A-20's are A-1" focuses on use of A-20 aircraft against the Nazis in Tunisia; "Liberators in the Middle East" describes the defeat of Field Marshal Rommel's Afrika Korps; "Hell-Bent" describes the crucial role of American vehicles and radio equipment in the battle of Kasserine Pass; "Rolling into Action" reports on the performance of American automotive equipment in the North African campaign; "It's Got Everything," a sound recording made on the North African battlefront, describes the P-38 aircraft attacks against the Nazis; "Stranger Than Fiction" and "Number 311" describe action on the North African battlefront.

Smithsonian Institution—African Diaspora Program Music Collection See entry N1.

D6 Traditional Music Documentation Project (TMDP)

1. a. *3740 Kanawha Street, NW*
   Washington, D.C. 20015
   363-7571

b-c. Interested researchers should call Mr. Wittig for appointment.

   d. Curt Wittig, Director

2. TMDP is an independent nonprofit organization which seeks to identify and document extant examples of traditional African music. The Documentation Project is primarily a research library containing an extensive collection of records; several hundred hours of music recorded on tape; oral data; and books and periodicals on African music. Though an exact count of the total holdings is not possible, it is certain that the collection is an extremely valuable resource for Africanists and contains many items which are unique and not available elsewhere. These materials are primarily from Nigeria, Zimbabwe, Southern Africa, Mozambique, and Zaire.

3. TMDP has so far released 12 albums on its Kaleidophone label. These are excellent examples of traditional music from Kenya, Tanzania, Uganda, Mozambique, Malawi, Zaire, Rhodesia, South Africa, Zambia, and Rwanda and include a vast spectrum of music—praise songs, chants, masquerade music, and varied instruments such as mbira, strings, drums, lute, bells, gourd flutes, rattles, guitars, and horns. The record collection also includes Duro Lapipo's *Oba Koso,* which dramatizes the last days of the powerful 15th-century Yoruba King Shango; and the complete set of Hugh Tracey's *The Music of Africa* series, which represents the pioneering work of Tracey in recording the music in Central and Southern Africa. In addition, the record library also has other labels, such as Folkways, Caprice, Ocora, Barenveiter, Vogue Disc, and Teuveren, all of which focus on traditional African music.

    TMDP also maintains a comprehensive collection of reference books and periodicals on ethnomusicology and African music. These include the following noteworthy titles: *African Arts; African Society Journal, Black Perspectives in Music; Ethnomusicology Society Journal;* and *Journal of the African Music Society* (issues dating back to the 1950s).

4. a. Listening equipment available.

    b. Researchers should call ahead to make arrangements for a visit.

    c. No fee charged.

    d. Selected albums available for purchase.

5. Traditional Music Documentation Project's *Kaleidophone Record Catalog, 1976,* is available free on request.

E Map Collections

Map Collections Entry Format (E)

1. General information
   a. *address; telephone number(s)*
   b. hours of service
   c. conditions of access
   d. reproduction services
   e. name/title of director and heads of relevant divisions

2. Size of holdings pertaining to Africa

3. Description of holdings pertaining to Africa

4. Bibliographic aids facilitating use of collection

Central Intelligence Agency Map Collection See entry K5·

E1 Defense Mapping Agency Hydrographic/Topographic Center

1. a. *6500 Brookes Lane*
      Washington, D.C. 20315
      227-2036 (Topographic Data Base Division)

   b. 7:30 A.M.-3:30 P.M.   Monday-Friday

   c. The Defense Mapping Agency Map and Chart Collections are not open to the public. Researchers are restricted to the Department of Defense Mapping, Charting, and Geodetic Community.

   d. Selected maps and charts are available for purchase from the DMA Office of Distribution Services.

   e. Col. John R. Lund, Director, DMA Hydrographic/Topographic Center
      Mr. Philip McAvoy, Chief, Topographic Data Base Division

2-3.   The DMA Hydrographic/Topographic Center Library Collection contains approximately 1,495,000 maps, 2,800 charts, 75,000 books, peridicals, and documents. The number of Africa-related maps and charts is difficult to estimate. The library contains predominantly topographic maps (depicting special features such as vegetation, roads, and railroads, land and ocean areas, cities, towns, and airfields) but also stores aeronautical charts (depicting essential topography, obstructions, aids to navigation, and other pertinent information for air use) and nautical charts (showing navigable waters and adjacent or included land areas, marine obstructions, aids to navigation, and other pertinent information for mariners).

In addition, there are selected topical maps on related subjects, such as administrative divisions and transportation and urban areas. The maps generally range in scale from 1:50,000 to 1:2,000,00. Many maps are classified. The classification is usually related to source, scale, and date, or restrictions imposed by international agreements with foreign countries.

4. A substantial number of maps produced by DMA are available to the public in the DMA Map and Chart Depository Program. Each depository collection contains over 1,000 maps of Africa. George Washington University Library and other depository libraries maintain a catalog of depository maps.

    Selected topographic maps, aeronautical, and nautical charts are available for purchase, such as the Africa, Series 2201. For further information and a copy of the *DMA Price List of Maps and Charts for Public Sale,* contact Defense Mapping Agency, Office of Distribution Services, Washington, D.C. 20315.

E2 Geological Survey Library (Interior Department)—Map Collection

1. a. *12201 Sunrise Valley Drive, Fourth Floor*
    Reston, Virginia 22092
    (703) 860-6679

    b. 7:45 A.M.-4:15 P.M.   Monday-Friday

    c. Open to the public.

    d. Researchers wishing to obtain copies of maps in the collection should seek the assistance of the staff, who will direct them to local photoduplication firms which provide such services for a fee.

    e. George H. Goodwin, Jr., Librarian

2. The library's map collection contains approximately 266,000 sheet maps, of which an estimated 2,000 are Africa-related. A measurement of the maps shelflist indicates that there are roughly 475 maps of West Africa, 325 of North Africa, 400 of East Africa, 275 of Central Africa, and 320 of Southern Africa.

3. Maps are arranged by subject and geographic area and further classified by region and country. The collection consists largely of geologic and

earth-science maps, divided into numerous categories: agriculture, mineral resources, water, vegetation, soils, climate, and coal.

4. At the present there exists no published catalog or inventory of the entire map collection. However, in the future, the holdings will be placed in a computerized system to facilitate easy access. For maps published by the Geological Survey, the following catalogs should prove of use to researchers:

Publications of the Geological Survey, 1879–1961 and *Publications of the Geological Survey, 1962–1970. New Publications of the Geological Survey,* issued monthly with annual cumulations, provides information on current maps. For further information, scholars should contact USGS Public Inquiries Office, Room 1-6-402 National Center, 12201 Sunrise Valley Drive, Reston, Virginia 22092.

Note: Also see entry A14.

E3 Library of Congress—Geography and Map Division

1. a. *845 South Pickett Street*
   Alexandria, Virginia 22304
   (703) 370-1335 (Reading Room or Map Reference Inquiries)
   (703) 370-1216 (Main Office)

   Mail: Washington, D.C. 20540

   b. 8:30 A.M.-5:00 P.M.   Monday-Friday
   8:30 A.M.-12:30 P.M.   Saturday

   c. Open to the public.

   d. Photoreproduction services available through the Library of Congress Photoduplication Service.

   e. John A. Wolter, Chief
   Richard W. Stephenson, Head, Reference and Bibliography Section
   Andrew W. Modelski, Bibliographer

2-3. The Geography and Map Division of the Library of Congress has the world's largest and most comprehensive cartographic collection, consisting of 3.6 million maps; 42,000 atlases; over 250 globes; and some 8,000 reference books. The collection is all inclusive, but it is especially strong in historical maps and atlases. Specific African material includes an estimated 340 atlases; 14,000 single uncataloged maps, published for the most part prior to 1968; 1,750 cataloged single maps received since 1968; and 57,000 individual sheets of large and medium-scale set maps and charts.

   The reference collection in the Geography and Map Reading Room contains geographic and cartographic reference books, bibliographies, gazetteers, and current issues of over 200 periodicals, all of which are available for consultation. Miscellaneous vertical files contain pamphlets and newspaper clippings.

ATLASES

The division's unique collection of atlases dates from the earliest printed editions of Ptolemy's *Geography* and includes representative and noteworthy volumes of every period in cartographic history dating from the 15th century. The collection contains over 55 printed editions of Ptolemy's *Geography* and a good representation of various editions of the atlases of Ortelius, Mercator, Blaeu, and other 17th-century publishers.

The extensive collection of African atlases covers the African continent, regions, individual countries, states, counties, and cities. Also included are special subject or topical atlases which provide historic, physical, economic, geological, linguistic, and ethnographic data.

A dictionary card catalog is available; however, many of the atlases are not listed in this catalog. A survey of the shelflist showed the following number of atlases: General and Colonial Africa, 67; North Africa, 54 (including 26 for Egypt); West Africa, 52 (including 12 for Nigeria); Central Africa, 62 (including 42 for Zaire); East Africa, 46 (including 11 for Tanzania and 9 for Ethiopia); and Southern Africa, 59 (over half are Republic of South Africa).

The contents of most of the division's atlases are described in Library of Congress, *A List of Geographical Atlases in the Library of Congress,* compiled by Philip Lee Phillips (Washington, D.C.: Government Printing Office, 1909-74), 8 volumes.

SINGLE MAPS

Maps obtained prior to 1968 are almost totally uncataloged. Holdings are arranged on the basis of geographic area, thereby making it relatively easy to identify and retrieve African materials. This massive collection of African sheet maps is arranged in 351 flat files with an average of 40 maps in each file. The map files are organized by continent, region, subregion, and country, and then further subdivided by chronological period (coverage extends back at least through the 17th century), by subject, e.g., agriculture, physical features, minerals and mines, ethnography, climate, economics, transportation and communications systems, missionary societies), by subnational region, by political/administrative subdivision, and by city. A survey of the African map files produced the following total numbers of maps by region (using a rough estimate of 40 maps per file drawer): General Africa, 2,000; North Africa, 3,280 (including 880 for Egypt); West Africa, 2,680 (including 760 for Nigeria); Central Africa, 1,600 (including 880 for Zaire); East Africa, 2,500 (including 520 for Tanzania); Southern Africa, 1,680 (including 360 for Zimbabwe-Rhodesia).

Single maps acquired by the division since 1968 (but dating from every historical period) are filed separately in the MARC collection (retrievable through the Library of Congress MARC computerized catalog). The MARC collection is arranged according to the same format as the one referred to earlier. African maps are arranged in 87 flat files with an average of 40 maps in each file drawer. A survey of the shelflist shows a total of some 4,570 African maps. The regional breakdown is as follows: North Africa, 1,340 (including 630 for Algeria,

200 for Egypt, 100 for Sudan); West Africa, 900 (including 250 for Nigeria, 110 for Ghana); East Africa, 700 (including 150 for Kenya, 100 for Uganda); Central Africa, 375 (including 150 for Zaire, 50 for Angola); Southern Africa, 925 (which includes 350 for the Republic of South Africa, 150 for Zimbabwe-Rhodesia, and 110 for Zambia).

Researchers can also find in the MARC collection maps published by the National Geographic Society, Central Intelligence Agency, United Nations, Defense Mapping Agency, African Geological Surveys, Michelin, Great Britain's Foreign and Commonwealth Offices, and the U.S. Army Map Service.

SERIES MAPS

The series or set maps are often extremely detailed and are arranged in the same type of flat file first by country, and then further divided by subject, region, and city. There are a total of 1,238 series for Africa. The following data refer to particular series: General Africa, 53; North Africa, 348 (including 145 for Egypt); West Africa, 264 (including 98 for Nigeria); Central Africa, 122 (including 62 for Zaire); East Africa, 250 (including 55 for Madagascar); Southern Africa, 201 (including 55 for the Republic of South Africa and 55 for Zimbabwe-Rhodesia). Contents include topographic, hydrographic, geologic, soil, mineral, and resource maps. The Nautical Chart Collection consists of nautical and aeronautical charts published by the major maritime powers. Predominant among these are charts produced by the British Admiralty and by Southern African governments. Virtually all materials in this collection date from the 19th and 20th centuries. At the present, there exists only a preliminary cataloging of the set maps; however, a series map shelflist is maintained by the division.

RARE AND VALUABLE MATERIALS

A large collection of unique and valuable items is stored in a special vault. These include extensive holdings of original manuscript, engraved and lithographed atlases, and facsimile editions of rare and historical volumes. African material in the vault consists of 4 drawers of early printed maps and manuscripts dating from the 12th to the 18th centuries. Especially noteworthy items among these uncataloged materials include numerious editions of Claudius Ptolemaeus, *Geographia,* the earliest of which dates from 1475 (the division also has other editions, notably Bologna 1477, Florence 1482, Ulm 1482, etc.); Abraham Ortelius, *Theatrum Orbis Terrarum* (1570); Nicolas Sanson, *L'Afrique, en Plvsiers Cartes Novvelles, et Exactes, &c. en Divers Traitez de Geographie, et d'Histoire* (Paris, 1667 [?]), and a rare 17th-century wall map portraying Africa, which is a 1669 Jaillot edition of Blaeu's map of Africa and is a unique and hitherto unrecorded copy and one of the earliest large-scale representations of the continent. (It is unusual and distinctive in having the title, inscriptions, and place names in French rather than Latin; it is described in Yusuf Kamal, *Monumenta Cartographica Africae et Aegypti* (Cairo, 1926–51), Walter W. Ristow, "America and Africa: Two Seventeenth-Century Wall Maps" in the *Quarterly Journal of the Library of Congress* (January

1967); and the collection of the American Colonization Society (25 maps).

A shelflist of the vault's holdings is maintained by the division.

4.   There does not exist any single comprehensive catalog of the division's entire holdings; card and book catalogs provide access to the specialized collections. An indispensible reference tool is the Geography and Map Division, *The Bibliography of Cartography* (Boston: G. K. Hall & Co., 1973), 5 volumes with a supplement. This is a comprehensive index to the literature of cartography. It provides author, title, and subject access to books and periodical articles. The supplement contains special subject headings and a list of 275 serials and periodicals. The division has also published several bibliographies and checklists which describe various cartographic groups; and in 1968 a computer-assisted cataloging system was initiated for current accessions of single-sheet maps. A descriptive brochure, *Geography and Map Division* (Library of Congress, 1977) and a *List of Publications* (1975), are available.

E4   National Archives and Records Service (NARS) (General Services Administration)—Center for Cartographic and Architectural Archives

1.   a. *8th Street and Pennsylvania Avenue, NW*
     (Entrance from Pennsylvania Avenue only)
     Washington, D.C. 20408
     523-3062

   b. 8:45 A.M.-5:00 P.M.   Monday-Friday

   c. Open to all researchers. Researcher identification card required and can be obtained from the Central Reference Division, Room 200 B.

   d. Various types of photoduplication services available.

   e. Ralph Ehrenberg, Director

2.   Africa-related maps are scattered in many different record groups.

3.   The maps and charts which cover a wide range of subjects and time periods can be found in the following groups:

   RG 8: Records of the Bureau of Agricultural Engineering. Contains records of drainage and irrigation investigations.
   RG 18: Records of the Army Air Forces. Maps of airports, air facilities in French Congo and Abyssinia, 1942–43, and maps of target areas in North Africa, especially Algeria.
   RG 23: Records of the Coast and Geodetic Survey. Gravity and magnetic observations made by E. D. Preston, who accompanied the naval eclipse expedition to the west coast of Africa in 1889; planimetric map of Liberia, showing highways, trails, towns, forest areas, and mountains, 1955.
   RG 30: Records of the Bureau of Public Roads. Road maps of Ethiopia and Egypt.
   RG 37: Records of the Hydrographic Office. The published nautical charts of this office consist of over 2,000 Africa-related items con-

taining charts relating to the African coast, harbors, islands, and hydrographic information. The numbered archives file contains several maps of Liberia, a map of the southwest coast of Madagascar and of Johanna Island, 1889.

RG 38: Records of the Office of the Chief of Naval Operations; maps relating to Suez Canal. The cartographic records of the Office of Naval Intelligence relating to Africa contain 2 maps of Algeria.

RG 43: Records of International Conferences, Commissions, and Expositions. Includes some copies of German and French maps of Central Africa.

RG 45: Naval Records Collection of the Office of Naval Records and Library. Contains maps of the Cape Palmas area, 1853–55.

RG 46: Records of the United States Senate. Map "Maryland in Liberia," 1853, shows various counties and cities along the coast and an inset of Cape Palmas.

RG 54: Records of the Bureau of Plant Industry, Soils, and Agricultural Engineering. Maps of African date palms, 1889–1914.

RG 59: General Records of the Department of State. Diplomatic and consular files contains several maps. Included are maps showing settlements on lower Congo; Liberian boundary, 1809; Kasai-Sankuru region, 1920–21; Stanley Falls area, 1893; numerous maps of roads, railways, bridges, and harbors in Dakar, 1929; Liberia, 1910–29; Portuguese Guinea, 1910–29; Italian East Africa, 1930–39; Egypt, 1910–29; Algeria, 1940–49; and French West Africa, 1940–49. In addition there are some 76 items scattered among Foreign Security Inspection Reports, Cartographic Records of the Division of Geography and Cartography, Consular Trade Reports, and the Numerical Map File. These maps show political boundaries and subdivisions, cities, mineral resources, trade and communications, population density and ethnic groups, U.S. consular districts, and foreign service posts.

RG 76: Records of Boundary and Claims Commissions and Arbitrations. A map of Africa showing European settlements.

RG 77: Records of the Office of the Chief of Engineers. Contains general cartographic records comprising maps of North Africa, Senegal, and the Belgian Congo; headquarters map file of the Office of the Chief of Engineers, 1800–1935; War Department map collection showing defenses of the Suez Canal, colonial possessions in Africa, war zone in South Africa, and the area involved in the Ashanti war, 1900; maps of the Army Map Service (2,000 items) showing physical features, place names, boundaries, roads, and rivers; and a British map relating to the East Africa Protectorate, 1941–45. (*Note:* RG 77 is probably one of the more important cartographic resources at the archives. It contains a total of 2,073 items pertaining to Africa.)

RG 83 Records of the Bureau of Agricultural Economics. Maps of political subdivisions in Egypt, Union of South Africa, and North Africa, 1920–40; dot maps showing agricultural production and livestock in Algeria, Egypt, and South Africa.

RG 95: Records of the Forest Service. Published maps of forest regions.

RG 115: Records of the Bureau of Reclamation. Maps relate to reclamation activities, including water supply, irrigation, and colonization of new lands.

RG 120: Records of the American Expeditionary Forces (World War I). Topographic maps cover areas of Egypt, Sudan, and South Africa.

RG 151: Records of the Bureau of Foreign and Domestic Commerce. Map of the African airway system.

RG 160: Records of Headquarters Army Service Forces. Task force maps of operations in the North African Theater, 1942–44; map of Trans-Africa Railway.

RG 165: Records of the War Department General and Special Staffs. Maps in file 6591 deal with French expedition for the relief of Fez, 1911; those in file 6903 with operations of the Italian Expeditionary Corps in Tripoli; map of area surveyed by Army Air Force during North African campaign, 1942–43; maps dealing with British military operations in South Africa, 1901; general cartographic records of the Military Intelligence Division; and maps of the Geographic and Topographic branch of the Intelligence Division.

RG 226: Records of the Office of Strategic Services. Forty-seven printed and manuscript maps of city plans, communication systems, minerals, railroads, agricultural regions, and theater maps; approximately 345 maps containing political boundaries and subdivisions, population distribution, ethnic and religious groups, and related subjects.

RG 234: Records of the Reconstruction Finance Corporation. More than 30 maps prepared by the Madagascar Department of Mines, mainly in the 1930s; maps and graphs relating to shipments of strategic minerals from Africa, containing information about mineral resources in the Belgian Congo, Angola, northern and southern Rhodesia, Mozambique, South West Africa, Gold Coast, and Rwanda-Urundi.

RG 242: National Archives Collection of Foreign Records seized. Maps and charts showing geographic features of various African areas and the location of troops in North Africa; 23 published maps comprising general maps of North Africa, military maps seized from the records of German Field Commands, cartographic records of the OberKommando der Kriegsmarine relating to naval strongholds and coastal fortifications of Southern African harbors, Portuguese East Africa coasts, and harbors of Portuguese Atlantic Islands; 23 published maps of North Africa; maps showing position of Allied and German units on the African front; maps of targets in Egypt, French North Africa, Libya, and Tunisia.

RG 253: Records of the Petroleum Administration for War. Contains maps relating to petroleum-producing areas, mainly Egypt and Morocco.

RG 256: Records of American Commission to Negotiate Peace. Maps deal with trade and economic relations. In addition to these there are 29 maps showing population density and distribution according to religion and "racial" type, suitable areas for colonization, natural resources, and Cape-to-Cairo railway; and 49 which deal with crop, farm, and livestock distribution and land classification and forested areas.

RG 291: Records of the Property Management and Disposal Service. Maps deal with mines and metallurgical plants.

RG 319: Records of the Army Staff. Maps and charts dealing with Africa-Middle East Theater of operations; geological surveys of diamond deposits in the Gold Coast and water reservoirs in Uganda.

RG 331: Records of the Allied Operational and Occupations Headquarters, World War II. Sixty-five operational maps of North Africa, 1941–45, showing progress of campaign and position of forces; 18 items arranged by geographical area showing tactical information on traffic mobility in North Africa.

RG 418: Records of St. Elizabeth's Hospital. Map showing routes of modern explorers in Central Africa.

4.   There is no single comprehensive catalog of NARS's African map collection. Researchers should, however, find National Archives and Record Service, *Guide to Federal Archives Relating to Africa* (1977) useful for locating cartographic materials. Most of the information given above comes from this publication.

Other guides which may be of some use include Charlotte M. Ashby et al., *Guide to Cartographic Records in the National Archives* (1971) and United States Hydrographic Office, *Manuscript Charts in the National Archives, 1838-1908*, compiled by William J. Heynen (Washington, D.C. 1978).

Note: Also see entries B3, D5, and F26.

E5 National Geographic Society—Cartographic Division Map Library

1. a. *Membership Center Building*
      11555 Darnestown Road (Maryland Route 28)
      Gaithersburg, Maryland 20760
      857-7000, Ext. 1401

    b. 7:30 A.M.-4:00 P.M. Monday-Friday

    c. Not open to the public. Serious researchers may, however, be permitted to examine the collection. They should contact the map librarian for permission.

    d. Xerox machine available.

    e. Margery Barkdull, Map Librarian

2-3.   There are an estimated 100,000 maps in the collection, which comprises U.S. and worldwide maps (topographic, administrative, subject, and highway maps), lunar maps, nautical and aeronautical charts, and city plans. The library has a copy of every map ever produced by the National Geographic Society. There is also worldwide coverage of atlases, reference books, and gazetteers.

It was not possible to estimate the number of African maps in the collection. Many of the young African countries have not yet developed mapping programs and as a result the African map collection is not extensive.

4.   The collection is arranged by geographical region and country.

Note: The National Geographic Society has published numerous excellent maps which are available for purchase at the Explorers Hall sales desk (857-7589) at 17th and M Streets, NW.

F Film Collections (Still Photographs and Motion Pictures)

Film Collections Entry Format (F)

1. General information
   a. *address; telephone number(s)*
   b. hours of service
   c. conditions of access
   d. name/title of director and key staff members

2. Size of collection pertaining to Africa

3. Description of holdings pertaining to Africa

4. Facilities for study and use
   a. availability of audio-visual equipment
   b. reservation requirements
   c. fees charged
   d. reproduction services

5. Bibliographic aids facilitating use of collection

F1 African Directions, Inc·—Education Division Film Collection

1. a. *884 National Press Building*
      Washington, D.C. 20045
      347-6638

   b. 9:00 A.M.-5:00 P.M. Monday-Friday

   c. Open to the public.

   d. Crispin D. Chindongo

2-3. The Education Division of *African Directions* maintains a small collection of approximately 270–300 color slides and several 8 x 10 black-and-white photographs. Subject matter includes African art and culture, African personalities, and scenes of modern Africa.

4. Prints can be purchased.

F2 Agency for International Development (AID)—Photo Collection

1. a. *AID Office of Public Affairs*
      State Department Building, Room 4886
      21st Street and Virginia Avenue, NW
      Washington, D.C. 20523
      632-9309

   b. 9:30 A.M.-5:30 P.M.   Monday-Friday

   c. Open to researchers. Call ahead for appointment and clearance. No phone calls or written requests can be processed.

   d. Kay Chernush, Photographer

2-3.   AID photo collection contains approximately 10,000 black-and-white prints and over 4,500 slides of Africa, Ethiopia, Egypt, Senegal, Upper Volta, Niger, Mali, Kenya, Tanzania, and Sudan. Coverage includes AID-sponsored development projects in the field of agriculture and rural development, nutrition, drought relief, education, and training, as well as the activities of AID field personnel and scenes of African people and conditions.

   The photographs and slides are arranged alphabetically by country and region.

   In addition, the Office of Public Affairs also has available for loan (without charge) two 16mm documentary films, "Survival in the Sahel" and a new film to be released shortly entitled "The Fly that Would be King" which deals with efforts to eradicate the tsetse fly and the disease it carries.

4. d. Reproduction services available for a fee.

F3 Agency for International Development (AID)—Training and Development Division—Film Collection

1. a. *Training and Development Division (PM/TD)*
      Operations Training Branch
      Room 405-B
      235-9098

   b. 9:00 A.M.-5:00 P.M.   Monday-Friday

   c. Open to researchers for on-site use.

   d. Michael Guido

2-3.   The collection is primarily meant to service AID personnel. There are 91 titles pertaining to Africa. Subject matter of these films includes: politics, economic development, agriculture, history, society, culture, and ethnic groups.

4. a. Audio-visual equipment is available for on-site use only.

   b. Researchers who wish to view the films are advised to call ahead for appointment.

c. No fee charged.

5. Agency for International Development, *Film Catalogue* (Washington Training Center, July 1978) provides a list and description of the films. The catalog, however, is for staff use only.

F4 Air Force Central Still Photographic Depository (Air Force Department)

1. a. *1361st Audio-visual Squadron*
   1221 South Fern Street
   Arlington, Virginia 22202
   695-1147

   b. 7:45 A.M.-4:30 P.M.   Monday-Friday

   c. Open to the public.

   d. Margaret Livesay, Chief

2-3. The depository maintains an Overseas File which contains approximately 1,600 unclassified black-and-white photographs pertaining to North Africa. There are alphabetically arranged in 32 books by region and country.

   Most of the photos deal with U.S. Air Force Operations during World War II and include U.S. Air Force aerial reconnaissance activities, airfield sites, air force installations and personnel, ceremonies involving U.S. officers and dignitaries.

4. d. Reproduction services are available for a fee.

F5 American Film Institute (AFI)

1. a. *John F. Kennedy Center for the Performing Arts*
   2700 F Street, NW
   Washington, D.C. 20566
   828-4000

   b. 10:00 A.M.-5:00 P.M.   Monday-Friday

   c. Open to the public.

   d. George Stevens, Jr., Director

2-5. The American Film Institute occasionally presents an African film series which includes recent and/or classic films.

   It also maintains an Information Services Library (ext. 88/89) which has a Foreign Information Section containing a few monographs on African cinema. In addition, the institute has a clipping file comprising reviews of African motion pictures, by country.

   Volume 10 of the AFI *Fact File* series focuses on *Third World Cinema* and is a useful reference guide for sources on African film-making.

F6 American Red Cross Photograph Collection

1. a. *Office of Communications Resources—Photograph Department*
   18th Street between D and E Streets, NW
   Washington, D.C. 20006
   857-3428

   b. 8:30 A.M.-4:45 P.M.   Monday-Friday

   c. Open to the public. Researchers who wish to view the collection should call ahead for an appointment.

   d. Carolyn Smith, Photo Librarian

2. The total collection consists of more than 20,000 black-and-white photographs and some 1,000 color transparencies.

3. Coverage includes nursing and relief activities of the Red Cross and its humanitarian efforts in the aftermath of natural calamities, disasters, and warfare. Most of the photographs deal with the period since 1950.

4. d. Photoreproduction service is available. Researchers should check with the staff regarding fees.

5. The Africa-related prints are arranged chronologically, by country, in an International Services File.

F7 Army Audio-Visual Center (Army Department)

1. a. *The Pentagon, Room 5A486*
   Washington, D.C. 20310
   697-2806 (Reference Library)

   b. 10:00 A.M.-4:30 P.M.   Monday-Friday

   c. Access to the Pentagon is restricted. Researchers wishing to examine the photographic collection should telephone the Reference Library from the Pentagon entrance desk to obtain clearance.

   d. Vickie Destefano, Chief, Reference Library

2. The collection contains more than 1 million still photographs, of which several hundred pertain to Africa.

3. The collection deals with the period from World War II to the present. Coverage includes U.S. military operations and activities in North Africa, troop movements, equipment, defense installations, and ceremonies involving U.S. officers and visiting dignitaries.

4. d. Photoreproduction services are available for a fee. Researchers should obtain an information sheet from the library which lists the charges and other details.

5. There are several card indexes arranged alphabetically by geographical areas and country and by subject.

F8 District of Columbia—Martin Luther King, Jr., Memorial Library—Audio-Visual Division

1. a. *Audio-Visual Division*
   Room 226
   901 G Street, NW
   Washington, D.C. 20001
   727-1265

   b. 9:00 A.M.-9:00 P.M.   Monday-Thursday
   9:00 A.M.-5:30 P.M.   Friday-Saturday

   c. All persons who are 21 years of age or older and who live, work, or own property in the District of Columbia are eligible to borrow films, free of charge. Films and other video equipment are loaned to borrowers for an overnight period.

   d. Diane Henry, Chief, Audio-Visual Division
   Lynne Bradley, Video Librarian

2-3. The entire collection of the division comprises over 3,000 film titles, some 700 filmstrips, and numerous slides covering a wide range of subjects. Of these some 45 films pertain to Africa. These include 37 titles on general Africa, 3 on Nigeria, 2 on Morocco, 2 on the Republic of South Africa, and 1 on art. Coverage includes art, history, city life, animals, music, and culture.

4. a. There are no facilities for viewing films. Video viewing facilities are available.

   b. Reservations must be made 5 days in advance.

   c. No fee charged for loan of films.

5. Assorted out-of-date printed catalogs are available. Researchers can consult *Films: A Descriptive Catalog of 16mm Sound Films for Free Loan* (Washington, D.C.: D.C. Public Library, 1971). The video collection is cataloged by title and subject in a card catalog in the Audio-Visual Division.

F9 Embassy of Egypt—Film Collection

1. a. *2200 Kalorama Road*
   Washington, D.C. 20008
   265-6400

   b. 9:00 A.M.-5:00 P.M.   Monday-Friday

   c. Individuals and institutions may borrow films free of charge. Reservations should be made in advance.

   d. Mr. Mohsen, Cultural Attaché.

2-3. The embassy's film collection contains an estimated 18 titles. Coverage includes art and archeology, the life of the pharoahs, social and economic conditions in Egypt, sports, etc.

4. Viewing equipment not available.

5. List of films and slides available from the embassy.

F10 Embassy of Liberia—Film Collection

1. a. *1050 17th Street, NW*
Washington, D.C. 20036
331-0136

   b. 9:00 A.M.-5:00 P.M. Monday-Friday

   c. Individuals and institutions may borrow films free of charge. Films should be reserved in advance.

   d. Mr. Tarty Teh, Research and Information Officer

2-3. Approximately 10 titles. Films deal with President Tolbert, mining and industry in Liberia, economic development, and tourism.

4. Viewing equipment is not available.

5. List of films is available from the embassy.

F11 Embassy of Libya—Film Collection

1. a. *1118 22nd Street, NW*
Washington, D.C. 20037
452-1290

   b. 9:00 A.M.-4:00 P.M. Monday-Friday

   c. Individuals and institutions may borrow films free of charge. Reservation is required.

   d. Cultural Attaché

2-3. 20 titles. Films on tourism and development, folklore, medicine, etc.

4. Viewing equipment is not available.

5. List of films is available from the embassy.

F12 Embassy of Nigeria—Film Collection

1. a. *2201 M Street, NW*
Washington, D.C. 20037
223-9300, Ext. 208/209

   b. 9:00 A.M.-5:00 P.M. Monday-Friday

    c. Individuals and institutions may borrow films free of charge. Films should be reserved in advance.

    d. Mr. Eke, Information Officer

2-3.   Thirty-nine titles. Subject matter includes Nigerian art and archeology, festivals, safari travel, Chief of Jos, and history.

4.   Viewing equipment is not available.

5.   List of films can be obtained from the embassy.

F13 Embassy of South Africa—Film Collection

1. a. *3051 Massachusetts Avenue, NW*
Washington, D.C. 20008
232-4400

    b. 9:00 A.M.-12:30 P.M., and 2:00 P.M.-5:00 P.M.   Monday-Friday

    c. Films available upon written or oral request.

    d. Mrs. Huppert, Information Office

2.   52 titles.

3.   Coverage includes the geography, peoples, industry, arts and crafts, and game reserves of South Africa.

4. a. Projector available only for on-site viewing.

    b. Advanced reservation required.

    c. No fee charged.

5.   A title list with descriptions of films is available by mail.

F14 Embassy of Tunisia—Film Collection

1. a. *2408 Massachusetts Avenue*
Washington, D.C. 20008
234-6644

    b. 9:00 A.M.-5:00 P.M.   Monday-Friday

    c. Individuals and institutions may borrow films free of charge. Films should be reserved at least 2 months in advance.

    d. K. Kaak, Cultural Attaché

2-3.   Six titles cover history, agriculture, industry, tourism, archeology, and education in Tunisia.

4.   Viewing equipment is not available.

5.   List of films can be obtained from the embassy.

F15 Embassy of Uganda—Film Collection

1. a. *5909 16th Street, NW*
      Washington, D.C. 20011
      726-7100

   b. 9:00 A.M.-5:00 P.M. Monday-Friday

   c. Individuals and institutions may borrow films free of charge. Requests for films should be made well in advance.

   d. Information Attaché

2-3. Collection consists of 10 film titles and some color slides. Subject matter of the films includes tourist sights in Uganda, Makerere University, dairy farming, tea production, and wildlife.

4. Viewing equipment not available.

5. List of films and color slides is available from the embassy.

F16 Embassy of Zambia—Film Collection

1. a. *241 Massachusetts Avenue, NW*
      Washington, D.C. 20008
      265-9717

   b. 9:00 A.M.-5:00 P.M. Monday-Friday

   c. Individuals and institutions may borrow films free of charge. Films should be requested in advance.

   d. Mr. Belemu, Press Information Officer

2-3. Over 50 titles.

4. a. A film projector is available for viewing films on the premises.

5. A list of films is available from the embassy.

F17 Howard University—Center for Learning Systems

1. a. *Center for Learning Systems*
      College of Liberal Arts
      Room 265, Locke Hall
      Howard University
      636-6737/6738

   b. 8:00 A.M.-5:00 P.M. Monday-Friday

   c. Open to serious researchers.

   d. J. Edwin Foster, Director

2-3. The center has an extensive collection of 16mm sound films, 8mm cartridge films, filmstrips, slides, records, and audio tapes. Only a few of these pertain to Africa. They include: "Africa in Ferment," "The Arab World," "Black and White in South Africa," "Black World, I and II" (deals with the black man's position in the world), "Heritage of Slavery," "In Search of a Past," "Islam," "The Rain Forest," "The River Nile."

4. a. Viewing equipment available.

   b. Reservations required.

   c. No fees charged.

5. Center for Learning Systems. *Audiovisual Materials Catalog* is available free of charge. The titles are arranged alphabetically by subject.

F18 Howard University—Institute for the Arts and the Humanities— Video-Media Documentation Unit

1. a. *Institute for the Arts and the Humanities*
   Howard University
   P.O. Box 723
   Washington, D.C. 20059
   636-7738

   b. 9:30 A.M.-5:30 P.M.   Monday-Friday

   c. Open to the public

   d. Stephen E. Henderson, Director
   Harold L. Burke, Education Media Specialist

2. A primary concern of the institute is to document and preserve significant artistic, cultural, social, and political events that relate to the life and history of black people. The institute's video-tape collection contains over 400 hours of programs recorded by the Video-Media Documentation Unit. These programs cover a wide range of subjects, from performing arts, literature, and folklore to public affairs and social issues.

3. Some of the more noteworthy video-tape materials in the collection include: proceedings of the Sixth Pan-African Conference in Dar es Salaam, Tanzania, June 1974, including an interview with Julius Nyerere; proceedings of the 3-day National Conference of Afro-American Writers, 1974, IAH, Howard University; the literature series, including Chinua Achebe, Atu Kwei O Kai, Ghanaian poet Leon G. Damas, and Sterling Brown; African Liberation Day March, May 1974; Washington Task Force on African Affairs, 1974; visual arts programs, including the Senegal National Dance Company, African Heritage Dance Company, and traditional dances of Tanzania; the Arrival of President Tolbert of Liberia in Washington, D.C., and his appearance at the National Press Club, 1976; President L. S. Senghor's 70th birthday

celebration; and the Conference on Culture and Development, October 1976, in Dakar, Senegal.

4. a. Viewing facilities available.

b. Advance reservations required.

c. No fees for on-site use of tapes.

d. Copies of selective tapes available. Contact the Education Media Specialist for further information.

5. *Video-Tape Catalog, 1975-76* is available for reference purposes. The catalog is currently being revised and updated.

Note: Also see entry B1.

F19 International Bank for Reconstruction and Development (World Bank)—Photo Library

1. a. *801 19th Street, NW, Room N-260*
   Washington, D.C. 20433
   676-1638 and 676-1585

   b. 10:00 A.M.-5:00 P.M. Monday-Friday

   c. Open to the public by appointment only.

   d. Yosef Hadar, Photo Editor and Producer
   Leah Suffin, Photo Librarian
   Martha-Elena Yanez, Library Assistant

2-3. The Photo Library contains over 30,000 black-and-white and color slides that cover some 70 developing countries of the world. Approximately 10,000 slides in this collection pertain to Africa.

   Subject matter of the photo collection consists of 5 major categories— agriculture, industry, people, social services, and transportation, with various subcategories.

4. a. Reproduction services available without charge. Photography is freely reproducible, except for advertising purposes.

5. Researchers should write or call for the *World Bank Photos Catalogue*, which includes separate sheets for each region, e.g., East Africa, Europe, the Middle East, North Africa, and West Africa.

F20 International Labour Organization (ILO)—Washington Branch Office Photograph Collection

1. a. *Room 330*
   1750 New York Avenue, NW
   Washington, D.C. 20006
   634-6335

   b. 8:30 A.M.-5:00 P.M. Monday-Friday

   c. Open to the public.

   d. Patricia S. Hord, Librarian

2.   The collection consists of over 2,000 black-and-white prints. Approximately 400-450 of these relate to Africa.

3.   Most of the photographs have as their focus ILO projects and programs. Subjects include agricultural and industrial workers, labor conditions, education, housing, employment, women workers, vocational rehabilitation, family planning, youth, rural development, and apartheid.

   The collection is arranged by topic, and within each topic-file there is considerable Africa-related material.

   In addition to the black-and-white prints, the ILO office also provides 16mm sound films on a free loan basis. There are 7 films dealing with Africa. Coverage includes vocational rehabilitation in Ethiopia, handicrafts in Morocco, a land-reclamation project in Burundi, unemployment and population growth in Africa and the land of Senegal.

4.   No reproduction services, but prints can be made available to researchers without charge.

5.   The ILO headquarters in Geneva, Switzerland, has a larger and more comprehensive photo library. *The ILO Photo Library: Catalogue* (Geneva, 1973) describes the content of the collection and provides a list of photographs by subject and by geographical area and country. The Washington office staff can assist researchers in obtaining prints from Geneva.

   A list of *ILO Films* is also available on request. For more information, contact Susan Goldstein of the Washington branch office.

F21 Library of Congress—Motion Picture, Broadcasting, and Recorded Sound Division: Motion Picture and Television Collections

1. a. *Thomas Jefferson Building (Annex), Room 1053*
    2d Street and Independence Avenue, SE
    Washington, D.C. 20540
    287-5840

   b. 8:30 A.M.-4:30 P.M.   Monday-Friday

   c. Open to serious researchers.

   d. Erik Barnouw, Chief
    Paul Spehr, Assistant Chief
    Barbara Humphrys and Emily Sieger, Reference Staff

2-3.   The Library of Congress has one of the largest archival collections of commercially produced motion pictures in the world. The total size of the collection is estimated at 75,000 titles, or more than 250,000 reels. Over 2,000 titles, including television films and videotapes, are added each year through copyright deposit, purchase, gift, or exchange. Since the emphasis of the collection is on American films, African holdings are rather limited. Furthermore, it is often difficult to identify and locate

African materials, as the motion picture collection remains largely un-cataloged. There is a shelflist which is arranged by title rather than by subject. Researchers must know the title of a motion picture before they can refer to the shelflist to determine if that particular title is in the collection. Researchers should consult the staff of the division, who can assist them in identifying relevant materials.

The division receives films ordered by the Africa and Near East Sections of the library (e.g., "Katutura," "Survival in the Sahel," and others from Egypt and the Republic of South Africa). It also receives selected films copyrighted in the United States, which occasionally include titles with African themes (e.g., "The African Queen"). The motion picture holdings include the Copyright Deposits Collection and other special collections acquired through gift, purchase, or placement by government agencies. The more relevant collections are described below.

Films Seized During World War II. This group of German and Italian newsreels and films was confiscated by the U.S. government after the war and transferred to the Library of Congress. In 1963 the copyrights were returned to the original owners, but the library retained permanent custody of the prints and screening privileges. Both these collections contain Africa-related films, especially relating to the North African campaigns. The German documentaries (including ethnographic and educational films) and newsreels dating from 1919 to 1944 include such titles as "Africa Corps Installations," "Afrika-Einsatz," "Tobruk," "Afrikanische Affen," "Afrikanische Steppenfahrt," "France is an Empire," "Weltspiegel," and "Koloniale Wochenschau." The Italian collection comprises reference prints of the *Istituto Luce* newsreels (1938–44) and *Luce* shorts (1930–54), which include some African material, and a few titles like "Africa Orientale: L'Avanzata Delle Truppe" and "Al Fronte Somalo con Dubat." There are separate card catalogs for the German and Italian newsreels. The films are arranged by title.

Paper Print Collection (1894–1912). The Paper Print Collection consists of some 3,000 titles, which include some material on Africa. The collection is described and indexed in Kemp R. Niver, *Motion Pictures from the Library of Congress Paper Print Collection, 1894–1912* (Berkeley and Los Angeles: University of California Press, 1967). The subject matter of the African films includes Egypt (architecture, market scenes, River Nile, inhabitants, irrigation); animals and hunting; and ethnic groups and their ceremonies.

George Kleine Collection, 1898–1926. This is the private film collection of Kleine, a pioneer in the American motion picture industry. The limited number of African films in this collection dates from the period between 1911 and 1915 and pertains to subjects such as Egypt (sports, monuments), South Africa (gold and diamond mines, ostrich farming), and the Ethiopian frontier. Reference prints are available for most of the titles. There is a computer file of this collection with subject indexing. A published printout by title is available for on-site reference use.

Theodore Roosevelt Association Collection, 1909–1930s. This collection consisting of 375 titles was received from the Theodore Roosevelt Association through the National Park Service. The collection includes footage of President Roosevelt's trip in 1909–10 to East Africa and includes titles such as "TR in Africa," "Scenes of African Animals," "TR Planting a Tree in Africa," "African Natives," etc.

The collection is described in "Theodore Roosevelt on Film," in the *Quarterly Journal of the Library of Congress* (vol. 34, no. 1 [January 1977], pp. 39-51). A descriptive catalog of the collection with indexing by subject, date, place, and name will be published in the near future.

Copyright Deposits Collection, 1942-Present. This collection comprises films selected from copyright deposits since 1942 and includes feature-length and short entertainment films; educational, scientific, religious, and business-sponsored films; and television documentary, educational, and entertainment programs. African materials in this collection are predominantly educational and documentary films, and include the "Africa In Change" series, "African Folklore" series, "The African Scene" series, and "Face of Change" series.

Television documentaries produced by the 3 major networks (CBS, NBC, and ABC) include coverage of Africa. A careful survey of the television holdings file should yield useful material on the Republic of South Africa, the Middle East War, Rhodesia, Uganda, the Congo, and U.S. foreign policy towards Africa.

The division maintains a separate television holdings file in which the holdings are indexed by "content descriptors."

There does not exist any single comprehensive finding aid for this collection. The shelflist and Television Productions File include the copyright deposits, and the Directors File, though still incomplete, should also be consulted. The *Catalog of Copyright Entries: Motion Pictures,* a semiannual publication prepared by the Copyright Office, lists all materials registered for copyright in the U.S.; however, it does not indicate which items were selected for the LC collection. The *Library of Congress Catalog—Audiovisual Materials,* issued quarterly and in annual cumulation, contains information on films which are of general interest to libraries, schools, and individuals, though not all of them are added to the LC collection.

4. a. Viewing facilities available for serious researchers. No interlibrary loan service.

    b. Viewing times must be scheduled in advance.

    c. No fees are charged.

    d. Some material may be reproduced subject to copyright laws and donor restrictions.

5. The division maintains a reading room with a reference collection of 1,500 books and some 20 current periodicals. Vertical files are arranged by subject and by title. The former includes a folder on Africa with distributor lists of available films and brochures. In the latter, one finds clippings from *Variety* and elsewhere about films, stills from films, and reviews of television shows. Also available are descriptions, including synopses, pressbooks, and scripts, for films and television program registered for copyright in the United States since 1912.

    Finding aids located in the offices of the Motion Picture, Broadcasting, and Recorded Sound Division include:

Directors File. Arranged alphabetically by name of director. Each entry contains the titles of films by that director which are in the library's collection. Concentration exclusively on theatrical films.

Nitrate Shelflist. Films arranged by title, company, and date.

Shelflist. Although not fully reliable, this card catalog contains an entry, by title, for each motion picture in the LC collection (includes safety film only). Entry cards may include information on director, production date, a synopsis, credits, and notes on the availability of a reference print.

Silent Film Files. Arranged by title, company, and date.

Special Collections Card Catalog. Arranged by collection with an entry for every motion picture in a specific collection.

Published finding aids which can prove useful to researchers in putting together a list of titles include: Library of Congress, Copyright Office, *Catalog of Copyright Entries: Motion Pictures; Library of Congress Catalog—Audiovisual Materials* (N.B.: both these catalogs do not indicate which titles are available in the LC collection); and Kemp R. Niver, *Motion Pictures from the Library of Congress Paper Print Collection, 1894–1912,* edited by Bebe Bergsten (Berkeley: University of California Press, 1967).

Descriptive catalogs of the Theodore Roosevelt and the George Kleine Collections are in press.

F22 Library of Congress—Prints and Photographs Division

1. a. *Library of Congress Annex (Thomas Jefferson Building)*
    Room 1051, First Floor
    2d Street and Independence Avenue, SE
    Washington, D.C. 20540
    287-5836

    b. 8:30 A.M.-5:00 P.M. Monday-Friday

    c. Open to the public.

    d. Jerry L. Kearns, Head of Reference
    Karen Beall, Curator of Prints
    Gerald Maddox, Coordinator and Collections Planner
    Bernard Reilly, Curator of Popular and Applied Graphic Arts
    Elena Millie, Curator of Posters
    Beverly Brannan, Curator of Photographic Collections
    George Hobart, Curator of Documentary Photographs
    Elizabeth Betz, Cataloging Specialist
    C. Ford Peatross, Curator, Architectural Collections

2. This division has custody of an estimated 10 million items, comprising prints, photographs, negatives, posters, and other pictorial materials which provide a visual documentation of "people, places, and events in America and throughout the world." It is difficult to locate items systematically on a geographic basis, as most still photographs (including the African materials) are arranged by "lot" rather than by individual piece. There is a "lot" card catalog (alphabetically arranged

by person and place name). A survey of the card catalog revealed the following number of "lots" for Africa: Africa (General)—69 lots; North Africa—87 (of which Egypt, 49); West Africa—37 (of which Liberia, 17); Central Africa—5 (of which Angola, 2); East Africa—37 (of which Ethiopia, 1; Italo-Ethiopian war, 5) and Southern Africa—16 (of which the Republic of South Africa, 13).

3. Some noteworthy items of interest to Africanists include: an extensive collection of North African photographs, mostly pertaining to World War II (these deal with North African campaign, civilian participation in the war, portraits of war-time officials, etc.); the Liberian collection, comprising many photographs from the American Colonization Society; photographic record of the drought in West Africa; and the Republic of South Africa "lots" which focus on the 1899–1902 war between Afrikaners and Great Britain.

There are also 3 separate Foreign, Geographical, and Historical Files arranged in alphabetical, self-indexing order, which contain about 100 old woodcuts, etchings, lithographs, and engravings; several hundred miscellaneous photoprints; and approximately 1,500 stereopticon cards of the Anglo-Boer War, Egypt, Algeria, and Zaire (called the Belgian Congo).

The poster collection consists of American and foreign posters ranging in date from the 1850s to the present. It contains some items from Egypt. A few African artists are represented in the litho collection, but the name of the artist must be known in order to locate the relevant material. The poster collection is cataloged by country and by artist within each country.

The Prints and Photographs Division also maintains several special collections, including the following:

American Colonization Society Collection. This contains some 550 photoprints and 30 original daguerreotype plates from the second half of the 19th century. Subject matter includes Liberian officials, scenes from daily life, mission schools, and various ethnic groups.

Carpenter Collection. This is an extensive collection of travel photographs (numbering over 2,500) made or collected by Frank G. Carpenter, primarily between 1910 and 1925. The emphasis is on travel, scenery, local inhabitants and their environment, animals, public buildings, etc. The Carpenter Collection files are arranged by continent and subject, with country and locality headings interfiled.

Harmon Foundation Collection. Subject matter deals with African artists and their work.

Johnson Collection. Approximately 30 photographs of topography, rock formations, villages in southern Tunisia (1900–10).

Kenya Colony Collection. Some 400 photoprints of Kenya Colony from the period between 1940 and 1946. Subjects represent white settlers and Africans, scenic views of Nairobi, agricultural activities, etc.

"Look" Magazine Collection.

Matson Collection. Approximately 20,000 original negatives provide visual record of persons, places, and events in Palestine and the Middle East.

Office of War Information Collection. Some 600 photographs pertaining to activities and events of World War II.

     Theodore Roosevelt Collection. Safari photographs taken during Roosevelt's travels in Africa from 1909 to 1925.

     U.S. Navy Expedition Collection. Photographs of a naval expedition in 1889.

4. d. Most materials may be reproduced subject to copyright laws.

5.   There is no comprehensive published catalog of still pictures. The only published reference tool is the Library of Congress, *Guide to the Special Collections of Prints and Photographs in the Library of Congress* (Washington, D.C., 1955) compiled by Paul Vanderbilt. This is, however, quite outdated. In the meanwhile, the best finding aids are the several card catalogs: the card catalog for the general collections is arranged by subject, photographer, and collector. In addition there are separate card catalogs for fine prints, for historical prints, posters, and master photographs. The *Look* Magazine Collection has its own index. Also see Milton Kaplan, "Africa Through the Eyes of a Camera," in the *Quarterly Journal of the Library of Congress,* (vol. 27, no. 3, [July 1970], pp. 222–237), and Library of Congress, Prints and Photographs Division, *Viewpoints, A Selection from the Pictorial Collections of the Library of Congress* (Washington, D.C., 1975). Reference specialists in the reading room can assist researchers in locating African materials.

F23 Middle East Institute—Film Library

1. a. *Office of Educational Programs*
   1761 N Street, NW
   Washington, D.C. 20036
   785-1141

   b. 9:00 A.M.-5:00 P.M. Monday-Friday

   c. Films are available to academic, cultural, and other organizations at a nominal fee. Reservations required. Orders may be place by phone if followed by confirming letter.

   d. Niecy Armstrong, Film Librarian

2.   MEI's film library contains more than 70 films, of which approximately 25 pertain to Egypt and North Africa.

3.   Films focus on the history, culture, religion, and the political and economic development of North African nations. There are 6 films on general topics relating to the Middle East, 13 on the Islamic religion, 8 on Egypt, 4 on Libya, and 2 on Tunisia. Coverage includes portrayal of the life of Egyptian fellahin (villagers), the Nile River, Egyptian archeology and art treasures, Berber villages in southern Tunisia, modernization in Tunisia, economic and social development in Libya, Bedouin and oasis lifestyles, traditional values and contributions of Islam, Sufism, and the history and culture of the Middle East.

5.   Film catalog is available, free of charge, from the Middle East Institute.

F24 Museum of African Art—Eliot Elisofon Archives

1. a. *330 A Street, NE*
    Washington, D.C. 20002
    547-6222

    b. 9:00 A.M.-5:30 P.M. Monday-Friday

    c. Access is by appointment. Some materials do circulate, and films such as "Tribute to Africa" are rented or sold. Slides and photographs are also available for sale.

    d. Edward Lifschitz, Archivist
    Dorothy Huete, Archives Assistant

2-3. The archives was established in 1973 on the basis of 100,000 photographs, slides, films, manuscripts, and other materials bequeathed to the museum by the late Eliot Elisofon, a former *Life* magazine photographer. Archival material is collected from other photographers so that the archival collection will continue to grow.

   About 35,000 color slides taken in Africa are arranged by subject. Six large cabinets on the main floor house these slides. Another 35,000 black-and-white images are also arranged by subject and stored in card files. Both collections cover Elisofon's travels in Africa from 1947 to 1973. Elisofron took pictures mainly in Sahel, Guinea Coast, Central Africa, and Egypt. He also produced a photo essay on the River Nile (published in *Life* magazine, November 20, 1950). Subsequently he prepared a book, *The Nile* (Viking Press, 1964). The archives owns 1,270 pictures he took for the Nile project, but, unlike the other collections, the negatives are not in the museum's possession.

   Elisofon's photographs of African art in the Berlin Museum and in the British Museum are also available, along with 5,000 4 x 5 mounted black-and-white prints of art in major public and private collections. They have been placed in a card file and are arranged by geographic region, then by ethnic group or country, art form, collection (e.g., Chaim Gross, Yale University, Paul Tishman, Nigerian Museum, Tervuren).

   Elisofon also made some 16mm films, notable among which are "African Sculpture," "Akan Gold," and "Black African Heritage Series." In addition to this core collection, 4 drawers of Elisofon research notes, diaries, and correspondence are stored here.

   Besides the unique Elisofon collection, the archival holdings also include an anonymous donation of 1,150 lantern slides from a trip to the Belgian Congo from 1910 through 1925; 25 16mm films, including "Survival in the Sahel," and 700,000 feet of Elisofon "outs and work prints."

4. a. Audio-visual equipment available.

    b. Reservations are required. They may be made in person, by mail, or by phone.

    c. No fees charged.

5. The staff is in the process of preparing finding aids and guides to the collections. Preliminary inventories that should provide much useful

information to researchers include the following unpublished finding aids: "Classification Code—Art in Collections" and "Field Photographs" (leaflets) and "Film Holdings."

In the interim, the following published materials with photographs by Eliot Elisofon may be used to indicate the scope of the archives' collection: Eliot Elisofon, *The Sculpture of Africa* (New York: Frederick A. Praeger, 1958), text by William Fagg; and *Tribute to Africa: The Photography and the Collection of Eliot Elisofon* (Washington, D.C.: Museum of African Art, 1974).

F25   National Anthropological Film Center (NAFC)—Smithsonian Institution

1. a. *Smithsonian Institution*
    Washington, D.C. 20560
    381-6537

    b. 8:45 A.M.-5:15 P.M.   Monday-Friday

    c. Open to bona fide scholars. Access to certain films may be restricted for a limited period of time.

    d. E. Richard Sorenson, Director

2-3.   The National Anthropological Film Center was established in 1975 to utilize the full potential of film as a tool of inquiry in anthropological research. The main purpose of the center is to identify, study, document, and preserve visual/auditory data on vanishing cultures and ways of life.

At the present, NAFC has very limited resources on Africa. The researcher may, however, find some material of interest in its world ethnographic film sample. This includes: 2,000 ft. of original film on Ghana— Edwuma healing ritual of the Church of the Twelve Apostles (1975); 34,000 ft. of film on Nigeria—cross-cultural comparison of dance styles —Georgia, Haiti, Nigeria (1930); and 70,992 ft. of film on western Kenya—"Maragoli," a documentary film depicting cultural change (1975).

NAFC projects in the near future will include some work in Africa, particularly among the Dinka people in the Sudan.

4. a. Viewing equipment is available.

    b. Researchers interested in using the audio-visual facilities should call ahead for appointment.

    c. No fees are charged for use of the facilities.

F26   National Archives and Records Service (NARS) (General Services Administration)—Audio-visual Archives Division

1. a. *8th Street and Pennsylvania Avenue, NW*
    Washington, D.C. 20408
    523-3267 (Motion picture)

523-3054 *(Still picture)*
523-3236 *(Division as a whole)*

b. 8:45 A.M.-5:00 P.M.   Monday-Friday

c. Open to the public. Research identification card required, obtainable from the Central Reference Division, Room 200-B.

d. James Moore, Director
William Murphy Chief, Motion Picture and Sound Recording Branch
Joe Thomas, Chief, Still Picture Branch

2. The Africanist will find many unique and fascinating items in the various record groups. Though a complete inventory of the African holdings does not exist, this is undoubtedly one of the most comprehensive and valuable depositories of films and still pictures on Africa in Washington, D.C.

3. The description of NARS's motion pictures and photographic collections is based primarily on *Guide to Federal Archives Relating to Africa* (1977) and a survey of the card catalog.

MOTION PICTURES

RG 18: Records of the Army Air Forces. This is one of the more important sources for motion pictures relating to Africa. All the films pertain to the World War II period. These include approximately 10 reels showing combat and noncombat operations; some 462 reels of edited and unedited films showing flight routes, city and airport scenes, and landing facilities in various geographic areas, mainly in North and West Africa; and an undetermined number of films relating to AAF activities during the war.

RG 24: Records of the Bureau of Naval Personnel. Film "Our Navy in the Near East" shows sailors viewing local sights in Egypt.

RG 33: Records of the Federal Extension Service. Deals with agriculture and topographical features of Madagascar and Mahafaly Plateau.

RG 59: General Records of the Department of State. There are an undetermined number of Africa-related films in this record group. They focus on a wide range of subjects, including economic activities, manners and customs of African peoples, and political events in Africa, 1910–49.

RG 70: Records of the Bureau of Mines. A few films of gold mines in Southern Africa and oilfields in North Africa.

RG 111: Records of the Office of the Chief Signal Officer. Films deal with the Italian invasion of Ethiopia; end of the war in Ethiopia and Haile Selassie reviewing troops; North African campaigns, 1939–45; and French colonial troops in the war. In all there are 44 reels. Also in this record group are some 100 reels which show combat operations, training of troops, and military preparations during the war in North Africa.

RG 151: Records of the Bureau of Foreign and Domestic Commerce. Deal with trade, commerce, and the economy.

RG 170: Records of the Bureau of Narcotic and Dangerous Drugs. Seven reels on drug traffic and enforcement in Egypt.

RG 200: National Archives Gift Collection. Contains films showing

President Eisenhower's trip to the Near East and Africa, 1959; a German film describing Nazi industry in the Cameroons; East African shots produced by the Department of Agriculture; the Ford Historical Film Collection dealing with the Ford Motor Company's activities in Africa, as well as short features and newsreels distributed to theaters all over the world; and, the Harmon Foundation Collection comprising some 49 reels. These deal with various facets of African life and depict daily life, arts and crafts, religious and mission work among Africans; and approximately 60 newsreels relating to political, military, diplomatic, social, and economic events in Africa. Includes coverage of Ghana's independence, independence struggle in Algeria, Dr. Albert Schweitzer in French Equatorial Africa, and Patrice Lumumba before a Pan-African Congress in 1960; Africa-related newsreels produced by Paramount News, 1941–57; and over 1,000 reels in the Universal Newsreel Collection, 1929–67. (Note: there is a detailed card index to the films in this series arranged by geographic areas.)

RG 208: Records of the Office of War Information. Approximately 35 reels. A majority of these are newsreels which focus on military campaigns and operations in North Africa and major political events during the war period.

RG 226: Records of the Office of Strategic Services. All 13 reels focus on the North African Campaign.

RG 242: National Archives Collection of Foreign Records Seized. Contains some 36 reels of film, mainly German and Italian newsreels. Also included in this are motion pictures produced during World War II in the Axis nations, which focus on the North African campaigns.

RG 306: Records of the United States Information Agency. Contains approximately 30 reels dating from 1945–52 and arranged chronologically. They consist of German-language newsreels shown throughout British and American zones of occupied Germany and Austria.

RG 342: Records of the United States Air Force Commands, Activities, and Organizations. Contains films concerning the activities of the Army Air Force and news reviews, 1955–59.

Note: Recent accessions which contain substantial numbers of Africa-related items include Records of the United States Information Agency (RG 306), Records of the Peace Corps (RG 362), and Records of the Agency for International Development (RG 286). These record groups which contain valuable material for the Africanist will be made available to researchers in the not-too-distant future. For more information on these and other Africa-related films, contact Donald Roe (523-3294) in the Motion Picture Branch.

STILL PICTURES

RG 18: Records of the Army Air Forces. Approximately 3,300 aerial and ground-level photographs of airports, landing fields, cities, rivers, mountains, and activities of military and civilian personnel.

RG 24: Records of the Bureau of Naval Personnel. Some 20 glass-plate negatives of Egyptian scenes.

RG 26: Records of the United States Coast Guard. Some 10 photographs showing Coast Guard participation in the North African campaign.

RG 38: Records of the Office of the Chief of Naval Operations. Included in this series are photographs of Allied leaders by Maurice Constant, a U.S. Navy photographer during World War II.

RG 59: General Records of the Department of State. Includes photographs of Kasai-Sankuru region, 1920–21; military activity in Alexandria, September 1938; Ethiopian coronation, 1930; road construction in Italian East Africa; southern Morocco; local peoples and scenes in Egypt, 1948; Trans-Saharan railroad; death and funeral of Moncef Bey, 1947; 44 photographs of African products and industry in the Congo, Nigeria, and Liberia.

RG 66: Records of the Commission on Fine Arts. Contains 5 items relating to historic sites in Egypt.

RG 78: Records of the Naval Observatory. Several photographs relating to Naval Astronomical Expeditions to Study Solar Eclipses.

RG 80: General Records of the Department of the Navy. Approximately 3,000 photographs, many relating to various naval operations in North Africa.

RG 131: Records of the Office of Alien Property. Contains prints and photographs of numerous African ports visited by the Hamburg-American and North German Lloyd Steamship Lines, 1920–40.

RG 151: Records of the Bureau of Foreign and Domestic Commerce. Contains some 800 Africa-related items arranged alphabetically by geographic area or country. Prints provide information on local industries and modes of transportation.

RG 160: Records of Headquarters Army Service Forces. Contains photographs of Trans-Africa Railway; supply installations for U.S. Army Forces in Central Africa; and a few additional items.

RG 165: Records of the War Department General and Special Staffs. Contains 33 photographs of Liberian people and scenes and a few items on U.S. military operations.

RG 169: Records of the Foreign Economic Administration. Contains photographs of local scenes and goods in British East Africa and approximately 500 photographs of the activities of the American Food Mission for North Africa.

RG 200: National Archives Gift Collection. The Harmon Foundation Collection has over 3,600 items pertaining to Africa. These materials are arranged in 4 series: artworks by African artists, 1947–67; photographs showing Nigerian life and culture; photographs and slides of artworks by African school children; and photographs of activities at the Abuja Pottery Center in Nigeria. This record group also contains some 35 color slides of scupture by African artists. These are arranged by country.

RG 208: Records of the Office of War Information. Contains photographs of military operations in North and West Africa, African personalities, local scenes, outstanding personalities of the World War II period, Allied activity in Africa, African delegations at the U.N. Conference on International Organization at San Francisco, and President Roosevelt at the Casablanca Conference.

RG 234: Records of the Reconstruction Finance Corporation. Contains several photographs of mines and minerals in Southern Africa, the Gold Coast, Liberia, and the Belgian Congo.

RG 242: National Archives Collection of Foreign Records Seized. Contains 2,800 photographs from General Rommel's collection, most of which deal with military activities in North Africa; photographs of Tunisia, 1943; aerial photographs of targets in Egypt, Libya, Tunisia; 700 aerial photographs used by German X Air Corps; some 50 photographs taken by German Army Propaganda Companies; 1,500 items in the Photographic Collection of the Germany Army Photographic Archives; and some 250 prints and slides of German troops in North Africa.

RG 306: Records of the United States Information Agency. Contains photographs and prints pertaining to various African expeditions, 1920–34; *New York Times* prints of African cities, scenes, daily life, and culture; photographs of African leaders and personalities, 1923–50; photographs of military activities in North Africa; some 100 items pertaining to the Seabrook-Wauthier expedition to Timbuktu; photographs of African leaders in the U.S.; and photographs of activities of United States Information Center Service field centers in African countries.

A careful search of this record group would reveal many more items of interest.

RG 319: Records of the Army Staff. Photographs of the Africa-Middle East Theater of Operations originally held by U.S. Armed Forces in the Middle East.

RG 350: Records of the Bureau of Insular Affairs. Contains some photographs relating to the Congo Free State.

RG 351: Records of the Government of the District of Columbia. Includes a few photographs of the visits of African dignitaries to Washington, D.C.

RG 418: Records of St. Elizabeth's Hospital. Slides depicting cities, buildings, street scenes, and local people in Egypt and Central Africa.

4. a. Individual screening equipment for 16 and 35mm films are available in the motion-picture research room.

    b. Researchers are advised to reserve the viewers by calling in advance.

    c. All services are free except for reproduction.

    d. Subject to copyright laws and other restrictions, the division staff can provide reproduction services for both still and motion pictures. There is a fee for these services.

5. No published finding aids are available at the present time; however, researchers should consult the several mimeographed caption lists and preliminary inventories. Card catalogs located in the division are also useful in locating Africa-related materials. Other available aids include:

    Mayfield S. Bray, *Still Pictures in the Audiovisual Archives Division of the National Archives* (1972);

    ———and William T. Murphy, *Motion Pictures in the Audiovisual Archives Division of the National Archives* (1972);

    ———, *Audiovisual Records in the National Archives Relating to World War II;*

    Contemporary African Art from the Harmon Foundation: Select Audiovisual Records (Washington, D.C.: Government Printing Office, 1975);

Aloha South, *Guide to Federal Archives Relating to Africa* (1977). The subject index in this guide can prove invaluable in locating relevant materials (see under "photographs" and "motion pictures").

F27 National Museum of Natural History (Smithsonian Institution)— Anthropological Archives Photograph Collection

1. a. *Natural History Building, Room 60-A*
      Constitution Avenue at 10th Street, NW
      Washington, D.C. 20560
      381-5225

   b. 9:00 A.M.-5:00 P.M.   Monday-Friday

   c. Open to the public. Visitors should notify the staff prior to their arrival.

   d. Herman Viola, Director
      James R. Glenn, Archivist

2-3. The Photograph Collection consists of an estimated 90,000 items (mainly black-and-white photographs), the majority of which date from the 1860s to the 1930s. Since the primary focus of the collection is Native American peoples, coverage on Africa is relatively limited.

4. Photoduplication services are available for a fee.

5. A card index is maintained.

F28 United Nations Information Centre—Washington Office—Film Collection

1. a. *United Nations Information Centre*
      2101 L Street, NW
      Washington, D.C. 20037
      296-5370

   b. 9:00 A.M.-1:00 P.M.   Monday-Friday

   c. Films may be borrowed by local schools, colleges, and interested individuals, without charge.

   d. Vera Gathwright, Reference Librarian

2-3. There are approximately 100 titles in this film collection, of which some 15–20 pertain to Africa. Coverage includes such subjects as agriculture, the Sahel, apartheid, the struggle for freedom, Arab refugees, African culture, Namibia, and Southern Africa.

4. b. Reservations advisable.

   c. No fees charged.

   d. All U.N. films are also available for purchase.

5. The *United Nations 16mm Film Catalogue, 1977–78* lists all U.N. films. Also see "Films Available for Distribution" (January 1978), which lists all the films available for loan locally.

G Data Banks

Data Banks Entry Format (G)

1. General information
   a. *address; telephone number(s)*
   b. hours of service
   c. conditions of access (including fees charged for information retrieval)
   d. name/title of director and key staff members

2. Description of data files (hard-data and bibliographic-reference) pertaining to Africa

3. Bibliographic aids facilitating use of storage media

G1 Agency for International Development (AID) Development Information System

1. a. *Office of Development Information and Utilization*
      AID Bureau for Development Support
      Room 570, Pomponio Plaza
      1735 North Lynn Street
      Arlington, Virginia 22209
      (703) 235-9207

   b. 9:30 A.M.-4:00 P.M.   Monday-Friday

   c. The Development Information System is primarily for the use of AID personnel. However, private researchers may on occasion be allowed to use the terminals to undertake bibliographic searches.

   d. Lida Allen, Director
      Maury D. Brown, Deputy Director

2. This is a computerized storage and retrieval system which contains technical and financial data on over 1,500 AID development projects since 1974. (Materials on projects prior to 1974 are available in the National Archives.)

Data have been abstracted from project experience documents which include project goals, evaluations, and reports; feasibility studies; and contract research studies and World Bank development-project evaluations. The data cover a broad spectrum of subjects including agriculture and rural development, population and family planning, health and nutrition, education, and economic indicators (national accounts, central-government expenditures, international trade, agricultural and food production) for each African country. In addition, each African country will have 3 sector files: Agriculture, Health and Nutrition, and Education and Human Resources.

The Tape Library contains cross-section and longitudinal micro-data sets. The initial purpose of the Tape Library is to procure and maintain data tapes produced by various international and national organizations in the U.S. and elsewhere.

In addition, the staff is presently developing a micro-data bank (MIDAB) which will contain data sets for developing countries obtained from questionnaires and household surveys. Its scope is limited primarily to the period from the late 1960s to the present. MIDAB data sets are divided into broad geographic regions, volume 1 dealing with Africa. There are approximately 140 data sets for Africa which are arranged alphabetically by country and divided into demographic (79) and socioeconomic (61) categories. They include information on fertility, family planning, migration, income level and distribution, manpower, education, rural/urban development, and attitudes.

3. In the past, many of the data bank's statistics were available in printed, hard-copy form in the publications of the AID Statistics and Reports Division. As a result of recent reorganization, these statistics are not currently being published. Researchers should contact the Economic and Social Data Division for further information.

G2 Agency for International Development (AID)—Economic and Social Data Bank (ESDB)

1. a. *Economic and Social Data Division*
    Development Information and Policy Analysis Review Services
    Bureau for Program and Policy Coordination
    Room 633, Pomponio Plaza
    1735 North Lynn Street
    Arlington. Virginia 22209
    (703) 235-9161

    b. 8:45 A.M.-5:30 P.M.   Monday-Friday

    c. The Data Bank is primarily for the use of AID personnel. Private scholars who wish to utilize the facility should contact the Economic and Social Data Division for conditions of access.

    d. Hunt Howell, Acting Division Chief

2-3. ESDB is the single automated agency-wide source of economic and social data. It is composed of 2 components, the File System and the Tape Library. The former contains the agency's official macro-data files, data on loans and grants, and other country-specific information. The country-data files contain information produced within the agency and other data obtained from the World Bank, IMF, U.N., and U.S. Department of Agriculture extending over a 30-year period. Included are major social indicators (population, birth/death rates, life expectancy, literacy, etc.) and data on economics and transportation. Each project is indexed by 20-40 project subcomponent descriptors.

Note: Also see entries A2, F2, F3, and K1.

G3 Agriculture Department—Data Service Center

1. a. *500 12th Street, SW*
    Washington, D.C. 20250
    447-8824

    b. 8:30 A.M.-5:00 P.M.   Monday-Friday

    c. Open to researchers with special permission.

    d. Marge Bever, Special Assistant for International Data

2. Data files contain a USDA-compiled index of world agricultural production (1950–present); USDA-generated data on international grain-crop acreage and yields; international trade data compiled by the Untied Nations (1967–present); U.N. Food and Agriculture Organization trade and production data (1961–74); and U.S. Agency for International Development population data, by country (1950–present).

Note: In addition, the Agriculture Department's Foreign Agricultural Service (see entry K2) maintains a Data Systems Division which has USDA-generated machine-readable data on agricultural production, supply, and distribution in various African countries (1960–present), as well as extensive U.S. Census Bureau data on U.S. trade with the countries of Africa.

G4 Commerce Department Data Bases

1. *Main Commerce Building*
    14th Street between Constitution Avenue and E Street, NW
    Washington, D.C. 20230
    377-2000 (Information)

2. There is no single, centralized facility which stores all the machine-readable data bases generated within the Commerce Department. Data files containing African material are available in several departmental bureaus and offices.
    Bureau of Economic Analysis. The bureau compiles data on U.S. private investment in Africa. Tapes are available on a commercial basis from the division's Data Retrieval and Analysis Branch (523-0981).
    Bureau of Export Development. The Office of Export Development's "Foreign Traders Index" contains data on non-U.S. foreign business firms and products in Africa.

Census Bureau. The Foreign Trade Division sells tapes containing U.S.-African trade statistics.

The Population Division's International Demographic Data Center (763-2834) holdings include data from census volumes and machine-readable materials from 1958 to date. These include census statistics (population, fertility, etc.).

G5 Defense Documentation Center (Department of Defense)

1. a. *Cameron Station, Building 5*
    Alexandria, Virginia 22314
    (703) 274-7633 (Document Information)
    (703) 274-6881 (Public Affairs)

    b. 7:30 A.M.-4:00 P.M.   Monday-Friday

    c. Open only to Department of Defense (DOD) personnel and authorized staff members of research organizations under DOD contract or grant.

    d. Hubert E. Sauter, Administrator

2. The Defense Documentation Center (DDC) is a computerized repository of over 1.2 million classified and unclassified research reports produced or funded by DOD. The primary focus of the collection is the physical sciences, technology, and engineering as they relate to defense and military matters. Some social-science research on international affairs (including Africa) may also be stored in the data base. The bibliographic data base is on computer tape; full research reports are available on microfiche. Unclassified materials in the data base are generally available to the public through the National Technical Information Service (entry K6).

3. No bibliographies of the center's holdings are available. The center, however, does distribute a confidential biweekly *Technical Abstracts Bulletin* of recent acquisitions to registered users on DOD contracts.

G6 Educational Resources Information Center (ERIC)

1. a. *National Institute of Education (NIE)*
    Division of Information Resources
    1200 19th Street, NW
    Washington, D.C. 20208
    254-7095

    b. 8:00 A.M.-4:30 P.M.   Monday-Friday

    c. Fee schedules vary for different services of the clearinghouse (ERIC) and for other institutions or computer systems which allow access to ERIC data bases. These computer services are available from many university libraries, state departments of education, educational information centers, research centers, and commercial organizations. For a list of ERIC data base search services, contact:

User Services Coordinator
ERIC Processing and Reference Facility
4833 Rugby Avenue, Suite 303
Bethesda, Maryland 20014.
656-9723

2.   ERIC, which is operated by the National Institute of Education of the Department of Health, Education, and Welfare, is a unique service to educators throughout the country. It is composed of 16 subject-oriented clearinghouses which abstract, index, catalog, and annotate materials dealing with virtually every aspect of education. The system offers access to a collection of some 300,000 items that include journal articles and research papers, as well as unpublished educational materials such as project reports, speech texts, research findings, and conference proceedings.
      A check of indexes reveals that the system contains several references to Africa and African countries.
      At present 4 of the clearinghouses are located in the Washington area: those on higher education, teacher education, languages and linguistics, and handicapped and gifted children. Each of the clearinghouses publishes books, reports, and bibliographies on its subject every year. Researchers working with ERIC data bases should find the following publications useful: *Current Index to Journals in Education* (CIJE), and index of articles from more than 700 periodicals; *Resources in Education* (RIE), a monthly index arranged by subject (ERIC descriptions, author or investigator, and institution); *Thesaurus of ERIC Descriptions*, source of the system for the retrieval of documents and journal citations in ERIC collections.
      Using these tools, researchers can locate materials by country, author, subject, etc.

3.   NIE has published a number of handbooks and pamphlets, including: *How To Use ERIC;* Elizabeth Pugh, ed., *Directory of ERIC Data Services;* and Dorothy Slawsky, ed., *Directory of ERIC Microfiche Collection* (1978).

Health, Education, and Welfare Department—Alcohol, Drug Abuse, and Mental Health Administration (ADAMHA): National Clearinghouse for Mental Health Information; National Clearinghouse for Drug Abuse Information; and National Clearinghouse for Alcohol Information See entry A17.

G7 International Bank for Reconstruction and Development (World Bank)—Data Systems

1. a. *1818 H Street, NW*
        Washington, D.C. 20433
        477-1234 (Central Operator)

        477-2403 (Publications Unit)

2-3. The bank's operations are organized on a geographic regional basis. Therefore, the primary responsibility for collection and analysis of data at the country level lies with the Regional Offices.

The bank's economic staff also maintains a centralized data system of internationally comparable statistics. The principal statistics are available through regular publications.

Among the principal documents available are:

Borrowing in International Capital Markets (quarterly);
Commodity Trade and Price Trends (annual);
Economic and Social Indicators (quarterly);
The World Bank Atlas (annual);
World Bank Commodity Working Papers (occasional);
World Bank Country Studies (occasional);
World Bank Staff Working Papers (occasional);
The World Debt Tables (annual);
The World Tables (triennial).

These documents and others in current distribution are listed in an annually updated *Catalog of Publications,* which is available free of charge from the bank's Publications Unit.

G8 International Monetary Fund (IMF) Data Fund

1. a. *700 19th Street, NW*
   Washington, D.C. 20431
   477-3207

   b. 9:00 A.M.-5:00 P.M.   Monday-Friday

   c. Arrangements for visits should be made in advance. Copies of the Data Fund's magnetic tapes are available on an annual subscription basis. Each subscription consists of 12 magnetic tapes, the corresponding book publication, and documentation. The cost is $1,000 per year to single users and $400 to universities.

   d. Earl Hicks, Director, Bureau of Statistics
   Robert L. Kline, Chief, Data Fund Division

2-3. The Data Fund is a computerized system which makes available data in machine-readable form from the following IMF publications:

Balance of Payments Yearbook. Tape subscription contains about 35,000 time series on balance-of-payments statistics covering 116 countries. Annual data begins with 1965 or later. The other 2,000 time series correspond to the long-term data series, frequently dating back to the mid-1950s.

Direction of Trade. DOT tape subscription contains over 43,000 time series reported in *Direction of Trade* country pages. Data includes sources and destination of imports and exports for some 150 countries. Annual entries begin in 1948, and quarterly entries in 1969.

Government Finance Statistics Yearbook. Tape subscription contains approximately 13,000 annual time series of data reported in *Government Finance Statistics Yearbook.* Included are data on revenues, expenditures, grants, lending, financing, and debts.

International Financial Statistics (IFS). Tape subscription contains approximately 16,500 time series, including all series appearing on IFS country pages, and world tables; 14 major series on countries' relationships with IMF, as well as exchange-rate and international-liquidity series for all countries. Annual entries date back to 1948.

Library of Congress—MARC; SCORPIO; National Referral Center See entry A27.

National Aeronautics and Space Administration (NASA) RECON System See entry K19.

National Agricultural Library—AGRICOLA See entry A30.

National Library of Medicine—Data Bases See entry A34.

G9 *New York Times* **Information Bank—Washington Office**

1. a. *1111 19th Street, N*
       Rosslyn, Virginia 22209
       (703) 243-7220

    b. 9:00 A.M.-5:00 P.M.   Monday-Friday

    c. Open to the public.

2. This computerized data base contains over 1.7 million abstracts of news stories, editorials, and other significant items from the *New York Times* (since 1969) and over 70 national and international periodicals.

    Researchers may utilize the Retail Service of the Information Bank, which for a fee can search the base for Africa-related materials. Abstracts are of 3-50 lines in length.

Smithsonian Science Information Exchange See entry K23.

Transportation Department—"TRISNET" See entry K25.

G10 **United Nations Environment Program—International Referral System (UNEP/IRS)**

1. a. *U.S. National Focal Point*
       U.S. Environmental Protection Agency
       401 M Street, SW, Room 2902
       Washington, D.C. 20460
       755-1838

b. 8:00 A.M.-4:30 P.M.   Monday-Friday

c. Open to the public.

d. Carol Alexander, Director

2.   UNEP/IRS, an independent agency of the United Nations, is a computerized data base containing environmental information for participating U.N. members. The purpose of the system is to facilitate the transfer and use of environmental information on a global basis.

The major operating concept of the IRS calls for the establishment of "national focal points" in individual countries which in turn will be responsible for collecting sources of environmental information within that country and transmitting these sources to the system's central directory. In March 1975, the U.S. Environmental Protection Agency (EPA) was designated as the U.S. National Focal Point and began operation in October 1975. Referral services are provided free of charge and are available to interested organizations and individuals. However, there probably will be a charge for substantive information. Information is available in some 30 categories (e.g., water and energy resources, land use and misuse, pollution, nonrenewable resources, etc.).

3.   Copies of the United Nations Environment Program/International Referral System, *General Information* and UNEP/IRS, *Policy and User's Manual* are available free on request. For further information, contact Charlene S. Sayers (755-1836), Source Coordinator for the U.S. International Environmental Referral Center.

ORGANIZATIONS

H Research Centers and Information Offices

Research Centers and Information Offices Entry Format (H)

1. *Address; telephone number(s)*

2. Chief official and title

3. Parental organization

4. Programs and research activities pertaining to Africa

5. Library/research facilities

6. Publications

H1 Advanced International Studies Institute (University of Miami)

1. *Suite 1122, East-West Towers*
   4330 East-West Highway
   Bethesda, Md. 20014
   (301) 951-0818

2. Mose L. Harvey, Director
   Dodd Harvey, Director of Publications

3. The Advanced International Studies Institute is affiliated with the University of Miami (Coral Gables, Florida). It was formerly known as the Center for Advanced International Studies of the University of Miami.

4. The institute undertakes interdisciplinary research in international affairs with a primary focus on Soviet studies. Present and future research interests will, therefore, include Soviet activities and involvement in Africa and global trouble spots such as the Middle East and Sub-Saharan Africa.

5-6. Regular publications of the institute consist of *Occasional Papers in International Affairs,* which contain the results of specialized research produced by the staff; the *Monographs in International Affairs* series, which focuses on subjects of immediate policy implications; and the periodical *Soviet World Outlook,* which periodically contains Africa-related articles. The following monographs should be of special interest to Africanists:

Susan Frutkin, *Aime Cesaire: Black Between Worlds* (1973);

Lt. Gen. Daniel O. Graham, *The Crisis in Africa: U.S. Strategy at the Crossroads* (1977);

Walter F. Hahn and Alvin J. Cottrell, *Soviet Shadow Over Africa* (1976);

Foy D. Kohler, Leon Goure, and Mose L. Harvey, *The Soviet Union and the October 1973 Middle East War: Implications for Detente* (1974);

Roger LeRoy Miller, *The Economic Impact of Restrictions on Trade with Rhodesia: A Preliminary View* (1974).

H2 African Bibliographic Center, Inc. (ABC)

1. *Suite 901*
   1346 Connecticut Avenue, NW
   Washington, D.C. 20036
   223-1392

   Mailing Address:
   P.O. Box 13096
   Washington, D.C. 20009

2. Daniel G. Matthews, President and Executive Director

3. ABC is affiliated with the Washington Task Force on African Affairs

4. Founded in 1963 as an information center for the general public and for researchers. A long-term goal was the building of an informal constituency for Africa.

   The ABC research program is varied and flexible; part of it is ongoing, and part of its depends on contracts from governments and foundations. The ongoing program consists of a steady flow of bibliographies and information programs on the radio. In addition, the staff attempts to pinpoint research areas before they become well known and then to publish books of bibliographies for them. An example is Alula Hidaru and Dessalegn Rahmato, *A Short Guide to the Study of Ethiopia: A General Bibliography,* which was published at a time when Ethiopian politics became of great concern to American policymakers and intellectuals.

   The contract program involves consulting for the World Bank, African governments, the State Department, USAID, and various American universities.

   ABC also has served as a liaison office providing contacts for organizations and governments. It has coordinated conferences for agencies and foundations such as the one in 1975, "Changing Vistas in United States-African Economic Relations." It has also provided assistance to visiting African heads of state, particularly in the area of public relations.

5. Most publishers send their African-oriented books to ABC for reviewing, but about half the titles are then sent out to reviewers. Reference books and some journals are kept, as well as newsletters from African embassies in Washington. The working library totals about 10,000 titles, part of which is kept in storage.

    Serious scholars, students, and government researchers may use this library if the materials are unavailable elsewhere. An appointment is necessary. Consulting firms using these facilities will be required to pay a fee.

6. The most important single publication of ABC is *A Current Bibliography on African Affairs,* which appears 4 times a year ($35.00). Ten volumes have been published over the past decade, and each number in these volumes contains a series of essays on subjects of current interest (e.g., "The Nigerian Press" and "The Civil War in Angola"), several long book reviews, lists of recent articles and books arranged by theme and country, and an author index.

    ABC also publishes books on countries or vital issues:

    Mohamed A. El-Khawas and Francis A. Kornegay, Jr., *American-Southern African Relations: Bibliographic Essays* (Westport, Conn.: Greenwood Press, 1975); William B. Helmreich, *Afro-Americans and Africa: Black Nationalism at the Crossroads* (Westport, Conn.: Greenwood Press, 1977); Alula Hidaru and Dessalegn Rahmato, *A Short Guide to the Study of Ethiopia: A General Bibliography* (Westport, Conn.: Greenwood Press, 1976); and Mohamed Khalief Salad, *Somalia: A Bibliographical Survey* (Westport, Conn.: Greenwood Press, 1977). Each of these books contains an essay or essays about the subject and annotated bibliographies that often provide considerable information about books and articles listed.

    Thirdly, the staff prepares reading lists and special reports: Mohamed A. El-Khawas, *Angola: The American-South African Connection* (Washington, D.C.: African Bibliographic Center, 1978); Susan M. Papenfuss, *Af-Log II: African Affairs in Washington, D.C. 1977–78* (Washington, D.C.: African Bibliographic Center, forthcoming); and Francis A. Kornegay, *Who Speaks for Southern Africa? A Resource Guide to Current Materials for Study and Research* (Washington, D.C.: African Bibliographic Center, forthcoming).

    Fourth, ABC produces *Habari,* which is a free information and news service available on the telephone (659-2529). Listeners receive a few minutes of the daily news from and about Africa. These recordings are purchased by several radio stations for broadcast, and some countries have approached ABC for advice on the creation of similar services.

Note: Also see entries H35 and Q9.

H3 African Research and Development Corporation

1. *2430 Pennsylvania Avenue, NW*
    Suite 106
    Washington, D.C. 20037

    387-6700

2.   Kevin Anyanwu, Director

4.   African Research and Development Corporation is a public, nonprofit organization which seeks to promote economic, social, and educational development and cooperation between the developing and the developed countries and provide research support for governments and institutions internationally.

   Staff members of the organization conduct research and analysis in the following fields: science and technology; resource development; investment opportunities; technological transfer; and public policy. Though the scope of their projects is continent-wide, recent activities pertain to Cameroons, Nigeria, and Tanzania.

   For Africanists, this organization is a valuable source of information on economic matters and other related topics, such as population, health, and nutrition.

   In addition to its research activities, the African Research and Development Corporation also conducts seminars to inform and disseminate information about Africa, especially in the area of investment opportunities.

6.   Researchers who wish to obtain access to the various research reports and studies should contact the office (387-6700).

H4 American Enterprise Institute for Public Policy Research (AEI)

1.   *1150 17th Street, NW*
   Washington, D.C. 20036
   862-5800

2.   William J. Baroody, President
   Robert J. Pranger, Director of Foreign and Defense Policy Studies

4.   The American Enterprise Institute, established in 1943, is a nonprofit research and educational organization which studies and analyzes national and international issues. Areas of concentration are economics, law, government, and foreign policy. The institute's research on Africa falls within the purview of its Foreign and Defense Policy Studies program; however, most of its Africa-related research focuses on the Middle East.

   The institute awards a small number of fellowships to visiting scholars for research in international affairs and foreign policy. It also sponsors periodic conferences, seminars, and symposia on foreign-policy issues. These events are generally closed to the public, but interested researchers may request to be placed on AEI's foreign-relations mailing list.

6.   AEI has an extensive publications program. Among its more recent publications with some reference to Africa are:

   John Duke Anthony, ed., *The Middle East: Oil, Politics, and Development* (1975);
   George Lenszowski, ed., *Political Elites in the Middle East* (1975);
   Ralph H. Magnus, ed., *Documents on the Middle East* (1969);

Robert J. Pranger, *American Policy for Peace in the Middle East, 1969–1971* (1971);

———— and Dale R. Tahtinen, *Nuclear Threat in the Middle East* (1975);

Dale R. Tahtinen, *The Arab-Israel Military Balance Since October 1973* (1974);

————, *The Arab-Israeli Military Balance Today* (1973).

A publications catalog and the quarterly *Memorandum,* which lists AEI activities, are available on request.

H5 American Institutes for Research (AIR)—Washington Office

1. *1055 Thomas Jefferson Street, NW*
    Suite 200
    Washington, D.C. 20007
    342-5000

2. Dr. Robert E. Krug, Vice President and Director, Washington Office

4. The American Institutes for Research is an independent, nonprofit institution engaged in research in the behavioral and social sciences. AIR also provides development and project evaluation services and training programs for the government, industry, and educational organizations.

    AIR's Africa-related activities include training and evaluation services, curriculum development, and the development of manpower skills. They have undertaken considerable work in the field of vocational guidance. Through a series of experimental studies in Nigeria, an AIR research team developed a set of 21 scholastic and vocational ability tests for use at different educational levels. The effectiveness of these techniques resulted in their being extended to other dveloping countries. In addition to Nigeria, AIR has also been involved in projects in Liberia, Ghana, Kenya, Uganda, Malawi, Botswana, Lesotho, and Swaziland.

5. AIR maintains its own library. For information on library hours and conditions of access, researchers should call Ms. Lilly Griner, Librarian (342-5047).

6. The American Institutes for Research *Annual Report* contains information on its manifold activities. Research results are published in professional journals, books, and monographs. A majority of the staff reports are available through ERIC and NTIS.

H6 Arab Information Center

1. *1875 Connecticut Avenue, NW*
    Suite 1110
    Washington, D.C. 20009
    265-3210

2. Yassar Al-Askari, Head

3. The main office is located in New York City.

4. The Arab Information Center represents the Arab League, whose membership includes 9 countries of Africa. The primary function of the center is to disseminate information regarding activities of the league and to foster better understanding and friendship between the Arab countries and the host country.

5. The library is located in the center's New York headquarters. The Washington staff, with its proficiency in the Arabic language, should be a useful resourse for scholars undertaking research on North Africa.

   The center also maintains a small collection of films and slides which are available for loan purposes free of charge.

6. The center publishes *Arab Report,* a fortnightly political and economic bulletin, and *Palestine Digest,* a monthly magazine consisting of reprints from newspapers and journals.

   In addition to these 2 publications, the center also distributes material (books and pamphlets) on 22 Arab nations. These are available to the public free of charge.

H7 Battelle Memorial Institute—Washington Operations

1. *2030 M Street, NW*
   Washington, D.C. 20036
   785-8400

2. George B. Johnson, Director of Washington Operations
   William Paul McGreevey, Director, Population and Development Policy Program

3. The institute's headquarters is in Columbus, Ohio.

4. Battelle is a multinational organization engaged in a broad range of research, educational, and invention- and technology-development activities. Its staff of 6,900 scientists, engineers, and supporting specialists brings its skills and training in the physical, life, and social/behavioral sciences to bear on the problems and needs of contemporary society. Much of its research is performed for industry and government on a contract basis.

   Over the years, the various Battelle research centers in Europe and the United States have conducted a variety of studies in Africa. These include transportation studies in Central Africa, food studies in Ethiopia and the Sudan, redesign of the Sudan Institute for Science and Technology, and development of a new water pump used in Nigeria. One current Battelle program pertinent to Africa is the Population and Development Policy Program. This focuses on several social and economic issues related to family size, fertility rates, population and family-planning programs, etc. Studies are currently being undertaken for several African countries.

H8 Brookings Institution

1. *1775 Massachusetts Avenue, NW*
    Washington, D.C. 20036
    797-6000

2. Bruce K. MacLaury, President
    John D. Steinbruner, Director of Foreign Policy Studies

4. The Brookings Institution is a nonprofit private organization devoted
    to policy-oriented research and publication in economics, government,
    foreign affairs, and national security.
    No substantial Africa-related research currently is being undertaken
    at Brookings. Its Foreign Policy Studies Program is concentrated largely
    in 2 areas: national security and international economic policy. Regional
    studies are focused on the Far East.
    The Advanced Study Program at Brookings offers a wide range of
    programs for leaders in government, business, and the professions. They
    include conferences, seminars, and other activities designed to increase
    the participants' awareness and understanding of public policy issues.
    In addition, Brookings offers a limited number of predoctoral fellow-
    ships and guest scholar appointments without stipend.

5. The Brookings Institution maintains its own 55,000-volume library, of
    which African holdings total only some 350 volumes. They consist
    largely of secondary materials in the fields of economics, history, and
    international relations. The library is open to Brookings staff members
    only; outside researchers cannot obtain access to the collection except
    through interlibrary loan. For reference and interlibrary loan informa-
    tion, call 797-6234, 8:30 A.M.-5:00 P.M., Monday-Friday.

6. Brookings has an extensive publications program. Recent titles of poten-
    tial interest to Africanists include:

    Fred C. Bergsten, Thomas Horst, and Theodore H. Moran, *American
    Multinationals and American Interests* (1978);
    ————, and Lawrence B. Krause, eds., *World Politics and Interna-
    tional Economics* (1975);
    Barry M. Blechman and Stephen S. Kaplan, *Force without War: U.S.
    Armed Forces as a Political Instrument* (1978);
    William R. Cline, *International Monetary Reform and the Developing
    Countries* (1975);
    Ernest W. Lefever, *Crisis in the Congo: A U.N. Force in Action*
    (1965);
    ————, *Spear and Scepter: Army, Police, and Politics in Tropical
    Africa* (1970);
    ————, *Nuclear Arms in the Third World: U.S. Policy Dilemma*
    (1979);
    Toward Peace in the Middle East: Report of a Study Group (1975).

H9 Carnegie Endowment for International Peace

1. *11 Dupont Circle*
   Washington, D.C. 20036
   797-6400

   30 Rockefeller Plaza
   New York, New York 10020
   (212) 572-8200

2. Thomas L. Hughes, President

4. The Carnegie Endowment for International Peace is an operating (not a grant-making) foundation that conducts its own programs of research, discussion, publication, and education in international affairs and American foreign policy. Program concentrations include arms control; executive-congressional relations in foreign policy; the Middle East; U.S.-Soviet relations; South Africa; precrisis fact-finding on selected issues; and international law and organization. The endowment engages in joint ventures with other tax-exempt organizations to reinvigorate and extend domestic and foreign dialog on world affairs issues, and it publishes the quarterly *Foreign Policy.*

6. A number of the endowment's published works are of value to the Africanist. These include:

   John de St. Jorre, *Inside the Laager: White Power in South Africa,* reprint from *Foreign Affairs* (October 1976);
   ———, *A House Divided: South Africa's Uncertain Future* (1977);
   Tom J. Farer, *War Clouds on the Horn of Africa: A Crisis for Detente* (1976);
   ———, *War Clouds on the Horn of Africa: The Widening Storm* (1979) (revision of the 1977 edition);
   Anthony Lake, *The "Tar Baby" Option: American Policy Toward Southern Rhodesia* (New York: Columbia University Press, 1976);
   Jack Shepherd, *The Politics of Starvation* (1976) (deals with the participation of the international community in a cover-up of the Ethiopian drought of 1973).

H10 Center for Defense Information (CDI)

1. *122 Maryland Avenue, NE*
   Washington, D.C. 20002
   543-0400

2. Gene R. LaRocque, Director

3. Affiliated with the Fund for Peace.

4. CDI conducts research and analyses of U.S. defense and weapons policies. Recent research interests have included nuclear nonproliferation and U.S. arms sales overseas.

The organization disseminates its views and findings through publications, media, congressional testimony, and seminars and meetings.

CDI also offers internships and fellowships for research on defense-oriented issues.

5. The center maintains a 2,000-volume library which contains Defense Department documents and publications, congressional committee hearings on military affairs, periodicals, and numerous defense-related materials.

6. CDI publishes *Defense Monitor,* issued 10 times a year.

H11 Center for International Policy

1. *120 Maryland Avenue, NE*
   Washington, D.C. 20012
   544-4666

2. Donald L. Ranard, Director

3. The Fund for Peace

4. The Center for International Policy is a private, nonprofit research organization which seeks to inform and educate the public and Congress about U.S. relations with the Third World, with a primary focus on the U.S. foreign-aid programs.

   Until recently, the center's research activities have been primarily concerned with Latin America and East Asia. Several studies on U.S. and multilateral aid to the Republic of South Africa have been produced, and reports on U.S. arms transfers and economic aid include mention of the African recipients.

6. The center publishes an annual survey of *Human Rights and the U.S. Foreign Assistance Program,* and the bimonthly *International Policy Reports* series. Africanists should find useful material in Jim Morrell and David Gisselquist, *How the IMF Slipped 464 Million Dollars to South Africa* (1978).

H12 Center for National Security Studies

1. *122 Maryland Avenue, NE*
   Washington, D.C. 20002
   544-5380

2. Morton Halperin, Director

3. The Fund for Peace and the American Civil Liberties Union (ACLU)

4. The Center for National Security Studies is primarily involved in research and litigation pertaining to national security. It also monitors the activities of U.S. intelligence agencies at home and abroad. Since the major focus is on domestic intelligence reform, Africa does not

figure prominently in the center's research projects except indirectly in the investigation of covert CIA activities abroad.

The center also provides assistance to individual researchers in gaining access to government information through the use of the Freedom of Information Act.

5.   The center maintains a small research library which is open to researchers by appointment. The materials in the library deal with intelligence issues and include over 300 congressional committee hearing records and selected CIA documents.

6.   The organization publishes a monthly newsletter, *First Principles,* which is available on a subscription basis. Other publications of interest to Africanists include: *CIA's Covert Operations Versus Human Rights* (1977, out of print), and a handbook on Freedom of Information entitled *Litigation under the Amended Federal Freedom of Information Act, 1978* (4th ed.).

H13 Center for Strategic and International Studies (CSIS)—Georgetown University

1.   *1800 K Street, NW*
Suite 520
Washington, D.C. 20006
833-8595

2.   David M. Abshire, Chairman
Michael A. Samuels, Executive Director for Third World Studies
Chester Crocker, Director of African Studies

3.   The center is affiliated with Georgetown University. It is funded primarily by foundations, corporations, and private individuals.

4.   CSIS, a research institution, was founded in 1962 to foster scholarship and stimulate public awareness of current international issues. Emphasis is on an interdisciplinary approach and problem solving.

Research at the center covers a wide range of subjects, from global issues which affect business and policymakers to more specialized ones, such as terrorism.

Most of the Africa-related research is being undertaken by the center's Third World Studies Program. Under this program, analytical studies of political stability and economic development in several African countries including Algeria, Egypt, Morocco, Namibia, Nigeria, and Zaire have already been completed.

Ongoing studies include an in-depth analysis of the current situation in the Republic of South Africa and Rhodesia from the viewpoint of U.S. diplomatic options, and prospects for a peaceful transition of power. Dr. Chester Crocker, the director of African studies at CSIS, is currently engaged in a study which examines economic and financial relationships, military ties, and the political-psychological dimensions of bargaining between the West and white South Africa. Other studies have focused on the Horn of Africa, the changing nature of Arab relations with Africa, political implications of population growth, the Arab-Israeli conflict, and the meaning of Soviet and Cuban activities in Africa.

CSIS also organizes and sponsors lectures, seminars, and meetings, many of which would be of considerable interest to Africanists. (These meetings are generally closed to the public, but researchers should make inquiries concerning limited access.) Past lectures have featured Rev. Ndabaningi Sithole, President of the Zimbabwe African National Union; Bishop Muzorewa; Senegal's President Leopold Senghor; and other prominent African leaders. Seminars and discussion groups have focused on issues such as "U.S. Interests and Policy in Southern Africa," "Arab-Israeli Conflict," and "Horn of Africa."

5. The center does not maintain its own library.

6. CSIS has an extensive publications program. *The Washington Quarterly* is a journal that has articles of interest to Africanists and special supplements that focus on the complexities of a major international problem, such as the May 1978 issue on the Horn of Africa.

The center also publishes *The Washington Papers* series. Of the 10 issues published in 1977, at least 2 should be of use to researchers: R. Michael Burrell and Abbas R. Kelidar, *Egypt: The Dilemma of a Nation, 1970–1977* (no. 48), and Leonard Sussman, *The Mass Media and the Third World Challenge* (no. 46). Other valuable monographs and reports include: Chester A. Crocker, *From Rhodesia to Zimbabwe: The Fine Art of Transition* (1977) and *Report on Angola* (1976); Chester A. Crocker and Penelope Hartland Thunberg, *Namibia at the Crossroads: Economic and Political Prospects* (1979); and Francis Murray and Louis H. Bean, *World Food: A Three Dimensional View of Production, Demand, and Nutrition* (1977).

H14 Georgetown University—Institute for International and Foreign Trade Law

1. *Georgetown University Law Center*
   600 New Jersey Avenue, NW
   Washington, D.C. 20001
   624-8330

2. Don Wallace, Jr., Director

4. The staff of the institute conducts research and analysis on legal aspects of international economic affairs, including the legal implications of economic development in developing countries. Currently, the institute is not involved in any ongoing research program pertaining to Africa; however, the staff is considering the preparation of a series of basic guides to the laws of various nations. Should this plan materialize, Africanists will find it a useful resource.

The institute's Investment Negotiation Center conducts training courses and seminars for foreign officials and law students. Participants include Africans.

6. The institute's *Lawyer's Guide to International Business Transactions*, vol. 1 (1977) should be of use to researchers. Three more volumes will be available in the near future.

H15 Howard University—Center for Ethnic Music (CEM)

1. *Fine Arts Building, Room 3036*
   Howard University
   Washington, D.C. 20059
   636-7080

2. Wanda L. Brown, Director

3. Affiliated with Howard University. The center, established in 1972, developed from an earlier project in African and Afro-American Music in the College of Fine Arts.

4. The Center for Ethnic Music is a unique facility housing resources for advanced study and research in ethnic music. Its primary objective is to enrich the curriculum of schools and colleges by collecting and developing materials in ethnic music. The emphasis is on the cultural contributions of the dominant nonwhite minorities in the United States, namely, Afro-Americans, Native Americans, Chicanos, Puerto Ricans, and Latin Americans.

   The Research Laboratory of the center contains a large collection of indigenous African instruments, recordings, publications, and manuscripts, as well as a wide selection of slides, films, and filmstrips. The center is thus a major resource for information concerning African-derived music in the nation.

   The center's extensive collection of publications covers virtually all aspects of African music. Researchers and scholars will find invaluable material on ethnomusicology; folk, tribal, and contemporary African music; musical instruments; storytelling and children's songs; talking drums of the Yoruba; and African music survivals in the New World.

   The center also provides assistance to schools and colleges in developing courses and curricula in ethnic music education through consultant services and loan of resource materials.

   Workshops and conferences are held periodically and are conducted by visiting scholars, members of the Howard University faculty, and the CEM staff. The primary objective of these workshops is to assemble educators for the purpose of exchanging viewpoints and exploring the resources of ethnic music.

Note: Howard University's Fine Arts Library, located in Room 1014 of the Fine Arts Building, maintains a collection of African music consisting of some 150-200 records. The library is open from 8:30 A.M.-8:00 P.M. Monday-Thursday, and 8:30 A.M.-5:00 P.M. Friday. For more information contact Carrie M. Hackney (636-7071).

H16 Howard University—Institute for the Arts and the Humanities (IAH)

1. *Institute for the Arts and the Humanities*
   Howard University
   P.O. Box 723
   Washington, D.C. 20059
   636-7738

2. Stephen E. Henderson, Director

3. Howard University

4-5. The stated objective of the institute is "to preserve, study, disseminate, and celebrate the artistic and creative aspects of the Afro-American heritage." It is concerned with the full range of the black creative process. Though its initial focus was on art, music, literature, folklore, and drama, increasingly equal emphasis is being placed on social issues and public affairs.

   The program of the institute encompasses the following areas: archival and documentation (expanding and preserving the university's Afro-American holdings in print, videotape, records, films, and photographs); research (analysis and study of the black heritage); seminars; workshops designed to facilitate greater interaction between artists and writers within the black community; fellowships; publications; and an annual writers' conference.

   Especially significant for the Africanist is the institute's video coverage of the Sixth Pan-African Conference in Dar es Salaam (June 1974) and the Conference on Culture and Development held in honor of President Leopold Senghor in Dakar, Senegal (October 1976). These materials should yield valuable information to researchers (see entry F18). In addition, IAH also sponsors an annual conference of black folklorists and organized a forum on "The African Cultural Presence in the Americas" in 1975.

Note: Students can earn academic credits for participating in the workshops and seminars sponsored by the institute.

6. The Institute publishes *IAH News,* a biannual 12-page newsletter which gives coverage of special arts activities at Howard and other institutions. In addition to this regular publication, the institute has published the proceedings from the 1974 writers' conference. For up-to-date information on publications, contact Juliette H. Bowles, research assistant for publications (636-7738).

H17 Institute of International Law and Economic Development

1. *1511 K Street, NW*
   Suite 345
   Washington, D.C. 20005
   347-0277

2. Arnold H. Leibowitz, President
   Warren Weinstein, Political Analyst (Africa)

4.   The institute was founded in 1973 to study the impact of the new world order on economic and political structures, with a special focus on newly independent countries and small states. Its specialists concentrate on constitutional questions, human rights, and federal relations.

   The institute engages in contract research in the areas noted above. Recently, for example, personnel have been studying human rights in Francophone Africa. Secondly, self-generated research is undertaken by individual staff members and by the institute. One person is preparing a *Francophone Africa Legal and Political Textbook,* and the institute as a whole has launched a *Small Area Studies* series. Thirdly, personnel serve as constitutional advisors and have already assisted in the drawing up of the constitutions of several countries.

5-6.   A highly specialized library, open to serious researchers, contains about 1,500 titles concentrating on American overseas possessions (doctoral dissertations, government documents, and general books) and on Francophone Africa. A list of key holdings has been prepared to facilitate exchanges with other research organizations. A dictionary card catalog is available.

   The institute sponsors conferences on small states and their problems with economic development. In the summer of 1978, a conference on human rights in Francophone Africa was organized. Papers from these conferences are usually published and made available to researchers.

H18 International Center for Research on Women (ICRW)

1.   *2000 P Street, NW*
        Washington, D.C. 20036
        293-3154

2.   Mayra Buvinic, Acting President

4.   The International Center for Research on Women is a nonprofit organization concerned primarily with the role of women in the development of countries. In recent years, ICRW's research activities have included projects in Kenya which involve developing methodology for future research on women.

5.   ICRW's library containing over 1,000 items includes several unpublished papers and materials relating to Africa. The library is open to researchers by appointment, from 8:30 A.M. to 5:00 P.M., Monday-Friday.

6.   The center publishes the quarterly *ICRW Newsletter,* which is available free on request.

H19 International Food Policy Research Institute (IFPRI)

1.   *1776 Massachusetts Avenue, NW*
        Washington, D.C. 20036
        826-5600

2.   J. W. Mellor, Director

4.   The International Food Policy Research Institute (IFPRI), established in 1975, is an autonomous organization engaged in the study and review of the global food and agriculture situation and the analysis of major policy issues with international implications. The organization is intended to provide "a focal point for the exchange of ideas and the accumulation of knowledge on crucial issues, methodology, and approaches to their solution."

    In meeting these objectives, IFPRI cooperates with international organizations such as FAO, UNCTAD, the World Bank, etc. The institute is also establishing working relationships with research and development institutions in developing countries.

    IFPRI's research is divided into 4 programs: trends analysis, production policy, consumption policy, and trade policy. Since the emphasis is on Third World developing countries, IFPRI has numerous Africa-related programs and activities. These include analysis of alternate policies for land use in Africa; food needs of African nations and projections of production and consumption; Nigerian agricultural research; potential for increasing production from rain-fed land; and the economic trade-off between food and cash-crop production and optional food policy choices for East African countries.

5.   IFPRI's Information Services Program strives to develop continuing information exchange links with policymakers, administrators, and governmental and nongovernmental national leaders.

6.   IFPRI has an extensive publications program which includes *Occasional Papers* and *Research Reports,* many of which pertain to Africa. IFPRI's *Annual Report* and *Research Highlights 1978* are available on request.

H20 Joint Center for Political Studies (JCPS)

1.   *1426 H Street, NW*
Washington, D.C. 20005
638-4477

2.   Eddie N. Williams, President

4.   JCPS, a nonprofit organization, strives to increase the participation of blacks and other minorities in the political process. To accomplish this goal, the center engages in research and public-policy analysis and provides training, technical assistance, and information for blacks and other members of minorities who are elected and appointed officials.

    The center's activities focus primarily on blacks and minority groups within the United States. For this reason, it is not a major resource for Africanists. Occasionally a staff member may undertake research pertaining to African and other Third World countries.

6.   *Focus,* the center's monthly newsletter, provides analysis of major policy issues. A recent issue dealt with "U.S.–Third World Relations in Transition" (vol. 5, April 1977).

    The *Annual Report* of JCPS and a publication list are available on request.

H21 Middle East Institute (MEI)

1. *1761 N Street, NW*
    Washington, D.C. 20036
    785-1141

2. L. Dean Brown, President

4. MEI, a nonprofit organization, was founded in 1946 to promote better understanding between the peoples of the Middle East and the United States through dissemination of information and education of the American public.

    The institute provides a variety of public services in the form of panels, lectures, conferences, and seminars which focus on important contemporary issues now facing the countries of the Middle East and North Africa. In addition to an annual conference, the institute also holds economic seminars which examine and analyze the prospects for American business in and with countries of North Africa and the Middle East.

    MEI periodically sponsors cultural events, some of which would be of interest to the Africanist, such as exhibits of art from the Middle East and the documentary film on the rights of Egyptian women by Egyptian director Laila Abou-Saif, both of which were organized during the 1977–78 season.

    In 1970, MEI instituted an Arabic language program which has grown considerably in the past few years. The institute also offers other courses, among them: Islam and Arabic Culture, Arabic Calligraphy, and Foreign Policy in Transition: The U.S. and the Middle East.

5. MEI's George Camp Keiser Library contains over 15,000 volumes, of which some 1,500 are in Arabic, primarily major classical works. Most of the materials deal with modern history, international politics, economics and oil, and 19th-century travel accounts. The library's periodicals collection consists of some 400 titles. The library is open to the public Monday through Saturday for on-site reference use.

    MEI also has its own film library (see entry F23).

6. The *Middle East Journal*, a quarterly published by MEI since 1947, is a valuable research tool for scholars. It contains articles on contemporary political, social, or economic issues, a chronology of events of the quarter, state documents, book reviews, and a bibliography of periodical literature. A cumulative index to the *Journal* (1947–66) is also available. MEI has also published several bibliographies, which include:

    John Duke Anthony, *North Africa in Regional and International Affairs: A Selected Bibliography* (1974);

    ———— with Elda Stifani, *The United States and the Middle East: Changing Relationships. A Selected Bibliography* (1975);

    Aghil M. Barbar, *Libya 1969–74: A Bibliography* (1976);

    Leon Carl Brown, ed., *State and Society in Independent North Africa* (1966);

    Harry N. Howard, *The Middle East: A Selected Bibliography of Recent Works, 1960–69* (with supplements from 1970 to 1978);

Harvey Sobelman, ed., *Arabic Dialect Studies: A Selected Bibliography* (1962).

In addition to the above, MEI has several publications that focus on contemporary politics and events, and social, economic, and developmental issues. Reports of annual conferences and proceedings are also available in published form. For further information regarding publications, researchers should call or write for MEI's *Publications Catalog,* available without charge.

H22 Middle East Research and Information Project

1. *P.O. Box 3122*
    Washington, D.C. 20010
    667-1188

2. Judith Tucker, President

4. The Middle East Research and Information Project, founded in 1970, is a research center and information office which focuses on U.S. policies and interests in the Middle East and North and East Africa. Its primary function is to inform and educate the American public through dissemination of information and the use of the mass media.

    Other activities of the office consist of providing speakers on issues of vital importance to organizations and institutions and organizing film and radio shows for the public.

5. The Middle East Research and Information Project maintains a library.

6. *MERIP Reports,* published monthly, contain news and analysis on the Middle East and North and East Africa.

H23 Middle East Resource Center (MERC)

1. *1322 18th Street, NW*
    Washington, D.C. 20036
    659-6846

2. Priscilla Norris and George Bisharat, Coordinators

3. MERC, established in 1975, is the Washington office of Search for Justice and Equality in Palestine.

4-5. The center's major function is to inform the Congress, the Executive Branch, the media, and citizens' groups about the Middle East conflict.

    Activities of MERC include distributing an information packet of basic resource materials on the Middle East to key members of Congress; arranging news conferences on behalf of the rights of the Palestinian people; raising the issue of human rights in occupied territories; and arranging forums for the exchange of ideas and viewpoints between members of Congress, peace groups, religious organizations, and Middle East specialists.

6. Regular publications consist of the monthly *Palestine/Israel Bulletin,* which provides information and analysis on various aspects of the Middle East conflict. The center has also published a study of the Middle East positions of Republican and Democratic candidates in the 1976 presidential primary elections.

H24 National Planning Association (NPA)

1. *1606 New Hampshire Avenue, NW*
    Washington, D.C. 20009
    265-7685

2. John Miller, President
    Theodore Geiger, Director of International Studies

4. NPA, a private, nonprofit organization, conducts research on emerging economic problems confronting the United States at home and abroad, and seeks to encourage joint economic planning and cooperation by leaders from business, labor, and the professions.

    A large number of its research projects pertain to the developing countries in Africa, Asia, and Latin America.

6. Under contract from the U.S. Agency for International Development, NPA publishes the quarterly *Development Digest.* In addition, it also publishes *New International Realities* (quarterly) and research studies on specific economic issues.

H25 Overseas Development Council (ODC)

1. *1717 Massachusetts Avenue, NW*
    Washington, D.C. 20036
    234-8701

2. James P. Grant, President

4. The Overseas Development Council is an independent, nonprofit organization which conducts research on a broad range of socioeconomic issues confronting the developing countries and their impact on the United States and other developed nations. Through its programs of research, publications, conferences, and seminars, ODC seeks to educate and inform the American public about the problems of poverty, hunger, disease, and injustice affecting the Third World.

    The council's research and policy papers deal with subjects such as Third World development strategies and basic human needs; international economic systems and their impact on the U.S. economy; the interrelationship between development strategies and health, fertility, and mortality; energy needs of developing countries; and policy issues related to world hunger and food scarcity. The developing countries are, however, studied from a global rather than a regional perspective.

    In addition to its own staff, ODC provides opportunities to development specialists from academia, government, and business to work at

ODC as visiting fellows. ODC has also established a regular fellowship for a Third World Development specialist.

ODC sponsors a wide range of activities, including conferences, seminars, workshops, and media briefings. Several of the seminars have dealt with subjects which should be of interest to Africanists. These include Southern Africa, the Sahel, and the Horn of Africa.

6. ODC has an extensive publications program which consists of books, monographs, occasional papers, development papers, and communiqués. Some selected items of interest to Africanists include:

    Mayra Buvinic, *Women and World Development: An Annotated Bibliography* (1976);

    Guy F. Erb and Valeriana Kallab, *Beyond Dependency: The Developing World Speaks Out* (1975);

    Denis Goulet, *Looking at Guinea-Bissau: A New Nation's Development Strategy*, Occasional Paper No. 9 (March 1978);

    Perdita Huston, *Third World Women Speak Out* (New York: Praeger Publishers, 1979);

    Martin M. McLaughlin and the staff of ODC, *The United States and World Development: Agenda 1979* (New York: Praeger Publishers, 1979);

    John W. Sewell with Lairold M. Street, *Is the Sahel a Wasteland?* Communiqué No. 30 (August 1976);

    John G. Sommer, *Beyond Charity: U.S. Voluntary Aid for a Changing Third World* (1977);

    Irene Tinker and Michele Bo Bramsen, *Women and World Development* (New York: Praeger Publishers, 1976);

    Paul M. Watson, *Debt and the Developing Countries: New Problems and New Actors*, Development Paper No. 26, NIEO Series (April 1978).

    The Overseas Development Council's *Annual Report* and a publications list are available on request.

H26 Population Reference Bureau, Inc. (PRB)

1. *1337 Connecticut Avenue, NW*
    Washington, D.C. 20036
    785-4664

2. Dr. Conrad Taeuber, Chairman of the Board
    Robert M. Avedon, President

4. PRB collects, interprets, and disseminates information on national and world population trends and their social and economic implications. It is, therefore, a useful source for Africanists seeking statistical information on population trends in African nations, much of which is available from the publications listed below.

5. PRB maintains its own library and information service which is open to the public.

6. Publications include:

    Interchange, a newsletter published 4 times a year for teachers and other educators, which focuses on specific population topics. Each issue is accompanied by a teaching module or other tool to enhance the teaching of population issues;

Intercom, a monthly newsmagazine that gives up-to-date population-related news;

PRB Reports, issued periodically;

Population Bulletin, a bimonthly in-depth report on trends, problems, and policies in population and related fields. Vol. 30, no. 1, in this series deals with *Africa and Its Population Growth;*

World Population Data Sheet, published annually, includes Africa by region and country. Gives data on population, birth rate, death, natural increase, infant mortality, life expectancy, and urban population.

In addition to the above-mentioned regular publications, researchers should find the following useful: *Population Handbook,* "a quick guide to population dynamics for journalists, policymakers, teachers, students, and other people interested in people"; *Source Book on Population, 1970–1976,* which contains an annotated description of over 1,000 publications, periodicals, organizations, and sources of information in the field of population; and a 271-page report, *World Population Growth and Response, 1965–1975: A Decade of Global Action.*

H27 Rand Corporation—Washington Office

1. *2100 M Street, NW*
    Washington, D.C. 20037
    296-5000

2. Dr. George K. Tanham, Vice-President, Washington Operations
    Frederic S. Nyland, Director, Washington Office National Security Research

3. The Rand Corporation's headquarters is in Santa Monica, California.

4. The Rand Corporation is a private, nonprofit organization engaged in research and analysis on domestic and international issues affecting the U.S. public welfare and national security. Its work encompasses most of the major disciplines in the physical, social, and biological sciences. The Washington office's National Security Research Staff numbers approximately 30-35 professionals.

    Rand's National Security Research Divisions have produced numerous reports and studies of African politics, economics, and defense strategies. However, the bulk of this work is classified material and unavailable to private researchers.

5. The Washington office maintains its own library, which contains several thousand volumes, mostly in the social sciences. Access to the library is restricted to Rand personnel; however, nonclassified materials may be obtained through interlibrary loan service.

6. Rand has an extensive publications program. Unclassified Rand publications are disseminated to some 350 academic and public libraries in the United States on a subscription basis, including the Library of Congress, George Washington University Library, and the Army Library. Rand also maintains a number of special subject bibliographies containing

abstracts of its publications. Two of these should be of special interest to Africanists: *A Bibliography of Selected Rand Publications: Africa* (May 1978), which lists over 20 books, reports, and memoranda pertaining to Africa, and *A Bibliography of Selected Rand Publications: Middle East* (April 1978), containing abstracts of 60 publications. These selected bibliographies are available free, upon request.

In addition to the above bibliographies, *Rand Research Review,* published 3 times a year, contains information on Rand's research programs and is available free of charge.

Research reports and individual titles may be purchased from the Publications Department, The Rand Corporation, 1700 Main Street, Santa Monica, California 90406.

H28 Resources for the Future

1. *1755 Massachusetts Avenue, NW*
   Washington, D.C. 20036
   462-4400

2. Emery N. Castle, President

4. Resources for the Future is a nonprofit organization which conducts research, primarily from an economic perspective, on national and international policy issues relating to natural resources, energy, environment, food, agriculture, and population.

   Presently, none of the ongoing research work involves Africa.

6. The organization publishes a newsletter, *Resources* (3 times a year), and a series of books and monographs including Ronald Riker, ed., *Changing Resource Problems of the Fourth World* (Baltimore: Johns Hopkins University Press, 1976) and Ronald Riker, ed., *Population and Development* (working paper, 1976).

H29 Rhodesian Information Office

1. *2852 McGill Terrace, NW*
   Washington, D.C. 20008
   483-4468

2. Kenneth Towsey, Director

4. The main function of the Rhodesian Information Office is to provide general information on Rhodesia. Pamphlets, literature, and other types of materials are distributed free of charge.

5. The Information Office maintains a reading room which contains some 150-200 general reference books, and Rhodesian magazines and current newspapers, namely the *Herald* and the *Sunday Mail*. It also has a collection of government statistics. The reading room is open to the public from 9:00 A.M. to 5:00 P.M., Monday-Friday.

6. A monthly newsletter, *Rhodesian Viewpoint*, is published and distributed free. Interested persons can request to be placed on its mailing list.

H30 School of Advanced International Studies (SAIS)—The Johns Hopkins University—Washington Center of Foreign Policy Research

1. *1740 Massachusetts Avenue, NW*
    Washington, D.C. 20036
    785-6276

2. Simon H. Serfaty, Director

3. The Washington Center of Foreign Policy Reesarch is affiliated with the School of Advanced International Studies of Johns Hopkins University.

4. The center conducts research on major issues in U.S. foreign policy and international politics. Nine permanent faculty members of the School of Advanced International Studies, along with 15 associates and several visiting fellows, participate in research projects, seminars, and discussions.

6. The center publishes, through the Johns Hopkins University Press, a series entitled *Studies in International Affairs*.

H31 South Africa Foundation

1. *Suite 300*
    1925 K Street, NW
    Washington, D.C. 20006
    223-5486

2. John H. Chettle, Director
    J. Andre Visser, Deputy Director

4. The South Africa Foundation is a private organization which seeks to provide greater understanding of South Africa through research and dissemination of information.

    As an information office, the foundation provides up-to-date information on South Africa to the media, political observers, businessmen, investors, and the general public. It is also concerned with analyzing and explaining the sources and reasons for various international attitudes toward South Africa. The foundation is also responsible for arranging and sponsoring visits to South Africa by leaders in all fields.

    In recent years the foundation's activities have included testifying before the Africa subcommittees of both the Senate Foreign Relations Committee and the House Foreign Affairs Committee at hearings on U.S. investment in South Africa; participating in radio and television interviews; and providing speakers for various national and regional organizations and universities.

6. Important publications of the foundation include:

    Briefing Papers, providing concise, factual information on major subjects related to South Africa;
    Information Digest, an annual publication containing statistical information and an overview of the socioeconomic situation in South Africa;

South Africa Foundation News, a monthly publication containing reports and analyses of current events in South Africa;
South Africa International, a quarterly journal serving as a forum for debate on domestic and international developments that directly or indirectly affect South Africa.

H32 Southern African Research Association (SARA)

1. *Room 4133, Art/Sociology Building*
   University of Maryland
   College Park, Maryland 20742
   (301) 454-5937

2. Madziwanyika Tsomondo, Secretary
   Mariyawanda Nzuwah, Editor, *Journal of Southern African Affairs*

4. The Southern African Research Association is an international organization of scholars, researchers, and institutions pursuing research on Southern Africa. The areas covered are Angola, Zaire, Zambia, Tanzania, Malawi, Mozambique, Zimbabwe, Botswana, Namibia, Swaziland, Lesotho, and South Africa.
   The association's research activities are threefold. First, it sponsors seminars, workshops, symposia, and conferences. Each year the association in cooperation with the Afro-American Studies Program at the University of Maryland sponsors a conference focusing on important themes and vital issues in Southern Africa. In 1978, the theme was "Perspectives on Evolution and Revolution in Southern Africa." Second, the association supports relevant research on Southern Africa. Third, it publishes the *Journal of Southern African Affairs.*

6. In addition to the *Journal of Southern African Affairs,* the association's forthcoming publications should be of interest to Africanists. They include Mariyawanda Nzuwah, ed., *Organization of African Unity on Southern Africa: Documents, Declarations, and Resolutions of the Organization of African Unity on Southern Africa, 1963–1978,* and *Southern Africa and the Future: Strategies for Development in the Next Twenty Years.* This will be a collection of papers on development presented at the Third Annual Conference of the Southern African Research Association, June 1978.

H33 United Nations Information Centre

1. *2101 L Street, NW, Suite 209*
   Washington, D.C. 20037
   296-5370

2. Marcial Tamayo, Director
   Patricia O'Callaghan, Information Officer

3-4. The Centre provides services which reflect the main functions of the U.N. Office of Public Information. These include reference and publications and the use of press, radio, television, films, and exhibitions for the dissemination of information. The Centre's primary goal is to establish direct contacts with representatives of the local press and information media, educational institutions, governmental and nongovernmental organizations, and to cooperate with them in providing a greater understanding of the aims and functions of the United Nations.

5. The Centre also maintains a library (see entry A41).

6. The Centre plays an important role in the observance of special U.N. occasions such as U.N. Day and Human Rights Day, as well as publicity for current U.N. programs.

United Nations Development Programme

1. *2101 L Street, NW, Suite 209*
    Washington, D.C. 20037
    296-5074

2. Charles Perry, Liaison Officer

3. This office maintains a listing of the various development projects the UNDP is presently involved in, along with a description of each project. The *Compendium of Approved Projects* is issued annually.

H34 Washington Office on Africa

1. *110 Maryland Avenue, NE*
    Washington, D.C. 20002
    546-7961

2. Edgar Lockwood, Executive Director

4. The Washington Office on Africa is primarily an action-oriented lobby group which seeks to gain the support of the American people in order to influence U.S. policy on Southern Africa and facilitate majority rule. Activities comprise publication and dissemination of resource materials and organization of support on specific issues.

5. The Washington Office on Africa does not maintain a formal library. However, it has extensive vertical files that contain unique and valuable materials pertaining to Southern Africa and U.S. policy. Researchers may be allowed to consult these materials at the discretion of the staff.

6. Africanists should find the following publications useful:
    African Action, bulletins on congressional action, dealing with U.S. official policy issues in Zimbabwe, Namibia, and Southern Africa;
    Congressional Voting Record on Southern Africa, published approximately once a year;
    Washington Notes on Africa (quarterly).
    Washington Office on Africa also makes available leaflets such as "Zimbabwe: Winning Hearts and Minds."

H35 Washington Task Force on African Affairs (WTFAA)

1. *P.O. Box 13033*
    Washington, D.C. 20009
    223-1393

2. Daniel G. Matthews, President and Executive Director

3. Washington Task Force on African Affairs is the volunteer arm of the African Bibliographic Center (see entry H2).

4. WTFAA is primarily an educational and information office. Its primary function is to educate the American public and develop an informed constituency for Africa through dissemination of information and comprehensive coverage of African affairs.

    Besides serving as an information organization, the Task Force also offers a wide range of services including lecturers, consultants, and curriculum specialists. It undertakes research and analysis on a contractual basis for institutions such as the World Bank, AID, and the Ford Foundation.

    In addition, it provides daily news briefs on current African affairs. (See *Habari* in the publication and media section of this guide, entry Q9.)

5. The African Bibliographic Center maintains its own library consisting of some 10,000 volumes. The library is, however, for staff use only.

6. For a description of the publications of the African Bibliographic Center, see entry H2. Specific publications of the Washington Task Force on African Affairs include:
    AMA: Women in African and American Worlds. An Outlook, a series of information guides providing up-to-date information on women in Africa and the U.S., with a focus on foreign affairs and the role of women in economic development;
    Congress and Africa, an analysis of congressional voting on African issues and selected reading list;
    Habari Special Reports, a series of topical and analytical materials on African affairs.

Note: Also see African Bibliographic Center, entry H2.

H36 Woodrow Wilson International Center for Scholars (WWICS)

1. *Smithsonian Institution Building*
    1000 Jefferson Drive, SW
    Washington, D.C. 20560
    381-5613

2. James H. Billington, Director

4. The Woodrow-Wilson International Center for Scholars was created by the United States Congress as the nation's official living memorial to its twenty-eighth president. As a national institution with international in-

terests, the center seeks to encourage the creative use of the unique human, archival, and institutional resources in the nation's capital for studies illuminating man's understanding of his past and present.

The center's programs attempt to commemorate the Wilsonian connection between ideas and affairs, between intellect and moral purpose. At the heart of the center stands its Fellowship Program, which enables the institution to appoint fellows annually from the U.S. and abroad to conduct research on major projects at the center for periods ranging from 4 months to 1 year or more. The center has no permanent or tenured fellows. The center's Fellowship Program consists of 2 broad divisions (Social and Political Studies, and Historical and Cultural Studies) and 4 special programs (on Russia and the Soviet Union, on Latin America and the Caribbean, on international security issues, and on environmental problems). The center also operates a Guest Scholar Program for the short-term use of the center's facilities by a small number of visiting scholars and specialists.

Through these programs scholars specializing in African affairs are brought into the center to carry out research. The number varies from year to year. Since 1976, center fellows and guest scholars with African specialities have included: Zewde Gabre-Sellassie, Grace Stuart Ibingira, Carl Eicher, James L. Gibbs, Jr., Hollis Lynch, Frank M. Snowden, Peter Vanneman, Mansour Khalid, Emmanuel Obiechina, David and Marina Ottaway, and Raymond Tanter.

The center's activities include frequent colloquia, evening seminars, and other discussions designed to foster intellectual community among the participants. The scheduled events are announced in the monthly *Calendar of Events.*

5. The Wilson Center has a working library containing 15,000 volumes of basic reference works, bibliographies, and essential monographs in the social sciences and humanities. The library subscribes to and maintains the back files of about 300 scholarly journals and periodicals. As part of a National Presidential Memorial, the libary has special access to the collections of the Library of Congress and other government libraries. The librarian is Dr. Zdeněk V. David (381-5850).

6. The *Wilson Quarterly* carries occasional articles on Africa. The spring 1977 issue, in particular, included a series on the Union of South Africa. The center also sponsors the publication of *Scholars' Guides to Washington, D.C.* Available from the Smithsonian Institution Press, the *Guides* survey the collections, institutions, and organizations pertinent to the study of particular geographic areas, such as Africa, East Asia, Latin America and the Caribbean, Russia/Soviet Union, and other world regions.

H37 World Coffee Information Center

1. *1100 17th Street, NW, Suite 302*
   Washington, D.C. 20036
   296-8844

2. Samuel E. Stavisky, Executive Director

4.   The center carries out activities on behalf of the Brazilian Coffee Institute, New York, aimed at obtaining U.S. congressional approval of the International Coffee Agreement of 1976. The agreement comprises 67 member countries around the world, including Latin America, Africa, and Asia.

H38 Worldwatch Institute

1.   *Suite 701*
      1776 Massachusetts Avenue, NW
      Washington, D.C. 20036
      452-1999

2.   Lester Brown, President

4.   The Worldwatch Institute, a nonprofit organization, undertakes research, from a global perspective, on population, food, energy, environment, roles of women, and other such issues.

6.   The institute publishes *Worldwatch Papers* (8 to 10 per year) and books (through a commercial publisher).

J Academic Programs

Academic Programs Entry Format (J)

1. *Address; telephone number(s)*

2. Chief official and title

3. Degrees and subjects offered; program activities

4. Library/research facilities

J1 American University—Foreign Area Studies (FAS)

1. *5010 Wisconsin Avenue, NW
   Washington, D.C. 20016
   686-2769*

2. William Evans-Smith, Director

3. In 1954 the Department of the Army began to produce area handbooks through a contract with the Human Relations Area Files (HRAF), New Haven, Connecticut; a Washington branch (WAHRAF) opened at American University in 1955. Three years later the university became the sole producer as the HRAF contract terminated.

   FAS conducts the Area Handbook Program, preparing book-length studies about the social, economic, political, and military institutions—the people and society—of foreign countries. Aimed at the nonspecialist, with an emphasis on contemporary society, the books average about 350 pages in length and feature cartographic illustrations and tables. Annual production of the book exceeds 100,000 copies of the more than 100 titles in print. African countries covered by these studies are: Angola, Algeria, Burundi, Cameroon, Chad, People's Republic of Congo, Egypt, Ethiopia, Ghana, Guinea, Ivory Coast, Kenya, Liberia, Libya, Malagasy Republic, Malawi, Mauritania, Morocco, Mozambique, Nigeria, Rwanda, Senegal, Sierra Leone, Somalia, Republic of South Africa, Southern Rhodesia, Sudan, Tanzania, Tunisia, Uganda, Zaire, and Zambia.

4.	The library at FAS is an unusual facility. Designed to meet the special research needs of its staff, the holdings reflect an emphasis on current and reliable (secondary) sources of information on the nations covered in the books. Periodical subscriptions account for the major part of acquisitions. Some unusual scholarly materials may be found here which are not readily available elsewhere in the area. The library can provide bibliographic assistance for its own and other Washington collections, has photoduplication services, and is open to qualified researchers who, if interested, should call FAS for more information.

J2 The American University—School of International Service (SIS)

1.	*School of International Service*
	The American University
	Washington, D.C. 20016
	686-2470

2.	William C. Cromwell, Acting Dean

3.	The school offers three master's degrees—in international affairs, international communication, and international development—and a Ph.D. in international relations.

	The core of the SIS program lies in 6 fields: international relations, international law and organization, international communications, U.S. and comparative foreign policy, international development, world human needs, and regional international systems. Students may specialize in any of 6 geographic areas which include Africa and the Middle East. The school offers several Africa-related courses taught by specialists and faculty members from other departments. These include courses in African history, culture, politics, economic systems, literature, and international development.

	SIS has also been involved in research pertaining to Africa, most recently on the drought in the Sahel region, population and development, and Southern Africa's political, social, and economic development.

	Other activities which would be of interest to Africanists include periodic meetings, lectures, and conferences sponsored by the school (such as the symposia on world food resources and population, and housing needs and environment held in recent years, and the conference on world health needs held in 1979).

	For details concerning these meetings and other special events, researchers should contact the school.

4.	See entry A3 in the library section.

Economic Development Institute See International Bank for Reconstruction and Development, entry L42.

J3 George Mason University—Department of History

1. *Department of History*
    219 Thompson Hall
    4400 University Drive
    Fairfax, Virginia 22030
    (703) 323-2242

2. Dr. Joseph Harsh, Chairman

3. The department awards a B.A. and M.A. degree in history. Students may select any one of 3 areas of concentration: United States, modern Europe, or Latin America. Since African history is not offered as a major field of specialization, only a few courses are available. These include: "The Afro-American Experience in the United States: African Background to 1865," and "The Ancient Near and Middle East." For further information on Africa-related courses, interested persons should contact Dr. George Walker (323-2242).

J4 George Washington University—Department of Anthropology

1. *Building X, 2112 G Street, NW*
    Washington, D.C. 20052
    676-6075

2. V. K. Golla, Chairman

3. The department awards a bachelor of arts with a major in anthropology and a master of arts in the field of anthropology. Among the several courses offered are the following which pertain to Africa: "Cultures of Africa," "Cultures of the Near East," "Old World Prehistory: Paleolithic and Mesolithic," and "Hominid Evolution." Staff members with African interests frequently offer seminars with an African focus. During 1978–79, 2 Africa-related seminars were given: "Prehistory of Africa" and "Afro-Brazilian Religions." Staff members with African interests include R. K. Lewis, A. S. Brooks, J. E. Yellen, C. M. Turnbull, and M. Koch-Weser.

J5 George Washington University—School of Public and International Affairs

1. *School of Public and International Affairs*
    George Washington University
    Washington, D.C. 20052
    676-6244

2. Burton M. Sapin, Dean

3. The School of Public and International Affairs offers a program leading to an M.A. degree in the field of international affairs, within which students may select a regional field of concentration, including Africa.

Course work may be taken in the departments of anthropology, economics, geography and regional science, history, political science, and sociology.

4.   See entry A 15.

Note: George Washington University also offers a limited number of courses in African anthropology, history, economics, and art. These include: Cultures of South and East Africa (Anthropology 178), Culture of West and Central Africa (Anthropology 179), Islamic Art (Art 116), African Art (Art 165), History of Africa (History 116), Government and Politics of North Africa (Political Science 180), Politics of Middle and Southern Africa (Political Science 181), African International Politics (Political Science 182), Government and Politics of North Africa (Political Science 180), and Topics in African Politics (Political Science 281).

J6 Georgetown University—Center for Contemporary Arab Studies

1.   *Center for Contemporary Arab Studies*
Georgetown University
Washington, D.C. 20057
625-3128

2.   John Ruedy, Chairman
Michael C. Hudson, Executive Director

3.   The center is devoted to the study of the contemporary Arab world. Its interdisciplinary program is designed to serve the needs of individuals engaged in the private and public sector, as well as those seeking academic careers.

The center awards an M.A. in Arab studies within which students may select a field of concentration. At present, disciplinary concentrations are offered in economics, Arabic history, and international affairs. In addition, students are required to demonstrate proficiency in Modern Standard Arabic or in a major Arab dialect. The center also offers a certificate program in Arab studies, both at the masters and the doctoral level.

In addition to the full-time permanent faculty, the center also recruits and invites outstanding Arabists as visiting professors. The center's staff undertakes and promotes research on a wide range of topics, dealing with social, political, and economic development of the Arab world.

4.   See entry A 16.

J7 Howard University—African Studies and Research Program

1.   *African Studies and Research Program*
Howard University
Washington, D.C. 20059

2. Robert J. Cummings, Director

3. The African Studies and Research Program was established in 1953 to encourage and facilitate interdisciplinary research and to focus on research methodology as well as policy-oriented research. Since 1969, the program has offered Master of Arts and Doctor of Philosophy degree in African studies. The Ph.D. degree is available under the following rubrics: Development and Planning in African Studies; Language and Communication in African Studies; and Social Organization in African Studies. The program places great emphasis on language proficiency and research competence. Instruction is provided in various African languages, which include Swahili, Yoruba, Hausa, Zulu, Amharic, and Arabic.

   In addition, the program also offers training programs for U. S. specialists and technicians working in Africa and selected personnel from African nations.

4. See entries A19 and A20.

J8 Howard University—College of Fine Arts

1. *College of Fine Arts*
   Howard University
   Washington, D.C. 20059
   636-7040

2. Thomas J. Flagg, Dean
   Starmanda Bullock, Chairman, Department of Art
   Doris E. McGinty, Chairman, Department of Music

3. The College of Fine Arts was established in 1960, when the School of Music and the Department of Art and Drama were merged. In recognition of its responsibility to develop and reaffirm the values and expression of the black experience, the college offers numerous courses in African art and music.

   The Department of Art offers programs leading to a Bachelor of Fine Arts and a Masters of Arts degree. Courses in African art include the following: African Art I and II, Survey of African Art, West African Art, Central and East African Art, Islamic Art, African Cultural Expression, Contemporary African Art, and upper-level seminar courses.

   The Department of Music has an undergraduate and graduate program in music. Of the many courses offered in the program, 3 are of special interest to Africanists: Introduction to African Music, African and Afro-American Music Literature, and African Drumming and Dance. The College of Fine Arts periodically sponsors lectures and presentations on relevant topics which are open to the community.

4. The college also maintains a library which contains reference materials on visual arts, drama, and music. Listening rooms with turntables, tapedecks, and earphones are available.

   The Department of Arts owns a collection of 18,000 mounted photographs and 12,000 slides, a substantial number of which deal with various aspects of African art. These serve as unique source materials for researchers and Africanists. For a description of the African art collection and the research laboratory in the Center for Ethnic Music, see entries C5 and D1.

J9 Howard University—Department of Afro-American Studies

1. *Department of Afro-American Studies*
   P.O. Box 746
   Howard University
   Washington, D.C. 20059
   636-7253

2. Russell L. Adams, Chairman

3. The department, which was established in September 1969, offers a Bachelor of Arts degree to students seeking an interdisciplinary, comparative, Pan-African, liberal arts education. The program seeks to provide a fundamental understanding of the political, economic, and social forces which have shaped Afro-American experience in the New World and to facilitate research and creative effort in the area of Afro-American studies. The curriculum reflects the interdisciplinary nature of the program, with emphasis on various academic disciplines such as sociology, history, political science, economics, and the arts. At present, students may choose a wide range of courses leading to concentration in the following 3 areas: social analysis, political analysis, and cultural analysis.

   Though the focus is primarily on the black experience in the Western hemisphere, Africa and its historical background are given significant coverage in the curriculum.

4. See entries for Afro-American Resource Center and Howard University Libraries, A19, A20, and A21.

J10 Howard University—Department of History

1. *Department of History*
   Howard University
   Washington, D.C. 20059
   636-7030

2. Joseph E. Harris, Chairman

3. While it provides instruction in various specialized areas, the department places special emphasis on the Afro-American experience, Africa, and the African diaspora.

   At the undergraduate level students may select Africa as their area of concentration and are offered a wide selection of courses focusing on all geographical regions of Africa.

   The department also awards a Master of Arts and Doctor of Philosophy degree in African history. Over 32 courses are offered. They include: Problems in African History, The Religious Factor in African History, European Imperialism and Africa, Plural Societies in East Africa, African Economic History, History of African Nationalism, and

Comparative Colonialism and Nationalism in Africa. Over the past few years the department has had visiting professors from African universities.

In the past the department has sponsored guest lectures by distinguished speakers in Africa-related fields. These talks are open to the public. For more information, contact the department office.

4.   See the Founders Library, entry A20.

Note: In addition to the above-mentioned departments, the Department of Anthropology also offers some courses in the archeology and anthropology of Africa.

J11 Howard University—School of Communications

1.   *2600 4th Street, NW*
        Washington, D.C. 20059
        636-7690

2.   Lionel Barrow, Dean
        Ted Roberts, Acting Chairman, Radio, Television, and Film

3.   The Radio, TV, and Film Department of the school (636-7927) offers a wide range of courses leading to a B.A. in film and broadcasting. Of special interest to researchers should be the course in Third World cinema, with its strong emphasis on Africa. The department does not maintain its own collection of African films but rents them for class lectures.

4.   See entry A20.

J12 Johns Hopkins University—School of Advanced International Studies—Center of Middle East Studies

1.   *School of Advanced International Studies*
        Johns Hopkins University
        1740 Massachusetts Avenue, NW
        Washington, D.C. 20036
        785-6200

2.   Dr. Majid Khadduri, Director of Middle East Studies
        Gerald Lampe, Head of the Arabic Language Program

3.   SAIS offers an interdisciplinary program leading to a Masters of Arts and Doctor of Philosophy degree. It also offers a 1-year program leading to a Master of International Public Policy designed primarily for mid-career government officials and business executives (U.S. and foreign). Students generally select 1 geographic area, while taking courses in international economics (required), international law, and diplomacy. Those who select the Middle East as their field of concentration are required to obtain proficiency in the Arabic language. This program is directed principally toward training professionals, and therefore in ad-

dition to academic learning, emphasis is placed on methods of critical analysis and policy formulation.

More than 15 courses are offered on the Middle East alone. They focus on the history and politics of the Middle East, Islamic law and institutions, U.S. foreign policy in the Middle East, modern North African developments, economic problems of the Middle East, and related topics.

In addition to the academic program, the faculty and students of the Center of Middle East Studies are involved in a number of activities which should be of interest to Africanists. The faculty is engaged in several research projects, most of which result in published articles or books.

The center also has a long-standing association with the Middle East Institute (see entry H21). The 2 institutions share facilities, programs and, on occasion, personnel. In 1978 they cosponsored a conference which focused on "Changing Patterns in Partnership: The United States and the Middle East, 1978."

The Middle East Center also maintains a close working relationship with the Shaybani Society of International Law.

In addition to organizing conferences, seminars, and workshops, the center also sponsors a number of lectures by visiting scholars and specialists on Mideast issues. These lectures cover a wide range of subjects such as: "The Nile and Economic Development," "Approaches to the Study of the Middle East," "Political Dynamics in the Sudan," "Society and Politics in Egypt," "Southern Problems and National Integration in and Sudan," and several other topics relating to Africa.

The Middle East Club, a student organization, sponsors lectures, film showings, seminars, and meetings with Arab students in the Washington area.

4. See entry A37 for the SAIS Library.

J13 Johns Hopkins University—School of Advanced International Studies—Program of African Studies

1. *Room 414*
   1740 Massachusetts Avenue, NW
   Washington, D.C. 20036
   785-6253

2. Vernon McKay, Professor and Director

3. Three disciplines dominate this graduate school, namely, political science, history, and economics. Consequently, the focus of the Program of African Studies is on these 3 areas as they apply to non-Arab Africa. (For North Africa see The Center for Middle Eastern Studies.) Students enrolled in SAIS may concentrate in African affairs, and currently the program counts 34 M.A. candidates and 12 Ph.D. candidates. All participants are expected to learn French or another non-English language. In recent years the study of African languages has been encouraged.

In addition to the degree program, Professor Lystad directs seminars in diplomacy for diplomats from recently independent countries. Many

Africans from Washington embassies participate in this year-long program, which usually focuses on a theme such as American policy toward Africa.

The third part of the program is the parliamentary conference on Africa under the director, Professor McKay. Members of Congress, Members of Parliament, and Canadian legislators meet together to talk about major problems in Africa or between Africa and other countries.

The school also sponsors a Friday noon seminar in which scholars, government officials, visiting African intellectuals, and leaders make a presentation and discuss current problems of politics and development with students. Generally reserved for students, but permission may be granted to attend.

4. Students use the library of SAIS (see entry A37). In addition, 44 files of clippings, pamphlets, speeches, and documents belonging to Professor McKay are at the disposal of students.

J14 Maryland University—Afro-American Studies Program

1. *Room 2169, New Social Sciences Building*
    University of Maryland
    College Park, Maryland 20742
    (301) 454-5666

2. Al-Tony Gilmore, Director

3. The program awards a Bachelor of Arts and Bachelor of Science degree in Afro-American studies. The student may select any one of 3 areas of concentration—Africa, U.S., and the Caribbean. At least half of the courses offered in the program focus on Africa. They include introductory courses, courses in African ideology, economic development, political movements, and several others. The only African language currently offered is Swahili.

    The Afro-American Studies Program in cooperation with the Southern African Research Association sponsors an annual Conference on Southern Africa at which research papers and reports are presented by leading scholars. It also produces the *Journal of Southern African Affairs.*

4. The program maintains its own library which consists of general reference works, newspapers, periodicals, and monographs. (Also see entry A28.)

Note: Maryland University's Baltimore campus also offers a B.A. and M.A. degree in Afro-American studies.

J15 National War College—Department of International Studies

1. *Director of African Studies*
    National War College
    Washington, D.C. 20319
    693-8383

2. William B. Davis, Director of African Studies

3. The Department of International Studies of the National War College offers an elective course on Africa entitled "U.S. National Security Interests in Africa." This course focuses on the political, social, and economic developments in Africa from the colonial period to the present day, with particular emphasis on U.S. security interests.

    The department also has a regular guest lecture program. Ambassadors of African countries and other distinguished Africanists are invited to speak on a wide range of subjects.

J16 University of the District of Columbia—Department of History

1. *425 2d Street, NE*
    Washington, D.C. 20001
    727-2534

2. Dr. Ali Bakri, Chairman

3. The department awards a Bachelor of Arts degree in history. Students may select Africa as their major area of concentration. The program offers several Africa-related courses which include: Introduction to African History, I and II; History of Pan-Africanism; History of West Africa; History of East Africa and North East Africa; History of Islam in Africa; History of African Liberation Movements; African Diplomatic History; and Seminar in African History.

    In addition to the above courses, the department also sponsors lectures and workshops in African history.

K United States Government Agencies

United States Government Agencies Entry Format (K)

1. General information
   a. *address; telephone number(s)*
   b. conditions of access

2. Support for research and use of consultants (in-house research, contract research, research grants, employment of consultants)

3. Bibliographic resources (records of research sponsored by the government and/or private institutions, bibliographies issued)

4. Library or research facility

5. Publications by the agency of potential interest to researchers

---

K1 Agency for International Development (AID)

1. a. *State Department Building*
      320 21st Street, NW
      Washington, D.C. 20523
      655-4000 (Information)
      632-1850 (Freedom-of-Information inquiries)

   b. Not open to the public. Appointments with department personnel should be made in advance.

2. An agency of the State Department, AID is responsible for the foreign economic assistance programs of the United States. Development-assistance programs of AID focus mainly on agriculture, nutrition, health care, population planning, education, housing, and development planning. Less-developed countries are the major recipients of the programs.

   AID conducts a great deal of research on Africa. The bulk of this research is produced under contract. The agency provides research grants to universities and institutions and periodically employs specialists as consultants. The personnel of the various offices are pleased to engage in discussions with individual scholars, but prior appointment is advisable.

3. Specific information about bibliographic resources is under each division.

Summaries of agency-sponsored research studies are published in the quarterly *AID Research and Development Abstracts*. A multivolume series *Catalogue of Research Literature for Development* provides abstracts of cumulative AID-sponsored research since 1962, by subject.

4. Consult the section on the Development Information Center (entry A2) in this *Guide*.

BUREAU FOR AFRICA (AFR)

Office of the Assistant Administrator

There are many offices under the Office of the Assistant Administrator which the Africanist should be aware of. These include the Office of Development Resources; Development Planning; Regional Affairs; Eastern African Affairs; Central and Anglophone West African Affairs; Sahel and Francophone West African Affairs; and Southern African Affairs.

The Bureau for Africa is responsible for the planning, formulation, implementation, management, and evaluation of regional and bilateral development-assistance activities pertaining to Africa. The AFR works in close conjunction with the Office of Food for Peace, Office of Foreign Disaster Assistance, and the Office of Housing.

AID programs in Africa focus on the development of the continent and the economic well-being of its people. The Geographic Area Offices advise on the formulation of bureau and agency polices and strategies, direct and supervise the activities of the country desks, and oversee the country programs in the area.

The country-desk officers are the most valuable resource in the Africa Bureau for the researcher, as they maintain country-specific information and expertise on political, social, and economic matters relating to a specific country. They can provide researchers with unclassified agency materials, including field reports from AID missions, working documents, and program-evaluation studies. A particularly valuable source of information is the *Development Assistance Program* (DAP) field reports.

BUREAU FOR NEAR EAST (AA/NE)

Office of Egypt/Israeli Affairs (NE/EI)
James R. Roberts   632-9048
Office of Near Eastern/North African Affairs
Tunisia/Morocco
Louis C. Stamberg   632-8306

This bureau's responsibilities are similar to those of the Africa Bureau, except for the fact that the countries of North Africa fall under its jurisdiction.

SAHEL DEVELOPMENT PROGRAM

AID's development assistance to the Sahel dates back to the early 1960s, when the majority of the Sahelian countries obtained independence. Since the great drought of 1968-74, AID's activities in the Sahel have been intensified.

The Sahel Development Program is unique in its scope and ambition. It integrates the efforts of some 20 countries and international organizations. It provides for the development and support of a comprehensive long-term program to develop the Sahelian region under the overall aegis of the Club du Sahel. The goal is the complete economic and ecological reformation of the region, self-sufficiency, and sustained socioeconomic development. AID projects in the Sahel encompass agriculture, livestock, and fisheries; human resources; health, water, nutrition, and population; and ecology and reforestation.

The staff of the Sahel Development Program welcomes discussions with interested scholars and can also assist in obtaining further information.

The Reference and Documents Room of the Sahel Development Program contains unpublished reports, papers, and working documents of the Club du Sahel, all of which are available to researchers. For more information, call Cynthia Seck (632-3910). Some useful sources of information include:

AID, *Africa Programs Including Sahel Development Program: Fiscal Year 1978;*

————, *Opportunity for Self-Reliance: An Overview of the Sahel Development Potential* (1976);

————, *Reports to the United States Congress: Proposal for a Long-Term Comprehensive Development Program for the Sahel* (1976). Part I deals with "Major Findings and Programs" and Part II consists of "Technical Background Papers";

————, *United States Response to the Sahel Drought* (1977).

OFFICE OF FOOD FOR PEACE (FFP)

1. a. *Room 249, Pomponio Plaza*
1735 North Lynn Street
Arlington, Virginia 22209
(703) 235-9220

4.   This office is responsible for the coordination of AID's role in the Food for Peace Program in accordance with interagency agreements. It is the focal point in the agency for the implementation of PL 480 (The Agricultural Trade Development and Assistance Act of 1954). Under this program, food aid is supplied to Africa for economic development and humanitarian purposes, on a bilateral government-to-government basis as well as through voluntary organizations. For more information contact Stephen French (235-9173) for African programs and Buddy Dodson (235-9195) for North African programs.

Scholars should know about 2 useful publications which provide more information on AID food aid programs in Africa. They are: AID, *Report to the Congress on Famine in Sub-Sahara Africa* (June 1975) and AID, *U.S. Overseas Loans and Grants and Assistance from Inter-*

national Organizations (pp. 87-139 deal with AID programs in Africa and also provide a summary of programs by country and appropriation).

OFFICE OF U.S. FOREIGN DISASTER ASSISTANCE (OFDA)
632-8924

OFDA administers the U.S. government's international disaster assistance program. This program involves a wide range of activities which consist of providing emergency relief to victims of natural and manmade disasters; monitoring all potential and actual disaster situations; assisting in rehabilitation; and encouraging foreign disaster preparedness and supporting the efforts of international organizations and voluntary agencies involved in similar programs. The Office of U.S. Foreign Disaster Assistance publishes disaster relief case reports. There are over 36 case reports dealing with various disasters in individual countries of Africa. In addition, the office also publishes country profiles. Both these publications are available to researchers.

A regional disaster preparedness seminar is planned for the Sahelian region for next year.

BUREAU FOR INTRAGOVERNMENTAL AND INTERNATIONAL AFFAIRS (AA/IIAA)

Office of International Affairs (IIA/IA)
Kenneth M. Kauffman, Dept. Assistant Administrator 632-0833

This AID office is the liaison with international organizations such as OECD and UNDP.

BUREAU FOR DEVELOPMENT SUPPORT (DBS)
632-8558

The main function of this bureau is to provide technical expertise and support to AID field missions throughout the world. Within each of its numerous offices can be found staff members with technical expertise in African aspects of their field of specialization.

All the various offices in the Bureau for Development Support have programs pertaining to Africa. Researchers should contact the individual offices for pertinent information. These are: Office of Rural Development (703) 235-8918; Office of Agriculture (703) 235-8945; Office of Education and Human Resources (703) 235-9015; Office of Development Administration (703) 235-9027; Office of Health (703) 235-8929; Office of Population (703) 235-9677; and the Office of Urban Development (703) 235-8902. (N.B.: All offices are located in the Rosslyn Plaza Building, 1601 Kent Street, Arlington, Virginia 22209.)

BUREAU FOR PROGRAM AND POLICY COORDINATION (PPC)
Walter F. Stettner, African Coordinator 632-2602

The bureau is mainly responsible for policy development and analysis and review of development programs. The regional coordinator for Africa serves as a liaison between the global policy perspectives of the bureau and the regional policy interests of the Bureau for Africa.

OFFICE OF PROGRAM INFORMATION AND ANALYSIS
SERVICES (PPC/PIAS)

Statistics and Reports Division
Room 669, Pomponio Plaza
1735 North Lynn Street
Arlington, Virginia 22209
(703) 325-9836

The Statistics and Reports Division produces several unclassified publications of interest to Africanists. These include the AID, *Economic Data Book: Africa;* the periodically updated *Food and Total Agricultural Production in Less Developed Countries, 1950–   ,* which gives statistical indexes of food and agricultural production for Africa, by country; *Selected Economic Data for the Less Developed Countries;* and *U.S. Overseas Loans and Grants, and Assistance from International Organizations: Obligations and Loan Authorizations* (updated annually), which contains statistical data for Africa by region and country from 1946 to date.

OFFICE OF PUBLIC AFFAIRS (OPA)
Arnold H. Dadian, Freedom of Information Officer   632-1850

This office can provide assistance to researchers in gaining access to AID documents. It also handles freedom-of-information requests.

K2 Agriculture Department (USDA)

1. a. *Independence Avenue between 12th and 14th Streets, SW*
      Washington, D.C. 20250
      447-2791 (Information)

   b. Open to the public. Researchers are advised to call ahead for an appointment.

2. Research on agriculture in Africa and related topics is undertaken by many divisions of the department. Most of the research is done in-house.

3. Many of the research records and studies are accessible to scholars. As time permits, the staff in various divisions can assist scholars in locating these materials. Since these records are primarily intended for internal use, their availability is subject to limitations.

4. See Libraries section of this *Guide* for the National Agricultural Library (entry A30).

5. See under the pertinent divisions.

FOREIGN AGRICULTURAL SERVICE (FAS)

USDA South Building
14th Street and Independence Avenue, SW

Thomas Hughes, Administrator   447-3935
Arthur Bailey, International Economist (Africa)   447-7727

This division should be the first point of contact at USDA for Africanists.

Perhaps the most valuable resources for the researcher here are the personnel who have had extensive experience in Africa. The Foreign Agricultural Service maintains agricultural attachés in U.S. embassies and consulates of various African countries. These attachés provide current information on various aspects of the agricultural situation in their own areas, such as agricultural production, government regulations, supply-and-demand information, trade variants, etc. Their reports, most of which are unclassified, can be obtained from the FAS Communications, Reports and Records Office (447-6135).

International Trade Policy Division   447-4371

This unit administers and coordinates functions of the department relating to the General Agreement on Tariffs and Trade (GATT) and other matters bearing on international trade policies and programs.

Trade Operations Division

The division's main function is to plan and conduct bilateral consultations on trade issues and problems and maintain up-to-date tariff schedules, trade data for all countries, and GATT documents.

Foreign Commodity Analysis   447-7233

Staff economists of this unit analyze world agricultural commodities from the standpoint of production, trade, competition, marketing and supply, consumption, etc. This unit is organized into divisions for individual commodity groups. The focus is therefore worldwide, not on a geographical basis.

FAS publications which are available to researchers without charge include:

Foreign Agriculture, published weekly, provides current information and background on world agricultural developments of consequence to U.S. producers and exporters.

Foreign Agricultural Circulars. FAS issues a number of circulars at irregular intervals on various commodities and export services, as well as specialized publications pertaining to specific commodities. Researchers may obtain these free of charge by writing to the FAS Information Division, Information Services Staff, Room 5918 South, USDA, Washington, D.C. 20250. A few of these, particularly on oilseeds and products, cotton, cocoa, and coffee may be of special interest to Africanists.

Weekly Roundup of World Production and Trade gives news items and statistics on various commodities and a summary of developments in world production and trade.

FAS's miscellaneous *Special Reports* occasionally deal with Africa, e.g., *Coffee Production in Africa* (September 1975), *Cotton in Tanzania* (June 1970), and *Cotton in Uganda* (February 1970).

ECONOMICS, STATISTICS, AND COOPERATIVE SERVICE (ESCS)

Foreign Demand and Competition Division
Developing Countries Program Area

Robert E. Marx, Project Leader, Africa and the Middle East   447-8966

This division's main task is to keep abreast of the agricultural situation in the developing countries, with primary emphasis on agricultural development and trade (crops, livestock, irrigation, rural government projects, and agribusiness). The 6 members of the staff are each assigned several countries of Africa and the Middle East. They conduct extensive research and maintain up-to-date trade and production figures for these countries. In contrast to the FAS, this division focuses on countries, not commodities. As a result of its country orientation, this division is a major resource for country-specific information, including statistics and current data on various African countries.

The numerous publications of this office provide useful material not available elsewhere. This includes *Annual Reports,* periodic *Bulletins* on some specific aspect of trade and agriculture, and *Statistical Bulletins.* The Africanist should find the following of great value:

Economics of Agriculture: Reports and Publications Issued or Sponsored by USDA's Economic Research Service, October 1966–June 1974 (reprinted May 1976);

USDA Economic Research Service, *Africa and West Asia Agricultural Situation,* review of past year, outlook for the coming year, and highlights of the agricultural year for 32 countries in Africa and West Asia;

————, *Angola's Agricultural Economy in Brief,* Report no. 139;

————, *Indices of Agricultural Production in Africa and the Near East, 1956–1975,* Report no. 556;

————, *Mozambique's Agricultural Economy in Brief,* Report no. 116;

USDA, Economics, Statistics, and Cooperative Service, *FATUS* (Foreign Agricultural Trade of the United States), monthly, free on request;

World Agricultural Situation (published 3 times a year) and 7 regional reports.

National Economic Analysis Division
  Agricultural History Program
  Wayne Rasmussen, Supervisory Historian   447-8183
  Documentation Center   447-8684

The Agricultural History Program maintains 2 reference aids of potential significance to Africanists. The first is a bibliographic card index of books and articles published in the U.S., U.K., and Canada, pertaining to agricultural history. Material on Africa is organized on the basis of individual countries. The second is a comprehensive vertical file of documents relating to the agricultural programs of the USDA and other government agencies. Both reference tools are accessible to researchers.

WORLD FOOD AND AGRICULTURAL OUTLOOK AND SITUATION BOARD
J. Dawson Ahalt, Acting Chairman   447-8651

The board provides a focal point for the dissemination of reliable and consistent information on domestic and world agriculture. It assumes all the functions previously carried out by the Outlook and Situation

Board and, in addition, it is responsible for reviewing and coordinating Foreign Agricultural Service reports and other data on the world food and agricultural situations.

OFFICE OF THE GENERAL SALES MANAGER (OGSM)
447-2612

USDA South Building
14th Street and Independence Avenue, SW

James F. Keefer, Geographic Coordinator for Africa   447-6705

This office in collaboration with AID administers United States food aid and food sales programs in Africa. The Public Law 480 Food for Peace Program provides assistance to developing countries in their effort to eradicate hunger and malnutrition. This program also seeks to promote economic and community development in these countries and provide disaster relief.

The office publishes *Food for Peace,* an annual report on agricultural activities carried out under the PL 480 program. Title I of this program provides for the concessional sale of agricultural commodities to friendly countries. Egypt has been the major recipient in this category. Others include Tunisia, Ethiopia, Tanzania, and Guinea. Since 1967, all such sales agreements have contained self-help measures to which recipient nations have committed themselves.

Title II of PL 480 authorizes donations of food on behalf of the American people, to provide famine and disaster relief, combat malnutrition, and promote economic development.

U.S. Export Sales, a weekly statistical bulletin, gives information on the commercial sales of private U.S. food exporters.

INTERNATIONAL DEVELOPMENT STAFF (IDS)
James A. Black, Program Leader for Africa   235-2283

This office provides technical assistance advisers for African agricultural development projects sponsored by the U.S. Agency for International Development. It also coordinates agricultural training programs for foreign nationals in the United States.

K3 Air Force Department

1. a. *The Pentagon*
       Washington, D.C. 20330
       545-6700

    b. Security clearance required to enter the Pentagon.

2.   The bulk of research on Africa is handled in-house.

OFFICE OF INFORMATION

Public Information Division   695-7793

   Magazine and Book Branch   695-7793
   Community Relations Branch   695-1128

Researchers who wish to gain access to Air Force records or who need clearance must first contact the Office of Information. The staff provides assistance to scholars in locating relevant materials. All research must also be cleared by the Office for Security Review (697-3222).

OFFICE OF AIR FORCE HISTORY
Maj. General John W. Huston, Chief

Bolling Air Force Base, 4th floor, Building 5681
Washington, D.C. 20332

This office may be the most important resource for Africanists in the Air Force Department. The office maintains a library containing government documents and personal papers of Air Force personnel. A careful search should unearth interesting items. Most of the relevant items pertain to the World War II period. The following publications should be of use in locating Africa-related materials:

Albert F. Simpson Historical Research Center, *Personal Files in the U.S. Air Force Historical Collections* (June, 1975);

———, *U.S. Air Force Oral History Catalog* (1977);

Samuel Duncan Miller, comp., *An Aerospace Bibligraphy* (Government Printing Office, 1978);

Lawrence J. Paszek, comp. *United States Air Force History: A Guide to Documentary Sources* (1973).

For further information researchers should contact William Heimdahl, Archivist (767-5088).

ADMINISTRATIVE ASSISTANT TO THE SECRETARY

Research and Analysis Division
Harry Zubkoff, Chief   695-2884

This division maintains vertical file collections. The materials are arranged by subject and chronologically.

DIRECTORATE OF ADMINISTRATION

Documentation Systems Division
Documentation Information and Services Section
Kip War, Chief   695-4992

This section handles requests for information based on the Freedom of Information Act.

K4 Army Department

1. a. *The Pentagon*
      Washington, D.C. 20310
      545-6700

   b. Access to the Pentagon is limited to persons with security clearance.

2.   Much of the agency research is performed in-house by its own personnel. Occasionally the department will engage individuals and institutions for contract work.

4.   Also see entry **F7.**

CHIEF OF PUBLIC AFFAIRS   697-4122

Public Information Division   697-2351

This should be the first point of contact for researchers seeking information and materials on Africa. Scholars should, however, be forewarned that both the Army Department and the Air Force are minor resources for the Africanist. Furthermore, what little information they possess is not easily accessible, because of the sensitive nature of their operations.

THE ADJUTANT GENERAL   695-0163

Records Management Division
Guy B. Oldaker, Chief   693-7830
Forrestal Builidng, Room GA 084
1000 Independence Avenue, SW
Washington, D.C. 20314

> Access and Release Branch
> W. Anderson, Chief   693-1847

> Program Branch
> Wendell Boardman, Chief   693-1937

> Declassification Operations Branch
> John Hatcher, Chief   (301) 763-2742

Researchers trying to locate specific Army historical records and documents should contact this division. The Access and Release Branch not only grants clearance and access to classified materials but also handles Freedom of Information requests.

DEPUTY CHIEF OF STAFF FOR OPERATIONS AND PLANS   695-2904

This division is mainly concerned with questions of strategy, war plans, and politico-military affairs. African countries have not traditionally figured prominently in its work.

DEPUTY CHIEF OF STAFF FOR RESEARCH, DEVELOPMENT, AND ACQUISITION   697-8186

This office is mainly concerned with technical matters such as armaments, munitions, and the like.

U.S. ARMY CENTER OF MILITARY HISTORY   693-5002

Forrestal Building, Room 6A 015
1000 Independence Avenue, SW
Washington, D.C. 20314

Dr. Maurice Matloff, Chief Historian

The center focuses on virtually all aspects of the U.S. Army and its activities, at home and abroad. Most of the center's research is done by staff specialists. The center's collection consists of 5,000-6,000 unpublished manuscripts which should be of interest to students of military history.

The Africanist will discover considerable matter here which deals with U.S. operations in North and Northwest Africa during World War II. The following unpublished manuscripts should be noted:

Africa-Middle East Theater, Headquarters. *History of the United States Army Forces in Liberia (USAFIL)* 1942–1946.

Africa-Middle East Theatre, Office of AC of S, G-2, Historical Section. *History of Africa-Middle East Theatre United States Army (Including USMNAN and USAFIME) to 30 April 1946* (8 volumes). Deals with U.S. Army operations in North Africa, Eritrea, West Africa, Libya, Tripoli, and Benghazi, as well as Liberia.

Persian Gulf Command, Headquarters, U.S. Army. Office of Technical Information. *History of the Persian Gulf Command* (7 volumes).

In addition to the titles listed above, there are over 100 files (shelved under "Historians' background material files," arranged geographically) comprising war diaries, dispatches, telegrams, radio-news-broadcast press releases, operations reports, and statistics which deal with U.S. Army operations in North Africa–Tunisia and the Middle East.

Presently there is no published catalog of the center's holdings. The existing card catalog is not a reliable indicator of the holdings, as a large amount of the material has been removed or discarded without removing the appropriate cards. Researchers should consult Hannah M. Zeidlik, Chief of the Historical Record Branch, for help in locating relevant materials.

Plans are under way for a new up-to-date card catalog.

K5 Central Intelligence Agency (CIA)

1. a. *Langley, Virginia*
    (703) 351-1100 (Information)
    (703) 351-7676 (Public Affairs)

    b. Closed to anyone without a security clearance.

2. The CIA occasionally funds contract research, primarily for technical studies and for research on methodology and model-building. The agency also employs foreign-area specialists as outside consultants. Research and consultant contracts are administered by the Coordinator for Academic Relations and External Analytical Support, James King (351-5075).

3. Most of the work undertaken by the CIA is classified, and information concerning the agency is often difficult to obtain. African specialists in the Office of Political Research and Analysis, the National Foreign Assessment Center, and other offices, study and analyze African affairs; however, private researchers do not have access to them. Outside researchers who wish to obtain any information should first contact the Public Affairs Office.

Internal records of the CIA are accessible only through Freedom of Information Act (FOI) processes. Information and Privacy Coordinator Gene Wilson (351-7486) handles all FOI matters.

At present, there is no centralized collection of CIA records released through the Freedom of Information Act. Many such documents are, however, listed in the *Declassified Documents Quarterly Catalog* published by the commercial Carrollton Press of Arlington, Virginia. Selected declassified CIA materials may be more easily available from the National Archives and Records Service (see entry B3).

4. The CIA Library (351-7701) is inaccessible to private researchers. However, some materials may be obtained through institutional interlibrary loan channels. The library's unclassified book holdings are indexed in the computerized Ohio College Library Catalog (OCLC), Columbus, Ohio.

The CIA's large map collection contains both classified and unclassified materials. The latter holdings are generally duplicated by the map collections of the Library of Congress (see entry E3) and the Interior Department's Geological Survey (see entry E2).

5. The CIA releases most of its unclassified publications through the Document Expediting (DOCEX) Project of the Library of Congress. Since 1972, when this program was initiated, a large number of unclassified agency publications have been distributed on a subscription basis. Most of these publications pertain to foreign economic and political affairs and are listed in an annually updated catalog: National Foreign Assessment Center, *CIA Publications Released to the Public through Library of Congress DOCEX* (July 1978). Items of interest to Africanists include: *Annotated Bibliography on Transnational and International Terrorism* (December 1976); *Arms Flow to LDCs: US-Soviet Comparisons 1974–1977* (November 1978); the monthly *Chiefs of State and Cabinet Members of Foreign Governments; Communist Aid to the Less Developed Countries of the Free World, 1976* (August 1977); *Handbook of Economic Statistics, 1977; International Terrorism in 1976* (July 1977); the semiannual *National Basic Intelligence Factbook* (which contains political, military, and economic data on foreign countries); and *Potential Implications of Trends in World Population, Food Production, and Climate* (August 1974). Private researchers interested in obtaining these publications should contact Photoduplication Service, Library of Congress, Washington, D.C. 20540. For information concerning subscription service, write to the Document Expediting (DOCEX) Project, Library of Congress, Washington, D.C. 20540.

In addition, the CIA also produces general reference maps of foreign countries. These multicolored maps identify major roads, population density, industries, location of natural resources, and other specific features. Individual maps are available for the following African countries: Egypt, Ethiopia, Guinea, Ivory Coast, Kenya, Liberia, Libya, Madagascar, Mauritius, Morocco, Mozambique, Nigeria, Senegal and Gambia, and Tunisia. Africanists would also find the following of considerable use: *Africa* (1977, volume 2 of the *Maps of the World's Nations*) and *Atlas: Issues in the Middle East* (1973). Maps and atlases may be ordered from the Superintendent of Documents, Government Printing Office, Washington, D.C. 20402, or by calling 783-3238.

K6 Commerce Department

1. a. *14th Street and Constitution Avenue, NW*
      Washington, D.C. 20230
      377-2000 (Information)

   b. Open to the public.

2. Some divisions of the department engage in research on Africa and/or employ scholars on contract research or as consultants.

4. Consult the libraries section of this *Guide* for a description of the main library and its branches (entry A7).

5. The department publishes a biweekly news magazine, *Commerce America*, which contains information on foreign and domestic business conditions. A semiannual issue deals with the world trade outlook. Researchers will find the *Commerce Publications Catalog and Index* useful. Call the Office of Publications (377-3721) for copies and information.

INDUSTRY AND TRADE ADMINISTRATION (ITA)   377-5087

The primary function of the Industry and Trade Administration (formerly the Domestic and International Business Administration) is to provide information and assistance to U.S. business firms in improving and expanding their overseas operations. The focus is on the development of export markets.

Bureau of Export Development

Office of International Marketing   377-4231
Africa Division
Max Miles, Country Marketing Manager   377-4927

The staff of this division provides information and guidance to American businesses on trade openings, state of economy, export quotas and tariffs, and business opportunities in African countries. Its main function is to assist in establishing buyer-seller contacts through provision of marketing informational and promotional activities. The latter consists of organizing seminar and trade missions, catalog shows, and participating in international trade fairs such as the one held in Lagos in November 1977.

There is a separate "country marketing manager" for the Near East and North Africa.

The Office of International Marketing produces in-depth foreign-country market research surveys and studies (on a foreign contract research basis). It also publishes a series of periodicals. These include:

Country Market Sectoral Surveys;
Foreign Economic Trends and Their Implications for the United States

(mainly country-reports from U.S. embassies abroad, containing statistical data);
Global Market Surveys;
International Marketing News Memos, periodic publications highlighting some significant trends;
Overseas Business Reports, which are updated annually.

The office also maintains an International Marketing Information Center (377-2470). Located in Room 4051, this center, which contains published and unpublished reports, is open to researchers.

Bureau of International Economic Policy and Research (BIEPR) 377-3022

The bureau is responsible for the department's international economic research, analysis, and policy planning.
Office of Country Affairs 377-4506

In this office, specialists monitor trade and economic patterns in Africa. This is, therefore, the most important resource within the Commerce Department for country-specific information.

Office of International Economic Research 377-5638

This office collects and studies U.S. and foreign trade and economic data. It publishes the monthly *Trends in U.S. Foreign Trade,* which contains data for Africa by country and commodity; and annual *Market Share Reports* series (by country), which compares U.S. market performance with that of other major supplier nations; and a quarterly statistics report, *International Economic Indicators.* Other publications include: *Selected Basic References on Trade Barriers and International Trade Flows* (1976); *Survey of Current International Economic Research,* a periodically updated bibliography; and *U.S. Trade with Developing Economies: The Growing Importance of Manufactured Goods* (1975).

There are 2 reference facilities, both of which are open to the public. The U.S. Foreign Trade Reference Room (377-2185), located in Room 5889, is a mini-library that contains a complete set of U.S. trade statistics from 1947 to date; Census Bureau statistics and trade reports; and extensive unpublished material (mainly trade data) on microfilm and microfiche. The World Trade Reference Room (377-4855), in Room 5899-A, maintains a collection of the official trade-statistics publications of all foreign nations.

Office of International Trade Policy 377-5327

The office is mainly concerned with international trade negotiations, foreign tariffs, and import quotas.

Office of International Finance and Investment 377-4925

The broader responsibilities of this office consist of assessing the impact of U.S. assistance programs for international development and advising the department on the formulation of investment policies. Its work will be only of peripheral interest to Africanists.

BUREAU OF THE CENSUS   (301) 763-7662

Suitland Road and Silver Hill Road
Suitland, Maryland

Mail: Department of Commerce
Washington, D.C. 20233

The bureau collects and maintains demographic and census materials for all countries, including Africa.

Note: There is a daily shuttle bus service between the Main Commerce Building in downtown Washington and the Census Bureau offices.

Foreign Trade Division

Federal Office Building 3
Suitland, Maryland 20233

This unit collects statistical data on U.S. exports and imports. Useful publications include the following:
   U.S. Bureau of Census, *Guide to Foreign Trade Statistics* (July 1975);
   ———, *U.S. Exports: World Areas by Commodity Groupings* (Report FT 455). Organized by continent and country of destination, it has a section on Africa;
   ———, *U.S. General Imports: World Areas by Commodity Groupings* (Report FT 155). Also has an index of world areas by continent and country.
   Monthly trade statistics and more detailed and current information are available on microfilm at the division.

Population Division

Scuderi Building
4235 28th Avenue
Marlow Heights, Maryland 20031

International Demographic Statistics Staff   (301) 763-2870

Country analysts in the Population Division's International Demographic Statistics Office collect in-depth data on all foreign countries including those in Africa. *World Population,* its annual publication, contains population statistics by country dating back to 1950. The Country Demographic Profiles series gives more detailed statistics, which include data on urban population, age-sex distribution, marital status, migration, fertility, mortality, family planning, education, labor force by occupation, etc.
   The unit's International Demographic Data Center (763-2834) can assist researchers in obtaining additional information and data.

BUREAU OF ECONOMIC ANALYSIS (BEA)   523-0777
Tower Building

14th and K Streets, NW
Washington, D.C. 20230

The Bureau of Economic Analysis monitors the state of the U.S. domestic economy. Its monthly *Survey of Current Business* will occasionally contain data pertaining to Africa. Its Reference Room (523-0595) in Room B-7 maintains the entire collection of BEA periodicals and staff papers.

International Investment Division   523-0660

This division studies the impact of multinational corporations and collects data on U.S. direct investments overseas. Its publications include: *Special Survey of U.S. Multinational Companies, 1970* (1972); *Survey of Current Business;* and *U.S. Direct Investment Abroad.* Though information on investments of individual companies in Africa cannot be made available, the staff can provide researchers with aggregate data on U.S. investments.

Balance of Payments Division   523-0620

This unit analyzes the United States' balance of payments and the international investment position. These statistics are published in the *Survey of Current Business.*

MARITIME ADMINISTRATION

Office of International Activities   377-5685

Researchers can confer with the staff regarding the administration's work relating to Africa, such as shipments of grain and other commodities to Africa.

Office of Trade Studies and Statistics   377-4758

This office compiles statistical data on U.S. ocean-borne trade with other countries, by country.

NATIONAL OCEANIC AND ATMOSPHERIC ADMINISTRATION (NOAA)   (301) 443-8910

Washington Science Center
6010 Executive Boulevard
Rockville, Maryland 20852

NOAA has several divisions scattered all over the D.C. area. It is, however, a minor resource for Africanists. Researchers who desire to obtain general information about the administration's activities should contact the Office of International Affairs (377-2977).

NATIONAL TECHNICAL INFORMATION SERVICE (NTIS)

425 13th Street, NW
Washington, D.C. 20004
557-4600 (General Information)

National Technical Information Service (NTIS)
5285 Port Royal Road
Springfield, Virginia 22161
(703) 557-4650 (Sales desk)

NTIS is a central source for the public sale of government-sponsored research, analyses, and reports. This voluminous information is provided in a variety of forms—microfilms, microfiche, and machine-processable data files.

NTIS' collection now exceeds 100,000 titles. Researchers can locate relevant items from the federally sponsored research reports published since 1964 by using the agency's on-line computer search service (NTISearch). In addition, the following publications may be of use: *Government Reports Announcement and Index; NTIS Information Services General Catalog; Subject Guide to the NTIS Information Collection; Weekly Government Abstracts.*

K7 Congress

1. a. *The Capitol*
   Washington, D.C. 20510
   224-3121

   b. The Senate and the House of Representatives galleries, as well as most committee hearings, are open to the public.

2. Both houses of Congress are in session throughout the year, wth periodic recesses. Congressional committees and subcommittees with jurisdiction over African matters are listed below. The manifold activities of the various committees can yield valuable information and material to the researcher. Committee staff members are often the most significant resource, for they possess not only expertise in a specific area but also maintain up-to-date information. They are generally willing to confer with scholars. The committees hold periodic meetings and convene hearings, which are open to the public. The law requires that these meetings and hearings be announced ahead of time. The announcements of committee activities appear in the *Daily Digest* section of the *Congressional Record* and are also published in the *Washington Post* each morning.

   Experts from the academic community and elsewhere frequently testify at the hearings, which can yield substantial oral and written testimony. Proceedings of these committee hearings are eventually published. Researchers who want to obtain the publications issued by a committee may request to be put on its mailing list.

   The Congressional Research Service is the principal research arm of the Congress. African specialists on its staff can also provide useful information on congressional activities relating to Africa.

4. The Library of Congress is described in the libraries section, entry A27.

5. The proceedings of the Senate and House of Representatives appear in the *Congressional Record,* published daily when Congress is in session. Committee publications are available both from the office of the committee and also commercially from the Government Printing Office (GPO) bookstores (see entry Q8). Subject bibliographies of congressional publications prepared by GPO are available without charge.

STANDING COMMITTEES OF THE SENATE

Agriculture, Nutrition, and Forestry   224-2035
Russell Senate Office Building, Room 322

This committee deals with agriculture in general (farm credit and security, crop insurance, soil conservation, etc.), also matters relating to food, nutrition, and hunger. Includes a Subcommittee on Foreign Agricultural Policy.

Armed Services   224-3871
Russell Senate Office Building, Room 212

The committee deals with military affairs and national defense, development of weapons systems and strategic materials. Includes a Subcommittee on Intelligence.

Banking, Housing, and Urban Affairs   224-7391
Dirksen Senate Office Building, Room 5300

The committee concerns itself with banking and currency and economic controls. It has a Subcommittee on International Finance (224-2854).

Finance   224-4515
Dirksen Senate Office Building, Room 2227

This committe reviews matters of reciprocal trade agreements, taxes, tariffs, import quotas, and foreign trade. It has a Subcommittee on International Trade.

Foreign Relations   224-4651
Dirksen Senate Office Building, Room 4229

The primary focus of this committee is relations with foreign nations, treaties, protection of American citizens abroad, the International Red Cross, Diplomatic Service, foreign interventions and declarations of war, the United Nations, and foreign loans. It has subcommittees on Foreign Economic Policy, Foreign Assistance, International Operations, Arms Control, and Near Eastern and South Asian Affairs.
    This is one of the most important committees for the Africanist.

Judiciary   224-5225
Dirksen Senate Office Building, Room 2226

The Judiciary Committee's concerns include immigration and natuarlization, espionage, and protection of trade and commerce. It has a Subcommittee on Immigration.

Select Intelligence   224-1700

The committee has legislative and budgetary authority over the CIA, FBI, and other components of the federal intelligence community.

STANDING COMMITTEES OF THE HOUSE OF REPRESENTATIVES
(No description is included for committees with interests that coincide with the Senate committees of the same name.)

Agriculture   225-2171
Longworth House Office Building, Room 1301

Appropriations   225-2771
The Capitol, Room H-218

The committee includes a Subcommittee on Foreign Operations.

Armed Services   225-4151
Rayburn House Office Building, Room 2120

Banking, Finance, and Urban Affairs   225-4247
Rayburn House Office Building, Room 2129

This committee includes a Subcommittee on International Development, Institutions, and Finance, and a Subcommittee on International Trade, Investment, and Monetary Policy.

International Relations   225-5021
Rayburn House Office Building, Room 2170

The jurisdiction of this committee includes foreign relations, establishment of boundary lines between the U.S. and foreign nations, foreign loans, international congresses and conferences, international trade, P.L. 480, export controls, international education, interventions abroad, and declarations of war. Researchers should make note of the following subcommittees:

Subcommittee on Africa

This is clearly the most important congressional committee for the Africanist, since it focuses specifically on Africa. The Africanist with a special interest in United States relations with Africa should follow the activities of this subcommittee closely. Over the past year, standing committee meetings have discussed matters such as: Southern African policy of the U.S.; economic assistance to Africa for fiscal year 1978; U.S.-Southern African relations; Rhodesian policy; aid policy; Soviet interests in Africa; security assistance for Africa; the African Bureau at AID; and U.S.-Uganda relations.

Subcommittee on Europe and the Middle East
Subcommittee on International Development Assistance
Subcommittee on International Economic Policy and Trade
Subcommittee on International Operations
Subcommittee on International Organizations
Subcommittee on International Security and Scientific Affairs

Interstate and Foreign Commerce   225-2927
Rayburn House Office Building, Room 2125

Merchant Marine and Fisheries   225-4047
Longworth House Office Building, Room 1334

Ways and Means   225-3625
Longworth House Office Building, Room 1102

This committee is concerned with reciprocal trade agreements, customs, etc.

JOINT COMMITTEES OF THE CONGRESS

Joint Economic Committee   224-5171
Dirksen Senate Office Building, Room G-133

This committee has a Subcommittee on International Economics.

Note: In addition, various Select and Special Committees of the Senate or House will occasionally focus on Africa-related topics.

K8 Congressional Research Service (CRS)

1. a. *Library of Congress, Main Building*
      10 1st Street, SE
      Washington, D.C. 20540
      287-5700

   b. Not open to the public.

2-3.   The Congressional Research Service provides reference and research assistance to members of Congress and the congressional committees. Staff members in the Foreign Affairs and National Defense Division produce research reports and background studies on African policy issues of current concern to Congress. These services are not available to private researchers. Individuals who wish to obtain specific research studies should contact the congressional member or committee which requested the work.

4.   See Library of Congress, entry A27.

5.   *Issue Briefs* published by CRS deal with major policy issues and provide a summary of pertinent legislative matters. They are distributed only to members of Congress. A monthly digest of CRS studies, the *CRS Review,* is also disseminated for congressional use. For copies of these publications, scholars should contact their congressional representatives. CRS also indexes periodical articles on current public policy issues (including foreign affairs, by country) from over 1,500 journals. This "Bibliographic Citation" file is available to researchers in machine-readable form through the Library of Congress' SCORPIO automated data base.

K9 Defense Department (DOD)

1. a. *The Pentagon*
      Washington, D.C. 20301
      545-6700

   b. Access limited to those with security clearance. Others should call to arrange for an appointment.

2.   Some divisions of DOD do undertake limited in-house research. Most research is, however, done on a contract basis.

3-4. See DOD Documentation Center, entry G5.

Africanists seeking materials for research purposes at DOD are likely to confront 2 problems—first, the difficulty of gaining access to the available materials (since most of the department's work deals with military and defense matters) and second, the paucity of materials on Africa. (Compared to other areas like Europe, China, and the U.S.S.R., interest in Africa until quite recently has been minimal.)

OFFICE OF THE SECRETARY OF DEFENSE (OSD)—PUBLIC AFFAIRS

Philip A. Farris, Staff Assistant for Public Correspondence   697-5737

This should be the first point of contact for researchers who need assistance in locating the relevant offices in the DOD.

ASSISTANT SECRETARY FOR INTERNATIONAL SECURITY AFFAIRS (ISA)   695-4351

Near Eastern, African, and South Asian Affairs
Robert J. Murray, Deputy Assistant Secretary   695-5223

The primary function of this office, which is responsible for all security matters, is to monitor political and military developments in Africa, the Near East, and South Asia. It also functions as a liaison between the State Department and the military. The in-house research undertaken by the agency specialists is largely unpublished and classified. The office also supports a limited amount of contract research.

ISA does not make available to the public any bibliographies of its published studies. Interested researchers should contact the staff for assistance in gaining access to the declassified materials. Examples of recent work sponsored by ISA include:

Kenneth L. Adelman, *U.S. Security Interests and Options in Central Africa* (Stanford Research Institute, International Strategic Studies Center, December 1977);

Nigeria: U.S. National Security Interests and Issues. Report sponsored by the Assistant Secretary of Defense for ISA (1977). The study deals primarily with Nigeria's U.N. voting behavior; the transition to civilian rule; and an analysis of policy alternatives on the Southern Africa problem.

ASSISTANT SECRETARY FOR INTELLIGENCE (DIRECTOR OF DEFENSE INTELLIGENCE)   695-0348

Defense Intelligence Agency   697-7072

DIA conducts substantial in-house research related to its defense intelligence activities, but all its work is classified. It has its own library, but nonagency researchers are prohibited access. Scholars interested in the declassified material at DIA should contact Mr. Louis E. Foster, Freedom of Information Officer, DIA, Washington, D.C. 20301.

Deputy Director of Defense Attaché System
Middle East and Africa Division   694-8666

The main function of this system is the management of the various defense attaché offices in Africa, and the selection, training, and evaluation of the personnel.

Office of the Secretary
Defense Security Assistance Agency   695-3291

This office implements the Military Assistance Program (MAP) of the DOD.

ADVANCED RESEARCH PROJECTS AGENCY (ARPA)   694-3032

Architect Building, Room 802
1400 Wilson Boulevard
Arlington, Virginia 22209

ARPA does not undertake any research of its own. The bulk of it is performed on a contract basis in such fields as strategic technology, material and natural sciences, nuclear monitoring, and cybernetics technology.

K10   Energy Department (DOE)

1. a. *20 Massachusetts Avenue, NW*
    Washington, D.C. 20001

   b. Access is monitored. Researchers should call ahead for an appointment.

2. DOE supports both in-house and contract research.

4. The Energy Library functions as a major repository for energy-related information. Its holdings consist of over 100,000 cataloged volumes, 4,000 periodical titles, and over 750,000 reports mostly on microfilm. Africa-related materials in the library are scattered among the various reports but can be retrieved by a literature search using the various data bases. The holdings of the library can be located in the computer-produced catalogs and indexes.

5. *Selected DOE Headquarters Publications Received by the Energy Library* is a useful bibliography which provides listings of publications issued from the U.S. Department of Energy.

ASSISTANT SECRETARY FOR INTERGOVERNMENTAL AND INSTITUTIONAL RELATIONS

Office of Public Affairs
James Bishop Jr., Director   252-5466
Public Inquiries Branch, Patrick Donnelly   566-7834

Office of Education, Business, and Labor Affairs
Lawrence Steward, Director   376-4070

ASSISTANT SECRETARY FOR INTERNATIONAL AFFAIRS
Harry E. Bergold Jr., Assistant Secretary   252-5800

This office has 5 primary elements corresponding to its responsibilities for international energy policy, programs, research and intelligence, trade and resource, and various key program support activities. It should be the first point of contact for the researcher.

Office of International Policy Development
Sarah Jackson, Deputy Assistant Secretary   254-6840

This office is responsible for overall international energy-policy analysis and development and for formulating export-import policies. It also has the task of promoting international cooperation involving energy resources and technologies.

Office of International Programs
J. Vanderryn, Director   376-4319

This office maintains current information and data on the energy sources and technologies of various foreign nations, negotiates bilateral and multilateral cooperative arrangements, and develops and implements nuclear policy. This office is also responsible for management of the Lesser Developed Countries' Program.

Office of International Trade and Resources
Peter Borre, Deputy Assistant Secretary

The main function of this office is to monitor world energy markets and trade to determine their impact on the price and security of U.S. energy supplies.

K11 Environmental Protection Agency (EPA)

1. a. *Waterside Mall West Tower*
      401 M Street, SW
      Washington, D.C. 20460
      755-2673

   b. Not all EPA offices are open to the public. Researchers should call ahead for an appointment.

2. The agency supports both in-house and contract research. Agency staff does engage in research relating to Africa, especially Egypt.

3. The library issues *EPA Reports Bibliography* (and quarterly *Supplements*). These are available from National Technical Information Service (NTIS).

4. The EPA headquarters library contains over 3,000 books; 1,100 periodical titles; and more than 200,000 reports and documents. It is at the present not a major resource for Africanists.
   The library, which supports agency programs by providing ready access to pertinent information on environmental pollution and control, is open to researchers and the public for on-site use. The library is located in Room 2404 Waterside Mall (PM-213) and is open from 8:00 A.M. to 4:30 P.M. Monday-Friday. For more information call 755-0308.

A valuable research facility at EPA is the United Nations' Environment Program International Referral System. See entry G10 in the Data Banks section of this *Guide*.

OFFICE OF INTERNATIONAL AFFAIRS   755-2780

This office, which deals with the worldwide and long-range nature of environmental problems, is responsible for supporting resolutions and programs which would maximize international cooperation in the efforts to improve the environment. To accomplish these objectives, the agency maintains close contacts with scientists and policymakers in various multilateral organizations and countries.

Bilateral Programs Division
Donald Oakley, Director   755-8712

EPA specialists participate in joint projects under bilateral agreements with several countries.

At present, Egypt is the only country in Africa in which the EPA is actively involved. Under the auspices of the Scientific Activities Overseas (SAO) Program, excess foreign currency funds are being utilized to conduct basic research in several environmentally related fields in Egypt. There are some 10 ongoing projects which include: water quality studies in River Nile and Lake Nasser; systems analysis of Mediterranean desert ecosystems of northern Egypt; studies on water pollution control and abatement; effects of insecticides on animals and plants; air pollution control; and impact of phosphate mining.

The Office of International Affairs is currently negotiating a reimbursable program in Nigeria. It will involve providing technical assistance and advice to Nigeria on specific problems such as waste treatment and air and water pollution control.

The majority of EPA reports, both domestic and international, are available to researchers. Additionally, the staff is willing to confer with scholars and interested persons.

OFFICE OF INTERNATIONAL ORGANIZATIONS AND WESTERN HEMISPHERE

Jack Thompson, Director
755-0430

On occasion, the activities of this office may relate to Africa.

K12   Export-Import Bank of the United States (EXIMBANK)

1. a. *811 Vermont Avenue, NW*
       Washington, D.C. 20571
       566-2117

    b. Open to the public.

2.   Eximbank is an independent corporate agency of the United States. It provides long-term financing for major foreign projects and facilitates

the export of U.S. goods and services. Its activities and projects encompass virtually every country in Africa.

DIRECT CREDITS AND FINANCIAL GUARANTEES

Africa and Middle East
Clayton Norris, Vice President   566-8919

International economists and country-loan officers in the Africa and Middle East Division maintain loan-project files and prepare country and regional studies.

In fiscal year 1977, Eximbank's financing assistance in the form of loans and guarantees to African nations amounted to over $600 million. Loans were provided for a wide range of projects and goods, such as financing for a natural gas plant, diesel electric locomotives, sugar-cane planting and harvest equipment, a hydroelectric project, and cement plant equipment.

The staff of the Africa and Middle East Division welcomes telephone inquiries from interested scholars.

4.   The Eximbank has its own library (see entry A11), which contains over 15,000 books and 950 periodical titles. Holdings fall primarily in the economics subject category, in the fields of banking, finance, trade, and other topics related to the mission of the agency. The library has a useful "country collection" arranged geographically. A survey of the shelflist indicated over 350 titles pertaining to Africa.

The library also subscribes to the *Quarterly Economic Review*, published by the Economist Intelligence Unit Ltd., which gives in-depth coverage of over 53 African countries. In addition it provides a concise summary and analyses of the latest economic indicators in various countries, along with relevant economic data. Another item of potential interest for the Africanist would be the *Marchés Tropicaux et Méditerranéens*, a weekly economic review from France which has special issues on African countries.

The library is open to the public. For further information contact Theodora McGill, Librarian.

5.   The Public Affairs Office (566-8990) makes available the following publications without charge: Export-Import Bank, *Annual Report; Eximbank News,* and a semiannual *Report to the U.S. Congress on Export Credit Competition and the Export-Import Bank of the United States.*

K13 Health, Education, and Welfare Department (HEW)

1. a. *330 Independence Avenue, SW*
    Washington, D.C. 20201
    245-6296

   b. Open to the public.

2.   The department supports both in-house and contract research.

4. See entries for the National Library of Medicine (A34) and National Institute of Education—Educational Research Library (A33).

EDUCATION DIVISION

Office of Education—Division of International Education (DIE) 245-9691

Regional Office Building 3
7th and D Streets, SW
Washington, D.C. 20202

DIE plans and administers a variety of programs and services to promote the international dimensions of American education. Emphasis is on foreign langauge and area studies and the non-Western world. Many of its programs would be of potential interest to the Africanist. A brief description of each is given below.

International Services and Research Branch (ISR)   245-9425

Comparative Education Section (CE)   245-9425

The Comparative Education staff's main function is to prepare and publish resource materials which would facilitate a better understanding of the educational systems of various countries. These studies are undertaken by staff specialists or selected outside consultants.
    Several studies have been published on education in Africa:
    Jerry Bolibaugh, *Educational Development in Guinea, Mali, Senegal, and Ivory Coast* (1972);
    Education Media Resources on Egypt (1977);
    Betty George, *Eduation in Ghana* (1976);
    Selected Bibliography of Education Materials: Maghreb, Algeria, Libya, Morocco, Tunisia, compiled for the Office of Education, HEW, and the National Science Foundation (1976);
    Selected Bibliography of Egyptian Educational Materials (Cairo, 1978);
    James R. Sheffield, *Education in the Republic of Kenya* (1971);
    Karen L. Wenk, *The Educational System of Tunisia* (1974).

The International Organizations Section (IO)   245-2761

The staff maintains contacts with international organizations like UNESCO, IBE, OAS, ILO, WHO, and OECD and cooperates on educational programs and conferences.

International Exchange Branch   245-2454

The Teacher Exchange Program (245-9700) provides opportunities for U.S. teachers to work abroad and also includes arrangements for the direct exchange of educators. The Educational Development Program (ED) enables foreign teachers to receive educational training, while the International Visitors Section assists visiting foreign educators through itinerary planning.

International Studies Branch (ISB)   245-2356

This office gives grants to educational institutions to establish inter-disciplinary studies and develop foreign language and area studies programs and instructional programs in international studies. The office awards several research grants and fellowships.

Ethnic Heritage Studies (EHS)   245-2293

Under this program, grants are made to individuals, institutions, and organizations to enable them to understand their own heritage and develop ethnic heritage programs through curriculum materials development, teacher training, and community activities. Interested researchers should obtain a copy of the annual *Ethnic Heritage Studies Factbook*.

Two informative pamphlets, *Selected Programs and Services of the Division of International Education* and *Selected U.S. Office of Education Publications to Further International Education,* are available without charge from the Clearinghouse (245-7804).

NATIONAL INSTITUTE OF EDUCATION (NIE)

Educational Resources Division

Educational Reference Center
Marsh Building
1832 M Street, NW
Washington, D.C. 20208   254-7934

A significant resource for researchers is the Educational Resource Information Center (ERIC), with computerized data bases (see entry G6). The ERIC system contains bibliographic information on international (including African) education and related subjects. Two useful NIE publications available free are: *Directory of ERIC Collections in the Washington, D.C. Area* and *Survey of ERIC Data Base Search Services.*

PUBLIC HEALTH SERVICE

Office of the Assistant Secretary for Health
Office of International Health
Parklawn Building
5600 Fishers Lane
Rockville, Maryland 20857

Office for Africa and Eastern Mediterranean
Robert N. Evans, Director (301) 443-4540

This office is the focal point and coordinating body for public-health services in Africa. Its main function is to assist and advise the U.S. government in developing programs and activities in Africa. Presently the most important activity and undertaking of this office is the U.S.-Egypt Joint Working Group on Medical Cooperation. This working group, established in 1974 under the U.S.-Egypt Joint Cooperation Commission, provides the mechanism under which bilateral health activities can be promoted in the fields of biomedical research; health manpower education; environmental health; strengthening health services; and pharmaceuticals, biologics, and medical projects.

Bilateral activities and research projects have also been established in Morocco and Tunisia. These comprise mainly health research activities such as training and health services delivery programs.

For more information researchers should write to the Office for Africa, Room 1875.

A unique resource for the student of comparative health systems is the *Syncrisis Studies* prepared by the Division of Program Analysis of the Office of International Health. These multivolume series describe and analyze health conditions of a specific country and its impact on socioeconomic development. At present these syncrisis studies are available for the following African countries: Liberia, Ethiopia, Ghana, Botswana, Lesotho, Swaziland, Zaire, Tunisia, Egypt, Morocco, and Senegal.

National Institutes of Health (NIH)
Fogarty International Center for Advanced Study in the Health Sciences
9000 Rockville Pike
Bethesda, Maryland 20014

The center conducts international exchange programs and administers postdoctoral fellowships and grants for research in the biomedical sciences.

The center's International Cooperation and Geographic Studies Branch (496-5903) publishes studies on foreign health systems.

Alcohol, Drug Abuse, and Mental Health Administration (ADAMHA)
International Activities Office   (301) 443-2600
Parklawn Building
5600 Fishers Lane
Rockville, Maryland 20852

This office dispenses grants and contracts for research in the biological, epidemiological, behavioral, and social sciences. Research projects are presently being undertaken in several countries of Africa and plans are under way to initiate new projects in Botswana, Rwanda, Tanzania, and Zambia in the near future. The International Activities Office maintains contract-research project files and can assist researchers in locating pertinent sources of information. For further information, scholars should contact: National Clearinghouse for Mental Health Information, (301) 443-4517; National Clearinghouse for Drug Abuse Information (301) 443-6500; and National Clearinghouse for Alcohol Information, (301) 948-4450.

K14 Housing and Urban Development Department (HUD)

1. a. *451 7th Street, SW*
    Washington, D.C. 20410
    755-5111 (Information)

    b. Open to the public.

4.   The library is described in entry (A18). Also see the international information system under the Information and Technology Division.

OFFICE OF INTERNATIONAL AFFAIRS

International Programs Division   755-5770

HUD's Office of International Affairs assists the Department of State in formulating U.S. positions with the United Nations and other bilateral and multilateral organizations involved in urban policy and programs. The International Programs Division thus serves as a liaison with international organizations.

In the past, HUD's International Programs Division was actively involved in various activities and programs in Africa. These included providing technical assistance to African countries (such as training facilities, recovery operations, building materials, social services, and disaster recovery) and supporting research and educational programs in Africa. This foreign assistance program was withdrawn in 1973. At the present time, the only program of consequence is in the area of housing. The staff renders advisory services, provides documentation and consultations in response to written requests, and assists in planning procedure and project evaluations.

The Office of International Affairs publishes:

HUD International Country Profiles, a publication on housing and urban affairs in individual nations;

HUD International Information Sources, an irregularly published series of bibliographies and research bulletins on foreign housing and finance;

HUD International Newsletter, a monthly which contains articles, abstracts of periodical literature, and brief descriptions of HUD's international activities;

HUD International Special Reports, a series providing in-depth studies on specific subjects.

Copies of these publications are available free from the Technology and Documentation Division.

Technology and Documentation Division   755-5770
Susan Judd, Information Specialist

This division maintains an extensive collection of documents, reports, and publications on foreign (including some African) housing, urban affairs, and related topics. These numerous documents are stored in the division's international information system, a computerized bibliographic data base. Entries in the system are indexed by subject, country, and author. The staff will run searches of the data base for researchers without charge.

A quarterly *International Cumulative Accessions* list is published by the division.

K15   Interior Department

1. a. *18th and C Streets, NW*
        Washington, D.C. 20240
        343-3171 (Public Affairs)

    b. Most offices are open to the public.

4.   See entries in the library section for the Interior Department—National Resources Library (entry A22) and the Geological Survey Library (A14).

The first contact point for the agency should be the Office of the Assistant to the Secretary and Director of International Programs (343-3101). This office can assist researchers in obtaining information about the activities of the various branches in the department that involve Africa.

BUREAU OF MINES

Columbia Plaza
2401 E Street, NW
Washington, D.C. 20241

Division of International Data and Analysis
     Africa and the Middle East Area Office
     Ebraham Shekarchi, Chief   632-5066

The Africa and the Middle East Office consists of 6 foreign country specialists who do in-house research and gather data on mineral wealth, mineral technology, new deposits, investment potential, industry growth, and nationalization. The emphasis here is on in-depth study of mineral economies on a country rather than commodity basis.

The office also maintains a reference library open to the public for on-site use, which can yield valuable material to the researcher. It contains foreign government publications, unpublished reports, reports on field trips undertaken by the staff, and other relevant materials.

Useful publications include the *Minerals Yearbook,* an annual publication in 3 volumes which provides data on a geographical area basis, and U.S. Department of Interior, Bureau of Mines, *Mineral Industries of Africa* (Washington, 1976). A similar volume on *Mineral Industries of the Middle East* is expected to be available in the near future.

U.S. GEOLOGICAL SURVEY (USGS)

National Center
12201 Sunrise Valley Drive
Reston, Virginia 22092
(703) 860-6118

The U.S. Geological Survey has several programs which involve Africa. These consist of cooperation with earth science agencies and institutions in Africa in investigating geological and mineral resources, environmental and land-use problems, and geological hazards. (Recent projects include irrigation feasibility studies and survey of water resources in Senegal, Mali, Mauritania, Kenya, and Cape Verde, and geologic studies of gold at Tarkwa, Ghana.) In addition to scientific and technical cooperation on subjects of mutual interest, USGS is also actively involved in technical assistance and participant-training programs. These programs provide training to African geologists in a wide range of scientific disciplines and technical assistance to African nations in the task of organizing and strengthening their own geological institutions. In fiscal year 1976, scientists from Egypt, Kenya, and Malagasy Republic were trained in the U.S. in the fields of remote sensing, cartography, typography, and seismology, while several USGS personnel were assigned to these countries and to Algeria, Central African Republic, Morocco, Niger, Nigeria, the Republic of South Africa, and Sudan.

In recent years, the USGS has also become increasingly involved in joint scientific studies of geological phenomena, as well as supporting international commissions and symposia.

Researchers who desire more information on the African activities of USGS should contact the following international units: Office of International Geology (Alfred H. Chidester, Chief, Branch of African Geology, 860-6551); Water Resource Division (J.R. Jones, Chief, Office of International Hydrology, 860-6548); and the Topographic Division's Branch of International Activities (860-6241). These offices can refer scholars to individual staff members who are specialists with expertise on Africa.

Publications of the survey which should interest Africanists include:

Bibliography of Reports Resulting from U.S.G.S. Participation in the United States Technical Assistance Program, 1940–67 (USGS Bulletin 1263);

Bibliography fo Reports Resulting from U.S. Geological Survey Technical Cooperation with Other Countries, 1967–74 (Washington, D.C.: U.S. Government Printing Office, 1976), with a bibliographic supplement for 1975 through June 1977;

U.S. Geological Survey International Activities, 1977.

K16 International Communications Agency (ICA)

1. a. *1750 Pennsylvania Avenue, NW*
   Washington, D.C. 20547
   724-9103

   b. Agency offices, except for the library, are open to the public. Researchers should call for an appointment.

2. The agency engages in substantial in-house research and occasionally also supports contract research.

4. See ICA Library in the libraries section (entry A23).

ICA represents a consolidation of the functions and personnel of the former United States Information Agency, Voice of America, and the Bureau of Educational and Cultural Affairs in the Department of State. The primary function of this newly created agency is to encourage and assist the broadest possible exchange of ideas and people between the U.S. and other nations, to provide a better understanding of U.S. policies, and to assist in the development and implementation of a comprehensive national policy on international communications.

OFFICE OF THE DIRECTOR FOR AFRICAN AFFAIRS
John L. Hedges, Director   724-9084

Office of West Africa—Anglophone
Dennis Shaw, Country Officer   724-9556

Office of West Africa—Francophone
John Anderegg, Acting Country Officer   724-9574

Office of Central Africa
Robert Gibbons, Country Officer   724-1350

Office of East Africa
Virginia Warfield, Country Officer   724-9572

Office of Southern Africa
Charles L. Bell, Country Officer   724-9575

The office of the Director for African Affairs should be the first point of contact for researchers at ICA. It is the focal point for all policies and programs relating to Africa. It is also responsible for the management and oversight of posts and programs in Africa.

The ICA currently operates in some 30 countries of Africa. (Reflecting increased U.S. interest in Africa and its people, 5 additional posts on the continent were recently opened in the Republic of Congo, Burundi, Rwanda, Mauritania, and Mauritius.)

Agency officers serving in various parts of Africa provide the most direct and substantive links with these countries. They are undoubtedly the most important resource because of their experience and area expertise.

ICA activities in each African country include an information program (lectures, seminars, and symposia); a library which makes available reference materials, books, and news about the U.S.; educational exchange programs; and cultural exchanges.

Country-desk officers are accessible and willing to confer with scholars regarding ICA programs in their respective countries of responsibility.

OFFICE OF CONGRESSIONAL AND PUBLIC LIAISON
Michael Pistor, Director   724-9103

The office functions as a liaison and its chief responsibility is to keep the Congress, media, and the public in general, informed about the activities of the agency.

OFFICE OF DIRECTOR (PRESS AND PUBLICATIONS)

Publications Division
1776 Pennsylvania Avenue, NW
Washington, D.C. 20547

Daniel Endsley, Chief   724-9718
Andrew Bardagjy   724-9540

The Publications Division produces some 14 magazines in 16 languages. However, only 2 are of potential interest to the Africanist. These include *Topic,* published 8 times a year in English and French for distribution in Sub-Sahara Africa, and *Al-Majal,* a monthly publication in Arabic for dissemination in Near East and North African countries. The contents of these magazines consist largely of reprints from American periodicals and focus on U.S.-African and U.S.-Near East relations.

These publications are distributed only in Sub-Sahara Africa and the Near East.

The Press Divisions' African branch produces a daily teletype news-service which is made available to African news media. Coverage includes texts of addresses and statements by U.S. leaders, background stories on U.S. domestic issues and foreign policies, and other topics of general interest.

OFFICE OF ASSOCIATE DIRECTOR OF BROADCASTING (VOA)
R. Peter Straus, Director

Africa Division
William Minehart, Chief   755-4160

Near East and South Asia Division
Allan E. Baker, Chief

Arabic Branch
Kamel O. Taweel, Head

VOA broadcasts to Sub-Saharan and North Africa are the prime responsibility of these units. The backbone of the programming is news and news analysis. Tapes of newscasts and commentaries are supplied to African radio stations by ICA field offices. Details regarding the broadcasting activities of the units can be found under VOA in the Media and Publications section of this *Guide* (entry Q22).

The greatest resources of VOA are the 80 or so staff members—writers, editors, broadcasters, and translators, most of whom have extensive broadcasting skills and media expertise and have travelled extensively in Africa. Their experience and background make them an invaluable resource for African scholars.

OFFICE OF ASSOCIATE DIRECTOR OF EDUCATIONAL AND CULTURAL AFFAIRS
724-9032

Office of Academic Programs
Susan Hanke Murphy, Academic Program Officer for Africa   724-9398

The Academic Exchange Programs Division administers various programs which should be of interest to Africanists. These include the awarding of individual grants to scholars, American and African, for a wide range of activities, including the exchange of academic faculty. Each year some 45 professors from Sub-Saharan Africa are awarded grants for research and postdoctoral work in the U.S., while over 60 U.S. professors receive 1-year grants to teach at various African universities. This division also administers student programs, under which more than 60 students from Africa come to the United States every year for higher education. Other programs include short-term visits to the U.S. by African educators and administrators.

Note: The Office of Academic Programs does not receive applications for fellowships and grants. These must be filed through embassies overseas. For more information on student and faculty grants, call 883-8400 and 833-4977, respectively, or contact the Institute of International Education (entry M30).

The Office of Educational Affairs now operates all those programs which were previously administered by the State Department's Bureau of Educational and Cultural Affairs. Thus, in addition to academic exchange programs for students, teachers, and scholars, it has other programs involving visits by leaders in the fields of government, labor, science, mass-media, education, etc., and numerous cultural exchange programs.

OFFICE OF RESEARCH   724-9545
Harold Engle, Acting Director

This office conducts sociological and demographic research on attitudes and audience reactions to ICA programs and related subjects. Research and media reaction staff also prepare material for the White House, Department of State, and other agencies of the government. These *Agency Research Reports* are available to interested persons at some 40 depository libraries in universities and institutions.

K17 Justice Department

1. a. *Constitution Avenue and 10th Street, NW*
        Washington, D.C. 20530
        737-8200

    b. Some departmental divisions, such as the FBI, are not generally open to the public. Researchers should contact individual offices for conditions of access.

CRIMINAL DIVISION

Foreign Agents Registration Unit   739-3154

All representatives of foreign governments are required to register with this unit and provide it with a detailed description of their activities in the United States. They must also file a copy of all material they disseminate in this country. All of these records are accessible to researchers and are available for examination purposes from the:

    Public Office   739-2332
    Federal Triangle Building
    Room 100
    315 9th Street, NW
    Washington, D.C. 20530

The *Annual Report of the Attorney General* gives a list of foreign agents registered with this unit.
    The Office of Management and Finance's Legal Information Systems Group has a data retrieval system called JURIS. For further information call 376-8280.

FEDERAL BUREAU OF INVESTIGATION (FBI)   324-5352

J. Edgar Hoover Building
Pennsylvania Avenue between 9th and 10th Streets, NW
Washington, D.C. 20535

The FBI's Public Affairs Office (324-5352) should be the first point of contact for researchers. The bureau's Intelligence Division and Criminal Investigation Division coordinate the counterespionage and counterintelligence activities of FBI field offices in the United States. Internal Records are classified and accessible only via Freedom-of-Information Act channels.

IMMIGRATION AND NATURALIZATION SERVICE

Information Services Division
425 I Street, NW
Washington, D.C. 20536

The Statistical Branch of the Immigration and Naturalization Service's Information Services Division monitors African immigration into the United States.

The *Annual Report* of the Commissioner of Immigration and Naturalization contains useful statistical data, including immigration figures by sex, occupation, and country of origin.

The Statistical Branch's library is open to the public.

K18 Labor Department

1. a. *New Department of Labor Building*
      200 Constitution Avenue, NW
      Washington, D.C. 20210
      523-8165

   b. Department offices are open to the public.

BUREAU OF INTERNATIONAL LABOR AFFAIRS

Office of Foreign Labor Affairs
Daniel C. Lazorchick, Director   523-7571
Casimir (Ed) Scoon, African Area Advisor   523-6388
James Mattson, Near East and South Asian Area Advisor   523-6234

The bureau has responsibility for formulating and developing all aspects of international and trade policies. It assists in representing the U.S. in bilateral and multilateral trade negotiations with such international bodies as the General Agreement on Tariffs and Trade (GATT), the International Labor Organization (ILO), and the Organization for Economic Cooperation and Development (OECD). The bureau is also involved in developing trade policies toward developing countries. Labor attachés are assigned to several African countries. The recruitment, training, and assignment of these attachés is one of the important tasks of the bureau. Besides providing guidance to these labor attachés at embassies abroad, the bureau is also involved in technical assistance programs overseas and trade-union exchange programs for foreign visitors to the U.S.

An important source of information for the researcher would be the reports prepared by the Labor attachés assigned to the various African nations. These periodic reports deal with significant trends and events, such as labor strikes. The researcher may face some difficulty in obtaining these, as many are classified. A more accessible source of information would be the *Annual Labor Reports* for individual countries.

The Bureau of International Labor Affairs is currently undertaking 2 new projects of potential interest to scholars. The first involves the preparation and publication of *Labor Digests* for some 30 countries, which will provide brief descriptions of labor conditions in each country: manpower and equipment, labor management, labor organizations, legislation, etc. Tentative plans include *Digests* for Nigeria, the Republic of South Africa, Senegal, Kenya, Tunisia, and Morocco. The second project is the publication of a series of monographs on matters pertaining to international labor. Through these monographs, the department hopes to stimulate discussion and encourage further study by providing vital information and analyses. For further information on these monographs, contact the Foreign Publications Group, 523-6378.

BUREAU OF LABOR STATISTICS

Division of Foreign Labor Statistics and Trade
John Chandler, Chief   523-9291

The division collects and analyzes data on foreign labor and trade.

K19 National Aeronautics and Space Administration (NASA)

1. a. *600 Independence Avenue, SW*
      Washington, D.C. 20546
      755-2320

   b. Some offices are closed to the public. Appointments recommended.

2. NASA supports substantial in-house as well as contract research in the field of aeronautical and space development.

3-4. The library has 2 bibliographic resources which should be useful to researchers. The first is the NASA/RECON computerized system, which enables users to conduct extensive literature searches. All reports, publications, and other relevant materials in aeronautics and astronautics are stored in this system.

   A literature search conducted by the library staff revealed over 560 bibliographic citations for Africa alone (this does not include other scientific materials and technical reports for individual African countries) and some 39 items for Egypt. These materials deal with a wide range of subjects, such as Landsat satellites, photogeology, mineral exploration, satellite-borne photography, thermal mapping, and satellite observations.

   The other bibliographic resource is a card file maintained by NASA which contains materials on astronautics and aeronautics.

5. NASA publications are listed in *Scientific and Technical Aerospace Reports* (STAR) issued by the Government Publications Office.

Note: NASA is at best a minor resource for Africanists. Its limited activities and programs relating to Africa are all administered by the Office of International Affairs, a brief description of which follows.

ASSOCIATE ADMINISTRATOR FOR EXTERNAL RELATIONS
Arnold W. Frutkin, Room 7021

Office of International Affairs
Norman Terrell, Director

This office should be the first point of contact in NASA. Its international activities are planned to demonstrate the peaceful purposes of space research and exploration by the United States, and to provide opportunities for scientists and agencies of other countries to participate in the space programs.

NASA programs which should be of interest to Africanists include: (1) the Cooperative Ground-based Projects for Remote Sensing. Several countries of the world, including Zaire, have agreements with NASA under which they establish Landsat receiving, processing, and data-distribution facilities; (2) the Communications Satellite Projects in Cameroon, Central African Republic, Ivory Coast, Kenya, Libya, Mali, Sierra Leone, Liberia, Morocco, Sudan, U.A.R., and Upper Volta. AID and NASA use the experimental communications satellite to broadcast films and live discussions on remote sensing, communications, and disaster relief technologies and their applications for development; and (3) the Meteorological Satellite Project in South Africa. This project involves the employment of satellites for meteorological and oceanographic experiments. In addition, senior scientists from several African countries have visited NASA facilities.

K20 National Endowment for the Humanities (NEH)

1. **a.** *806 15th Street, NW*
   Washington, D.C. 20506
   724-0386

   b. Open to the public.

2. The National Endowment for the Humanities offers fellowships and research grants in a wide range of disciplines, including literature, linguistics, history, philosophy, religion, foreign policy, jurisprudence, archeology, anthropology, and the arts.

   The Division of Fellowships (724-0376) provides stipends to individual scholars.

   The Division of Research Grants (724-0341) funds collaborative projects and work relating to the development of research tools and the editing of humanistic texts.

5. An annually updated booklet, *Program Announcement,* describes NEH activities and provides information on application procedures and deadlines.

The *Annual Report* contains detailed information about NEH programs, including lists of grant recipients and the amounts awarded to them.

These and other miscellaneous publications of the NEH are available free of charge from the Office of Public Information.

K21 National Science Foundation (NSF)

1. a. *1800 G Street, NW*
   Washington, D.C. 20550
   632-7970 (General Information)

   b. 8:30 A.M.-5:00 P.M.   Monday-Friday
   Open to the public.

2. The NSF was established in 1950 to promote scientific progress in the United States. The foundation supports and sponsors scientific research and education in the fields of mathematical, physical, environmental, biological, social, and engineering sciences and promotes scientific information and exchange. Funding is in the form of research grants and the award of contracts.

5. The NSF has numerous publications. These include annual reports, publications of the National Science Board, descriptive brochures, science resources studies, special studies, and periodicals. Researchers are advised to obtain the National Science Foundation's *Organizational Directory* and list of publications, both of which are available free on request. The NSF's *Guide to Programs* provides summary information about the foundation's programs for each fiscal year and is intended for individuals and institutions interested in participating in these programs.

DIRECTORATE FOR SCIENTIFIC, TECHNOLOGICAL, AND INTERNATIONAL AFFAIRS (STIA)

The directorate has 4 divisions, each of which may have programs of some relevance to Africanists. The most important is:

Division of International Programs
Bodo Bartocha, Director   632-5798

Africa and Asia Section
Roger W. Doyon, Section Head   632-5796

Africa Regional Programs
Gerald Edwards, Acting Program Manager   632-5797

U.S.-Egypt and U.S.-Tunisia Programs
Selim Selcuk, Program Manager   632-4342

The main function of the Division of International Programs is to promote international cooperation and understanding through joint efforts and programs between the U.S. and other nations in the areas of science and technology.

The United States-Africa Cooperative Science Program seeks to build cooperative linkages between African and U.S. scientists and scientific institutions. Through this program, the foundation supports (a) cooperative research projects, (b) scientific seminars and workshops, and (c) scientific visits. At the present time, these cooperative ventures involve Egypt and Tunisia.

The INT also oversees the Scientists and Engineers in Economic Development (SEED) Program. Under this program, teaching as well as travel grants are made to U.S. scientists to enable them to apply their experience to development problems in other nations. The SEED projects are far-ranging and have in the past included the study of soil erosion in Ghana, minerals in Nigeria, and artificial breeding of cattle in Kenya. Over 17 African nations have participated in this program.

Under the Special Foreign Currency Program, U.S.-owned foreign currencies have been used to support a wide range of scientific activities and research in various countries. Under this program, projects have been undertaken in Egypt and Guinea. (Note: the list is subject to change.)

Division of Science Resources Studies (SRS)
2000 L Street, NW
Washington, D.C. 20550
634-4634

The division sponsors studies of the scientific (human and capital) resources of foreign countries. The primary objective is the development of factual and analytical information.

The other 2 divisions of the directorate, each with international sections, are Policy Research and Analysis (PRA) (632-5990) and Information Science and Technology (DIST) (254-3020).

DIRECTORATE FOR BIOLOGICAL, BEHAVIORAL, AND SOCIAL SCIENCES (BBS)
632-7867

The directorate supports scientific and related activities in the biological, behavioral, and social sciences. Among others, it includes programs in anthropology, linguistics, social and developmental psychology, and psychobiology. Programs also provide funds for doctoral dissertation research, research conferences, international travel to selected scientific meetings, acquisition of specialized equipment and materials, and construction of specialized research facilities.

Anthropology Program
John E. Yellen, Program Director 632-4208

The Anthropology Program, one of the programs in the Division of Behavioral and Neural Sciences, was established in October 1975. It supports research in social and cultural anthropology, archeology, and physical anthropology. The program, which encompasses all topics, geographic areas, and methodologies, emphasizes research on specific problems. Summary descriptions of all research projects can be obtained for a small fee.

Linguistics Program
Young-Key Kim-Renaud, Assistant Program Director   254-6326

The program supports research in all aspects of linguistics: syntactic, semantic, phonological, and phonetic properties of individual languages; acquisition of language by children; social influences on and effects of language and dialect variation; and biological foundations of language.

K22 Navy Department (and the Marine Corps)

1. a. *The Pentagon*
   Washington, D.C. 20350
   545-6700

   b. The Pentagon and most other departmental buildings are closed to those without security clearance.

2. The Navy Department is a minor resource for the Africanist since it does not engage in any substantial research relating to Africa. The Office of Naval Research does, however, contract with outside institutions to perform research on specific topics.

OFFICE OF NAVAL RESEARCH (ONR)   692-4258

Ballston Center Tower One
800 North Quincy Street
Arlington, Virginia 22217

The ONR is divided into several branches and divisions which engage in a wide range of activities. The only program of potential interest to Africanists is in the field of biological sciences and is described below.

Biological Sciences Program
Dr. Arthur J. Emery, Jr., Chief   696-4056

The office does not perform any in-house research; rather, it contracts with universities, institutions, and industry to do research. Most of this research is in the area of epidemiology (locating and identifying diseases and their mode of transmission and devising methods of prevention and cure); naval biology (including pollution control and sewage treatment); and microbiology.

At the present time, there is only one ongoing project in Africa, in Egypt. NAMRU (Naval Medical Research Unit) has set up medical laboratories in Egypt. There used to be a very successful medical research program in Ethiopia, but it has been discontinued.

The technical reports emanating from these projects would be a useful source of information for medical researchers. There is no bibliography or index of these materials, but the staff welcomes inquiries and is extremely helpful in assisting scholars in locating relevant materials.

Oceanic Biology Program

This division has initiated an overseas program in oceanic biology. Currently it has a project in Egypt.

Researchers should note that other offices such as the Geography Branch (Code 462) of the Earth Sciences Division and the Psychological Sciences Division (Code 450), which at present have virtually no material for Africanists, may in the future become involved in some Africa-related programs.

OFFICE OF NAVAL INTELLIGENCE

The Pentagon
Rear Admiral Donald P. Harvey, Director   695-3944

Due to the sensitive nature of its operations, virtually all of the office's work is classified. Researchers seeking specific information should write directly to the office, citing the Freedom of Information Act.

Naval Intelligence Command (1975), a useful book of information, and an organizational chart are available on request.

NAVAL OCEANOGRAPHIC OFFICE   (301) 763-1140

Suitland, Maryland
Mail: Washington, D.C. 20373

The office, previously located in Suitland, Maryland, has moved to the National Space Technology Labs in Bay St. Louis, Mississippi.

The office, which focuses on marine biology, climatology, chemistry, and related subjects, is a relatively insignificant resource for Africanists. Researchers may write for the free *Catalog of Naval Oceanographic Office Publications.*

Naval Historical Center   433-2210

This center undertakes research and publication programs in the field of U.S. naval history. In addition, it operates the Naval Memorial Museum (433-3519) and the Historical Research Branch (433-2364). All are located in Building 220, Washington Navy Yard.

Two useful publications of the center are: Dean C. Allard and Betty Burn, comp., *U.S. Naval History Sources in the Washington Area and Suggested Research Subjects* (3d rev. ed., 1970), and W. Bart Greenwood et al., comp., *United States Naval History: A Bibliography* (6th ed., 1972).

Naval Records Management Division   695-1929

Freedom of Information Act requests are handled by the staff of this division.

U.S. MARINE CORPS

History and Museums Division
Washington Navy Yard, Building 58
Washington, D.C. 20374

The earlier Marine Corps records are held in the National Archives. The division, however, houses personal papers and oral history collections. The staff can assist researchers in locating relevant materials.

K23 Smithsonian Institution

1. a. *Headquarters:*
      1000 Jefferson Drive, SW
      Washington, D.C. 20560
      628-4422

   b. Most Smithsonian buildings (with the exception of administrative offices) are open to the public.

2. The Smithsonian Institution supports research of all kinds, both in-house and on contract basis through numerous programs.

3. The Smithsonian Science Information Exchange (SSIE), located at 1730 M Street, NW, Washington, D.C. 20036 (381-4211), is perhaps the most important bibliographic resource of the institution.
   The SSIE is a center for the collection and dissemination of information on research in progress. It seeks to provide a central source for the exchange of information on recently completed and current projects, thereby preventing unnecessary duplication. Research projects of federal, state, and local government agencies, nonprofit organizations, foundations, academic institutions, and private investigators are entered in the computerized list. Notice of Research Project (NRP) gives the relevant information on each project, with the supporting organization's name and project number, project title, and a brief description of the work. Search services are available on a fee basis.

4. The libraries and archives of the Smithsonian are listed under the names of the appropriate museums and galleries (consult the Name Index under "Smithsonian Institution").

5. The monthly *Smithsonian* magazine contains articles on subjects of general interest and additionally gives news of the institution and its varied activities.
   The Smithsonian, established in 1846, is a scientific, educational, and cultural institution which administers several national collections, museums, and art galleries; supports and conducts scientific and scholarly research; maintains archives and laboratories; and runs educational programs. These varied activities are described in the appropriate sections of this *Guide*. Some divisions not described elsewhere are mentioned below.

INTERNATIONAL EXCHANGE SERVICE

1111 North Capitol Street
Washington, D.C. 20002

John E. Estes, Director   381-5311

The primary function of the service is to oversee the exchange of all official U.S. publications with various countries, including those in Africa. Under this program, books and other selected materials, mainly in medicine and related fields, are sent as gifts to African countries. (The Republic of South Africa is the major recipient.) Incoming publications from these countries go directly to many libraries, e.g., the Libray of Congress, National Library of Medicine, and the National Agricultural Library.

DWIGHT D. EISENHOWER INSTITUTE FOR HISTORICAL RESEARCH

National Museum of History and Technology
Constitution Avenue between 12th and 14th Streets, NW
Washington, D.C. 20560

Forrest Pogue, Director   381-5458

This institute, established in 1975, undertakes research mainly in the field of military history. Presently, none of its research relates to Africa, but future research may touch upon subjects of potential interest to Africanists.

SMITHSONIAN ASSOCIATES   381-6264

The Smithsonian Associates Program is open to all. Individuals can become associates by paying the membership dues. This membership entitles them to certain benefits.

This division also sponsors a series of Foreign Study Tours and Foreign Charter Tours for Associates. The Foreign Study Tours headquarters is in the main Smithsonian Institution building (381-5520); the Foreign Charter Tours office is located in the Arts and Industries Building, Washington, D.C. 20560 (381-5635).

For visitors to the area, the Smithsonian offers a round-the-clock reference service which provides information on events and exhibits of current interest: Dial-a-Museum, 737-8811.

K24   State Department

1. **a.** *2201 C Street, NW*
    Washington, D.C. 20520
    655-4000 (Information)
    632-0772 (Freedom-of-Information Staff)

    b. The building is not open to the public. Appointments with department personnel should be made in advance to ensure admittance.

2. A substantial amount of research on Africa is conducted by the numerous offices of the State Department. Both the Bureau of African Affairs and the Bureau of Intelligence and Research contract for research on Africa and employ Africanist scholars as consultants. As time permits, and within the limits imposed by security regulations, State Department personnel are willing to confer with researchers.

3. Specific information on bibliographic sources is given under each division.

    State Department publications include the weekly *Department of State Bulletin* (contains excerpts from news conferences of the president, secretary of state, and other officials; press releases; texts of treaties and international agreements; discussion on international affairs; and lists of congressional documents pertaining to foreign policy); the monthly *Department of State Newsletter;* and *Gist,* a series of brief reference aids on current world issues.

4. Consult the State Department Library in the libraries section of this *Guide* (entry A38).

5. Bibliographies include *Major Publications of the Department of State: An Annotated Bibliography* (revised edition, 1977), and *Publications of the Department of State* covering the periods 1929–52, 1953–57, and 1958–60.

BUREAU OF AFRICAN AFFAIRS (AF)   632-0322
Assistant Secretary of State Richard M. Moose

Office of Executive Director (AF/EX)   632-1298

Economic Policy Staff (AF/EPS)   632-2623

Office of Inter-African Affairs (AF/I)   632-0754

Public Affairs Staff (AF/P)   632-2683

Office of Central African Affairs (AF/C)   632-2080

This office is responsible for Zaire, Congo, Rwanda, Burundi, Angola, Gabon, Cameroon, Equatorial Guinea, Central African Republic, São Tomé and Principe.

Office of East African Affairs (AF/E)   632-9742

This office is responsible for Ethiopia, Somalia, Djibouti, Tanzania, Uganda, Kenya, Seychelles, Biot, Malawi, Zambia, Republic of Madagascar, Mauritius, Sudan, Comoroes, Diego Garcia.

Office of Southern African Affairs (AF/S)   632-7786

This office is responsible for the Republic of South Africa, Namibia, Botswana, Lesotho, Swaziland, Mozambique, Southern Rhodesia.

Office of West African Affairs (AF/W)   632-0902

This office is responsible for Benin, Gambia, Ghana, Guinea, Guinea-Bissau, Ivory Coast, Liberia, Mali, Mauritania, Niger, Nigeria, Senegal, Sierra Leone, Togo, Upper Volta, Chad, Western Sahara, Cape Verde.

The Bureau of African Affairs coordinates and supervises U.S. diplomatic activities and roles in Africa. Country-desk officers are the primary resource in the bureau and can provide country-specific information. They will also make relevant unclassified documents available to researchers.

The Bureau of African Affairs has a wide range of activities, many of which would be of potential interest to scholars. These include organizing and convening periodic seminars and conferences which focus on a specific topic or region of Africa. Africanist scholars from universities and academic and research institutions are invited to participate and present papers at this conference. These meetings are held 5 or 6 times a year. The conference in July 1978 focused on "The Sudan and Its Potential." Scholarly papers presented at such meetings could be valuable to researchers.

Another significant activity of the Africa Bureau is the Scholar-Diplomat Seminar held twice a year. The purpose of these seminars is to initiate a meaningful dialog between the bureau and the academic community and to provide an opportunity for an exchange of views on the State Department's Africa policy. A seminar held in November 1977 dealt with topics such as: "The Rhodesian Peace Proposal"; "Namibia Transition: A Study in International Diplomacy"; "U.S. Policy Toward Africa: The Congressional Perspective"; "Development of U.S. Policy in Response to Recent Events in South Africa"; "The Formulation of U.S. Policy Toward Uganda"; and "Recent Developments in the Horn of Africa."

The Bureau of African Affairs also conducts a summer internship program in Africa for highly qualified graduate students. Selected candidates are placed at American embassies in Africa for the duration of the summer. For further information on this program, call 632-0322.

Two useful publications include the weekly *AF Press Clips,* which contain excerpts from various newspapers dealing with current events of importance in Africa, and *Background Notes,* a series of general information fact sheets by country (updated every 2 years).

BUREAU OF NEAR EASTERN AND SOUTH ASIAN AFFAIRS (NEA)   632-9588

Algeria, Libya, Morocco, Tunisia (NEA/AFN)   632-0840
Egypt (NEA/EGY)   632-2365

This bureau is the counterpart of the Bureau of African Affairs and has virtually the same responsibilities and functions. The staff of NEA assists and advises the State Department on matters concerning the Near East.

BUREAU OF INTERNATIONAL ORGANIZATION AFFAIRS (IO)   632-9600

This bureau coordinates United States participation in the United Nations. Selected staff members in the various offices monitor the activities of the African delegations and analyze the implications of U.S. policy positions within the U.N. General Assembly and Security Council. The numerous functional offices focus on U.N. political affairs, international economic affairs, labor affairs, human rights, health and narcotics, agriculture, development and humanitarian programs, transportation and communications, etc.

The bureau maintains a file of U.N. documents.

BUREAU OF PUBLIC AFFAIRS (PA)   632-9606

Office of the Historian
515 22d Street, NW
Washington, D.C. 20520

David F. Trask, Historian   632-1931
William Z. Slany, Chief, Foreign Relations Division   632-1902

The primary function of this office is to prepare a documentary record of U.S. foreign policy for publication in the series *Foreign Relations of the United States*. This series, begun in 1861, consists of important telegrams, diplomatic notes, memoranda, and other materials. (The 1949 volume deals with Africa.)

Other publications of the Historical Office include *American Foreign Policy—Current Documents*, 12 volumes (1956–67), and the State Department *Bulletin* (the official monthly record of U.S. foreign policy). The former series (which ceased publication in 1967) includes records of speeches, public statements, press releases, etc., and should provide considerable information on U.S. recognition of newly independent African nations.

The staff of the office is available for consultation and research guidance.

Freedom of Information Staff (PA/FOI)   632-0772

This unit receives Freedom of Information Act declassification-review requests. Declassified documents can be examined by researchers in the units public-access reading room.

BUREAU OF INTELLIGENCE AND RESEARCH (INR)   632-0342

Office of Research and Analysis for Africa (INR/DDR/RAF)
C. Thomas Thorne, Jr.   632-6130

Office of Research and Analysis for Near East and South Asia (INR/DDR/RNA)
Philip H. Stoddard   632-8397

These 2 offices are the principal research arms of the State Department for Africa and the Near East respectively. Research is undertaken on all aspects of African affairs—political, military, economic, and social. Virtually of all their information is, however, classified.

Office of External Research (INR/XR)
E. Raymond Platig, Director   632-1342

The Office of External Research is the institutional unit which fulfills the research requirements of the department. Its primary role is to identify and meet the department's needs for professional research assistance, commission scholarly research on subjects likely to affect foreign policy concerns in the future, and coordinate government-sponsored research on foreign affairs.

The numerous programs and activities of the Office of External Research are aimed at fulfilling this role. They include the maintaining of the Foreign Affairs Research Documentation Center (which collects and disseminates government-funded studies and other unpublished research materials); arranging and sponsoring symposia, conferences, and seminars for researchers in and out of government; supporting research contracts and consultant studies; and promoting interagency collaboration on research projects.

The office publishes an annual computerized inventory of *Government-Supported Research Projects on Foreign Affairs* (unclassified).

Researchers may also find the following publications useful: Larry Moses, *Kenya, Uganda, Tanganyika, 1960–1964, A Bibliography* (External Research Service, 1964); U.S. Department of State, External Research Staff, *Africa;* U.S. Department of State, External Research Division, *Middle East;* and U.S. Department of State, Office of Intelligence Research and Analysis, *Research on Middle East.*

In addition, the Office of External Research administers the:

Foreign Affairs Research Documentation Center
Room 4111, Pomponio Plaza East
1800 North Kent Street
Arlington, Virginia 22209

Barbara Morlet, Deputy Director of Research Services   (703) 235-8079

This center collects and disseminates government-funded research studies and unpublished research papers produced by individual scholars, universities, and research centers. The main objective is to facilitate the exchange of information between the government and the academic community, maximize the benefits of research, and avoid duplication.

Currently the center houses some 15,000 papers in anthropology, sociology, history, economics, demography, geography, international relations, law, philosophy, and political science. Private researchers have acccess only to those studies funded by the State Department. Requests for all other studies should be made directly to the author of the sponsoring agency. The center maintains a geographic as well as dictionary card catalog.

The FAR Documentation Center publishes a monthly accessions list, *Foreign Affairs Research Papers Available.* In addition, a *Special Papers Available* series contains an annual volume on Africa-Sub-Sahara, and another on Near East, South Asia, and North Africa.

Office of Economic Research and Analysis   632-2186

This office is primarily involved in research and analysis of international economic issues, incluing U.S.-African economic relations.

The Office of Economic Research and Analysis also produces *Intelligence Reports;* however, most of them are classified and restricted to interagency use. Researchers can request copies of the unclassified publication *Communist Aid to the Less Developed Countries of the Free World* from the Communist Economic Relations Division (632-9128).

Office of Political-Military Affairs and Theatre Forces   632-2043

This office conducts research (some pertaining to Africa) on international arms sales, military production and capabilities, and other defense-oriented subjects.

Office of Strategic Affairs   632-2086

Virtually all of this office's work is classified.

Office of the Geographer
Robert D. Hodgson, Geographer   632-1428

This office studies international boundaries and law of the sea and publishes *Geographic Notes, International Boundary Studies* (irregularly), and *Limits of the Sea.*

BUREAU OF ECONOMIC AND BUSINESS AFFAIRS (EB) 632-0396

Many of the bureau's offices have some degree of involvement with matters concerning Africa. The bureau has primary responsibility within the State Department for the formulation and administration of U.S. foreign economic policy. In discharging these responsibilities, the bureau's staff oversees and monitors the economic policies of African nations, conducts bilateral and multilateral negotiations on economic matters, and represents the U.S. at international conferences.

Other bureau offices with some degree of involvement with Africa include the Office of Monetary Affairs (632-1114), Office of International Trade (632-2534), Office of Investment Affairs (632-1128), Office of Development Finance (632-9426), Office of International Commodities (632-7952), Office of Food Policy and Programs (632-3090), Office of Commercial Affairs (632-8097), and Office of Fuels and Energy (632-1420).

BUREAU OF POLITICO-MILITARY AFFAIRS (P/M)   632-9022

The bureau is primarily concerned with defense and security matters, and virtually all of its work is classified. The bureau has a functional, not a geographic basis. Some important offices are listed below:

Office of International Security Policy (632-2056)
Office of Security Assistance and Sales (632-3882)
Office of International Security Operations (632-1616)

BUREAU OF HUMAN RIGHTS AND HUMANITARIAN AFFAIRS (HA)   632-0334

The bureau monitors human-rights conditions all over the world and assists the department on policy decisions regarding human rights and humanitarian affairs.

Office of Human Rights (HA/HR)
Robert H. Maxim, Human Rights Officer for Africa   632-1255

This office monitors human-rights conditions in Africa and renders policy recommendations concerning economic development and military assistance to Africa. It is also responsible for the preparation of country reports (presented to the Congress annually) on human rights in those African countries which receive U.S. economic or military aid. Presently there are 39 such reports. These *Country Reports on Human Rights Practices* are available to the public.

Office of Refugee and Migration Affairs (HA/ORM)
Graham Mettson, Jr., Refugee Affairs Officer for Africa   632-2362
Lawrence L. Arthur, Officer for African Political Asylum   632-2551

This office is mainly concerned with humanitarian issues, namely refugee and disaster relief.

BUREAU OF OCEANS AND INTERNATIONAL ENVIRONMENTAL AND SCIENTIFIC AFFAIRS (OES)   632-1554

The bureau deals with foreign policy questions as they relate to oceans and fisheries, environmental and population issues, nuclear and energy technology, and applied science and technology. The bureau is concerned primarily with global issues and maintains close ties with international organizations.

None of the bureau's current activities deals with Africa. For more information, call Information Officer Pamela Smith (632-2398).

OFFICE OF THE LEGAL ADVISER

Michael J. Matheson, Assistant Legal Adviser for African Affairs   632-3736

David H. Small. Assistant Legal Adviser for Near Eastern and South Asian Affairs   632-9501

This office renders legal advice to the various bureaus of the State Department. Staff lawyers can provide scholars with information on African legal issues, treaties, and international agreements.

Publications of the office include the annual *Digest of United States Practice in International Law, Treaties in Force.* and *United States Treaties and Other International Agreements* (UST) (containing texts of all treaties and agreements of the U.S. since 1950). The multivolume *Treaties and Other International Agreements of the United States of America, 1776-1949* is also available, but contains little information of interest to an Africanist.

BUREAU OF ADMINISTRATION (A)   632-1492

Foreign Affairs Document and Reference Center (FADRC)
John S. Pruden, Director   632-0394

FADRC administers the official centralized files of State Department records comprising cables, airgrams, overseas post records, papers and memoranda, etc.

There exists a computerized index for all material received since July 1973. Neither the index nor the record files is open to outside researchers. Access is only through the Freedom of Information Act.

The FADRC publishes the *Country Fact Sheets* (one volume deals with Africa), an extremely valuable source for information on basic facts on each country. *Country Fact Sheets* is regularly updated and is distributed to the libraries of several U.S. government agencies.

FOREIGN SERVICE INSTITUTE

1400 Key Boulevard
Arlington. Virginia 22209
(703) 235-8750

George S. Springsteen. Director

The Foreign Service Institute provides training and instruction to employees and officers of the State Department and other government departments in the field of foreign relations and languages.

Center for Area and Country Studies
W. Lawrence Dutton, Dean   235-8839

Near East and North Africa
Peter K. Bechtold, Chairperson   235-8844

Africa Sub-Sahara
John L. Collier, Chairperson   235-8835

This is the focal point for the promotion of area and country knowledge. Personnel from the State Department and other foreign-affairs agencies receive interdisciplinary training in Sub-Saharan Africa and North Africa. The training programs consist of regularly scheduled 2-week seminars which give an overview of the history, politics, economics, geography, and culture of an area and advanced area courses offiered in conjunction with the institute's language-training program. Other programs include family workshops which provide general orientation and language training to family members of officers assigned abroad and some periodic specialized courses.

Currently the Department of Near Eastern and African Languages in the School of Language Studies provides instruction in Amharic, Swahili, Arabic, and Afrikaans. For more information, contact Dr. James Snow, Chairman of the Department of Near Eastern and African Languages.

The Foreign Service Institute maintains its own library. It contains over 40,000 books and some 300 periodical titles. Access is restricted to U.S. government employees, but serious scholars may obtain special permission to use the library for on-site reference purposes.

The library contains over 1,900 items on Sub-Saharan Africa and some 1,250 on North Africa and the Near East. For further information, contact Mary C. Schloeder, Librarian, (703) 235-8717.

Two useful publications of the institute include: Department of State, Foreign Service Institute, School of Area Studies, *A Selected Functional and Country Bibliography for Africa, Sub-Sahara* (August 1974) and *A Selected Functional and Country Bibliography for Near East and North Africa* (January 1978). These guides are generally updated every 2 years. The institute also publishes a self-study guide and syllabus, but it is primarily intended for use by institute personnel.

K25 Transportation Department (DOT)

1. a. *400 7th Street. SW*
      Washington, D.C. 20590
      426-4000

   b. Open to the public.

2. The Office of International Transportation Programs is responsible for programs which involve international cooperation with numerous foreign countries in the area of transportation and exchange of research and information.

3. TRISNET (Transportation Research Information Services Network) is an extensive computerized data base maintained by DOT in conjunction

with the Transportation Research Board (TRB), National Research Council, and other organizations. It contains a vast amount of bibliographic information for the U.S. and other countries in the field of transportation, specifically on subjects such as highways, railroads, bridges, air transport, etc. This bibliographical tool is a valuable resource for Africanists for material not easily available elsewhere.

4.   See the DOT library (entry A40).

OFFICE OF INTERNATIONAL TRANSPORTATION PROGRAMS 426-4368

Technical Assistance Division
Richard L. Braida, Chief of Division   426-4196

The Office of the Secretary has a Resource Support Services Agreement (RSSA) with AID to provide technical assistance in the field of transport planning and economic evaluation of selected projects. A staff member of this office is presently assigned to the Africa Desk. His primary function is to render advice on the allocation of development projects, to assist AID in finding solutions to specific investment and planning programs, and to evaluate and review programs. Emphasis is placed on devising modes of transportation to service the agricultural sector in Africa.

Recent projects include one undertaken in the Shaba region to develop feeder roads to service agriculture and another to develop transportation networks in the Sahel.

FEDERAL AVIATION ADMINISTRATION (FAA)   426-8521

800 Independence Avenue, SW
Washington, D.C. 20590

Office of International Aviation Affairs   426-3213

This office is involved in a number of projects in Africa which range from providing assistance in procurement of equipment to flight inspection services and training programs in ground control. At the present time, FAA has programs in Egypt, Cape Verde Islands, Lesotho, Malawi, Somalia, Sudan, Tanzania, and Libya.

K26   Treasury Department

1.   a. *15th Street and Pennsylvania Avenue, NW*
         Washington, D.C. 20220
         566-2000

     b. Access to the building is restricted. Appointments should be made in advance.

2-3.   Staff economists in the Office of the Assistant Secretary for International Affairs (OASIA) analyze international monetary and fiscal issues and maintain records of government research. A substantial part of this is, however, classified material.

The library issues *Treasury Notes,* a monthly review of current literature which may occasionally contain pertinent information for the Africanist.

4.   The Treasury Department Library, located in the main Treasury Building in room 5030, is open to the public. It has a fairly extensive collection of publications and material in the fields of economics and finance. Its holdings on Africa are insignificant and the library is thus a minor resource for Africanists. (Librarian: Ann E. Stewart, 566-2777.)

OFFICE OF THE ASSISTANT SECRETARY FOR
INTERNATIONAL AFFAIRS (OASIA)   566-5363

Deputy Assistant Secretary for Developing Nations
Arnold Nachmanoff   566-8243

Office of International Development Bank
Colin Bradford   566-8171

African Development Fund and African Development Bank
Robert Chlebowski   566-2067

OASIA advises and assists the secretary of the treasury and other departmental officials in the formulation and implementation of international economic, financial, monetary, and trade policies and programs. The office is divided into divisions responsible for monetary affairs, developing nations, trade and raw materials policy, and energy and investment pjolicy. The African Development Fund and African Development Bank analyze policies and programs. Specific research studies prepared by the staff in connection with the above activities are usually classified. The office will, however, answer inquiries from serious scholars.

OFFICE OF DEVELOPING NATIONS' FINANCE
Robert Pelikan   566-2373

The main task of this office is to follow the financial policies and economic developments of selected African countries, specifically the oil-producing countries and nations having balance-of-payment problems. African countries which come under its scrutiny include: Nigeria, Libya, Morocco, Sudan, Algeria, Egypt, Gabon, Ghana, Zambia, Zaire, and Tanzania.

Other departmental offices may from time to time become involved in short-term programs, such as conducting seminars and workshops for African businessmen.

Note: *A Select List of Treasury Publications* is available from the Office of Public Affairs (566-2041).

L African Embassies and International Organizations

African Embassies and International Organizations Entry Format * (L)

1. General information
    a. *address; telephone number(s)*
    b. hours/conditions of access

2. Reference facilities

3. Publications

4. Programs and research activities

---

   * In the case of large, structurally complex international organizations, each relevant division or subunit will be described separately, following the information on the organization as a whole.

L1 Embassy of Algeria

1. a. *2118 Kalorama Road, NW*
       Washington, D.C. 20008
       234-7246

    b. 9:00 A.M.-5:00 P.M.   Monday-Friday

3.   *Algeria News Report,* published twice a month by the embassy, contains national news and general information concerning Algeria's foreign and economic policies.

L2 Embassy of Benin

1. a. *2737 Cathedral Avenue, NW*
       Washington, D.C. 20008
       232-6656

    b. 9:00 A.M.-5:00 P.M.   Monday-Friday

L3 Embassy of Botswana

1. a. *4301 Connecticut Avenue, NW*
   Suite 404
   Washington, D.C. 20008
   244-4990

   b. 9:00 A.M.-5:00 P.M.   Monday-Friday

3. The embassy publishes a monthly news letter which is distributed to the public, free of charge.

L4 Embassy of Burundi

1. a. *2717 Connecticut Avenue, NW*
   Washington, D.C. 20008
   387-4477

   b. 9:00 A.M.-5:00 P.M.   Monday-Friday

2. The embassy receives a daily newspaper, *Le Renouveau du Burundi.*

L5 Embassy of Cameroon

1. a. *2349 Massachusetts Avenue, NW*
   Washington, D.C. 20008
   265-8790

   b. 9:00 A.M.-1:00 P.M. and 2:00 P.M.-5:00 P.M.   Monday-Friday

2. The embassy maintains a small public-reference library containing some 300-400 books, newspapers, and magazines. It also receives the daily newspaper *Cameroon Tribune.*

3. *Cameroon News,* a monthly news bulletin, is published by the embassy.

L6 Embassy of Cape Verde

1. a. *1120 Connecticut Avenue, NW*
   Washington, D.C. 20036
   659-3148

   b. 10:00 A.M.-5:00 P.M.   Monday-Friday

3. The embassy receives a weekly, *Tchuba,* published in Rhode Island, which contains news and information about Cape Verde, and current and past issues of *Voz d'i Povo,* a weekly newspaper.

L7 Embassy of Central African Empire

1. a. *1618 22d Street, NW*
   Washington, D.C. 20008
   265-5637

b. 9:00 A.M.-12:30 P.M. and 2:00 P.M.-5:00 P.M.   Monday-Friday

L8 Embassy of Chad

1. a. *2600 Virginia Avenue, NW*
   Washington, D.C. 20027
   331-7696

   b. 9:00 A.M.-5:00 P.M.   Monday-Friday

L9 Embassy of Egypt

1. a. *2300 Decatur Place, NW*
   Washington, D.C. 20008
   234-0980

   b. 9:30 A.M.-5:00 P.M.   Monday-Friday

2. The embassy distributes general-information literature to the public. A collection of documentary films and slides is also available (see entry F9).
   In addition, the embassy receives several Egyptian newspapers, which include: the *Egyptian Gazette, El-Ahram, El-Akhbar,* and *El-Gomhouria.*

L10 Embassy of Ethiopia

1. a. *2134 Kalorama Road, NW*
   Washington, D.C. 20008
   234-2281

   b. 9:00 A.M.-5:00 P.M.   Monday-Friday

2. The embassy currently receives 2 daily newspapers—*Addis Zemen* (Amharic) and the *Ethiopian Herald*—and the weekly *Yzareyitu Ethiopia.*

L11 Embassy of Gabon

1. a. *2034 20th Street, NW*
   Washington, D.C. 20009
   797-1000

   b. 9:00 A.M.-Noon and 1:30 P.M.-4:30 P.M.   Monday-Friday

L12 Embassy of Ghana

1. a. *2460 16th Street, NW*
   Washington, D.C. 20009
   462-0761

   b. 9:00 A.M.-12:30 P.M. and 2:00 P.M.-5:30 P.M.   Monday-Friday

2. The embassy maintains a public reference library containing approximately 300-400 book titles and other materials such as periodicals, government statistics, and yearbooks. Some 5 newspapers are also currently received. For further information, call the Press and Information Office (462-0761).

3. A monthly general-information newsletter, *Ghana News,* is published and distributed by the Information Section of the embassy.

L13 Embassy of Guinea

1. a. *2112 Leroy Place, NW*
    Washington, D.C. 20009
    483-9420

    b. 9:00 A.M.-4:30 P.M.   Monday-Friday

2. A small reference collection of general-information literature and government publications is maintained for public use.

3. Current and past issues of *Horoya,* a weekly news magazine of PDG (Organe Central du Parti-Etat), are distributed on request.

L14 Embassy of Guinea-Bissau

The embassy's duties are temporarily handled by the Permanent Mission of Guinea-Bissau to the United Nations, 211 East 43d Street, New York, New York 10017. For information call (212) 661-3977.

L15 Embassy of Ivory Coast

1. a. *2424 Massachusetts Avenue, NW*
    Washington, D.C. 20008
    483-2400

    b. 9:00 A.M.-5:00 P.M.   Monday-Friday

2. The embassy receives a small number of daily newspapers and assorted magazines.

L16 Embassy of Kenya

1. a. *2249 R Street, NW*
    Washington, D.C. 20008
    387-6101

    b. 9:00 A.M.-1:00 P.M. and 2:00 P.M.-4:00 P.M.   Monday-Friday

2. The embassy maintains a small reading room which contains books, newspapers, and periodicals from Kenya. Government publications and statistical yearbooks are also available.

The embassy's Information Section has a small film and slide collection available for loan, without charge. Interested persons should write to the embassy for a list of available films.

3. The embassy disseminates *Kenyan Newsletter*. Researchers may request to be placed on the mailing list.

L17 Embassy of Lesotho

1. a. *Caravel Building, Suite 300*
    1601 Connecticut Avenue, NW
    Washington, D.C. 20009
    462-4190

    b. 9:00 A.M.-5:00 P.M.   Monday-Friday

L18 Embassy of Liberia

1. a. *5201 16th Street, NW*
    Washington, D.C. 20011
    723-0437

    b. 9:00 A.M.-5:00 P.M.   Monday-Friday

2. The embassy's Information Center and Reading Room, located in Room 330, 1050 17th Street, NW, Washington, D.C. 20036 (331-0136), maintains a small collection of reference books and general-information literature for public use.
    The embassy has a few films for loan. See entry F10.

L19 Embassy of Libya

1. a. *1118 22d Street, NW*
    Washington, D.C. 20037
    452-1290

    b. 9:00 A.M.-4:00 P.M.   Monday-Friday

2. The embassy has a small film collection for loan, without charge. See entry F11.

L20 Embassy of Madagascar

1. a. *2374 Massachusetts Avenue, NW*
    Washington, D.C. 20008
    265-5525

    b. 9:30 A.M.-Noon and 2:30 P.M.-5:00 P.M.   Monday-Friday

L21 Embassy of Malawi

1. a. *1400 20th Street, NW*
      Washington, D.C. 20036
      296-5530

   b. 9:00 A.M.-5:00 P.M. Monday-Friday

2. A small reference library containing newspapers, magazines, and government publications is maintained by the embassy. It also currently receives the *Daily Times*.

L22 Embassy of Mali

1. a. *2130 R Street, NW*
      Washington, D.C. 20008
      332-2249

   b. 9:00 A.M.-5:00 P.M. Monday-Friday

2. The embassy receives the daily and weekly newspaper *L'Essor*.

L23 Embassy of Mauritania

1. a. *2129 Leroy Place, NW*
      Washington, D.C. 20008
      232-5700

   b. 9:00 A.M.-5:00 P.M. Monday-Friday

2. The embassy receives *Chaab*, a daily newspaper in French and Arabic.

L24 Embassy of Mauritius

1. a. *4301 Connecticut Avenue, NW*
      Washington, D.C. 20008
      244-1491

   b. 10:00 A.M.-4:00 P.M. Monday-Friday

2. The embassy currently receives several daily newspapers from Mauritius. These include *Cerneen, L'Express, Le Mauricien, Nation, Le Populaire,* and *The Star*.

L25 Embassy of Morocco

1. a. *1601 21st Street, NW*
      Washington, D.C. 20009
      462-7979

   b. 9:30 A.M.-1:00 P.M. and 2:30 P.M.-5:00 P.M. Monday-Friday

L26 Embassy of Niger

1. a. *2204 R Street, NW*
    Washington, D.C. 20008
    483-4224

    b. 9:00 A.M.-5:00 P.M. Monday-Friday

2.   The embassy currently receives the daily newspaper *Le-Sahel* and the weekly *Sahel-Hebdo*.

L27 Embassy of Nigeria

1. a. *2201 M Street, NW*
    Washington, D.C. 20037
    223-9300

    b. 9:30 A.M.-Noon and 2:00 P.M.-4:30 P.M. Monday-Friday

2.   The Nigerian embassy maintains a public reference library containing several hundred general reference books on African history, literature, social and economic development, and art; government statistics; Central Bank of Nigeria reports and statistics; development plans; and an extensive collection of regional and federal *Official Gazettes*. In addition, the library receives all the major Nigerian newspapers, including *Daily Sketch, Daily Times, New Nigerian, Nigeria Standard, Nigerian Chronicle, Nigerian Herald, Nigerian Observer, Nigerian Tribune, Star*, and *Sunday Express*.

   For further information regarding the library's resources, researchers should call 223-9300, ext. 305.

   The embassy also has a collection of films and slides available for loan, without charge. Seen entry F12.

3.   *Federal Nigeria,* a quarterly newsletter, was published and disseminated by the embassy until recently. The Information Section of the embassy plans to resume its publication in the not-too- distant future.

L28 Embassy of Rwanda

1. a. *1714 New Hampshire Avenue, NW*
    Washington, D.C. 20009
    232-2882

    b. 9:00 A.M.-12:30 P.M. and 2:30 P.M.-5:00 P.M. Monday-Friday

L29 Embassy of Senegal

1. a. *2112 Wyoming Avenue, NW*
    Washington, D.C. 20008
    234-0540

b. 9:00 A.M.-1:00 P.M. and 2:30 P.M.-5:00 P.M.   Monday-Friday

2.   The embassy currently receives 2 newspapers from Senegal: the weekly *Jeune Afrique* and the daily *Soleil* (French).

L30 Embassy of Sierra Leone

1. a. *1701 19th Street, NW*
Washington, D.C. 20009
265-7700

b. 9:00 A.M.-5:00 P.M.   Monday-Friday

2.   The embassy maintains a small library which it hopes to enlarge in the near future. Currently it contains general-reference material on Sierra Leone, including newspapers and periodicals.

3.   The embassy disseminates a monthly newsletter.

L31 Embassy of Somalia

1. a. *600 New Hampshire Avenue, NW*
Washington, D.C. 20037
234-3261

b. 9:00 A.M.-5:00 P.M.   Monday-Friday

2.   The embassy currently receives the daily Somali newspaper *October Star.*

L32 Embassy of South Africa

1. a. *3051 Massachusetts Avenue, NW*
Washington, D.C. 20008
232-4400

b. 8:30 A.M.-12:30 P.M. and 1:30 P.M.-5:00 P.M.   Monday-Friday

2.   The embassy maintains a small library which contains a reference collection of government publications, newspapers, periodicals, and other general-information literature. For the embassy's film collection, see entry F13.

3.   The information counselor of the embassy publishes on an ad hoc basis (approximately 10 times a year) the *Backgrounder Series,* which covers a wide range of subjects. Recent issues have focused on: "South Africa: Scope for Investment"; "The Cape Route—Strategic Ocean Passage"; "South Africa's Vital Minerals"; "South Africa's New Constitutional Plan"; "Sport in South Africa"; and "South-West Africa/Namibia: South Africa's Case." These and other materials are distributed free of charge. For further information, call the information counselor (232-4400).

L33 Embassy of Sudan

1. a. *600 New Hampshire Avenue, NW*
   Washington, D.C. 20037
   338-8565

   b. 10:00 A.M.-Noon and 2:00 P.M.-4:00 P.M. Monday-Friday

2. The embassy maintains a small reference library for public use. This consists of books and some 150 M.A. theses and Ph.D. dissertations.

3. A newsletter, *Sudan Press,* is distributed by the embassy, along with *Sudan News,* an economic bulletin published by the Economic Office.

L34 Embassy of Swaziland

1. a. *4301 Connecticut Avenue, NW*
   Washington, D.C. 20008
   362-6683

   b. 9:00 A.M.-5:00 P.M. Monday-Friday

L35 Embassy of Tanzania

1. a. *2139 R Street, NW*
   Washington, D.C. 20008
   232-0501

   b. 9:00 A.M.-5:00 P.M. Monday-Friday

2. The embassy currently receives the *Daily News* and *Uhuru* from Tanzania.

3. A newsletter is distributed by the Information Section.

L36 Embassy of Togo

1. a. *2208 Massachusetts Avenue, NW*
   Washington, D.C. 20008
   234-4212

   b. 9:00 A.M.-5:00 P.M. Monday-Friday

2. The embassy currently receives only 1 newspaper, *Togo Press* (in French).

L37 Embassy of Tunisia

1. a. *2408 Massachusetts Avenue, NW*
   Washington, D.C. 20008
   234-6644

b. 9:00 A.M.-1:00 P.M. and 2:00 P.M.-5:00 P.M.   Monday-Friday

2.   The embassy currently receives the major French and Arabic language newspapers from Tunisia. It also maintains a small collection of films which are available for loan (see entry F14).

L38 Embassy of Uganda

1. a. *5909 16th Street, NW*
      Washington, D.C. 20011
      726-7100

   b. 9:00 A.M.-5:00 P.M.   Monday-Friday

2.   The embassy disseminates general-information literature. It currently receives the 2 leading newspapers from Uganda: *Sunday Voice* and *Voice of Uganda*. For the embassy's film collection, see entry F15.

3.   A regular newsletter is published and distributed by the embassy.

L39 Embassy of Upper Volta

1. a. *5500 16th Street, NW*
      Washington, D.C. 20011
      726-0992

   b. 9:00 A.M.-5:30 P.M.   Monday-Friday

2.   The embassy currently receives 3 newspapers in French from Upper Volta.

L40 Embassy of Zaire

1. a. *1800 New Hampshire Avenue, NW*
      Washington, D.C. 20009
      234-7690

   b. 9:00 A.M.-Noon and 2:00 P.M.-4:00 P.M.   Monday-Friday

2.   Some general-information literature is maintained for public use. The embassy also receives 2 newspapers—*Mwanashaba* (Swahili) and *Salongo* (Lingala).

L41 Embassy of Zambia

1. a. *2419 Massachusetts Avenue, NW*
      Washington, D.C. 20008
      265-9717

   b. 9:00 A.M.-5:00 P.M.   Monday-Friday

2.   The embassy disseminates general-information literature about Zambia to the public. It currently receives 2 daily newspapers: *Times of Zambia* and *Zambia Daily Mail.* See entry F16 for the embassy's film collection.

3.   Press releases of the embassy are made available to the public.

L42 International Bank for Reconstruction and Development (World Bank)

1. a. *1818 H Street, NW*
        Washington, D.C. 20433
        477-1234
        Robert S. McNamara, President

    b. Scholars should call ahead for appointments with the staff.

3.   See entry A26 for the Joint Bank-Fund Library.

4.   The main objective of the World Bank (formally, the International Bank for Reconstruction and Development) and its 2 affiliates—the International Development Association (IDA) and the International Finance Corporation (IFC)—is to provide financial and technical assistance for economic development. Since the bank is primarily concerned with making or guaranteeing loans for reconstruction and development projects, most of its activities pertain to developing countries. Bank and IDA operations encompass the following areas: agriculture and rural development, education, energy, industrial development and finance, population and nutrition, power, technical assistance, telecommunications, transportation, urban development, and water supply and sewerage. The bank assesses and takes into account the environmental impact and health aspects of its projects.
      The World Bank is a valuable resource for research in the field of African economics in these areas.

The bank's operational structure is organized into 6 regional offices, 3 of which deal with Africa (East Africa, West Africa, and Middle East and North Africa).
      The regional offices are responsible for the planning and management of the World Bank's development assistance programs. They are divided into projects and programs departments, dealing with the countries in each region. The regional offices are complemented and supported by the Central Projects Staff and Development Policy Staff dealing specifically with sectoral work and research.
      The bank's Information and Public Affairs Department has public-affairs specialists who carry out the department's public-affairs effort in developing countries on a regional basis and provide information services to those regions. These regional specialists are the first point of contact with the bank and will guide interested persons and scholars to the ap-

propriate departments or specialists in the regional offices. All inquiries should be directed to:

Public Affairs Specialist (Africa)
Information and Public Affairs Department
1818 H Street, NW
Washington, D.C. 20433

676-1625

Approximately one-third of the bank's staff (excluding support staff) is engaged in programs or projects relating to Africa. The bank, therefore, is an invaluable source of information on Africa as well as other countries, especially material pertaining to the sectors mentioned above. The Africanist can find this information in numerous publications of the bank dealing with a wide range of subjects, such as planning in Morocco; options for long-term development in Nigeria; Kenya's development since 1963; economic performance of the Ivory Coast over the past 25 years; Senegal's economic and Zambia's agricultural development; and African experiences with rural development.

Statistical information may be found in the *World Bank Atlas,* published annually, which gives population, total and per capita gross national product, and growth rates for 185 countries and territories, including those in Africa, and *World Economic and Social Indicators* (quarterly).

The *World Bank Staff Working Paper* series, in addition to dealing with specific countries and areas, disseminates the results of the bank's research and information on economic subjects of special importance to the bank's work. The *Sector Policy Paper* series discusses important trends in the bank's sector and project work.

Researchers should consult the *World Bank Annual Report,* which highlights specific areas of the bank's activities and policy decisions during each fiscal year (July 1-June 30), gives details of operations by region and a summary of projects assisted during the fiscal year, and reviews technical assistance and aid coordination activities. The report includes a statistical annex on the debt situation of developing countries and on foreign and international bond issues, the financial statements of the World Bank and IDA, and appendices giving cumulative totals of lending by major purpose and region and by country.

In addition to the numerous free publications which are available to serious researchers on request, books are published on behalf of the World Bank by a number of publishing houses (for example, The Johns Hopkins University Press in the United States, Oxford University Press in the United Kingdom, Editorial Tecnos in Spain, and others). The books may be bought in bookstores or ordered from the publisher.

The bank's publications, free and for sale, are listed in the *World Bank Catalog of Publications* which is published annually. The catalog is organized by subject matter. Country studies are listed alphabetically by country. This section also has a cross-reference listing of papers dealing with specific countries or regions that may be found under other subject categories.

Requests for the World Bank catalog and for free publications should be addressed to:

> World Bank
> Publications Unit
> 1818 H Street, NW
> Washington, D.C. 20433
>
> 477-2403

Audio-visual Program   676-1633

The World Bank's Information and Public Affairs Department maintains an extensive library of photographs on a wide range of projects which have been assisted by the bank in the various member countries. Many of these would be of interest to Africanists, who should call the Photo Library in order to view them.

Additionally, the World Bank has also started producing slideshows and motion pictures, which are available for viewing and borrowing by individuals and institutions. Inquiries regarding the availability of films, radio-tapes, and photographs should be made to the Chief, Audio-visual Division, Department of Informaiton and Public Affairs.

ECONOMIC DEVELOPMENT INSTITUTE (EDI)

1800 G Street, NW
Washington, D.C. 20433
477-2203

Raymond Frost, Director

The Economic Development Institute was established by the World Bank with the aim of improving the quality of economic management in developing countries by providing training for officials involved in development programs and projects. Participants in the training courses are nominated by the developing countries on the basis of their experience, background, and their potential for making a significant contribution to the development of their countries. Presently, courses are offered in agriculture and rural development; industry and development banking; education; and urbanization, water supply, and transportation. EDI courses are not open to the public.

The institute's publication program, which currently consists of some 15 titles, is primarily aimed at emeting its own requireemnts for teaching materials. These *EDI Seminar Papers* include the following, which should be of interest to the Africanist: *Selected Bibliography on Agricultural Project Evaluation* (EDI Seminar 1); *Some Aspects of Financial Policies and Central Banking in Developing Countries* (EDI Seminar 11); and *Zambia: An Agricultural Development Strategy for the Next Twenty-five Years* (EDI Seminar 14).

Note: Also see entries A26, F19, and G7.

L43 International Monetary Fund (IMF)

1. a. *700 19th Street, NW*
   Washington, D.C. 20431
   477-7000
   Jacques de Larosière, Managing Director

   b. Appointments with personnel should be made in advance.

2. See entry A26 for the Joint Bank-Fund Library in the Libraries section of this *Guide*.

4. The main purpose of IMF is to promote international monetary cooperation, facilitate the balanced growth of international trade, and maintain exchange stability through consultation and collaboration by member countries.

   The Monetary Fund, like its counterpart the World Bank, is a major resource for the Africanist, especially in the subject category of economics. IMF's extensive list of publications provides a continuous and up-to-date source of statistics and other information on economic developments in African countries. Perhaps a more important resource at the fund is the staff members themselves, who are extremely knowledgeable in their fields and have country-specific expertise. Time permitting, these specialists are willing to confer with scholars.

The IMF has numerous departments and offices with activities that pertain to Africa. Some of the more important of these are discussed below.

AFRICAN DEPARTMENT
J. B. Zulu, Director   477-2888

Central African Division
Evangelos A. Calamitsis, Chief   477-6107

East African Division
Bo Karlstroem, Chief   477-6542

Equatorial African Division
Massimo Russo, Chief   477-3763

Midwest African Division
Grant B. Taplin, Chief   477-2852

North African Division
Christian A. François, Chief   477-3707

Southeast African Division
Joseph G. Keyes, Chief   477-5657

West African Division
Francis d'A. Collings, Chief   477-4973

The African Department comprises 7 divisions, each of which is assigned 6 countries. More than 70 economists in the department monitor balance-of-payments developments, exchange rates, foreign trade, and related economic trends in the various countries. They also render advice and technical assistance to member countries. As a result, much of their work is of a confidential nature and not accessible to outside scholars.

The researcher can, however, obtain useful material from the 7-volume series, *Surveys of African Economies,* published by the IMF. Available in separate English and French editions, these 7 volumes cover 36 countries in Africa. They contain extensive material on the monetary, fiscal, exchange-control, and trading systems for each country and also provide detailed information on natural resources, development planning, production, budgets and taxation, money, banking, foreign trade, and payments.

Staff Papers, a compilation of studies prepared by members of the fund staff, also frequently contain material on Africa. They cover a wide range of subjects, such as "The Economy of Swaziland and Botswana"; "Economic Integration in Central and West Africa"; "Stabilization Program in Sierra Leone"; "The Development of Capital Markets in Africa, with Particular Reference to Kenya and Nigeria," and so forth.

BUREAU OF STATISTICS
Werner Dannemann, Director   477-2963

The publications of the bureau contain statistical information and results of research conducted for each country or region.

International Financial Statistics (IFS), a monthly publication, is a standard source of international statistics on all aspects of domestic and international finance, with information for individual African countries. The monthly *Direction of Trade* gives the most up-to-date information on direction of trade in every country, including those in Africa. The annual cumulation provides data for a number of years along with summary tables for different areas of the world. The *Balance of Payments Yearbook* provides balance-of-payment statistics for over 100 countries. Besides the annual issue, there are monthly booklets and a supplement to the *Yearbook*. The *Government Finance Statistics Yearbook* (GFS) provides users with internationally comparable data on revenues, grants, expenditures, lending, financing, and debt of central governments. Detailed data for 1 to 3 years are given for some 90 countries.

The bureau also maintains a computer system, called Data Fund (see entry G8 in the section of this *Guide* on data banks).

IMF INSTITUTE
Gerard M. Teyssier, Director   477-3727

Technical assistance constitutes one of the fund's major activities and it includes the training of officials from the finance ministries and central banks of member countries. The IMF Institute has provided the fund's training facilities since 1964. It offers courses in financial analysis and policy, balance-of-payments methodology, and public finance.

Most of the participants come from developing countries, many of which are African.

Researchers may also obtain some information on Africa from the Middle Eastern Department (477-4401), which is responsible for the fund's activities relating to Sudan, Ethiopia, Libya, and Egypt, and from the Research Department (477-2981).

IMF issues a broad range of publications on its activities as well as related economic subjects. Scholars may write for a free brochure, IMF, *Publications* (Washington, D.C., 1978), which lists and describes all publications. Some of these have already been described under various departments. In addition, the following IMF publications may contain material of interest to Africanists: *Annual Report of the Executive Directors,* which contains a survey of the world economy; the *Annual Report on Exchange Restrictions,* which contains country-by-country descriptions of the exchange system; *Balance of Payments Manual* (4th ed., January 1978); *Finance and Development,* a quarterly published jointly by IMF and the World Bank, which provides information on current international monetary trends and might be of value to students of international economics; and *IMF Survey,* which is published 23 times a year with an annual index and occasional supplements.

Note: Also see entry A26 in the Libraries section of this *Guide.*

M Associations (Academic, Professional, and Cultural)

Associations (Academic, Professional, and Cultural) Entry Format (M)

1. *Address; telephone number(s)*

2. Chief official and title

3. Programs and activities pertaining to Africa

4. Library/reference collection

5. Publications

M1 Academy for Educational Development, Inc. (AED)

1. *1414 22d Street, NW*
    Washington, D.C. 20037
    862-1900

2. Alvin C. Eurich, President and Chief Executive Officer
    Stephen F. Moseley, Director of International Operations Division

3. AED was founded in 1961 to meet the growing needs of U.S. colleges and universities for long-range programs in education and finance. Since then, its activities have been considerably expanded and encompass many areas of education, including international affairs, in which it assists developing countries in the planning and implementation of educational programs.

    AED's Africa-oriented programs consist of studying short-term skill-training methods for the Sahel region; evaluating the benefits of educational TV for adults in the rural areas of Ivory Coast; preparing feasibility studies for the establishment of regional communications centers in Africa; planning nonformal educational programs in Tunisia, Central African Empire, Upper Volta, Gambia, and the Cameroons; studying health-related applications of communications technology in the Sudan; and providing resource experts in African countries during the AIDSAT demonstrations.

4. AED's Clearinghouse on Development Communication (CDC), supported by the Agency for International Development, maintains its own library, which consists of a specialized collection of print and nonprint materials. Valuable to the Africanist is their collection of country-specific materials on education and communications in the form of unpublished research and reports. The nonprint collection includes in-depth materials on educational TV in Ethiopia and Niger, rural radio programs in Zaire, educational films in Ghana, and educational radio programs in Kenya and Tanzania.

5. The Clearinghouse on Development Communications (CDC) serves as an international center for information and materials relating to the application of communication technology to development programs. It publishes a quarterly newsletter, *CDC Report,* and a series of information *Bulletins.* Additionally, CDC's *Project Profiles* provide up-to-date information on existing programs in developing countries.

M2 African-American Institute—Washington Office

1. *1320 19th Street, NW*
    Ground Floor
    Washington, D.C. 20036
    872-0521

2. Melvin A. McCaw, Director, Washington Office

3. The African-American Institute is a private organization founded in 1953 to promote African development, strengthen African-American understanding, and inform Americans about Africa.

    The institute supports a wide range of educational, training, and research activities which include: scholarship programs for undergraduate and graduate study for Africans at U.S. universities; counseling services to African students and Southern African refugees in the United States; short-term training for African university administrators; technical and practical training to help meet manpower needs in Angola, Cape Verde, Guinea-Bissau, Mozambique, São Tomé and Principé; and travel grants to students and educators from Africa.

    In addition to the abovementioned educational activities, the African-American Institute also sponsors conferences and seminars which focus on leading policy issues in African-American relations; disseminates information on Africa to U.S. senators, congressmen, and the public; supports disaster-relief efforts in Africa, including the Sahel; and presents African art and cultural exhibits.

5. Publications include the bimonthly *Africa Report, South Africa/ Namibia Update,* published approximately every 3 weeks, which provides up-to-date coverage of the economic and political developments in South Africa and Namibia, and an *Annual Report.* In addition, the African-American Institute also publishes reports of conferences, bulletins, and informational materials.

M3 African-American Scholars Council, Inc. (AASC)

1. *1001 Connecticut Avenue, NW*
   Suite 1119
   Washington, D.C. 20036
   387-4736

2. Constance B. Hilliard, Executive Director

3. AASC's primary goal is to encourage Afro-Americans to become involved in and make significant contributions to Africa's development.
   Its program, funded by the U.S. AID, seeks to stimulate and support
   academic and applied research which will contribute to the future socioeconomic development of the African continent. Its manifold activities
   include: (a) research grants program to facilitate scholar-exchange
   between Africa and the U.S. and promote cooperation and linkages
   between educational institutions. Under this program, research has been
   carried out in over 20 African countries in areas such as food and nutrition, health-care delivery, agriculture, communications, education, and
   women's issues; (b) conference participation grants to promote interaction between scholars and professionals; and (c) professional exchange grants which would enable Africans and Americans to establish
   joint projects of mutual interest.
   Additionally, the AASC periodically sponsors workshops and conferences which focus on key African development issues and serve as a
   forum for the exchange of ideas and information. Sessions in the past
   have dealt with a wide range of topics, such as: "Southern Africa:
   Research for Development"; "African Women and Societal Crises: Implications for Development Planning"; "Programmatic and Research
   Strategy for the Control of Major Endemic Diseases in Africa"; and
   the conference on the Sahel held in October 1978, "New Adaptive
   Social Mechanisms Evolving Among Sahelian Populations Affected by
   the Drought."
   AASC also supports applied-research field projects in which teams of
   researchers investigate vital issues in African development and provide
   technical assistance. These applied-research studies are undertaken in collaboration with African governments and research institutions and have
   included the following: adaptive mechanisms evolving among Sahelian
   populations; Zimbabwe-Namibia: anticipation of economic and humanitarian needs; transition problems of developing nations in Southern
   Africa; and a study of continuities between the methods of traditional
   and scientific African health-care practitioners.

5. *African-American Scholar,* a bimonthly publication.

M4 African Cultural and Religious Society ASUOGYEBI Shrine of Washington, D.C.

1. *2021 Martin Luther King, Jr., Avenue, SE*
   Washington, D.C.
   678-9776

2.   Nana Kwabena Brown, Chief Priest

3.   The African Cultural and Religious Society is an organization of Ghanaians and black Americans who share common beliefs and the worship of ASUOGYEBI. In addition to their religious work, members of the society are involved in educational, social, and recreational activities and community work. Some of its teachers are from Africa, and they strive to retain close ties with Africa.

5.   A general-information leaflet is available on request.

M5   African Directions, Inc.

1.   *884 National Press Building*
     Washington, D.C. 20045
     347-6638

2.   Crispin D. Chindongo

3.   African Directions, Inc., is primarily concerned with the collection and dissemination of information about Africa on a large number of topics, such as African traditional thought, music and dance, art and religion, and oral traditions and history, as well as contemporary political, economic, and social affairs.

     The Education Division sponsors lectures, seminars, research projects, study tours, and cultural and trade shows. It also maintains a small collection of slides, films, and still photos.

5.   *African Directions,* a quarterly magazine, focuses on African affairs, art, culture, religion, economy, and education. (See entry Q2.)

M6   African Heritage Studies Association (AHSA)—Washington Office

1.   *Department of Political Science*
     Howard University
     2401 6th Street, NW
     Washington, D.C. 20059
     636-6999

2.   Dr. Ronald Walters, AHSA Representative in Washington

3.   AHSA is a professional organization of scholars whose main objective is to encourage research and writing on Africa and the African diaspora and facilitate greater contact among scholars. The association sponsors an annual conference and periodic seminars.

5.   Until recently, AHSA published the bimonthly *Newsletter,* which contained information on its activities. Back issues are available on request.

M7 African Marketing Corporation, Ltd.

1. *1614 Newton Street, NE*
    Washington, D.C. 20018
    526-2619

2. Oluwole Oduba, President

3. The African Marketing Corporation, Ltd., a private commercial export-import enterprise, is primarily engaged in the export of domestic merchandise and commercial and industrial equipment to West African countries. The bulk of its business undertakings are with Nigeria, though it hopes to expand its activities in the near future.

M8 African Methodist Episcopal Church Service and Development Agency, Inc.

1. *2311 M Street, NW*
    Washington, D.C. 20007
    965-9313

2. Bishop Henry W. Murph

3. The AME Church was founded in 1787 by Richard Allen with the establishment of Mother Bethel Church in Philadelphia. From its inception, the African Methodist Episcopal Church has been active in Africa, and currently there are numerous AME churches on the African continent. The church is divided into 18 episcopal districts, 5 of which serve the African population in the following countries and areas: Ghana, Liberia, Nigeria, Sierra Leone, Southwest Africa, Northern and Southern Rhodesia, Central Africa, Swaziland, Botswana, Bechuanaland, and East Africa.

    The AME Church Service and Development Agency is involved in humanitarian and educational work in Africa. Its primary goal is to help the African people develop their talents and the resources of their country.

4. AME church archives, a valuable resource for the Africanist, are open to serious scholars. Those who wish to examine the manuscripts and papers in this collection should contact Bishop Murph's office (628-6371) for permission.

5. AME Church publications include the *AME Review;* a monthly newspaper, *Christian Recorder;* and *Voice of Missions.* General-information materials are available on request.

M9 African Students Service Association

1. *1010 Vermont Avenue, NW*
    Suite 414
    Washington, D.C. 20005

2. K. A. Apori, Director

3. The association, which was established in 1972, renders assistance and guidance to African students seeking admission to U.S. colleges and institutions of learning. It helps them find suitable housing and aids them in dealing with immigration and other problems.

    All African students are eligible to become members of the association.

M10 African Wildlife Leadership Foundation

1. *1717 Massachusetts Avenue, NW*
    Washington, D.C. 20036
    265-8394

2. Robinson McIlvaine, Executive Vice President
    Sandra Price, Director of African Operations

3. The African Wildlife Leadership Foundation was founded in 1961 with the idea of providing a constructive wildlife training program for the Africans who would, in the final analysis, determine the fate of their wildlife.

    AWLF helped to establish and continues to support 2 colleges of wildlife management which provide training for park and game wardens. Graduates of these 2 schools now fill most of the positions formerly held by expatriates. AWLF also supports broadbased educational programs and pioneering research projects, as well as the advanced training of African ecologists. The foundation also provides equipment and technical assistance to parks and reserves.

    AWLF is the only international conservation organization that maintains a field office in Africa.

5. *Wildlife News* is published 3 times each year from the Nairobi office.

M11 Africare

1. *1601 Connecticut Avenue, NW*
    Washington, D.C. 20009
    462-3614

2. C. Payne Lucas, Executive Director

3. Africare, a charitable and welfare organization, is primarily concerned with rural health in Africa. It seeks the eradication and amelioration of the health problems of Africans through material and human resources.

    Africare is actively involved in the fields of nutrition, maternal and child health, health planning, water resources, and paramedical training.

4. The African Resource Information Center is a library cum resource center which contains materials on the Sahel, Southern Africa, and

health-related topics. The center, which also maintains a Personnel Data Bank, is open to the public from 9:00 A.M. to 5:30 P.M. Monday-Friday. Researchers should call ahead for appointments.

5. Publications of Africare include an *Annual Report* which describes the programs and activities of the organization and a quarterly *Newsletter.*

M12 America—Mid East Education and Training Services (AMIDEAST)

1. *1717 Massachusetts Avenue, NW*
Suite 100
Washington, D.C. 20036
797-7900

2. Orin Parker, President

3. AMIDEAST, formerly known as American Friends of the Middle East, seeks to further understanding between the peoples of the Middle East and North Africa and the people of the United States through educational exchange programs. The organization renders a wide range of educational services which include: educational counseling; placement of students from the Middle East and North Africa in U.S. institutions of learning; orientation seminars; and the administration of scholarship programs.

 AMIDEAST also maintains information on the universities in the Middle East and North Africa.

5. Publications include a quarterly *Report* and the biannual *Study and Research in the Middle East and North Africa.*

M13 American Anthropological Association (AAA)

1. *1703 New Hampshire Avenue, NW*
Washington, D.C. 20009
232-8800

2. Edward J. Lehman, Executive Director

3. The American Anthropological Association is a professional society of anthropologists, students, educators, and others interested in advancing the discipline of anthropology. Individual members of the association engage in research pertaining to Africa which is published in scholarly journals, books, and monographs. The society also sponsors lectures and conferences and maintains a placement service and speakers' bureau.

5. Publications include: *American Anthropologist* (quarterly), *American Ethnologist* (quarterly), *Anthropology Newsletter,* and *Guide to Departments of Anthropology* (annual). In addition, several of the association's *Anthropological Studies, Monographs,* and *Selected Papers* should be of interest to Africanists. A *Publications List* is available free on request.

M14 American Association for the Advancement of Science (AAAS)

1. *1776 Massachusetts Avenue, NW*
    Washington, D.C. 20036
    467-5441

2. William D. Carey, Executive Officer
    J. Thomas Ratchford, Acting Head, International Science

3. The primary objective of AAAS is to encourage and promote scientific research and foster scientific freedom and responsibility. In fulfilling these objectives, AAAS supports a wide range of activities, which include: planning and support of annual meetings and symposia; special programs in science education, international cooperation, science, and public policy; and opportunities in science.

    AAAS's Africa-related programs are administered by its Office of International Science, which is responsible for coordinating all international activities. These activities consist of greater cooperation and communication between AAAS and the members of its Consortium of Affiliates for International Science, and foreign associations for the advancement of science, on issues of mutual interest. An example of such joint endeavors is AAAS's participation in 1977 at meetings sponsored by several scientific associations which included the West African Science Association, the East African Academy, and the Tanzania National Scientific Research Council. An AAAS representative attended the inaugural meeting of the Association of Faculties of Science of African Universities. AAAS was also actively involved in and cosponsored the Nairobi Seminar on Desertification held in August 1977. Africans and Africanists were included in workshops organized by AAAS in preparation for the 1979 U.N. Conference on Science and Technology for Development.

    In 1977, AAAS completed a 3-year project which stressed the role of cultural factors in population programs. This project has direct relevance for development programs and population policies in developing nations of Africa.

    The Office of International Science sponsors annually a series of seminars for science attachés of various African and other countries.

5. A major concern of the association is to increase public understanding and appreciation of science. As a result, AAAS has an extensive publications program. Since 1900, it has published *Science,* a weekly magazine that contains scholarly articles and current information on vital scientific concerns and issues. AAAS also publishes the proceedings of selected symposia and meetings. For a complete list of its publications, researchers should obtain the current *Catalog* by calling 467-4304/4305.

M15 American Association of State Colleges and Universities (AASCU)—Office of International Programs

1. *Suite 700*
   1 Dupont Circle, NW
   Washington, D.C. 20036
   293-7070

2. Maurice Harari, Director, Office of International Programs

3. AASCU represents some 330 state colleges and universities, many of which have programs and activities pertaining to Africa. In the past, under the auspices of the Office of International Programs, selected educators visited various African countries on exchange programs. Currently, however, there are no ongoing programs involving Africa.

M16 American Association of University Women (AAUW) Educational Foundation

1. *2401 Virginia Avenue, NW*
   Washington, D.C. 20037
   785-7736

2. Marjorie Bell Chambers, President
   Helen B. Wolfe, General Director

3. The primary objective of the AAUW is to initiate, encourage, and support creative programs to provide intellectual growth for women and service to society. The main focus is on women, education, cultural interests, international relations, and the community. Of the foundation's numerous activities, special mention needs to be made of the African Educators Program. This program, which was established in 1963, provides African women (mainly educators and administrators) with the opportunity to visit and study American educational institutions. The program provides a variety of educational and cultural experiences and facilitates crosscultural exchange of ideas and values.

   The Educational Foundation also awards over 35 fellowships every year to outstanding women of countries other than the United States, for advanced study and training in the U.S. Several African women have been recipients of this International Fellowship Program.

4. The foundation has its own library and an archival collection on women. The library, which is open to members only, has a small collection of books pertaining to Africa (mainly on women, economic and rural development, education, and history). It also contains a complete collection of the *AAUW Journal,* the official publication of the association.

5. *AAUW Journal,* which began as a quarterly, has since 1970 become an annual publication. See *AAUW Journal Index: 1882–1975* (Washington, D.C., 1977).

M17 American Bar Association (ABA)—Joint Committee on International Legal Exchange (ILEX)

1. *1800 M Street, NW*
   Washington, D.C. 20036
   331-2258

2. Kathrine Lee Ebert, Staff Director

3. The ABA's ILEX administers short- and long-term training and internship and seminar programs for members of the legal profession from the U.S. and other countries.

5. Program literature is available on request.

M18 American Council of Education—Overseas Liaison Committee

1. *Overseas Liaison Committee (OLC)*
   11 Dupont Circle, NW
   Washington, D.C. 20036
   833-4674

2. Charles H. Lyons, Director

3. The Overseas Liaison Committee (formerly known as Africa Liaison Committee), consisting of university scholars and administrators with a specialized knowledge of and commitment to higher education, seeks to promote greater communication between the American academic community and higher education in Africa and facilitate socioeconomic development in Africa through sharing of information, experience, and knowledge.

   The committee has undertaken several cooperative projects in conjunction with regional and national educational associations in Africa. Noteworthy among them is the Rural Development Network (RDN), which involves a wide range of rural development activities.

5. Publications include: *International Directory for Education Liaison* (American Council of Education, 1973), an annotated bibliography on rural development in Africa; *Rural Development Network Bulletin,* a quarterly in English, French, and Portuguese; *Rural Development Papers;* and miscellaneous reports.

M19 American Federation of Labor and Congress of Industrial Organizations (AFL-CIO)

1. *815 16th Street, NW*
   Washington, D.C. 20006
   637-5000

2. Lane Kirkland, President

3. The AFL-CIO's longstanding interest in Africa and African trade unions led to the creation of the African-American Labor Center in 1964. The primary goal of the AALC is to strengthen the labor movements in Africa and support them in their struggles for economic and social independence. Its activities include trade-union education, leadership training, vocational education, economic research, provision of social services, and the development of cooperatives and credit unions.

   AALC has a close working relationship with African missions at the U.N., the Economic Commission for Africa, OAU, the Organization of African Trade Union Unity, and other international organizations. It is actively involved in over 340 programs in some 41 countries of Africa and has 14 field representatives in Africa. Though AALC's office is located in New York, the Washington AFL-CIO can provide researchers with considerable information on its varied activities.

5. The African-American Labor Center publishes a monthly newsletter *Reporter,* which contains information concerning AALC projects and other trade-union developments.

M20 American Historical Association (AHA)

1. *400 A Street, SE*
   Washington, D.C. 20003
   544-2422

2. Mack Thompson, Executive Director

3. AHA is a nonprofit professional organization which is the principal representative of historians in the United States. It seeks to encourage and improve the study and teaching of history, including African historical writing.

   The annual convention of the AHA, held each December, provides an opportunity for Africanists to meet one another and remain up-to-date on the most recent research and writing in their fields of interest.

5. AHA issues a series of pamphlets which provide recent interpretations in specific areas and also cover questions of methodology and approach. The pamphlets contain select bibliographies which are useful for students and teachers. Two of the pamphlets in the series deal with Africa: Philip Curtin, *Precolonial African History* and Joseph C. Miller, *Equatorial Africa.*

   Additionally, AHA publishes the *American Historical Review,* issued 5 times a year, which contains scholarly articles in all fields of history, and the AHA *Newsletter.* Since 1976 the association has published a valuable index to periodical literature on individual countries and regions. *Recently Published Articles* is issued 3 times a year.

American Home Economics Association See entry N5.

M21 American Near East Refugee Aid (ANERA)

1. *900 Woodward Building*
   733 15th Street, NW
   Washington, D.C. 20005
   347-2558

2. Peter Gubser, President

3. ANERA is a charitable and welfare organization which renders assistance to Palestinian refugees and other civilian victims of the Mideast war. It also seeks to further American understanding of the Arab refugee problem by disseminating informaton on the Middle East crisis.

   The American Middle East Rehabilitation (AMER) is the medical division of the American Near East Refugee Aid. It solicits and sends medical supplies for use by refugees. For more information on its activities, researchers should contact Robert L. Fisher, Director (347-2558).

5. ANERA's *Annual Report* describes the activities of the organization. It also disseminates a quarterly *Newsletter*.

M22 American Political Science Association

1. *1527 New Hampshire Avenue, NW*
   Washington, D.C. 20036
   483-2512

2. Evron Kirkpatrick, Executive Director

3. The American Political Science Association is a professional and scholarly organization which seeks to promote, improve, and enhance the study of political science. Its membership, drawn predominantly from the ranks of the academic community, also includes journalists, government workers, and other interested persons.

   Individual members of the association frequently engage in research relating to Africa, specifically in the sphere of domestic and international politics and government.

   The association sponsors annual conventions, at which there are always some sessions devoted to African government and politics.

5. The *American Political Science Review*, a quarterly, publishes articles and reviews of books in the field of African studies. *The Proceedings of the Annual Meeting* are also available on microfilm.

M23 American Public Health Association (APHA)—International Health Programs

1. *1015 15th Street, NW*
   Washington, D.C. 20005
   789-5600

2. William H. McBeath, M.D., Executive Director

3. The American Public Health Association (APHA), a professional organization of over 50,000 public health workers, strives to improve personal and environmental health through its domestic and international programs.

   APHA's International Health Programs are designed to provide leadership in international health development; to improve and increase health services and manpower in developing countries; and to promote basic preventive and curative health services. The programs encompass many areas of public health: food and nutrition, maternal and child health, population, education, environment, and epidemiology.

   Africa-related activities of the Office of International Health Programs include: (a) operational and management support for primary health-care and family-planning programs. In collaboration with international organizations, African regional organizations, and 20 West and Central African governments, it seeks to strengthen training institutions, promote epidemiological surveillance, and improve primary health care facilities; (b) assessments of health and environmental status in 8 countries in the Sahel region, and studies of low-cost health delivery systems in Africa; (c) training and consultative services; and (d) sponsorship of conferences and workshops on primary health care. It should be pointed out that many staff members of the Office of International Health Programs have had extensive field experience in Africa, and their expertise and knowledge should be of considerable use to researchers.

4. The American Public Health Association serves as a resource center in Washington for the collection and dissemination of information and materials on health systems. The Office of International Health Programs maintains extensive data on primary health-care projects around the world, including Africa. These include data on health education, manpower utilization, health-care services, and planning and evaluation. For further information, contact Barry Karlin (467-5007).

5. APHA has an extensive publications program, which includes the following: *American Journal of Public Health* (monthly); Abram S. Berenson, ed., *Control of Communicable Diseases in Man,* 12th ed. (American Public Health Association, 1975); and *Salubritas,* a quarterly newsletter published in English, Spanish, and French, which deals with problems of primary health care in developing countries.

   In addition, APHA has a large body of information pertaining to disease patterns in the Sahel states. Researchers can obtain a list of publications of APHA by calling 467-5027.

M24 American Sociological Association (ASA)

1. *1722 N Street, NW*
   Washington, D.C. 20036
   833-3410

2. Russell R. Dynes, Executive Officer

3.　　ASA is a professional and scholarly organization devoted to the promotion and furtherance of research and teaching of sociology.

　　ASA's Committee on World Sociology has under it various liaison groups for different regions of the world, including a Subcommittee on Africa. Researchers who wish to know more about this subcommittee's activities should contact David Wiley, (517) 353-1700.

　　ASA sponsors annual conventions at which scholarly papers are presented and which also serve as a meeting place for sociologists.

5.　　ASA's publications include: *American Sociological Review* (bimonthly); *American Sociologist* (quarterly); *Contemporary Sociology* (biannual); *Journal of Health and Social Behavior; Social Psychology Quarterly;* and *Sociology of Education* (quarterly). These publications may contain occasional articles of interest to Africanists.

M25 Amnesty International U.S.A.—Washington Office

1.　　*413 East Capitol Street, SE*
Washington, D.C. 20003
544-0200

2.　　Stephanie Grant, Director of Washington Office

3.　　Amnesty International is an independent nonpartisan, worldwide human-rights organization concerned with prisoners. It advocates fair and early trials for all prisoners and seeks "the release of men and women imprisoned anywhere for their beliefs, colour, ethnic origin, language, or religion, provided they have neither used nor advocated violence."

　　The organization has over 2,000 adoption groups and national sections in 35 countries of the world, including Africa and the Middle East, and a worldwide individual membership. Members of each adoption group are responsible for at least 2 prisoners of conscience each, whose rights and interests they try to defend.

　　Amnesty International acts on the basis of the United Nations Universal Declaration of Human Rights and cooperates with other international organizations. It is also a member of the Coordinating Committee of the Organization of African Unity's Bureau of Placement and Education of African Refugees.

5.　　Several publications of Amnesty International would be of interest to the Africanist. These include:

Amnesty International Annual Report 1978, which describes the work of the organization over a 1-year period and contains a country-by-country survey;

Amnesty International Briefing Papers, a series containing papers for *Guinea* (June 1978); *Malawi* (August 1976); *Morocco* (October 1977); *Namibia* (April 1977); and *Rhodesia/Zimbabwe* (March 1976);

Human Rights in Rhodesia: Testimony of Malcolm Smart, Amnesty International to the Subcommittee on Africa of the Committee on International Relations of the House of Representatives, April 2, 1979;

Human Rights in Uganda: A Report by Amnesty International (June 1978);

Human Rights Violations in Ethiopia (November 1978);

Political Imprisonment in South Africa: An Amnesty International Report (1978);

Tunisia: Imprisonment of Trade Unionists in 1978: Amnesty International Report (February 1979).

In addition to the above-mentioned publications, Amnesty International also distributes free of charge its monthly newsletter *Amnesty Action* and *Matchbox*, a quarterly publication. Background papers and updates on human-rights violations are also available for many countries not listed above.

M26 Association for the Study of Afro-American Life and History

1.   *Carter G. Woodson Center*
       1401 14th Street, NW
       Washington, D.C. 20005
       667-2822

2.   Charles Walker Thomas, President
       J. Rupert Picott, Executive Director

3.   The association was founded in 1915 by Carter G. Woodson "as an instrument to promote appreciation of the life and history of the Black American, to encourage an understanding of present status, and to enrich the promise of the future."

       The activities of the association are varied, but its central focus—presentation of the Afro-American and African experience—is consistent. Its 2 major publications (see section 5 below) carry articles about Africa and the African diaspora (e.g., "Africa's Elevation and Changing Racial Thought at Lincoln University, 1854-1886," and "Marcus Garvey's Impossible Dream").

       The association also convenes an annual meeting at which scholarly papers are presented by some 60 panels (cassette recordings of these papers can be purchased). In addition, the association sponsors a Black History Month during which towns, schools, mass media, and businesses are encouraged to present programs about Africa and the Afro-American experience. The National Historical Marker Program places plaques at the birthsites or places of achievement of historically significant individuals or at historic sites associated with blacks. In addition, the ASALH sells kits to schools to celebrate Black History Month.

4.   The library is relatively new, and only about half of its 4,000 titles are cataloged. No purchases are made, but books arrive for review in the *Journal*. There are some 300 titles of Africa-oriented books, and there are others in offices. The library is mainly for the benefit of the association and its staff, but individuals are admitted. It is open from 9:30 A.M. to 2:30 P.M.

       Titles of note include all publications of the ASALH, about 200 pre-Civil War titles (biographies of former slaves, *A Plea for Africa* [second edition, 1837]), and Congressman Dawson's personal library. There are some vertical files with assorted material, of which a few items concern Africa, and assorted unclassified African periodicals. A shelflist and a dictonary catalog are also available.

5.   The association publishes the *Journal of Negro History* (quarterly) and the *Negro History Bulletin* (bimonthly).

The publishing agency of the association is Association Publishers, Inc., which has currently more than 50 titles in print, including Andrew F. Brimmer, *Economic Development: International and African Perspectives* (Washington, D.C.: Associated Publishers, Inc., 1976), and Carter G. Woodson, *African Heroes and Heroines* (reprint ed., Washington, D.C.: Associated Publishers, Inc., 1969). A catalog of publications is available on request.

M27 Association of Ghanaians in North America (AGHANA)

1.   *P.O. Box 14029*
Washington, D.C. 20044
277-5043

2.   Kojo Darley, President

3.   The association serves as a link between Ghanaians in North America and their mother country. It keeps them informed about the political, social, and economic events in Ghana and encourages them to make contributions toward their country's development.

AGHANA also seeks to promote cultural understanding between the Ghanaians and the American people. It sponsors lectures and cultural activities.

5.   A monthly publication, *Afajato,* focuses on political and economic issues.

M28 Association of Seventh-Day Adventist Educators (ASDAE)

1.   *c/o General Conference, Department of Education*
6840 Eastern Avenue, NW
Washington, D.C. 20012
723-0800

2.   W. J. Brown, Executive Secretary

3.   ASDAE, with a membership drawn from the ranks of administrators and educators, is mainly concerned with promoting the ideals and principles of Christian education and with fostering greater understanding and cooperation between peoples of different nations.

5.   The association publishes the *Educational Newsletter* and a bimonthly *Journal of Adventist Education.*

M29 Association on Third World Affairs (ATWA)

1.   *3114 Rodman Street, NW*
Washington, D.C. 20008
966-9326

2. Lorna Hahn, Executive Director

3. Founded in 1966, ATWA is a membership organization composed of educators, lawyers, diplomats, and others who share a common interest in promoting cooperation between Americans and peoples of the developing countries.

    The association is actively involved in a wide range of Africa-related activities which include study, research, and dissemination of information; interviews with prominent African leaders, such as Bishop Abel Muzorewa and Chief Jeremiah Chirau; and regular meetings to discuss issues of global importance. Guest lecturers at these meetings are frequently African leaders, such as Chief Gatsha Buthelezi, President of the National Cultural Liberation Movement and Chairman of the South African Black Alliance, and the foreign ministers of Zambia and Tanzania.

5. The association publishes a bimonthly newsletter, *Third World Forum*.

    In addition, ATWA also publishes a series of occasional papers which deal in depth with controversial issues of concern to the U.S. and to Third World countries. The first in this series is Lorna Hahn, *South Africa and Transkei: Some Alternative Approaches* (1978).

M30 Institute of International Education (IIE)—Washington Office

1. *Suite 200*
    11 Dupont Circle, NW
    Washington, D.C. 20036
    483-0001

2. Peter D. Pelham, Director of Washington Office

3. The Institute of International Education, with its headquarters in New York, is a private, nonprofit organization which administers a number of educational and cultural exchange programs on behalf of the U.S. government, private foundations, foreign governments, and institutes. These include the Fulbright-Hays Mutual Educational Exchange Program; UNESCO Fellowships; Ford Foundation Graduate Fellowships; University of North Carolina Population Center Internships; and the Harvard University Institute for International Development projects in economic planning and development.

    IIE also provides technical assistance services to U.S. specialists working in the fields of agricultural and economic development, population, urban planning, and related areas in developing countries, including those in Africa.

    IIE maintains branch offices in Nairobi, Kenya, Lagos, and Nigeria.

    The Washington office is mainly involved in the U.S. government's International Visitors Program and disseminates information on exchange programs.

5. The organization's reference materials and information brochures include: *Basic Facts on Foreign Study* (1976); Gail A. Cohen, ed., *Summer Study Abroad* (1977); *Scholarships and Fellowships for Foreign Study: A Selected Bibliography* (1975); Robert Spencer and Ruth

Awe, *International Educational Exchange: A Bibliography* (1970); *Teaching Abroad* (1976); and *U.S. College-Sponsored Programs Abroad* (1977).

IIE staff is currently working on the *Handbook on International Study for U.S. Nationals—Volume III*, which will focus on Africa and the Near East. This will be a useful source for Africanists.

A publications list, an annual report, a summary of sponsored projects, and the quarterly newsletter *IIE Reports* are available on request.

M31 International and Multicultural Development Center—University of the District of Columbia

1.   *929 E Street, NW*
      Suite 203
      Washington, D.C. 20004
      727-2731

2.   Barbara C. Patterson, Director

3.   The International and Multicultural Development Center's supportive services and programs are designed to assist foreign students and U.S. bilingual/bicultural students in meeting their education and career goals. The center provides counseling and advisory services which include: career placement; legal assistance; tutoring in English, math, and study skills; and financial aid and employment opportunities.

      In addition the center also sponsors intercultural conferences, seminars, lectures, exhibits, educational tours, visitors' programs, and other activities which seek to promote intercultural and understanding.

5.   Publications include the monthly *International-Multicultural Bulletin*.

M32 International Council of Goodwill Industries

1.   *9200 Wisconsin Avenue*
      Washington, D.C. 20014
      (301) 530-6500

2.   George Soloyanis, Director of International Operations
      Robert Ransom, Africa Programs Coordinator

3.   The International Council of Goodwill Industries has 38 affiliates in 24 countries of the world, including 5 in Africa. The council works in partnership with private nonprofit organizations in African countries which are working with handicapped persons. Its main function is to help local organizations extend and improve vocational rehabilitation services for the handicapped and to provide employment opportunities for them. Goodwill Industries' consultants have provided guidance to organizations in Togo, Nigeria, Sierra Leone, Mauritania, and Senegal, in the establishment and development of national vocational rehabilitation programs in these countries.

5.   Publications which describe the council's activities in Africa include:

Goodwill Industries of America, Inc., *Annual Report* (1977 and 1978);

International Council of Goodwill Industries, *Annual Yearbook and Statistical Report* (1977 and 1978);

———, *Progress Report, Africa Programs Development* (April 1978 and January 1979).

M33 International Institute for Cotton (IIC)

1. *Room 203, Solar Building*
    1000 16th Street, NW
    Washington, D.C. 20036
    223-5876

2. Peter Pereira, Executive Director

3. IIC is an intergovernmental market-development organization. Its membership is open to all cotton-producing countries belonging to the U.N. and includes Ivory Coast, Nigeria, Tanzania, and Uganda. The primary objective of the institute is to promote greater demand for cotton and its products in Western Europe and Japan and thereby help maximize the returns to cotton farmers and cotton-producing countries. To meet its objectives, IIC's several divisions focus on economic and market research; technical research and development of new and improved cotton products; and training programs and market-support programs aimed at stimulating consumer demand.

5. IIC publishes *Cotton and the Third World*. A small booklet entitled *Cotton's Importance to the Developing World* contains statistical information on cotton yields and exports of several African nations.

M34 International Institute for Environment and Development (IIED)

1. *1302 Eighteenth Street, NW, Suite 501*
    Washington, D.C. 20036
    462-0900

2. Barbara Ward, President

3. IIED is a nonprofit foundation which is primarily concerned with the issues of future energy and environment, development of sufficient shelter and clean water for mankind, and the utilization of science and technology for development, IIED maintains close contact with governmental and nongovernmental organizations, the U.N., and other international institutions.

    IIED's Africa-related programs include research and development of renewable energy resources in the Third World; assessment of the impact of national human settlements policies in Egypt, Sudan, Tunisia, Kenya, Niger, Nigeria, and Tanzania (these policies will be evaluated in light of the major recommendations of Habitat—the U.N. Conference on Human Settlements); and the examination of the problem of desertification.

Earthscan, IIED's media-information unit, is designed to increase public awareness of vital global environment-development issues. Its activities include newspaper features service, briefing documents, press briefing seminars, press conferences, and personal contacts.

IIED periodically organizes symposia and conferences in which researchers and representatives of governments and international agencies are brought together to discuss vital issues. Recent symposia include "National Human Settlements Policies" at the University of Sussex in February 1978 and "Marginal Settlements in Africa and Latin America" in Mexico, September 1977, which was attended by 10 researchers from Africa. Papers presented at these meetings are generally published in several languages.

5. IIED has an extensive publications program which includes several items of interest for the Africanist. Subjects include energy policies and options, desertification, food and hunger, and human settlements. Information pertaining to these publications can be obtained from the IIED *Annual Report* by writing to the institute.

M35 Islamic Center

1. *2551 Massachusetts Avenue, NW*
   Washington, D.C. 20008
   332-3451

2. Dr. M. A. Rauf, Director

3. The Islamic Center is a place of worship for the Muslim community as well as a cultural institution for the dissemination of information on Islam, its history and culture. The center conducts numerous activities aimed at fostering greater interest and understanding of the Islamic faith. These include a publications program (see entry 5), organization of periodic lectures on various aspects of Islam, and instruction in the Arabic language.

4. The center also maintains a small library. This collection, totaling over 4,000 books, consists mainly of standard works on Islamic law, history, philosophy, traditions, and biographies. A majority of these books are in Arabic and some may be of interest to the Africanist. The library is open to the public 7 days a week, 10:00 A.M. to 4:00 P.M. for reference use only.

5. The center's publications deal with the Islamic faith and related topics. Books are available on the Qur'an, the Prophet, Islamic beliefs and practices, law and society, etc. A publications list is available on request.

M36 National Academy of Sciences (NAS)

1. *2101 Constitution Avenue, NW*
   Washington, D.C. 20418
   393-8100

2. Philip Handler, President
    Murray Todd, Executive Director, Commission on International Relations

3. The National Academy of Sciences is an independent, nonprofit institution dedicated to the advancement of science and technology in the U.S. and abroad. Its principal function is to assist and advise the government on matters pertaining to science and technology. It is supported by government and private funds and also gives grants and fellowships to individual private scholars.

    The NAS has a longstanding interest in the application of science and technology to less-developed countries.

    The principal operating agency of the National Academy of Sciences and the National Academy of Engineering is the National Research Council (NRC), which in turn is divided into a number of assemblies and commissions comprising several different boards. This entry will, however, list only those which are of direct relevance to Africanists.

COMMISSION ON INTERNATIONAL RELATIONS

Board on Science and Technology for International Development (BOSTID)

The BOSTID programs have emphasized cooperation and collaboration with counterpart organizations in African countries in the application of science and technology to problems of social and economic development. Regional organizations such as the Scientific Council for Africa (CSA), and the Commission for Technical Cooperation in Africa South of the Sahara (CCTA), and the United Nations Economic Commission for Africa, have participated actively in these programs.

BOSTID programs in the past decade have centered on bilateral workshops, seminars, and conferences; visits by African scientists; and the exchange of scientific information and cooperation between scientists in the U.S. and Africa. Workshops were held in Egypt, Ghana, Nigeria, Sudan, Tanzania, Tunisia, and Zaire on a wide range of topics which included science policy and organization; natural resources; manpower and education; agriculture; medical sciences, public health and demography; and food and nutrition.

BOSTID studies have been undertaken on such topics as "Arid Lands of Sub-Saharan Africa," "More Water for Arid Lands: Promising Technologies and Research Opportunities," "Postharvest Food Losses in Developing Countries," "African Agricultural Research Capabilities," and several others.

ADVISORY PROGRAM ON THE SAHEL

The Sahel Program was established in May 1978 under the Board of Science and Technology for International Development. Its main objectives are twofold: first, to establish a cooperative relationship with institutions and agencies applying science and technology to development in the Sahel Region (Chad, Mali, Mauritania, Niger, Senegal, Upper Volta, Gambia, and Cape Verde Islands); second, to advise and assist AID in assessing the long-term ecological and environmenal consequences of development activities in the countries concerned to make the programs more effective in achieving their development objectives. This program is closely tied to the Sahel Documentation Center at Michigan State University and maintains links with scientific institutions and universities in the U.S. and overseas.

4. BOSTID maintains a working library of resource materials related to scientific and technological aspects of economic development, including African reference materials.

5. The NAS has an extensive publications program. These numerous scientific and technical publications originate in, or are sponsored by, NAS National Academy of Engineering, Institute of Medicine, and the National Research Council. All reports are available to the public. For a complete list see *Publications Listing, Titles in Print* (January 1977). The National Academy of Engineering and the Institute of Medicine are affiliates, organized under the NAS charter in 1964 and 1970 respectively.

M37 National Association of Negro Business and Professional Women's Clubs—International Affairs Committee

1. *1806 New Hampshire Avenue, NW*
   Washington, D.C. 20009
   483-4880

2. Yvonne Chappelle, Chairperson, International Affairs Committee

3. The primary goal of this organization is to create an atmosphere in which women can actively participate in bringing about meaningful change in society. Its membership is large and varied, consisting of black businesswomen and professional women in the United States and abroad, including some in Africa.
   The major resources here are the members of this organization, many of whom have expertise in African affairs.
   The International Affairs Committee also sponsors visits to Africa.

5. Publications include a quarterly magazine, *Communiqué,* and *President's Newsletter,* published irregularly.

M38 National Education Association (NEA)—Office of International Relations

1. *1201 16th Street, NW*
   Washington, D.C. 20036
   833-4105

2. Braulio Alonso, Director, Office of International Relations

3. The Office of International Relations provides information, training, and consultant and advisory services to teacher organizations in foreign countries. It maintains close ties with numerous teacher organizations in Africa and participates in joint projects. In April 1979, NEA's Office of International Relations will cosponsor a conference in Nigeria with

the Nigerian Union of Teachers (UTC) which will focus on the theme of developing leadership of women in teacher organizations.

M39 Overseas Education Fund of the League of Women Voters

1. *2101 L Street, NW, Suite 916*
    Washington, D.C. 20037
    466-3430

2. Willie Campbell, President
    Stanton E. Dreyer, Director, Planning and Programming
    Fay Williams, Chairman of the Africa Committee

3. The main objective of the Overseas Education Fund is to encourage and promote the active participation of women in the development of their countries. The emphasis is on providing leadership skills and improving economic standards in developing nations of Latin America, Africa, and Asia. These assistance programs help women acquire the necessary skills for community change and also enable them to reach their full potential as productive human beings.

    Presently, the OEF is actively involved in projects in Zambia and the Cameroons and is planning to establish new projects in other regions of Africa.

4. The fund maintains a resource center which is open to the public from 9:00 A.M. to 5:00 P.M. The center's holdings consist of a small collection of general reference books, periodicals, and numerous reports and papers on women in developing nations. There is also a vertical file collection which contains pamphlets, reports, clippings, and other material on women, education, economic development, family-planning programs, leadership, rural development, poverty, womens' rights, and technical-assistance programs. The Africanist will find some useful material in these files, which are arranged in boxes by countries as well as subjects. The resource center also has over 20 reports of TAICH (Technical Assistance Information Clearinghouse) called *Development Assistance Program of U.S.* which pertain to specific countries in Africa.

    At the present, a complete inventory of the center's holdings is not available, but interested scholars should contact Barbara Bennan for assistance in locating the materials.

5. A mimeographed list of the various publications of the Overseas Education Fund is available on request and is revised periodically.

M40 Population Crisis Committee (PCC)

1. *1120 19th Street, NW*
    Washington, D.C. 20036
    659-1833

2. Fred O. Pinkham, National Chairperson
    Lawrence R. Kegan, President

3.   The Population Crisis Committee is a nonprofit educational organization which seeks to stimulate public awareness, understanding, and action in the face of world population problems. Its primary goal is to cooperate with national and international agencies to devise effective means of reducing population growth by stimulating progress in areas such as food, resources, health, environment, and overall development. The committee members are also actively involved in generating interest and public support for the International Planned Parenthood Federation and the United Nations Fund for Population Activities. Many of its activities thus pertain to Africa.

4.   PCC maintains a small library which is open to the public. For further information call Janet L. Stanley, Librarian.

5.   Periodic reports are published which outline the activities of the organization.

M41 TransAfrica

1.   *1325 18th Street, NW*
        Suite 202
        Washington, D.C. 20036
        223-9666

2.   Randall Robinson, Executive Director

3.   TransAfrica, a membership organization founded in 1977, functions as a lobby group for Africa and the Caribbean. Its primary objective is to inform and organize public opinion in the United States to advocate policies and practices which will help bring about a more progressive U.S. foreign policy vis-à-vis Africa and the Caribbean.
        TransAfrica's staff members examine and study various foreign policy issues and assess their implications for the African world. They also communicate the foreign policy views of black Americans to elected officials, the administrations, and the media. The knowledge and expertise of TransAfrica's staff members on foreign policy issues are thus a valuable resource for Africanists.

5.   TransAfrica publishes a quarterly policy newsletter and action alerts on key issues.

M42 U.S.-South Africa Leader Exchange Program (USSALEP)

1.   *Suite 605*
        1717 Massachusetts Avenue, NW
        Washington, D.C. 20036
        232-6720

2.   Helen Kitchen, Executive Director

3.   USSALEP is a private, charitable, educational organization founded in 1958 under the auspices of the African-American Institute. Its objective

is "to promote fruitful communications, the transforming of relationships, and the broadening of options within and between the United States and South Africa."

USSALEP is involved in a wide range of activities which include exchange and team visits and symposia. Its Careers Development Project provides educational assistance and mid-career internships to black South Africans. Additionally, USSALEP also sponsors study tours for black businesswomen and a Nieman Fellow at Harvard University each year.

5. Publications include an *Annual Report, Occasional Papers,* and a brochure describing its programs.

M43 World Hunger Education Service

1. *2000 P Street, NW*
   Suite 205
   Washington, D.C. 20036
   223-2995

2. Patricia L. Kutzner, Director

3. The primary function of this nonprofit organization is to facilitate the exchange of information and insights on world food and development issues.

4. An open-shelf reading room with periodicals and reports from the U.N., U.S. federal, and U.S. nongovernmental agencies is available to the public during normal office hours.

5. The World Hunger Education Project publishes a monthly magazine *Hunger Notes,* which provides reports and analysis of domestic and international hunger issues: food aid, agrarian reform, malnutrition, population growth, rural development, and development education.

   Also available is a 32-page directory of governmental and private agencies and groups involved in the area of hunger, *Who's Involved With Hunger: An Organizational Guide,* published jointly with the American Freedom from Hunger Foundation (1976; a second edition is in preparation).

M44 World Population Society (WPS)

1. *1337 Connecticut Avenue, NW*
   Suite 200
   Washington, D.C. 20036
   833-2440

2. Philander P. Claxton, Jr., President
   Frank H. Oram, Associate Director

3. The World Population Society, established in 1973, is a nonprofit membership organization of scientists, professionals, and others who share

a common concern about world population problems and the need to ameliorate them.

The society's primary goal is to promote worldwide membership of populationists; to encourage multidisciplinary approaches to the solution of population problems; and to support the fulfillment of the World Population Plan of Action. The latter consists of allocation of more funds for population programs in developing countries, implementation of family planning programs which affect fertility and reduce infant mortality, and increased support for population research and educational curricula development.

5. The World Population Society publishes and distributes the monthly *World Population News.* Also available are proceedings and summaries of World Population Society International Conferences and Symposia.

N Cultural-Exchange and Technical-Assistance Organizations

Cultural-Exchange and Technical-Assistance Organizations Entry Format (N)

1. *Address; telephone number(s)*

2. Chief official and title

3. Programs and activities pertaining to Africa

4. Publications

N1 The African Diaspora Program (Smithsonian Institution—Division of Performing Arts

1. *2100 L'Enfant Plaza, SW*
   Washington, D.C. 20560
   381-6781

2. Dr. Bernice Johnson Reagon, Director

3. The African Diaspora Program, a component of the Festival of American Folklife, was initiated in 1972. Its primary goal is to examine and explore black American culture from the perspective of the diaspora (the dispersal of black people all over the world) and to document cultural linkages between black Americans and the peoples of Africa, Latin America, and the Caribbean.

   The annual Festival of American Folklife serves as a staging ground for performances and demonstrations in music, dance, oral traditions, and material culture. These numerous cultural forms are selected on the basis of extensive field research undertaken jointly by cultural historians and folklorists from the Smithsonian and the host countries. Participants from Africa have included groups from Ghana, Nigeria, Zaire, Liberia, Senegal and Benin.

   In the past, visitors to the Festival of American Folklife have had the unique opportunity of hearing a gonje group from northern Ghana render praise songs to the king of the Dogombas; guitar bands perform highlife music from Ghana; and religious presentations by the Yoruba from Nigeria. In addition to stage performnaces (dance, music, and oral traditions), there are craft and food demonstrations, which include cooking, hairbraiding, woodcarving, basketry, weaving, and jewelry-making.

The African Diaspora Program maintains recorded tapes of the various performances and interviews as well as extensive photographic archives of the Festival of American Folklife. These items are available to serious researchers and scholars for on-site reference use. Interested persons should call ahead for an appointment.

4.   Publications include: *African Diaspora Cookbook* (Festival of American Folklife, Smithsonian Institution, 1976) and *Black People and Their Culture: Selected Writings from the African Diaspora* (Summer 1976).

N2 African Heritage Center for African Dance and Music

1.   *2146 Georgia Avenue*
Washington, D.C. 20001
347-5589

2.   Melvin Deal, Director

3.   The African Heritage Center is a nonprofit professional company whose primary objective is to project a positive image of Africa and to develop a greater awareness of the African heritage through dance and music.

The company tours and performs in the United States as well as overseas, with frequent visits to Africa.

The multicultural center offers instruction in traditional African dance and music to teenagers, free of charge, and to adults for a fee.

N3 Agricultural Cooperative Development International (ACDI)

1.   *201 Continental Building*
1012 14th Street, NW
Washington, D.C. 20005
638-4661

2.   Donald H. Thomas, President

3.   ACDI is a nonprofit organization which provides technical assistance to agricultural cooperatives in developing countries. Activities include advisory and training services in the fields of agricultural credit, co-operative banking, agricultural marketing, supply, education, and policy planning. ACDI has assisted in the development of agricultural coopera-tives in several African nations and is active in Liberia, Kenya, and Tanzania.

ACDI is primarily funded by the U.S. Agency for International Development.

4. Publications include an *Annual Report* and a bimonthly newsletter, *News of Cooperative Development.* Additionally, ACDI publishes country reports on an irregular basis.

Note: ACDI also maintains a small library.

N4 American Council of Young Political Leaders

1. *Suite 300*
    1616 H Street, NW
    Washington, D.C. 20006
    347-7806

2. H. Joseph Farmer, Executive Director

3. The American Council of Young Political Leaders sponsors and administers international exchange programs for young political leaders and government officials from the United States and foreign countries. Recent exchanges include study tours to Liberia, Zambia, Tanzania, and Kenya by a U.S. delegation comprising state legislators, city councillors, and deputy mayors, and visits by delegations from the host countries.

4. Program literature is available on request.

N5 American Home Economics Association—International Family Planning Project

1. *2010 Massachusetts Avenue, NW*
    Washington, D.C. 20036
    862-8300

2. Betty Brabble, Director, International Family Planning Project

3. The American Home Economics Association's International Family Planning Project assists in the establishment and integration of family-planning and population programs in the school curricula of developing nations. Its activities include providing training services and educational materials. The project, which is funded by the U.S. Agency for International Development, has worked in several African countries, namely, Nigeria, Sierra Leone, Ghana, Gambia, Liberia, and Sudan.

    The International Family Planning Project also organizes periodic regional meetings in Africa, the most recent of which was held in Kenya in June 1979. Participants include home economists from select African nations.

4. Publications include resource and training materials for field personnel and a quarterly newsletter, *The Link.*

N6 American National Red Cross—Office of International Services

1. *17th and D Streets, NW*
    Washington, D.C. 20006
    857-3591

2. Dorothy Taaffe, Director, Office of International Services

3. The American Red Cross is a voluntary organization involved in humanitarian work aimed at providing relief to victims of natural or manmade disasters. It is affiliated with national Red Cross organizations in every African nation through the League of Red Cross Societies, based in Geneva, Switzerland.

   The League of Red Cross Societies is responsible for coordinating the relief operations in major foreign disaster and refugee situations. It has also provided training services and technical assistance to Red Cross organizations in many African nations. Currently, the Red Cross is actively involved in some 12 countries of Southern Africa. Its activities include developing training programs in such fields as first aid, disaster prevention and preparedness, development of blood centers, health care, and paramedical education.

   The National Headquarters Library of the American Red Cross (857-3491) has a number of resources of interest to Africanists. The library maintains an extensive vertical file collection which contains miscellaneous publications from African national Red Cross organizations, by country. The library is open to researchers from 8:30 A.M. to 4:45 P.M., Monday to Friday. Interlibrary loan and photoreproduction services are available.

4. The *Annual Report* of the League of Red Cross Societies, and a bimonthly periodical, *Panorama,* contains news and information about Red Cross societies and their activities in individual countries.

Note: Also see entry F6.

N7 CARE, Inc.

1. *1016 16th Street, NW*
   Washington, D.C. 20036
   296-5696

2. Wallace J. Campbell, President
   Louis Samia, Executive Director

3. CARE is an agency for voluntary international aid and development. CARE's primary concern has been with hunger; food is the basis of its operations. Besides providing food to the hungry and poor, it is active in a wide variety of self-help programs, which include health care and nutrition, agricultural development, school construction projects, community development projects, and training of medical personnel.

   CARE operates in the following African countries: Egypt, Chad, Kenya, Lesotho, Liberia, Mali, Niger, Sierra Leone, and Tunisia.

4. The Public Information Department prepares special promotional and informational materials, including CARE's *Annual Report,* which describes its activities.

N8 Checchi and Company

1. *1730 Rhode Island Avenue, NW*
    Washington, D.C. 20036
    452-9700

2. Vincent Checchi, President
    Vicki Macdonald, Coordinator of International Programs

3. Checchi and Company is a private, commercial, research and consulting
    firm which specializes in international development and works under
    contract for U.S. government agencies, the World Bank, and other
    organizations.
    The company has undertaken short- and long-term technical assistance
    projects in virtually all parts of Africa in the areas of agricultural devel-
    opment, small-scale industries, tourism and area planning, transportation,
    and regional development.
    Currently, the company has ongoing projects in Mali, Senegal, and
    Mauritania.

4. Published copies of reports can be obtained for a small fee through U.S.
    AID and the World Bank.

N9 Council for International Exchange of Scholars (CIES)

1. *11 Dupont Circle, Suite 300*
    Washington, D.C. 20036
    833-4950

2. Nancy S. Milburn, Chairman
    Adolph Y. Wilburn, Director

3. CIES is a private, nonprofit organization which supports and facilitates
    international exchanges in higher education and cooperates in the admin-
    istration of the Fulbright-Hays programs. Its programs provide research
    and teaching opportunities for U.S. scholars in 90 countries (including
    Africa) and also enables scholars from African nations to visit the
    United States.

4. For further information on the council's programs, researchers should
    consult 2 flyers, "Council for International Exchange of Scholars—Pro-
    grams, Activities, Organization" and "Scholars from Abroad."

N10 Credit Union National Association—Global Projects Office

1. *Suite 404*
    1120 19th Street, NW
    Washington, D.C. 20036
    659-4571

2.   Paul E. Hebert, Executive Assistant Managing Director
Thomas R. Carter, Director of Programs
Barbara M. Reno, Director of Communications

3.   As the apex organization of the organized credit-union movement, WOCCU promotes international credit-union development through service to regional credit-union associations and emerging credit-union organizations in 67 countries. The purpose is to encourage self-help development through member-owned and member-controlled savings and credit cooperatives. Emphasis is placed upon developing self-sufficient credit-union institutions and providing production credit programs for small farmers.

    Through its Global Projects Office based in Washington, D.C., the World Council of Credit Unions responds to technical assistance, training, and project-development requests made by WOCCU affiliates. WOCCU works closely with the African affiliate of the World Council of Credit Unions and the Africa Cooperative Savings and Credit Association (ACOSCA). ACOSCA represents savings and credit cooperative associations in 22 African countries.

4.   Periodic publications include the WOCCU *Annual Report, WOCCU Newsletter* (monthly), and *World Reporter* (quarterly).

N11 Development Alternatives, Inc. (DAI)

1.   *1823 Jefferson Place, NW*
Washington, D.C. 20036
833-8140

2.   Donald R. Mickelwait, President

3.   Development Alternatives, Inc., is a private consulting organization which specializes in the identification, design, implementation, and evaluation of development projects in Africa, Asia, and Latin America. The bulk of its work is undertaken on a contract basis for the U.S. Agency for International Development, the World Bank, and other international organizations.

    DAI has undertaken development work and provided technical assistance in the fields of agriculture (farmer training, livestock marketing, and seed multiplication); rural health; education, manpower development; and rehabilitation, to various African countries, including Cameroon, Egypt, Ethiopia, Ghana, Kenya, Liberia, Niger, Rwanda, Sierra Leone, Sudan, Tanzania, Upper Volta, and Zaire.

4.   A number of DAI-published studies, reports, and occasional staff papers should be of interest to Africanists. These include:
Bringing Developmental Changes to Rural Egypt: A Study of the Organization for the Reconstruction and Development of the Egyptian Villages, prepared for USAID/Cairo and the Arab Republic of Egypt, Ministry of Local Government (March 21, 1976);

Personnel Requirements for Project Development in East and Southern Africa, prepared for AID's Regional Economic Development Services Office (East Africa [October 17, 1977]);

A Seven-Country Survey on the Roles of Women in Rural Development (Boulder, Colo.: Westview Press, 1976);

Strategies for Small Farmer Development: An Empirical Study of Rural Development Projects, 2 volumes (Boulder, Colo.: Westview Press, 1976);

Strategies for the Reintroduction of Development Assistance to the Sudan, prepared for AID's Office of Eastern and Southern Africa Affairs (October 18, 1976).

Most DAI reports can be obtained through the U.S. Agency for International Development.

N12 Earth Satellite Corporation

1. *7222 47th Street*
   Bethesda, Maryland 20015
   652-7130

2. J. Robert Porter, President

3. The Earth Satellite Corporation is a private commercial firm which provides consulting services on a contract basis.

   Currently, its Africa-related work includes natural resource mapping of selected areas of Ghana, Benin, and Upper Volta, using Landsat imagery as a base and supplying photomaps of Libya.

4. Requests for *Project Reports* should be made directly to the appropriate client or funding agency.

N13 Experiment in International Living—Washington Office

1. *Suite 820*
   1346 Connecticut Avenue, NW
   Washington, D.C. 20036
   872-1330

2. Anne Lewis, Director, Washington Office

3. The Experiment in International Living is a private, nonprofit organization which sponsors international exchange programs and cross-cultural education programs for high school and college students.

   Under this program, selected U.S. students visit Kenya, Nigeria, or Ghana for a period of 8 weeks or more, and participate in work projects and "homestay" programs.

   The Experiment in International Living also offers hospitality to visitors from abroad, including Africa.

4. Publications include the monthly *Experiment Volunteer,* the quarterly newsletter *Odyssey International,* and numerous program brochures.

N14 General Federation of Women's Clubs (GFWC)—Care Education Program

1. *General Federation of Women's Clubs (GFWC)*
   1734 N Street, NW
   Washington, D.C. 20036
   347-3168

2. A. M. Quint (formerly Mrs. Oscar C. Sowards), President

3. The program (formerly called the GFWC-CARE Program in Africa) is a joint project of GFWC and CARE which focuses on raising funds to provide aid to developing countries of the world.

   In addition to providing food to hungry and malnourished children in Africa and other developing countries, the newly established International Affairs Program emphasizes education projects for the countries. These include a wide range of programs in the fields of nutrition, health-care training, vocational skills, agricultural development, fish production, reforestation, and school construction.

4. *GF Clubwoman Magazine* is published 9 times a year.

N15 Institute for the Preservation and Study of African-American Writing, Inc.

1. *P.O. Box 50172*
   Washington, D.C. 20004
   398-3175

2. Jonetta Barras-Abney, Director

3. The institute's primary objective is to inform and educate the Washington community about the literary contributions of African-Americans and to encourage meaningful interaction among writers.

   The institute organizes photographic exhibits and sponsors workshops, seminars, and lectures which focus on the work of African-American writers. A recent exhibit dealt with Negritude poets.

4. The institute has prepared an educational kit entitled "Washington, D.C. African-American Poets from 1900 to the Present," which is distributed to schools and academic institutions.

N16 International Voluntary Services, Inc. (IVS)

1. *1717 Massachusetts Avenue, NW*
   Suite 605
   Washington, D.C. 20036
   387-5533

2.   John T. Rigby, Executive Director

3.   IVS, a private, nonprofit organization, provides skilled technical assistance for rural development projects in the fields of agriculture, public health, small business, cooperative development, and engineering. Since its inception in 1953, IVS has met the need for skilled manpower in over 22 developing countries, through an international recruitment network. Presently IVS has programs in Botswana, Mauritania, and Sudan. Technical assistance is rendered in the following areas: horticulture, beekeeping, development of small enterprises, health programs and antituberculosis drives, training of mechanics, and the application of innovative technology in construction.

4.   IVS has numerous outlets for sharing the technical expertise and field experience of its personnel with interested researchers and those involved in development. These include *Technical Booklets* compiled by individual volunteers which are distributed through VITA (Volunteers in Technical Assistance). These are available from VITA, 3706 Rhode Island Avenue, Mt. Rainier, MD 20822. Particularly useful for individuals involved in educational extension programs is the *Index of Sources of Materials for Development Workers.*

    A new biannual publication, *Dialogue,* contains interesting articles, some of which focus on the field experience of volunteers in African countries.

N17 National 4-H Council

1.   *7100 Connecticut Avenue*
Washington, D.C. 20015
(301) 656-9000

2.   Grant A. Shrum, Executive Director
Melvin J. Thompson, Director, International Programs

3.   The National 4-H Council is a private, nonprofit educational organization which coordinates international programs on behalf of the 4-H youth program of the Cooperative Extension Service.

    The council conducts assistance, exchange, and training programs and serves as liaison with similar youth programs in 80 countries.

    Programs include the "International 4-H Youth Exchange" (IFYE), which provides opportunities for travel and study for young leaders from rural areas in the United States and other countries. The council also sponsors the "Professional Rural Youth Leader Exchange" (PRYLE) and the International Youth Development Project (YDP). Recent exchange programs have involved youth leaders from Botswana, Egypt, Swaziland, and Kenya.

4.   Program literature is available on request from the council or the offices of the Cooperative Extension Service.

N18 National Rural Electric Cooperative Association (NRECA)— International Programs Division

1. *1800 Massachusetts Avenue, NW*
   Washington, D.C. 20009
   857-9500

2. Samuel Bunker, Coordinator of International Programs
   George Doud, Administrator for Near East and Africa

3. The International Programs Division of NRECA renders technical assistance to foreign government agencies, cooperatives, and utility companies in the development and operation of rural electric systems and cooperatives. Activities include advisory and training services. In Africa, surveys have been carried out on the potential of rural electrification in Liberia and Tanzania.

4. Publications include *NRECA Overseas Report* and a monthly magazine, *Rural Electrification Magazine.*

N19 People-to-People Health Foundation, Inc. (Project HOPE)

1. *Project HOPE Health Sciences Education Center*
   Millwood, Virginia 22646
   (703) 837-2100

2. William B. Walsh, M.D., President

3. The People-to-People Health Foundation is a nonprofit corporation which provides educational and training programs in the health sciences (medicine, nursing, dentistry, family planning, nutrition, and health-care planning) to developing countries. It currently has programs in Tunisia, Egypt, and Morocco.

4. Publications include *HOPE News,* a quarterly newsletter, program reports for various countries, and over 15 *Educational Monographs.* Presently, none of the titles in the monograph series pertains to Africa.

N20 Phoenix Associates, Inc.

1. *1218 16th Street. NW*
   Washington, D.C. 20036
   347-3301

2. Robert W. Rafuse, President

3. Phoenix Associates, Inc., is a small private consulting firm which undertakes contract work for the U.S. Agency for International Development and other organizations.
   Phoenix Associates has provided consulting and evaluation services for housing projects in Botswana, Cameroon, Liberia, Mauritania, Sene-

gal, and Tunisia. The firm is presently involved in several ongoing development projects in Africa, all of which are in the field of housing.

N21 Public Welfare Foundation, Inc.

1.   *Suite 505*
      2600 Virginia Avenue, NW
      Washington, D.C. 20037
      965-1800

2.   Davis Haines, President and Chief Executive Officer

3.   The Public Welfare Foundation, Inc. is a private, charitable, nonprofit organization which provides grants to people whose need is genuine and urgent. The foundation, with a worldwide scope, seeks to alleviate human suffering and improve education, health, and living conditions of people all over the world. It has supported numerous projects in Africa which include: establishment of a mobile health clinic in Ikare, Ondo State, in Nigeria; support and evaluation of mobile health clinics in the Naroki and Kajiado districts of Kenya; and replacement of old buildings in Rwanda which serve as an education center for handicapped children.

4.   An *Annual Report* is available on request.

N22 Sister Cities International (Town Affiliation Association of the U.S., Inc.)

1.   *1625 I Street, NW*
      Washington, D.C. 20006
      293-5504

2.   Thomas Gittins, Executive Vice President

3.   Sister Cities International sponsors and coordinates educational, cultural, and technical exchange programs which link cities in the U.S. with cities overseas. Some 37 African cities are currently participating in this program as affiliates.

4.   Publications of this organization include 2 pamphlets, *Building a Sister City Program with an African City* and *Emphasis Africa,* and a bimonthly newsletter, *Sister City News.*

N23 Volunteer Development Corps (VDC)

1.   *1629 K Street, NW*
      Washington, D.C. 20006
      223-2072

2.   David W. Angevine, President

3.   Volunteer Development Corps is a private organization which provides short-term technical assistance (advisory and training services) to co-

operatives in developing countries. The organization's assignments in Africa include work in Botswana, Cameroon, Ethiopia, Ghana, Kenya, Lesotho, Liberia, Mauritius, Mozambique, Nigeria, Senegal, Sierra Leone, Togo, and Zambia.

The funding for Volunteer Development Corps comes from 2 sources: the U.S. Agency for International Development and United States cooperatives.

4. VDC volunteers report to requesting organizations. Copies of their reports may be available through VDC, with the requesting organization's approval.

N24 Volunteers in Technical Assistance, Inc. (VITA, Inc.)

1. *3706 Rhode Island Avenue*
    Mt. Rainier, Maryland 20822
    (301) 277-7000

2. Henry Norman, Executive Director

3. VITA, Inc. is a private nonprofit organization which provides, generally free of charge, technical and developmental information to developing countries. The organization maintains a skill bank of over 4,000 volunteers.

    Currently, VITA, Inc. is involved in projects in the Upper Volta, Nigeria, Zaire, and Tanzania.

    The organization is partially funded by the U.S. Agency for International Development. It also provides training sessions for Peace Corps personnel.

    For more information on Africa-related programs, researchers should contact Program Officers Christine Hollis and George Codrea, both of whom are knowledgeable on the subject.

    VITA, Inc., also maintains a technical library which is open to the public for on-site use. Researchers who wish to use the library should call ahead to make arrangements.

4. Publications include a quarterly newsletter, *VITA News*, over 50 project handbooks, and technical manuals and bulletins. Especially useful is VITA's *Village Technology Handbook* (VITA, April 1978), updated periodically.

P Religious Organizations

Religious Organizations Entry Format (P)

1. *Address; telephone number(s)*

2. Chief official and title

3. Programs and activities pertaining to Africa

4. Publications and information pertaining to Africa

African Cultural and Religious Society ASUOGYEBI Shrine of Washington, D.C. See entry M4.

African Methodist Episcopal Church Service and Development Agency, Inc. See entry M8.

P1 African Methodist Episcopal Zion Church

1. *1615 14th Street, NW*
   Washington, D.C. 20009
   667-3824

2. Dr. Reuben Speaks, Resident Bishop for Africa

3. The AME Zion Church is engaged in missionary and denominational work in Ghana, Liberia, and Nigeria.

P2 Baptist World Alliance

1. *1628 16th Street, NW*
   Washington, D.C. 20009
   265-5027

3.   Baptist World Alliance is a worldwide organization of 111 Baptist national church bodies. According to its estimates, there are more than 100 Baptist missions in Africa.

The alliance's humanitarian activities include the Baptist World Alliance Relief Fund, a program carried out under the direction of a worldwide Committee on Relief and Development which provides help to victims of famine, disaster, and other catastrophies.

The alliance convenes a general meeting or congress every 5 years. In addition, its General Council meets annually.

4.   The alliance publishes *The Baptist World,* a monthly magazine.

P3 General Conference of Seventh-Day Adventists

1.   *6840 Eastern Avenue, NW*
Takoma Park
Washington, D.C. 20012
723-0800

2.   Neal C. Wilson, President

3.   Organized in 1863, the General Conference of Seventh-Day Adventists has been active in relief, teaching, and mission work in virtually all parts of the African continent, except the Spanish Sahara, Mauritania, Somalia, and Djibouti.

The conference's Department of Archives maintains numerous files which contain records, correspondence from Adventist missionaries in Africa, histories of their activities in each African country, and biographical records of all overseas workers. Researchers who wish to examine these records should write for permission to the above address or call Maurice T. Battle (724-0800, ext. 391) for clearance.

4.   Publications of the General Conference include: *Annual Yearbook;* the weekly *Review and Herald,* which contains reports from African missions; and *World Missions Report,* a quarterly publication which also has substantial material pertaining to Africa.

P4 Holy Cross Foreign Mission Society, Inc.

1.   *4301 Harewood Road, NE*
Washington, D.C. 20017
526-2211

2.   Rev. Arnold A. Fell, C.S.C., Director

3.   Founded in 1924, the Holy Cross Foreign Mission Society is the central service-support agency for Holy Cross priests and brothers from the United States working overseas.

Presently some 35 to 40 members of Holy Cross are engaged in various activities in Africa (Uganda, Kenya, Tanzania, Ghana, and Liberia), mainly in teaching, parish works, social services, and communications.

P5 Holy Ghost Fathers

1. *Missionlane Building*
    Wheaton, Maryland 20902
    (301) 933-6130

2. Rev. Francis M. Philben, C.S.Sp., Director

3. Founded in 1703, the Holy Ghost Fathers have been active in Africa since 1842, mainly in Sierre Leone, Gambia, Ghana, Kenya, Malawi, Tanzania, and Zambia.

    Presently, there are an estimated 1,500 Holy Ghost Missionaries (priests and brothers) engaged in educational and humanitarian work on the continent of Africa. Currently, the organization maintains a residence in Washington for several of its priests.

4. The archives, records, and files of the organization are located at the central headquarters in Rome. Scholars who wish to examine these records should write to the Office of Information, Clivo di Cinna—195, 00036 Roma, Italy. Though the archives are located in Rome, the Development Office of the American Branch of the Holy Ghost Fathers (located in Wheaton, Maryland) can provide researchers with limited information regarding the international activities of the organization. A photographic file of black-and-white photographs taken in several African countries is maintained in the Wheaton office (933-6130). The photos are arranged by country and scholars are welcome to examine them after first calling the director at the number given above.

P6 Islamic Center

1. *2551 Massachusetts Avenue, NW*
    Washington, D.C. 20008
    332-3451

2. Dr. M. A. Rauf, Director

3. The mosque is open daily for 5 daily prayers, including the important congregational ceremony at noon on Fridays. The primary purpose of the center is to guide the Muslim community of the U.S. in the application of the faith and to promote a better understanding of the true principles and ideals of Islam.

    For more detailed information on the center's activities, see entry M35. The center is open 10:00 A.M. to 4:00 P.M. 7 days a week.

P7 Jesuit Missions, Inc.

1. *1717 Massachusetts Avenue, NW*
    Suite 402
    Washington, D.C. 20036
    387-3720

2.   Simon E. Smith, S.J., Executive Secretary

3.   The Jesuits have been active on the African continent since 1893. Presently there are an estimated 1,100 Jesuit fathers in Africa, mainly in Chad, Zaire, Madagascar, Cameroon, Rhodesia, Tanzania, Zambia, and Nigeria. They are engaged in evangelical activities and educational and social work.

4.   Publications include *JM Newsletter* and *Studies in the International Apostolate of Jesuits,* the latter published about twice a year. Of particular interest to scholars will be the report on the Jesuit Conference on Africa and Madagascar which has recently been published in a book: *Jesuit Response to the Challenge of Mission in Africa and Madagascar Today* (Washington, D.C.: Jesuit Missions, Inc., 1976). This book contains valuable information on the Jesuit presence in the various regions of Africa and statistical data concerning the Catholic Church and the Jesuit missions.

Researchers who want to undertake research in this field should also contact the staff of the Jesuit Conference (462-0400), whose primary function is to maintain liaison with the 6,000 Jesuits in the U.S. and Canada.

P8 Lott Carey Baptist Foreign Mission Convention

1.   *1501 Eleventh Street, NW*
Washington, D.C. 20001
667-8493

2.   Rev. Wendell C. Somerville, Executive Secretary and Treasurer
Myrtle Thompson, Secretary

3.   Lott Carey is a convention of Negro Baptists involved in foreign mission work in Africa, Haiti, India, and the USSR. It is named after Rev. Lott Carey, a Virginia slave who was the first black American missionary to travel to Africa in 1821 and work among the Bassa people. The Providence Baptist Church in Monrovia, established in 1822, was the first Protestant church erected in Africa by an American missionary.

The Lott Carey Foreign Mission Convention is engaged in evangelical and educational work in Liberia and Nigeria. Its activities include mission work; establishment of schools, nurseries, and vocational training centers; financial assistance to African students; and provision of elementary medical and nursing services.

4.   Publications consist of the *Annual Report* and the *Lott Carey Herald,* which has now been discontinued. The organization's records and correspondence files are available to scholars for examination, but prior permission must be obtained.

P9 United States Catholic Conference (USCC)

1.   *1312 Massachusetts Avenue, NW*
Washington, D.C. 20005
659-6600

3.   The conference provides assistance to American Catholic bishops in their evangelization, educational, and humanitarian activities in various parts of the world, including Africa. Several departments of the conferences have programs and activities in various African countries. Interested researchers should contact the following departments for information: Campaign for Human Development, Catholic Relief Services, Migration and Refugee Service, and Social Development and World Peace.

4.   USCC's office of International Justice and Peace maintains a small reference library which is open to scholars during regular office hours. It also publishes numerous leaflets and pamphlets, some of which pertain to Africa. A *Publications List* is available free on request. Some useful publications include: Rollins E. Lambert, *Focus: Africa,* which contains a series of articles on Southern Africa; and Thomas E. Quigley, *Developing Communities in the Third World;* and *U.N. Sanctions Against Rhodesia* (transcript of USCC testimony before Congress).

The United States Catholic Conference also publishes the monthly *NCCB/ISCC Report,* which contains information on its activities.

Q Publications and Media

Publications and Media Entry Format (Q)

1. *Address; telephone number(s)*

2. Chief official and title

3. Publications and programs pertaining to Africa

Q1 *A Current Bibliography on African Affairs*

1. *African Bibliographic Center*
    1346 Connecticut Avenue, NW, Room 901
    Washington, D.C. 20036
    223-1392

3. The *Bibliography* is a quarterly guide produced by the African Bibliographic Center which provides up-to-date information on research materials and literature on Africa. It contains scholarly articles, book reviews, and current bibliography on Africa. All inquires concerning subscription should be addressed to:

    Baywood Publishing Company
    120 Marine Street
    Farmingdale, New York 11735.

Q2 African Directions News Agency (ADNA)

1. *884 National Press Building*
    Washington, D.C. 20045
    347-6638

2. Crispin D. Chindongo, Editor in Chief

3. ADNA publishes a quarterly magazine, *African Directions*, which contains articles on all aspects of African life, such as African oral tradition

and history, art, culture, religion, philosophy, contemporary events, and economic affairs. In addition, the News Agency (organized in 1977) issues weekly African news reports, statements, press releases, commentaries, and editorials.

Q3 African Index

1.   *1835 K Street, NW*
      Washington, D.C. 20006
      223-6500

2.   Helen Kitchen, Editor

3.   African Index is a semimonthly news service which provides a coverage of the African political and economic scene. It is an invaluable resource for the Africanist. The index consists of in-depth articles and analysis of major developments in Africa; news briefs which are organized by country and subject; economic notes on action in commodities, finance, labor, markets, tariffs, trade pacts, etc.; and statistical information and charts.

Q4 "America's Black Forum"

1.   *904 National Press Building*
      Washington, D.C. 20045
      347-9168

2.   Glen Ford, President, Producer, and Moderator

3.   "America's Black Forum" is a nationally syndicated television program. Since its focus is on black-oriented news, coverage on Africa is extensive. Recent programs have included interviews of African ambassadors, discussion of black strategies toward Africa, and analyses of the Rhodesian situation. Programs are aired on Washington's WJLA television on Sundays at 7:30 P.M. and Mondays at 6:30 A.M. Transcripts of all programs are available for a small fee.

Q5 Arab News

1.   *National Press Building*
      Suite 359
      Washington, D.C. 20045

3.   This is the Washington bureau for 3 Saudi Arabian publications: *Arab News* (English-language daily published in Jeddah), *Asharq Al-Awsat* (Arabic daily published in London and Jeddah), and *Saudi Business* (English weekly published in Jeddah).
      The office maintains a file of back issues of these publications dating from January 1978. Researchers may find it useful to talk with the staff, who are knowledgeable and have Arabic language skills.

Q6 Associated Publishers

1. *1401 14th Street, NW*
   Washington, D.C. 20005
   667-2822

3. This is the publishing arm of the Association for the Study of Afro-American Life and History. It has published over 80 textbooks and other materials relating to Afro-Americans.

Q7 *Congressional Quarterly Weekly Report*

1. *1414 22d Street, NW*
   Washington, D.C. 20037
   296-6800

2. Eugene Patterson, Editor

3. The *Congressional Quarterly Weekly Report,* which is published by the Congressional Quarterly, Inc., is an indispensable publication for researchers who wish to follow U.S. legislation. It provides coverage of Congress, national politics, and the government.

   The Africanist should find much material in the *Weekly Reports* on congressional proposals and actions relating to Africa, particularly on defense and military issues, foreign policy, and trade questions.

Note: See Congressional Quarterly, Inc., Editorial Research Reports Library in the Libraries section of this *Guide* (entry A8).

Q8 Government Printing Office and Office of the Federal Register (General Services Administration)

Significant publications have been noted in the entries for government agencies. However, researchers should be aware of 2 important sources for obtaining government publications: the Government Printing Office (GPO) and the Office of the Federal Register.

1. *U.S. Government Printing Office*
   Washington, D.C. 20402
   783-3238

3. GPO's *Monthly Catalog of U.S. Government Publications* lists titles of most government publications which are available by writing to the Superintendent of Documents at the above address or by calling 783-3238. A semiannual index is also available. Out-of-print or out-of-stock publications are not available from this office.

1. *Office of the "Federal Register"*
   1100 L Street, NW
   Washington, D.C. 20408
   523-5240

3. Most of the publications of this office deal with the working of the U.S. government. Users of this guide may, however, find the following of some interest:

   > *Federal Register* (daily);
   > *Public Papers of the Presidents of the United States;*
   > *U.S. Government Manual* (annual), indispensable to researchers trying to find their way around the federal government agencies;
   > *Weekly Compilation of Presidential Documents,* containing transcripts of presidential news conferences, speeches, and press releases from the White House (indexed).

   These publications must be ordered from GPO.

Q9 Habari

1. *Washington Task Force on African Affairs*
   P.O. Box 13033
   Washington, D.C. 20009
   659-2529

2. Daniel G. Mathews, President and Executive Director

3. Habari is a 24-hour telephone news and information service (659-2529). It provides, free of charge, daily news briefs on current African affairs. It also includes information on new books, documents, films, meetings, and other relevant information relating to Africa.

   Transcripts of the Habari news service are available for purchase on a weekly, monthly, or quarterly subscription basis.

Note: For Africanists and researchers, the Habari News Service is an invaluable and indispensable source of up-to-date information on current African affairs.

Q10 *International Development Review*

1. *1346 Connecticut Avenue, NW*
   Washington, D.C. 20036
   296-3810

2. Andrew E. Rice, Editor

   International Development Review is a quarterly publication devoted to international affairs. *International News Review* is now published in Rome, Italy.

Q11 *Internewsletter*

1. *Internews Media Services*
   919 National Press Building
   Washington, D.C. 20045
   347-4575

2.   Marie-Benoite Allizon, Director

3.   *Internewsletter* is a French-language review of U.S. press coverage on Africa.

Q12 Joint Publications Research Service (JPRS)

1.   *1000 North Glebe Road*
      Arlington, Virginia 22201
      (703) 841-1050

3.   Joint Publications Research Service, established in 1957, provides translation services to all government agencies. Some of its work is for intelligence agencies and is, therefore, not published. With the exception of copyrighted materials which only the government agencies receive, all JPRS publications are sold by NTIS.

      JPRS does not index its own publications. The following list should prove useful in locating JPRS publications:

      Bibliography—Index to Current JPRS Translations: International Developments, Africa, Latin America, Near East, International Communist Developments (New York: Research and Microfilm Publications, CCM Information Corp. 1962–). Monthly.

      Catalog Cards in Book Form for United States Joint Publications Research Service Translations (New York: CCM Information Corp.). Semiannual. Began with volume for 1957/61. Superseded from 1971 by Transdex.

      Transdex: Bibliography and Index to the United States Joint Publications Research Service Translations (New York: CCM Information Corp., 1971–). Monthly with semiannual cumulation.

      Since 1958, JPRS translations have also been listed in the *Monthly Catalog of United States Government Publications.*

Q13 *Journal of Negro Education*

1.   *Bureau of Educational Research*
      Howard University
      P.O. Box 311
      Washington, D.C. 20059
      636-6750

2.   Charles A. Martin, Editor

3.   Established in 1932, the *Journal of Negro Education* (quarterly) focuses on Negro research and education.

Q14 *Journal of Negro History*

1.   *Association for the Study of Afro-American Life and History, Inc.*
      1401 14th Street, NW
      Washington, D.C. 20005
      667-2822

2.   Dr. Alton Hornsby, Editor

3.   The *Journal*, a quarterly academic publication, focuses on all aspects of black history.

Q15 *Journal of Southern African Affairs*

1.   *4133 Art/Sociology Building*
University of Maryland
College Park, Maryland 20742
(301) 454-5937/8

2.   Mariyawanda Nzuwah, Editor

3.   The *Journal* is a publication of the Southern African Research Association and Afro-American Studies, University of Maryland. It is an interdisciplinary quarterly of research and writing on politics, economics, international affairs, history, law, sociology, anthropology, and the cultures of Southern Africa. The geographic areas covered are: South Africa, Namibia, Swaziland, Lesotho, Botswana, Angola, Zambia, Zimbabwe, Malawi, Mozambique, and Tanzania.

Q16 Liberation Information Distributing Company

1.   *4206 Edson Place, NE*
Washington, D.C. 20019
667-1193

2.   Hodari Ali, President

3.   The Liberation Information Distributing Company is one of the largest distributors of books and magazines on Africa. It services bookstores and other outlets.

Q17 *Middle East Journal*

1.   *Middle East Institute, Publisher*
1761 N Street, NW
Washington, D.C. 20036
785-1141

2.   William Sands, Editor

3.   The *Journal* is a quarterly publication of the Middle East Institute. It carries articles on all aspects of the contemporary Middle East—political affairs, foreign relations, defense effort and buildup, and social and economic development.

Q18 *Negro History Bulletin*

1. *Association for the Study of Afro-American Life and History, Inc.*
   1401 14th Street, NW
   Washington, D.C. 20005
   667-2553

2. Thelma D. Perry, Editor

3. Established in 1937, the *Negro History Bulletin* is a monthly publication which focuses on the life and contributions of the Negro.

Q19 *New Directions*

1. *Department of University Relations and Publications*
   Howard University
   Washington, D.C. 20059

2. Paul R. Hathaway, Editorial Director
   Abdul Kadir N. Said, Editor

3. *New Directions* is a quarterly publication of Howard University which contains scholarly articles, essays, book reviews, poetry, and discussions of a wide range of issues focusing on the black experience, by faculty and other writers not connected with the university. Though its scope is not limited to Africa, nearly all issues of the magazine have some Africa- or Third World-related material.

Q20 *Quarterly Journal of the Library of Congress*

1. *Library of Congress, Publisher*
   Library of Congress Publishing Office
   Washington, D.C. 20540
   287-5093

2. Frederick B. Mohr, Editor

3. The *Quarterly Journal* provides information on the Library of Congress collections, new acquisitions, and programs. Articles of interest to Africanists are occasionally included.

Q21 *U.S. News and World Report*

1. *2300 N Street, NW*
   Washington, D.C. 20037
   333-7400

2. Marvin L. Stone, Editor

3. Established in 1933, *U.S. News and World Report* focuses on national and international news.

Q22 Voice of America (VOA)

1. *HEW Building*
    330 Independence Avenue, SW
    Washington, D.C. 20201
    755-4422

2. R. Peter Straus, Director of VOA

3. The Voice of America broadcasts to Africa are now administered by the newly created International Communication Agency's Office of Associate Director of Broadcasting.

    VOA is the global radio network of ICA. The backbone of the programming is news and news analysis, though cultural and special-interest programs are also broadcast.

    The Africa Division, headed by William Minehart, handles the broadcasts in the Sub-Saharan countries of Africa. Programs are currently being broadcast in English, French, Swahili, Hausa, and Portuguese.

    The Near East and South Asia Division, headed by Allan E. Baker, is responsible for programs in Egypt and North Africa. The Arabic Branch (Kamel O. Taweel, Head) broadcasts programs aimed at the Arab world. Currently, VOA programs total 7½ hours a day in Arabic; some, however, are aimed specifically at listeners in North Africa.

    Scholars who desire more information on broadcast contents should refer to *Content Report*, the daily publication which lists program titles and indicates in-house sources. See also VOA's "Broadcast Schedule" for pertinent languages.

Note: More information on VOA may be found in the Government Agencies section of this *Guide* under the International Communication Agency (entry K16).

Q23 WHUR

1. *2600 4th Street, NW*
    Washington, D.C. 20059
    265-9494

3. WHUR-FM is the radio broadcasting station of Howard University. It broadcasts a daily news report at 6:00 P.M. entitled "African Roundup." For further information researchers should contact WHUR Africa correspondent Mohamad Samoura.

Q24 WPFW-FM

1. *700 H Street, NW*
    Washington, D.C. 20001
    783-3100

3. WPFW, a noncommercial, community-supported radio station, sponsors "African Roots," an African music program every Saturday from 6:00

P.M. to 8:30 P.M. and the "Afro-Centric," a public affairs program on Tudesdays, 7:30 P.M. to 8:30 P.M., which focuses on issues relating to Africa. For further information, contact Cheikh Soumare, Producer.

Q25 *Washington Afro-American*

1. *The Afro-American Co., Publishers*
   2002 11th Street, NW
   Washington, D.C. 20001
   332-0080

2. Arthur M. Carter, Editor

3. Established in 1933, the *Washington Afro-American* is a weekly newspaper.

Q26 *World Affairs*

1. *American Peace Society, Publishers*
   4000 Albemarle Street, NW
   Washington, D.C. 20016
   362-6195

2. Cornelius W. Vahle, Managing Editor

3. *World Affairs* is a quarterly journal devoted to international relations and world affairs. Periodically, it contains articles on U.S.-Africa relations and other pertinent foreign-policy issues.

APPENDIXES

Appendix I.   Library Collections: A Listing by Size of African Holdings

The size of African holdings in the Washington, D.C., area library collections was difficult to determine, but the following table represents the best-informed estimates available.

More than 15,000 volumes:
   Library of Congress (A27)
   Howard University (Founders Library [A20] and Moorland-Spingarn Research Center [A21])

10,000-15,000 volumes:
   Joint Bank-Fund Library (A26)
   National Agricultural Library (A30)
   State Department Library (A38)

5,000-10,000 volumes:
   National Library of Medicine (A34)
   University of Maryland (A28)
   School of Advanced International Studies (SAIS)—
      Johns Hopkins University (A37)

2,500-5,000 volumes:
   Action Library (A1)
   Dumbarton Oaks (A10)
   George Washington University (A15)
   Georgetown University (A16)
   International Communications Agency Library (A23)

Appendix II. Bookstores

Introductory Note

The Washington area does not have any bookstore which specializes in African-language materials. A selective list of bookstores, which may prove useful to African area specialists, follows. Unless indicated otherwise, these stores carry mostly English-language textbooks and monographs. Researchers should contact individual bookstores for additional information on service hours, discount rates, etc.

DISCOUNT RECORDS AND BOOKS
1340 Connecteicut Avenue, NW
Washington, D.C. 20036
785-1133

This bookstore does not carry textbooks. It has a collection of general books on Africa, mainly in the fields of history, art, anthropology, religion, and politics. The store also has one of the best collections of import records, including African music recordings.

GLOBE BOOK SHOP
1700 Pennsylvania Avenue, NW
Washington, D.C. 20006

The store carries foreign-language materials, including a selection of reference works and learning tools in Swahili, Yoruba, and Hausa; also paperbacks, political science, and travel books.

HOWARD UNIVERSITY BOOKSTORE
2801 Georgia Avenue, NW
Washington, D.C. 20059
636-6656

This store may well have the areas's largest selection of books on Africa. The African Studies section of the store carries textbooks in all fields—history, political science, anthropology, arts, language and literature, and economics.

INTERNATIONAL LEARNING CENTER BOOKSTORE

1715 Connecticut Avenue, NW
Washington, D.C. 20009
232-4111

The center carries African language materials, mostly in Hausa and Swahili. It also has a small African area-studies section which has books on economic development.

KRAMER BOOKS, INC.

1347 Connecticut Avenue, NW
Washington, D.C. 20036
293-2072

This store sells used books, publishers' overstock books, etc.

MARYLAND BOOK EXCHANGE

4500 College Avenue
College Park, Maryland 20740
(301) 927-2510

The book exchange carries general reference works and books on African history.

MODERN LANGUAGE BOOK AND RECORD STORE

3160 O Street, NW
Washington, D.C. 20007
338-8963

The bookstore specializes in foreign-language materials. It carries a small selection of African verse in French and Spanish.

MUSEUM OF AFRICAN ART BOOKSHOP

316 A Street, NE
Washington, D.C. 20002
547-6222

This bookshop carries works on African art, culture, philosophy, and literature.

NEWMAN BOOKSTORE OF WASHINGTON

3329 8th Street, NE
Washington, D.C. 20017
526-1036

The store has a small selection of books on African religions and philosophy.

SECOND STORY BOOKS

5017 Connecticut Avenue, NW
Washington, D.C. 20008
244-5550

This store sells used and publishers' overstock books, with an emphasis on history and general reference works on Africa.

SIDNEY KRAMER BOOKS, INC.
1722 H Street, NW
Washington, D.C. 20006
298-8010

The store carries books on contemporary Africa, African politics, and economic development.

UNIVERSITY OF THE DISTRICT OF COLUMBIA— MOUNT VERNON CAMPUS BOOKSTORE
929 E Street, NW
Washington, D.C. 20004
727-2517

This bookstore specializes in textbooks.

Note: A most valuable resource for book-lovers in the Washington area are the major book sales held each year. These include the Vassar College and Brandeis University book sales held in the spring and the book sale organized by the Association of American Foreign Service Wives, held annually in the fall in the State Department building. All of these book sales have a foreign-language and an area-studies section in which the Africanist can often find many items. These sales are advertised in local papers such as the *Washington Post*.

Appendix III. Housing, Transportation, and Other Services

Introductory Note

This section is prepared to help outside scholars who come to Washington, D.C., for short-term research, to find suitable housing. It also contains data on local transportation facilities and information services. (Prices quoted are current as of April 1979 and are subject to change.)

HOUSING INFORMATION AND REFERRAL SERVICE

For anyone interested in leasing an apartment or house, *Apartment Shoppers' Guide and Housing Directory* (ASGHD) (updated every 3 months) is a valuable source of information. The directory, which quotes current rental prices, terms of leases, and directions to each of the facilities listed, is available at People's Drug Stores in the Washington area. It is published by an organization bearing the same name as the directory and located at 35 Wisconsin Circle, Suite 310, Washington, D.C. 20015. The ASGHD staff provides a housing referral service, free of charge, from 9:00 A.M. to 5:00 P.M., Monday through Friday. An up-to-date list of available apartments and houses is maintained at the office. For further information, call 652-1632 or 652-1633.

Scholars can also get help from the following local universities' housing offices:

George Washington University Off-Campus Housing Resources Center
676-6688 (Summer: 676-7221)
2121 I Street, NW (Rice Hall), 4th Floor
Washington, D.C. 20052

Summer: 9:00 A.M.-7:00 P.M.   Monday-Friday
Winter: 9:00 A.M.-5:00 P.M.   Monday-Friday

This office has listings of apartments and other housing in the Washington area. Open to the public, the office also distributes the *Apartment Shoppers' Guide and Housing Directory* (see above), maps of Washington, D.C., and a *Guide to Off-Campus Housing* (annual) prepared for the students by the office.

Georgetown University Off-Campus Housing Office
625-3026
Healy Building Basement, Room G08
Georgetown University
37th and O Streets, NW
Washington, D.C. 20057

1:00 P.M.-4:30 P.M.   Monday-Friday

Open to the public, this office offers services similar to those at the George Washington University Housing Resource Center.

Catholic University of America Off-Campus Housing Office
635-5618
St. Bonaventure Hall, Room 106
Catholic University of America
Washington, D.C. 20064

9:00 A.M.-5:00 P.M.   Monday-Friday (Call until 2:00 P.M.)

Open to the public, this office provides services similar to those of George Washington University.

Northern Virginia Community College—
Annandale Campus Housing Office
(703) 323-3143
Student Activities Center
Science Building, Room 225-A
8333 Little River Turnpike
Annandale, Virginia 22003

8:30 A.M.-5:00 P.M.   Monday-Friday

Its services are similar to those listed above.

Note: The off-campus housing offices of American University, Howard University, and the University of Maryland handle inquiries and requests from their own students and faculty members only.

HOUSING—SHORT-TERM

For those scholars who intend to stay for a short period of time (i.e., a few weeks to several months), the following facilities may be useful.

International Guest House
726-5808
1441 Kennedy Street, NW
Washington, D.C.

Rates: $8.50 per bed per day or $51.00 per week (breakfast with shared rooms); $4.25 for a child under 10; $3.25 per cot; and $2.00 per crib (daily rate).

International Student House
232-4007
1825 R Street, NW
Washington, D.C. 20009

Rates: $220.00 to $315.00 per month for room and board (2 meals, 7 days). Single and shared double or triple rooms are available. The house maintains a nationality quota policy that permits no more than 10 Americans or 3 citizens from any 1 foreign country at any time.

The Woodner Hotel
483-4400
3636 16th Street, NW
Washington, D.C. 20010

The hotel has furnished efficiency and 1-bedroom or 2-bedroom apartments. Rates: $420.00 and up for efficiency; $535.00 and up for 1-bedroom; and $620.00 and up for 2-bedroom apartments.

Hunting Towers
(703) 548-8484
1204 South Washington Street
Alexandria, Virginia 22314

Rates: For short-term (1-month) lease, $260.00 for furnished efficiency; $328.00 for furnished 1-bedroom apartment; and $428.00 for 2-bedroom apartments. All rates are reduced somewhat after a 3-month stay.

The Capitol Park
484-5400
800 4th Street, SW
Washington, D.C. 20024
(Near the Library of Congress)

Rates: Furnished 1-bedroom apartments: by the week $130.00; by the month $500.00; and furnished 2-bedroom apartment (3-month lease required), $510.00 per month including maid service.

The Coronet Apartment
547-6300
200 C Street, SE
Washington, D.C. 20003
(Near the Library of Congress)

Rates: Furnished efficiency, $375.00 per month for 1; $425.00 for 2; furnished 1-bedroom apartment, $425.00 for 1, $475.00 for 2, including maid service and linen 6 days a week and utilities. (Add $24.80 occupancy tax per month.)

LONG-TERM HOUSING

Those wishing to rent an apartment or house for 1 year or more should consult not only the *Apartment Shoppers' Guide and Housing Directory* and the local university housing offices, but also the following rental agencies:

Millicent Chatel	338-0500
Lynch	232-4100
Nyman Realty Co.	474-5700
Edmund Flynn Co.	554-4800 or 537-1800
H. A. Gill	338-5000
Shannon & Luchs	659-7000
Norman Bernstein	331-7500

Home and apartment rents vary greatly from one section to the other in the Washington area. Normally, rents are lower in suburban Virginia and Maryland than in Washington, D.C. One should also remember that it is difficult to find furnished apartments in the Washington area through regular real estate agents. People who need furnished quarters may have to take unfurnished apartments and rent furniture. Such an arrangement can be negotiated with the real estate brokers. Even under such an arrangement, linen, blankets, dishes, silverware, and cooking utensils must be furnished by the tenant.

TRANSPORTATION IN THE WASHINGTON AREA

Scholars should be advised that parking space in the nation's capital is limited, and that it is relatively expensive to park at commercial lots (e.g., $1.25 per hour). It may be preferable, therefore, to use either bus, Metro subway, or taxi to get around the downtown Washington area.

To National Airport

Metro bus No. 11 leaves every 10 minutes from 10th and Pennsylvania Avenues, NW. There is also a Metro subway train that leaves every 7 minutes from downtown stations for National Airport.

To Dulles International Airport

An airport bus leaves from the Capital Hilton Hotel, 16th and K Streets, NW, once every hour in the morning and every 30 minutes in the afternoon until 9:30 P.M. (fare: $4.25). There is a Metro bus (only 1 per day) departing at 8:25 A.M. from 11th and E Streets, NW. downtown Washington, and arriving at Dulles Airport at 9:45 A.M. Also, there is a limousine service daily to National Airport until 11:15 P.M. and the Dulles Airport until 12:00 P.M. For further information, call Greyhound Airport Service (471-9801).

To Baltimore-Washington (Friendship) International Airport

All buses leave from 16th and K Streets, NW, downtown Washington, making 1 stop at Greenbelt Station, Maryland. For further information, call (301) 441-2345. The tickets are $5.00 for a single trip, and $8.50 for a round trip.

Taxi

Fares in Washington, D.C., are based on a zone system and are reasonable when compared with other large cities in the United States. Taxi fares crossing state lines into and out of Virginia and Maryland are, however, fairly expensive.

Metro Subway System

Although the subway system is still under construction, parts of it have been completed, with the remainder to be operational within the next few years. It is a reasonably economical and efficient means of transportation in the Washington, D.C., area. Maps of the subway can be obtained at the National Visitor's Center, located at the site of the old Union Station (50 Massachusetts Avenue, NE). For further information, call Washington Metropolitan Area Transit Authority (637-2437).

Metro Buses

In order to get around town by Metro bus, which links almost every major corner of metropolitan Washington, scholars should get a copy of *Getting About by Metro Bus*, which is available at the Metro Headquarters, 600 5th Street, NW, Washington, D.C. 20001. For routes and schedule information, call 637-2437.

Train

Union Station (50 Massachusetts Avenue, NE) is the terminal for all trains serving Washington, D.C. Located near the Capitol, it is within minutes of the downtown hotel area. More detailed information pertaining to Washington, D.C., can be obtained from the National Visitors Center, which is located at Union Station.

INTERNATIONAL VISITORS INFORMATION SERVICE (IVIS)

IVIS is a private, nonprofit community organization that offers a diversified program of services to international visitors to the Washington area. Its programs are operated with the support of over 1,200 volunteers living in the Washington area. IVIS has 2 locations:

> Main Information and Reception Center
> 801 19th Street, NW
> Washington, D.C. 20006
> 872-8747

> Information Booth
> Dulles International Airport.

Multilingual staff and volunteers are available to help the visitor with sightseeing arrangements, hotel accommodations, and bilingual medical assistance. IVIS also provides tour brochures, maps, and information, and telephone assistance in 47 languages (operating 24 hours a day, 7 days a week). Persons in need of language assistance may call 872-8747.

For the foreign student enrolled in U.S. institutions of higher education, it may be useful to contact the Foreign Student Service Council of Greater Washington (FSSC), located at 1623 Belmont Street, NW, Washington, D.C. 20009 (tel. 232-4979). Its staff and volunteers provide home hospitality, sightseeing, and other services to the foreign students (local and transient).

OTHER SOURCES OF INFORMATION

Among several guidebooks to Washington, D.C., *Newcomers' Guide to Metropolitan Washington,* edited and published by the *Washingtonian Magazine,* is highly useful. It is updated annually. Also useful is *The Best of Washington: The "Washingtonian Magazine"'s Guide to the Nation's Capital* (Washington, D.C.: Washingtonian Books, 1977). Dated somewhat but still useful is Laura L. Babb, ed., *"The Washington Post" Guide to Washington* (New York: McGraw-Hill Book Co., 1976).

MAP

Free copies of the metropolitan Washington area map are available from the District of Columbia Department of Transportation. Also, one can obtain a copy of the same from the Map Office, Room 519, 415 12th Street, NW, Washington, D.C. 20004. Mail requests must include a stamped, self-addressed, 8" x 10" envelope. The office is open from 8:15 A.M. to 4:45 P.M. on weekdays.

Appendix IV. Standard Entry Formats

A. Libraries Entry Format

1. General information
    a. *address; telephone number(s)*
    b. hours of service
    c. conditions of access (including availability of interlibrary loan [ILL]) and reproduction facilities)
    d. name/title of director and heads of relevant divisions

2. Size of collection

3. Descriptions of holdings/Evaluation of subject strength

Subject Category	Number of Titles	Evaluation (A-D)*
History		
Philosophy and Religion		
Geography		
Anthropology		
Economics		
Sociology		
Politics and Government		
Foreign Relations		
Law		
Education		
Fine Arts		
Language		
Literature		
Military		
Bibliography and Reference		

North Africa
    Algeria, Canary Islands, Egypt, Libya, Morocco, Sahara, Tunisia
West Africa
    Benin, Cameroon, Cape Verde Islands, Dahomey, Gambia, Ghana, Guinea, Guinea-Bissau, Ivory Coast, Liberia, Mali, Mauritania, Niger, Nigeria, Senegal, Sierra Leone, Sudan, Togo, Upper Volta

Central Africa
Angola, Burundi, Central African Empire, Chad, Congo, Equatorial Guinea, Gabon, Rwanda, São Tomé and Principé, Zaire
East Africa
Comoro Islands, Ethiopia, Kenya, Madagascar, Mauritius, Mozambique, Reunion, Seychelles, Somalia, Tanzania, Uganda
Southern Africa
Botswana, Lesotho, Malawi, Namibia (Southwest Africa), Republic of South Africa, Swaziland, Zambia, Zimbabwe (Rhodesia)

*A—comprehensive collection of primary and secondary sources (Library of Congress collection to serve as standard of evaluation)

B—substantial collection of primary and secondary sources; sufficient for some original research (holdings roughly one-tenth those of the Library of Congress)

C—substantial collection of secondary sources, some primary; sufficient to support graduate instruction (holdings roughly one-half those of B collection)

D—collection of secondary sources, mostly in English; sufficient to support undergraduate instruction (holdings roughly one-half those of C collection); collections rated below D indicated by "D-"

4. Special collections (periodicals, newspapers, government documents, maps, films, tapes)

5. Noteworthy holdings

6. Bibliographic aids facilitating use of collection (guides, catalogs, computerized retrieval systems)

B. Archives Entry Format

1. General information
   a. *address; telephone number(s)*
   b. hours of service
   c. conditions of access
   d. reproduction services
   e. name/title of director and heads of relevant divisions

2. Size of holdings pertaining to Africa

3. Description of holdings

4. Bibliographic aids facilitating use of collection (inventories, finding aids, catalogs, guides)

C. Museums, Galleries, and Art Collections Entry Format

1. General information
   a. *address; telephone number(s)*

   b. hours of service

    c. conditions of access
    d. reproduction services
    e. name/title of director and heads of relevant divisions

2.   Size of holdings pertaining to Africa

3.   Description of holdings

4.   Bibliographic aids facilitating use of collection (catalogs, inventories, guides)

D. Collections of Music and Other Sound Recordings Entry Format

1.   General information
    a. *address; telephone number(s)*
    b. hours of service
    c. conditions of access
    d. name/title of director and key staff members

2.   Size of collection pertaining to Africa

3.   Description of holdings

4.   Facilities for study and use
    a. availability of audio-visual equipment
    b. reservation requirements
    c. fees charged
    d. reproduction services

5.   Bibliographic aids facilitating use of collection

E. Map Collections Entry Format

1.   General information
    a. *address; telephone number(s)*
    b. hours of service
    c. conditions of access
    d. reproduction services
    e. name/title of director and heads of relevant divisions

2.   Size of holdings pertaining to Africa

3.   Description of holdings pertaining to Africa

4.   Bibliographic aids facilitating use of collection

F. Film Collections (Still Photographs and Motion Pictures) Entry Format

1.   General information
    a. *address; telephone number(s)*
    b. hours of service
    c. conditions of access
    d. name/title of director and key staff members

2. Size of collection pertaining to Africa

3. Description of holdings pertaining to Africa

4. Facilities for study and use
   a. availability of audio-visual equipment
   b. reservation requirements
   c. fees charged
   d. reproduction services

5. Bibliographic aids facilitating use of collection

G. Data Banks Entry Format

1. General information
   a. *address; telephone number(s)*
   b. hours of service
   c. conditions of access (including fees charged for information retrieval)
   d. name/title of director and key staff members

2. Description of data files (hard-data and bibliographic-reference) pertaining to Africa

3. Bibliographic aids facilitating use of storage media

H. Research Centers and Information Offices Entry Format

1. *address; telephone number(s)*

2. Chief official and title

3. Parental organization

4. Programs and research activities pertaining to Africa

5. Library/research facilities

6. Publications

J. Academic Programs Entry Format

1. *Address; telephone number(s)*

2. Chief official and title

3. Degrees and subjects offered; program activities

4. Library/research facilities

K. United States Government Agencies Entry Format

1. General information
   a. *address; telephone number(s)*
   b. conditions of access

2. Support for research and use of consultants (in-house research, contract research, research grants, employment of consultants)

3. Bibliographic resources (records of research sponsored by the government and/or private institutions, bibliographies issued)

4. Library or research facility

5. Publications by the agency of potential interest to researchers

L. African Embassies and International Organizations Entry Format

1. General information
   a. *address; telephone number(s)*
   b. hours/conditions of access

2. Reference facilities

3. Publications

4. Programs and research activities

In the case of large, structurally complex international organizations, each relevant division or subunit will be described separately, following the information on the organization as a whole.

M. Associations (Academic, Professional, and Cultural) Entry Format

1. *Address; telephone number(s)*

2. Chief official and title

3. Programs and activities pertaining to Africa

4. Library/reference collection

5. Publications

N. Cultural-Exchange and Technical-Assistance Organizations Entry Format

1. *Address; telephone number(s)*

2. Chief official and title

3. Programs and activities pertaining to Africa

4. Publications

P. Religious Organizations Entry Format

1. *Address; telephone number(s)*

2. Chief official and title

3.   Programs and activities pertaining to Africa

4.   Publications and information pertaining to Africa

Q. Publications and Media Entry Format

1.   *Address; telephone number(s)*

2.   Chief official and title

3.   Publications and programs pertaining to Africa

Bibliography

Reference sources consulted for identification of collections and organizations included in this *Scholars' Guide*.

African Bibliographic Center. *AF-LOG: African Interests of American Organizations.* Washington, D.C., 1975.

American Association of Museums. *Official Museum Directory.* Washington, D.C.: American Association of Museums, 1975.

American Council of Voluntary Agencies for Foreign Service, Inc. *U.S. Non-Profit Organizations in Developmental Assistance Abroad Including Voluntary Agencies, Missions, and Foundations.* New York: Technical Assistance Information Clearing House of the American Council of Voluntary Agencies for Foreign Service, Inc., 1971.

Ayer Press. *'77 Ayer Directory of Publications.* Philadelphia: Ayer Press, 1977.

Benton, Mildred, ed. *Libraries and Reference Facilities in the Area of the District of Columbia.* 9th ed. Washington, D.C.: American Society for Information Science, 1975.

Brownson, Charles B., comp. *Congressional Staff Directory.* Mount Vernon, Va., 1976.

Center for a Voluntary Society. *Voluntary Transnational Cultural Exchange Organizations of the U.S.: A Selected List.* Washington, D.C.: Center for a Voluntary Society, 1974.

Chamberlin, Jim, and Ann Hammond, eds. *Directory of the Population-Related Community of the Washington, D.C. Area.* 3d ed. Washington, D.C.: World Population Society—D.C. Chapter, 1978.

Congressional Quarterly, Inc. *Washington Information Directory, 1977–1978.* Washington, D.C.: Congressional Quarterly, Inc., 1977.

Duignan, Peter, ed. *Handbook of American Resources for African Studies.* Stanford: The Hoover Institution on War, Revolution, and Peace. Hoover Institution Bibliographical Series 29 (1967).

Encyclopedia of Library and Information Science, Vol. 21. New York: Marcel Dekker, 1977.

Fisk, Margaret, ed. *Encyclopedia of Associations.* 11th ed. Detroit: Gale Research Co., 1977.

Grant, Steven A. *Scholars' Guide to Washington, D.C. for Russian/Soviet Studies.* Washington, D.C.: Smithsonian Institution Press, 1977.

Grayson, Cary T., Jr., and Susan Lukowski. *Washington IV: A Comprehensive Directory of the Nation's Capital . . . its People and Institutions.* Washington, D.C.: Potomac Books, Inc., 1975.

Green, Shirley L. *Pictorial Resources in the Washington, D.C. Area.* Washington, D.C.: Library of Congress, 1976.

Hamer, Philip M., ed. *A Guide to Archives and Manuscripts in the United States.* New Haven: Yale University Press, 1961.

Joyner, Nelson T., Jr. *Joyner's Guide to Official Washington.* 3d ed. Rockville, Md.: Rockville Consulting Group, 1976.

Mason, John Brown, ed. *Research Resources: Annotated Guide to the Social Sciences.* Santa Barbara, Cal.: American Bibliographical Center, 1968–1971.

Palmer, Archie M., ed. *Research Centers Directory.* 5th ed. Detroit: Gale Research Co., 1975.

Panther House. *Black List: The Guide to Publications and Broadcasting of Black America, Africa, Caribbean.* New York: Panther House, 1970.

Ruder, William, and Raymond Nathan. *The Businessman's Guide to Washington.* Rev. ed. New York: Macmillan Publishing Co., 1975.

Schmeckebier, Laurence Frederick, and Roy B. Eastin. *Government Publications and their Use.* 2d rev. ed. Washington, D.C.: Brookings Institution, 1969.

Schneider, John H.; Marvin Gechman; and Stephen E. Further, eds. *Survey of Commercially Available Computer-Readable Bibliographic Data Bases.* Washington, D.C.: American Society for Information Science, 1973.

Sessions, Vivian S., ed. *Directory of Data Bases in the Social Behavioral Sciences.* New York: Science Associates/International, 1974.

Smith, David Horton, ed. *Voluntary Transnational Cultural Exchange Organizations of the U.S.: A Selected List.* Washington, D.C.: Center for a Voluntary Society, 1974.

South, Aloha, ed. *Guide to Federal Archives Relating to Africa.* African Studies Association. Waltham, Mass.: Crossroads Press, 1977.

U.S. Department of State, Office of External Research. *Foreign Affairs Research: A Directory of Governmental Resources.* Washington, D.C.: U.S. Department of State, 1977.

————. *Government-Supported Research on Foreign Affairs: Current Project Information, 1976.* Washington, D.C.: Government Printing Office, 1977.

U.S. Government Documents Round Table, American Library Association. *Directory of Government Document Collections and Librarians.* Chicago: American Library Association, 1974.

U.S. Library of Congress, National Referral Center for Science and Technology. *A Directory of Information Resources in the United States: Federal Government.* Washington, D.C.: Library of Congress, 1974.

————. *A Directory of Information Resources in the United States: Social Sciences.* Rev. ed. Washington, D.C.: Library of Congress, 1973.

U.S. National Archives and Records Service. *United States Government Organizational Manual, 1977/78.* Washington, D.C., 1978.

Washington Booksellers Association. *Metropolitan Bookstore Guide.* Washington, D.C.: Washington Booksellers Association, 1975.

Washington, D.C. Area telephone directories.

Weber, Olga S., comp. *North American Film and Video Directory: A Guide to Media Collections and Services.* New York: R. R. Bowker Co., 1976.

Witherell, Julian W., comp. *The United States and Africa: Guide to U.S. Official Documents and Government-Sponsored Publications on Africa, 1785–1975.* Washington, D.C.: African Section, General Reference and Bibliography Division, Library of Congress, 1978.

Wynar, Lubomyr R. *Encyclopedic Directory of Ethnic Newspapers and Periodicals in the United States.* Littleton, Colo.: Libraries Unlimited, 1975.

————. *Encyclopedic Directory of Ethnic Organizations in the United States.* Littleton, Colo.: Libraries Unlimited, 1975.

Name Index

(Organizations and Institutions)

Entry symbols correspond to the following sections of the text:

A —Libraries
B —Archives
C —Museums, Galleries, and Art Collections
D —Collections of Music and Other Sound Recordings
E —Map Collections
F —Film Collections (Still Photographs and Motion Pictures)
G —Data Banks
H —Research Center and Information Offices
J —Academic Programs
K —United States Government Agencies
L —African Embassies and International Organizations
M —Associtions (Academic, Professional, Cultural)
N —Cultural-Exchange and Technical-Assistance Organizations
P —Religious Organizations
Q —Publications and Media

Personal-Papers Index

Alsop, Joseph W. B2

Bohlen, Charles E. B3
Breckinridge, Robert J. B2
Brown, Sterling B1

Cassell, Abayomi C. A21
Chaille-Long, Charles B2
Clarkson, Thomas B1
Coker, Daniel B2
Croffut, William A. B2
Crosby, Oscar T. B2
Cuffe, Paul A27, B2

Davis, John W. B1
Diggs, Charles B1
Durant, William West B2
Douglass, Frederick B1, B2

Eaker, Ira Clarence B2
Elisofon, Eliot F24

Foote, Andrew Hull B2
Force, Peter B2
Frazier, Franklin E. B1

Gardiner, Arthur Zimmerman B3
Gilchrist, Huntington B2
Green, Theodore Francis B2
Grimké, Archibald B1

Hansberry, William Leo B1
Harper, Robert Goodloe B2
Harrison, Jessie Burton B2
Hubbard, Charlotte Moton B1
Hughes, Charles Evans B2
Hunt. William H. B1
Hyvernat, Henri A5

Johnson, Mordecai W. B1

Kelly, John A16
Kipling, Rudyard A27
Kuh, Frederick R. A15

Langston, John M. B2
Lewis, Thomas Narven B1
Lima, Manoel de Oliveira A5
Livingstone, David and Family B2
Locke, Alain L. B1
Logan, Rayford B1
Lucas, Townsend McKinley B1

Mays, Benjamin B1
Miller, Kelly B1
Montgomery, Thomas B1
Moorland, Rev. Jesse E. A21
Morgan, John Tyler B2
Murphy, George B1
Murray, Daniel Alexander Payne B1
Murray, Freeman Henry Morris B1

Nassau, R. H. B2
Nelson, William Stuart B1

Petersen, Theodore C. A5
Phillipps, Thomas B2
Porte, Albert A21
Porter, Dorothy Burnett B1
Pulitzer, Joseph B2

Randolph, A. P. B2
Roche, Manoel Ribeiro A5
Roosevelt, Theodore A27, B2
Ruffin, George L. B1

Sevaried, Eric B2

Library Subject-Strength Index

This index identifies the most useful library collections in the Washington, D.C., area by subject. Evaluation ("A" through "C") is based on the following criteria:

A—comprehensive collection of primary and secondary sources (Library of Congress collection to serve as a standard of evaluation);

B—substantial collection of primary and secondary sources, sufficient for some original research (holdings roughly one-tenth those of the Library of Congress);

C—substantial collection of secondary sources, with some primary; sufficient to support graduate instruction (holdings roughly one-half those of a "B" collection).

The standard Library of Congress subject-headings have been used for categorization; however, some ratings are based on subcategories of major subject headings, since no other method could be devised which could include a few exceptionally valuable specialized collections. The reader's attention is also called to Appendix I: "Library Collections: A Listing by Size of African Holdings."

1. History
   A collections: A27
   B collections: A20, A21, A28, A37, A38
   C collections: A5, A15, A16, A20

2. Philosophy and Religion
   A collections: A27
   B collections: A5, A21
   C collections: A28

3. Geography
   A collections: A21, A27, A32
   B collections: A12, A28, A32, A38
   C collections: A3, A5, A15, A16, A20, A35, A37

4. Anthropology
   A collections: A27, A35
   B collections: A3, A5, A15, A16, A21, A28, A29, A32
   C collections: A20, A37, A38

5. Economics
   A collections: A26, A27, A30, A35
   B collections: A6, A21, A25, A28, A37, A38
   C collections: A1, A3, A7, A11, A15, A16, A24

6. Sociology
   A collections: A21, A27

B collections: A5, A15, A16,
A20, A23, A28, A35, A38
C collections: A1, A3, A9, A37

7. Politics and Government
A collections: A27
B collections: A20, A21, A28,
A37, A38
C collections: A3, A15, A16, A23

8. International Relations
A collections: A27
B collections: A3, A20, A21,
A23, A28, A37, A38
C collections: A8

9. Law
A collections: A27
B collections: —
C collections: A24

10. Education
A collections: A27

B collections: A21, A28, A33,
A38
C collections: A1, A37

11. Fine Arts
A collections: A27
B collections: A9, A20, A21,
A28, A29, A35
C collections: A3, A5

12. Language and Literature
A collections: A21, A27
B collections: A16, A28
C collections: A3, A5

13. Military
A collections: A27
B collections: A4, A21, A38
C collections: A20, A37

14. Bibliography and Reference
A collections: A21, A27
B collections: A20, A38
C collections: A16, A28, A37

Subject Index

The alphabetic code represents the following sections of the *Guide:*

A —Libraries
B —Archives
C —Museums, Galleries, and Art Collections
D —Collections of Music and Other Sound Recordings
E —Map Collections
F —Film Collections (Still Photographs and Motion Pictures)
G —Data Banks
H —Research Centers and Information Offices
J —Academic Programs
K —United States Government Agencies
L —African Embassies and International Organizations
M —Association (Academic, Professional, Cultural)
N —Cultural-Exchange and Technical-Assistance Organizations
P —Religious Organizations
Q —Publications and Media

The subject index which follows employs a topical as well as a geographic approach. It is necessary, however, to point out that the vast majority of library collections and organizations discussed in this volume focus on all the countries of Africa rather than exclusively on any single country or geographical region. As a result, most entries included in this *Guide* can be expected to contain resources for country-specific research. Where relevant, country headings have been included.

The author, Purnima Mehta Bhatt, was born in India in 1946. She attended Delhi University (B.A. 1965 and M.A. 1967) and obtained her Ph.D. in African history from Howard University (1976). She has taught at Delhi University, India, and Towson State University, and is presently Assistant Professor of Anthropology and Interdisciplinary Studies at Hood College, Frederick, Maryland.

The consultant, Daniel G. Matthews, is Executive Director of the African Bibliographic Center in Washington, D.C.

The consultant, Michael R. Winston, is Director of the Moorland-Springarn Research Center at Howard University.

The consultant, Julian W. Witherell, is Chief of the African and Middle Eastern Division in the Library of Congress.

The series editor, Zdeněk V. David, has been Librarian of the Wilson Center since 1974. Previously he served as the Slavic Bibliographer of the Princeton University Library and as Lecturer in the Department of History at Princeton University.